BOOKS LISTED IN TABLE INSIDE FRONT COVER

Aukerman, R.C. *Reading in the Secondary School Classroom.* New York: McGraw-Hill, Inc., 1972.

Burmeister, Lou E. *Reading Strategies for Secondary School Teachers.* Reading, Mass.: Addison-Wesley, 1974.

Burron, A., and Claybaugh, A. *Using Reading to Teach Subject Matter: Fundamentals for Content Teachers.* Columbus, Ohio: Merrill, 1974.

Herber, H. *Teaching Reading in Content Areas.* Englewood Cliffs, N.J.: Prentice-Hall, 1970.

Karlin, R. *Teaching Reading in High School.* 2nd ed. New York: Bobbs-Merrill, 1972.

Olson, A., and Ames, W. *Teaching Reading Skills in Secondary Schools.* Scranton, Pa.: Intext Educational Publishers, 1972.

Robinson, H. *Teaching Reading and Study Strategies: The Content Areas.* Boston: Allyn and Bacon, 1975.

Thomas, E., and Robinson, H. *Improving Reading in Every Class: A Source Book for Teachers.* Boston: Allyn and Bacon, 1972.

PERSONALIZING READING INSTRUCTION IN MIDDLE, JUNIOR, AND SENIOR HIGH SCHOOLS

PERSONALIZING READING INSTRUCTION IN MIDDLE, JUNIOR, AND SENIOR HIGH SCHOOLS

Utilizing a Competency-Based Instructional System

Martha H. Dillner
Associate Professor
University of Houston, Clear Lake City Campus

Joanne P. Olson
Associate Professor
University of Houston, Central Campus

Macmillan Publishing Co., Inc.
New York
Collier Macmillan Publishers
London

Macmillan Publishing Co., Inc.
866 Third Avenue, New York, New York 10022

Collier Macmillan Canada, Ltd.

Library of Congress Cataloging in Publication Data

Dillner, Martha H.
  Personalizing reading instruction in middle, junior, and senior high schools.

  Includes bibliographies and index.
  1. Reading (Secondary education)   I. Olson, Joanne P., joint author.   II. Title.
LB1632.D54   428'.4'0712   76-8192
ISBN 0-02-329790-5

Printing: 2 3 4 5 6 7 8   Year: 7 8 9 0 1 2 3

Preface

Project director of the "Right to Read" secondary school programs were recently reported as agreeing that

> it is not enough to have a remedial lab program or even a developmental reading course for secondary students—reading skills must be emphasized continuously throughout the entire curriculum. The primary focus . . . is the development of an all-school reading program—one which is aimed at all students and utilizes all faculty. The intent, however, is not just to improve reading skills, but to refine teaching strategies which also improve content area instruction and create an appreciation of and interest in reading.*

This also is the intent of *Personalizing Reading Instruction in Middle, Junior, and Senior High Schools.* This text concerns ways in which both the classroom teacher and the reading specialist may use content area materials to individualize learning. Since reading is a skill and not a content, the information included is applicable to any subject in which the student is expected to read—in short, almost any content area in the curriculum.

The authors gratefully acknowledge Dr. W. Robert Houston for his help and guidance in teaching us the competency-based approach to teacher education, Janice Guetzow for reading the entire manuscript, and Emma L. Ankele for reading and reacting to selected chapters.

M. H. D.
J. P. O.

Right to Read '75, bimonthly report on the National Right to Read Effort issued by the International Reading Association, November, 1975, Vol. 2, No. 4.

Contents

Part Four   Developing an Effective Reading Program

Part Five   Practicing Teaching Reading

Appendixes

Index   531

How to Use This Book

The purpose of this book is to help you develop the skills that you will need to teach reading in the secondary school classroom. The format differs from a traditional textbook in that each chapter contains six major sections as follows:

1. A **Prerequisite**, which tells what the participant needs to know or to have completed before proceeding with the chapter.
2. A **Rationale**, which includes a statement of why the chapter is important.
3. A delineated list of behavioral **Objectives**, which inform the participants of what they are expected to be able to do after they have completed the chapter.
4. A **Self Pre-Assessment** to determine whether the participant already knows the data contained in the chapter.
5. A list of **Enabling Activities**, which allows participants to engage in types of learning most comfortable to them—readings, audiovisual aids, and class sessions.
6. An **Information Given** section, which consists of expository material.

For these six major sections the authors have used a double-numeration system in which the number of the section consists of the chapter number, followed by a decimal point and the section number. For example, **1.1** indicates section 1 (**Prerequisite**) in Chapter 1. The double numerations are printed in boldface type.

Format Explanation

A close examination of a chapter will help to demonstrate the format mentioned above. Turn to Chapter 1. **Prerequisite 1.1** tells you what you should have successfully completed before proceeding with the chapter. If you can meet **Prerequisite 1.1**, read **Rationale 1.2** and then **Objectives 1.3**. Three explanations are in order regarding the objectives. First, though four objectives are listed, your instructor may not want you to complete all four. Second, blank lines have been provided in objectives 5, 6, 7, and 8 for additional objectives. Third, objective 9 is related to the content of Chapter 1 but refers to Chapter 13. Check with your instructor about objectives to be deleted or added and whether you should meet objective 9 now or later.

Self Pre-Assessment 1.4 should help you decide whether you need to complete any enabling activities in addition to those your instructor might require. The three given **Enabling Activities 1.5** for Chapter 1 include: (1) **Information Given 1.6**, which is the reading selection in this book, (2) a reading option from a basic text, and (3) a class session option. The blank lines following these suggested activities are provided so that you may add any other activities assigned by your instructor. Other such enabling activities could include additional readings, seminars, audiovisual aids—in short, anything that helps you meet the objectives.

Many of these options contain almost the same information, but each may present the data in a slightly different manner. Choices are offered to give you an opportunity to learn in a style most comfortable for you.

Information Given 1.6 is an expository description that should enable you to meet all four objectives listed in **Objectives 1.3**.

After you have completed as many enabling activities as are required, as well as those that you feel are necessary, take the Post-Assessment deemed appropriate by your instructor. Check with him about when and where this should be completed. If your post-assessment is satisfactory, then you have completed the chapter. If it is not satisfactory, ask your instructor for further directions.

Each chapter in this text is divided into the same six sections and should be approached in a manner identical to the one used above. Now that you are familiar with the procedure, you are ready to begin the text.

Part One

Understanding the Meaning of Reading

Chapter 1

Identifying the Role of the Secondary School Teacher in Reading Instruction

Prerequisite 1.1

Participants* should have successfully completed the objectives for an introductory course in education before attempting those in this text.

Rationale 1.2

Participants beginning this course of study often ask, "Why do I need to know how to teach reading? I plan to become a history, art, science, language, or literature teacher." This chapter attempts to answer this question by bringing attention to the scope of reading and the secondary teacher's role in reading instruction.

Objectives 1.3

Upon successful completion of this chapter, the participant will be able to:

1. Given a description of a teaching situation, state whether the teacher is giving reading instruction.
2. List the three major components of reading.
3. Given a grade level, state the approximate level on which (1) the

*Throughout this text, "participant" is used to describe the college student; "student" refers to the middle, junior, or senior high school pupil. "Teacher" refers to the middle, junior, or senior high school teacher. And, "instructor" designates the college professor. Also, the terms "secondary" and "middle and secondary" are used interchangeably to refer to grades 5-12.

weakest reader would be reading and (2) the strongest reader would be reading.

4. Describe the role of a teacher in his own teaching area in relation to reading.

5. (On the lines below, add other objectives according to your instructor's directions.) _____

_____

6. _____

_____

7. _____

_____

8. _____

_____

*   *   *   *   *   *   *   *   *   *   *   *   *   *

Chapter 13, Experience 1, extends Chapter 1 with this performance/consequence objective:

9. During this experience, the participant will interview one middle or secondary school teacher and one middle or secondary school student to elicit their views on reading and reading instruction.

*   *   *   *   *   *   *   *   *   *   *   *   *   *

Self Pre-Assessment 1.4

Can you complete all the activities listed in **Objectives 1.3**? Answer "yes," "no," or "not certain."

If you answered "yes" to the question, complete the enabling activities required by your instructor and take the Post-Assessment on the date assigned by him.

If you answered "no," refer to **Enabling Activities 1.5**. If you decide to do any activities that are not required, select those that best suit you as a learner. You need not complete all the optional activities or all parts of a particular optional activity. As soon as you have the information you need to complete the objectives, answer "yes" to the **Self Pre-Assessment 1.4** question and stop the activity.

If you answered "not certain" to the question, refer to **Enabling Activities 1.5**. Select the enabling activity that best suits your style of learning and peruse it. Then make a firm "yes" or "no" answer and proceed accordingly.

Enabling Activities 1.5

Complete only as many of the activities listed below as are required and which you need in order to meet the objectives.

1. *Enabling activity one* is a *reading* alternative. This is **Information Given 1.6.** It is a brief overview of the definition of reading and the secondary teacher's role in reading instruction.

2. *Enabling activity two* is another *reading* option. In this case, the material to be read is one of the textbooks used to expand the theoretical background for this course. See chart on inside front cover for keying in textbooks that may be used.

3. *Enabling activity three* is a *class session* option. Attend the class session(s) on the date(s), at the time(s), and at the place(s) announced.

_____	_____	_____
(Date)	(Time)	(Place)
_____	_____	_____
(Date)	(Time)	(Place)
_____	_____	_____
(Date)	(Time)	(Place)

4. *Enabling activity four* (These lines are left blank so that you may add other enabling activities as suggested by your instructor.)_____

_____

_____

5. *Enabling activity five*_____

_____

6. *Enabling activity six*_____

_____

_____

Now that you have completed the appropriate number of required and/or optional learning alternatives, look back at **Self Pre-Assessment 1.4.** If you feel you can answer "yes" to all of the questions, you are ready to proceed to the Post-Assessment. This may be given to you immediately or after completion of a series of chapters.

Three topics are discussed in this chapter. First, the scope of the skill *reading* is investigated. Second, the role of all teachers in relation to the teaching of reading at the middle, junior, and senior high school levels* is delineated. And, third, the remainder of the book is overviewed.

LASALLE JUNIOR–SENIOR HIGH SCHOOL

LaSalle Junior-Senior High School was located on the outskirts of a large metropolitan area. The students represented a wide variety of socioeconomic levels, cultural backgrounds, learning styles, abilities, and achievements.

Viewing Students' Reading Test Scores

Mark McNee and Sol Lentz taught social science to classes from grades seven through twelve. They received the reading scores on the standardized test administered by the school for the students in their classes. Mark McNee's grade seven class totaled thirty students who were randomly selected from all the grade seven students in the school. Their scores on the standardized reading test administered by the school are given in Table 1.1.

TABLE 1.1

Reading Scores for Mark McNee's Grade Seven Class

	Name	Grade Score		Name	Grade Score
1.	Henry	12.9	16.	Val	7.6
2.	Melinda	11.5	17.	Sharon Lea	7.5
3.	James	10.9	18.	Lily	7.4
4.	Richard	10.1	19.	Joan	7.3
5.	Martha	9.8	20.	Derek	6.9
6.	Sheng-Yen	9.7	21.	Ann	6.8
7.	Walter	9.3	22.	Jack	6.5
8.	Linda	8.9	23.	Diana	6.4
9.	Keith	8.8	24.	Frederic	6.3
10.	Sandra	8.6	25.	Carolyn	5.9
11.	Jefferson	8.5	26.	Justin	5.6
12.	Robert	8.3	27.	Sue Ann	5.3
13.	Nancy	7.9	28.	Philip	4.8
14.	Terence	7.8	29.	Jill	3.1
15.	Jeanne	7.7	30.	Rosemary	1.9

*In this text, "middle school level" will refer to grades five through eight, "junior high school level" will refer to grades seven through nine, and "senior high school level" will refer to grades nine or ten through twelve.

This table indicates the grade score for each student in reading. According to the scores shown, Rosemary, the student whose name appears last on the list, made the lowest score on the reading test. Her score indicates that she reads as well as the average child in the ninth month of grade one. Jill produced the next lowest score in the class. Her score indicates that she reads as well as the average child in the first month of grade three. The highest score on the reading test was made by Henry, who scored at level 12.9. His reading skills are equivalent to the average student in the ninth month of grade twelve. Seven students scored on the grade level in which they were actually enrolled, grade seven. An additional ten students scored within one year of their actual placement. These students' grade scores placed them on the grade six or grade eight levels. The remaining students scored above the grade eight level or below the grade six level. A summary of the reading scores of the average grade seven class is given in Figure 1.1.

| Grade and Description | Grade Score on Reading Test | | | | | | | | | | | | |
	1	2	3	4	5	6	7	8	9	10	11	12	Higher Than Grade 12
Grade 7 Randomly Chosen Class	1		1	1	3	5	7	5	3	2	1	1	
Grade 8 High-Achieving Class								7	8	7	5	2	1
Grade 9 Low-Achieving Class		2	2	3	3	4	5	8	3				
Grade 10 Randomly Chosen Class			1		1	1		2	6	8	7	3	1
Grade 11 Randomly Chosen Class			1		1		1	1	2	3	12	5	4
Grade 12 Randomly Chosen Class				1		1		1	1	2	4	12	8

Figure 1.1 Number of Students Scoring on Each Grade Level on a Reading Test

Mark McNee's grade eight class was made up of selected high-achieving students. The summary of this class's scores is shown in Figure 1.1. Again, a range of reading scores is evident, with the lowest scores being on a grade eight level and the highest scores being on a higher than grade twelve level. Most of the students read above grade level.

Sol Lentz's grade nine class was made up of low-achieving students. A range of reading scores from grade two through grade nine was evidenced. The majority of students read one or two years below grade level.

Students were not selected by achievement for the other classes in Figure 1.1. Therefore, a wide range of reading ability was found at each grade level. The majority of students' scores fell on or close to the grade level in which they were placed.

Viewing Teachers' Instructional Strategies

Susan Mathew was conducting a class in grade seven mathematics. The topic was *interest*. She had written the term *interest* on the chalkboard and was explaining its meaning through the following demonstration. She had divided the class into *bankers* and *borrowers*. Each *banker* was figuring out the amount that the *borrower* would pay him for a given sum of money. The *borrower* was figuring out the amount of interest he would pay.

Helen Echols, the home economics teacher, was leading her grade twelve class through a *consumer awareness* unit. Each student had been provided with a newspaper and was studying its advertisements to find examples of emotionally charged words designed to enhance the image of a product.

Mark McNee, a social science teacher, had taken his grade eight class to the library. He planned for each student to find information regarding one historical person in at least three sources other than the textbook and to take notes on the readings. He knew that if the class were to complete this project successfully, he would have to teach his students how to use the card catalog, how to find information in the encyclopedia, and how to take notes. He was beginning to teach the first of these skills.

Cheryl Scott was meeting with her grade eleven chemistry class. She had found a chemistry magazine containing information she believed would be of interest to her class. However, as the materials were not developed for high school use, she questioned whether her students would be able to understand the long, complex sentences and the numerous technical terms. Therefore, she was "trying the material out" on the students. If they appeared to be able to read the magazine, then she would continue to recommend it to them as a possible source of information. However, if her students encountered undue difficulty with the material, she would remove the magazine from the reading list.

Philip Edwall taught driver's education and physical education. His ninth grade class contained many students who had difficulty reading the state driver's handbook on which the written portion of the driver's test was based. Philip had, therefore, adopted a policy of introducing the major terms and giving the students questions to answer before they read the handbook. He had found that with this introduction the students learned more from their reading and increased their chances of passing the driver's test.

Frank Jackson taught English and reading. His tenth grade reading class included several boys who had little interest in reading and who could read nothing more difficult than material designed for third graders. Frank believed that his job in relation to these students was to lessen their dislike for reading and to teach them basic reading skills. Therefore, he had located books on mechanics written for boys who read on third grade level and below. With one

10

group, he was using these materials to teach the skill of finding the main idea. With a second group, he was using the same materials to reinforce the students' sight word skills.

READING DEFINED

Reading is a complex process that has no single definition. Definitions range from those that stress word recognition such as the "visual perception of word forms and their meaning" to "a process of meaning elaboration or thinking in relation to written symbols." (Harris 1969) Educators usually use more comprehensive definitions of reading such as the latter.

For the purpose of this book, the term *reading* will be used to include three interrelated skills—vocabulary, comprehension, and study skills.

Vocabulary skills include those skills that enable the reader to pronounce and/or give meaning to a printed word. *Comprehension skills* include those skills that enable the reader to understand and apply the written material. *Study skills* include those skills that enable the reader to use vocabulary and comprehension skills efficiently and effectively. Vocabulary skills, comprehension skills, and study skills will be further delineated in Chapters 2, 3, and 4.

The task of each of the teachers discussed earlier may now be examined on the basis of this conceptualization of reading.

Susan Mathew taught her students a meaning of the word "interest" that was new to them. She was teaching a vocabulary skill.

Helen Echols had her students locate emotionally toned words in advertisements. She was teaching a comprehension skill.

Mark McNee showed his students how to use the card catalog and encyclopedia and to take notes. He was teaching a study skill.

Cheryl Scott was trying to find out if the students in her class could read a chemistry magazine that she thought would be helpful to them. She was diagnosing her pupils' comprehension skills.

Philip Edwall introduced the major terms in the driver's handbook and gave the students questions to answer. He was teaching vocabulary and comprehension skills.

Frank Jackson gave some of his poorest readers mechanics books written on the third grade level. He was teaching a vocabulary skill and a comprehension skill.

THE MIDDLE AND SECONDARY TEACHER
TEACHES READING

Several research investigations in recent years have indicated that many North Americans lack adequate reading skills. Gray (1956) concluded that in the mid-1940s only one half of the American population could read at or above the ninth grade level. A more recent study, the *Survival Literacy Study* (1972), showed, among other findings, that 34 per cent of its subjects encountered difficulty completing a Medicaid application. A third study (Sticht et al., 1972) indicated that many men in military jobs lacked adequate skills to read the instructional manuals for their jobs; and, in addition, that a lack of reading skills often had a negative effect on job proficiency.

Most of a student's learning comes about through reading. The better a student's reading skills, the easier mastery of content will be. Thus every effort should be made to develop a student's reading skills to their fullest potential. Elementary teachers and secondary school reading and content area teachers share in this responsibility.

The basic reading skills are introduced and reinforced in the elementary school. However, most elementary school children are not taught the reading skills required by more complicated secondary level materials because they are not mature enough to deal with them. For example, elementary students may be able to outline a simple paragraph in a single book, but most could not learn to outline a high school textbook. Likewise, they might be able to understand the plot of the book *Animal Farm* at a literal level, but most would not be ready to deal with the more complex meanings intended by the author.

Therefore, all middle and secondary school teachers share a responsibility for reading instruction. While the job of the middle and secondary reading teacher is to increase the reading skills of all students, the function of the content teacher is *primarily* to teach students the substance of a particular subject matter. However, the learning of facts and concepts is greatly enhanced when the content teacher presents the subject material always considering the specific reading skills required for its understanding. The roles of the reading teacher and the content teacher will be further discussed in the sections following.

The Middle and Secondary Reading Teacher's Role

The middle and secondary reading teacher's role is to increase the reading skills of students. Classes should be offered for students who have ample reading skills as well as for those who have few reading skills. Many authorities, including Balow (1965), Bond and Tinker (1973), Early (1970), and Herman (1969) believe that unless reading skills that are taught in the lower grades are reinforced in the middle, junior, and senior high school, reading skills of the weak reader will not increase and may deteriorate.

The reading teacher should

1. Diagnose each student's reading skills to ascertain the grade level of the material that the student can read.
2. Diagnose each student's reading skills to determine, from a total list of skills, which specific ones have been mastered.

3. Be aware of the reading demands and teaching strategies of the content areas so that these skills can be highlighted and reinforced.
4. Provide instruction in these skills at the appropriate level of difficulty.

For example, Mr. Jackson diagnosed the reading levels of each member of his class. He found that one student, Faith, had a reading level of grade six and that another, Bentley, had a reading level of grade ten. After further diagnosis, Mr. Jackson discovered that Faith needed help in the comprehension skills and that the most necessary skills in this area in the light of her school courses were ascertaining sequence and locating cause-effect relationships. After diagnosing Bentley's reading skills, Mr. Jackson discerned that Bentley's greatest needs were in the study skill area. In view of the skills involved in the study skill area, Mr. Jackson decided to give instruction first in skimming, taking notes, and outlining. Mr. Jackson provided instruction in the above areas for Faith and Bentley by using materials on grade six and grade ten levels, respectively.

The Middle and Secondary Content Teacher's Role

The teachers of the physical sciences, social sciences, humanities, and other secondary content areas also have an important place in reading instruction. Whereas the secondary reading teacher's role is to provide students with those reading skills missing from their backgrounds, the role of the secondary content teacher is to help students apply their reading skills to enhance specific content mastery. The major role of the content area teacher in relation to reading is to

1. Diagnose each student's reading skills to ascertain the specific content area materials which can be read.
2. Ascertain which reading skills are needed in the content area and which students need instruction.
3. Provide instruction to students in relevant reading skills at an appropriate level of difficulty.
4. Provide learning routes that do not require reading if materials on an appropriate level of reading difficulty cannot be found.

For example, Cheryl Scott knew that Faith, who could comprehend material no more difficult than that written for sixth graders, would be wasting her time if she attempted to read the grade ten science book. Thus, for Faith and others with similar reading skills, Miss Scott provided simpler books that covered the same content as the grade level text. In addition, she provided these students with questions before they began to read so that they would know what to look for. After they had read the material, they discussed the answers. In these ways, Miss Scott hoped to improve the students' reading comprehension skills as well as their content mastery. When Miss Scott was unable to find materials that presented the same concepts as the textbook but were written on an easier level, she used teaching strategies that did not involve reading. In these cases, she provided the students with lectures, audio-tapes, films, and other audiovisual aids that did not require her students to struggle with a textbook that was impossible for them to read.

Cheryl Scott also taught reading to students like Bentley who were quite capable of reading the science textbook. In order to facilitate their ability to use the textbook, she had given instruction in such skills as note-taking, out-lining, and skimming.

All the content area teachers at LaSalle Junior-Senior High School felt a responsibility toward teaching some reading skills to their students. In short, all the teachers had become teachers of reading.

OUTLINE OF THE BOOK

The remainder of this book is designed to be of interest to both secondary reading teachers and secondary content area teachers. Part One of this book familiarizes the reader with the importance of teaching reading in the secondary school as well as with the reading skills that should be known by students in middle, junior, and senior high school programs. Chapter 1 discusses the role of the secondary school teacher in reading; Chapter 2 overviews the strategies needed to learn and expand vocabulary skills; Chapter 3 outlines the skills needed to comprehend written material; and Chapter 4 summarizes the skills needed to study efficiently.

Part Two of this book discusses the variance in reading achievement levels and methods by which content area materials may be adapted to meet the needs of students on all reading levels. Chapter 5 describes how the classroom teacher may use measures of reading achievement levels such as standardized reading tests and informal reading inventories. Chapter 6 identifies some of the major problems that students encounter when using content area text-books. Topics include factors inherent to the student, textbook readability, instructional focus, and inadequate use of textbook aids. Chapter 7 presents several ways in which the content area teacher may instruct students simul-taneously in the content areas and the reading skills. A five-step lesson plan and a directed reading lesson are described and sample lesson plans illustrating their relationship are given. Chapter 8 discusses ways in which the classroom teacher may design lessons to help the student read his content area textbook with maximum understanding. It presents means by which different types of materials may be used to teach the same concepts and also describes how all materials may be better understood by the middle and secondary school student through the use of guided reading sheets.

Part Three of this book specifically outlines how content area lessons may be adapted to teach a wide range of reading skills. Chapter 9 introduces the concept of diagnostic-prescriptive instruction and illustrates how to establish a reading program that includes selecting a scope and sequence of reading

14

skills, forming assessments, keeping records, planning lessons, and scheduling instruction. Chapter 10 demonstrates techniques by which all the reading skills discussed previously may be assessed and then presents a teaching suggestion for each skill that may be used by teachers of any content area.

Part Four of the book discusses materials and organizational approaches that may be used to teach reading. Chapter 11 presents information concerning commercially produced instructional and nontext reading materials. The chapter also delineates characteristics of the adolescent that alter the effectiveness of the materials that are used with him. Suggestions for teacher-made materials are also given. Chapter 12 describes several ways in which the teaching of reading may be organized in the middle and secondary school. It also discusses materials often used within each organizational approach and means by which middle, junior, and senior high school personnel may become involved as teachers of reading. In addition, techniques for conducting inservice activities in reading for content area teachers are described.

Part Five of the text contains only one chapter and requires practical application of Parts One, Two, Three, and Four. Participants are instructed to use all their previously learned knowledge in a teaching situation. Though this section is optimally designed for a course that allows participants to teach middle and secondary school students, most of the objectives can also be completed through peer teaching.

References and Bibliography

Balow, B. "The Long-term Effect of Remedial Reading Instruction." *The Reading Teacher*, 18:7 (April 1965), 581–586.

Bond, G. L., and Tinker, M. A. *Reading Difficulties: Their Diagnosis and Correction.* 3rd ed. New York: Appleton-Century-Crofts, 1973.

Caughran, A. M., and Lindlof, J. A. "Should the 'Survival Literacy Study' Survive?" *Journal of Reading*, 15:6 (March 1972), 429–435.

Early, M. "Reading: In and Out of the English Curriculum." Pages 237–250 in L. Josephs and E. R. Steinberg, eds., *English Education Today.* New York: Noble and Noble, 1970.

Gray, W. S. "How Well Do Adults Read?" *Adult Reading*, 55th yearbook, Part II, NSSE. Chicago, 1956, pp. 29–56.

Harris, T. L. *Encyclopedia of Educational Research.* New York: Macmillan, 1969, p. 1075.

Herman, W. "Reading and Other Language Arts in Social Studies Instruction: Persistent Problems." *A New Look at Reading in the Social Studies.* Newark, Del.: International Reading Association, 1969, pp. 1–20.

Sticht, T. G., et al. "Project REALISTIC: Determination of Adult Functional Literacy Skill Levels." *Reading Research Quarterly*, 7:3 (Spring 1972), 424–465.

Survival Literacy Study. Washington, D.C.: GPO, 1972.

Chapter 2

Identifying the Vocabulary Skills

Prerequisite 2.1

Participants should have successfully completed the objectives for Chapter 1 or should know the relationships between vocabulary skills, comprehension skills, and study skills before beginning this chapter.

Rationale 2.2

Students use basic strategies for identifying words: illustration clues, context clues, phonic analysis, structural analysis, dictionary skills, and sight word skills. The purpose of this chapter is to show middle and secondary teachers how these strategies aid the student in reading, to suggest ways in which they can reinforce the students' use of these skills, and to introduce the advantages and limitations of each technique. Methodologies for diagnosing and teaching the vocabulary skills are presented in Chapter 10.

Objectives 2.3

On successful completion of this chapter, the participant will be able to:

1. Define the following terms:
   (1) denotative meaning
   (2) connotative meaning

      (3) grapheme
      (4) phoneme
      (5) morpheme
      (6) sight word skills
      (7) borrowing
      (8) coining
      (9) acronym

2. State the circumstances under which each of the following should be used: word attack skills, sight word skills.

3. Identify the word attack skill being used when given situations that involve an adolescent's reading.

4. Construct and discuss an original example of an adolescent using a given vocabulary skill according to the following criteria: (1) the example must be from the content area in which the participant teaches, (2) the discussion should concern one advantage and disadvantage of the vocabulary skill presented in the original example.

5. State one advantage and one disadvantage of using each of the vocabulary skills.

6. State the reason why a reader should use a variety of vocabulary skills.

7. (On the lines below, add other objectives according to your instructor's directions.) _____

_____

8. _____

_____

9. _____

_____

10. _____

_____

*   *   *   *   *   *   *   *   *   *   *   *   *

Chapter 13, Experience 2, extends Chapter 2 with this objective:

11. During this experience, the participant will analyze a student's reading to identify the vocabulary skills being used.

*   *   *   *   *   *   *   *   *   *   *   *   *

Self Pre-Assessment 2.4

Can you complete all the activities listed in **Objectives 2.3**? Answer "yes," "no," or "not certain."

If you answered "yes" to the question, complete the enabling activities required by your instructor and take the Post-Assessment on the date assigned by him.

If you answered "no," refer to **Enabling Activities 2.5.** If you decide to do any activities that are not required, select those that best suit you as a learner. You need not complete all the optional activities or all parts of a particular optional activity. As soon as you have the information you need to complete the objectives, answer "yes" to the **Self Pre-Assessment 2.4** question and stop the activity.

If you answered "not certain" to the question, refer to **Enabling Activities 2.5** of this text. Select the enabling activity that best suits your style of learning and peruse it. Then make a firm "yes" or "no" answer and proceed accordingly.

Enabling Activities 2.5

Complete only as many of the activities listed below as are required and which you need in order to meet the objectives.

1. *Enabling activity one* is a *reading* alternative. This is **Information Given 2.6.** It is a brief overview of some of the vocabulary skills that middle, junior, and senior high school students should know.
2. *Enabling activity two* is another *reading* option. In this case, the material to be read is one of the textbooks used to expand the theoretical background for this course. See chart on inside front cover for keying in textbooks that may be used.
3. *Enabling activity three* is a *class session* option. Attend the class session(s) on the date(s), at the time(s), and at the place(s) announced.

(Date)	(Time)	(Place)
(Date)	(Time)	(Place)
(Date)	(Time)	(Place)

4. *Enabling activity four* (These lines are left blank so that you may add other enabling activities as suggested by your instructor.)_____

5. *Enabling activity five*_____

6. *Enabling activity six*_____

Now that you have completed the appropriate number of required and/or optional learning alternatives, look back at **Self Pre-Assessment 2.4.** If you feel you can answer "yes" to all of the questions, you are ready to proceed to the Post-Assessment. This may be given to you immediately or after completion of a series of chapters.

Information Given 2.6
Identifying the Vocabulary Skills

The teachers at Clarke Middle School and LaSalle Junior-Senior High School attended a workshop designed to help them learn how to teach the skills that their students needed in order to understand textbooks. The reading consultant had shown the teachers sentences from four different subject area texts to start the discussion.

History: "In June Moscow and Washington agreed on a 'hot line' to provide direct teletype communications between the two capitals to help prevent nuclear war by accident." (Todd and Curti 1972, p. 591)

Mathematics: "If the replacement set is U = {2, 4, 6, 8, 10}, list the elements in the set of each of the following sentences." (Payne, Zamboni, and Lankford 1972, p. 22)

Biology: "The chromatids from each chromosome move apart." (BSCS 1973, p. 359)

English: "The 'yes–no' question transformation may be applied to all of the basic patterns." (Guth and Schuster 1970, p. 139)

After reading the sample sentences, several teachers pointed out words that would not be known to some of the students. In doing this, the teachers showed that they realized that vocabulary development is a skill important to success in all content areas.

VOCABULARY DIFFICULTIES IN THE MIDDLE AND SECONDARY SCHOOL

A student's ability to pronounce and give meaning to the words in content area textbooks contributes much to the correct interpretation of the content, since misunderstanding even one important word could radically change the intended meaning of a sentence, paragraph, or an entire selection.

Technical Words

All words in textbooks can be roughly divided into two groups. One group consists of words that are common to all subject areas (e.g., *a*, *and*, *the*, *on*, *not*). The other group is made up of words that are unique to a specific subject area (e.g., *gerund*, *participle*). These are called *technical* words. There are three types of technical words: (1) words peculiar to the subject area, (2) words common to all content areas but used with special meanings in certain subjects, and (3) signs and symbols. Words peculiar to an area include *chromatids* and *chromosomes* (biology). Common words that have taken on technical meaning include *hot line* (history), *replacement set* and *elements* (mathematics), and *"yes–no" question transformation* and *basic pattern* (English). Signs and symbols include U = {2, 4, 6, 8, 10} (mathematics).

Using the classifications listed above, the teachers then developed lists of some of the technical words peculiar to their subject areas. Examples from history, mathematics, science, and English follow.

History
Words peculiar to subject area: aqueduct, Bolshevik, capitol, extraterritoriality, fascism, homestead.
Common words with special meaning: Allied Powers, Big Three, cold war, grandfather clause, yellow-dog contract.
Signs and symbols: coined words (acronyms) such as EPA, NATO, NRA, UN, UNESCO.

Mathematics
Words peculiar to subject area: abscissa, contrapositive, integer, monomial, polygon, quadrant, rectangle, vertex.
Common words with special meanings: acute, constant function, coordinate, direct variation, empty set, equivalent sentences, field.
Signs and symbols: =, { }, ϕ, $\sqrt{\ }$, $\in$, $\notin$, c, $\not\subset$.

Biology
Words peculiar to subject area: anthropoid, ecosystem, hybrid, oogenesis, paramecium, pseudopodium.
Common words with special meanings: conduct, collision, crop, elements.
Signs and symbols: Coined words (acronyms) such as BMR, DNA, FSH, LH, LSD, NADP, NADPH, PGAL, RNA.

English
Words peculiar to subject area: adjective, adverb, apostrophe, consonant, diacritical, pseudonym, vowel.
Common words with special meanings: active voice, case, dash.
Signs and Symbols: ¶, " ", !, ?, :, '.

Due to the number of technical words that are to be found in textbooks, it is impossible to teach students to recognize every term they encounter. Thus the teacher must select key terms to teach from each unit. Criteria for word selection might include (1) The importance of the word in comprehending the topic. A word that is vital to comprehension should be given priority for study. (2) The number of times the word is used. A word that is used often should be given priority over a word that is used only once or twice.

20

Multiple Meanings of Words

Another vocabulary difficulty middle and secondary students encounter is understanding the exact meanings of certain words. Few words may be defined in isolation since meaning is almost always dependent upon the way a word is used in context. Hence word study should help students recognize that most words have more than one meaning.

Perhaps the simplest starting point for secondary students to begin to learn to understand multiple word meaning is to look at words in terms of denotative meanings, connotative meanings, and figurative language.

Denotative Meanings of Words

In General Use. Reference to the dictionary verifies that many words have more than one literal meaning. The word *habit* may mean "costume," "characteristic condition of the mind or body," or "addiction."

In Technical Use. A technical definition of *habit* is also given in the dictionary. This is its biological meaning, "the tendency of a plant or animal to grow in a certain way." Other previously cited examples of words used technically include the terms *Big Three*, indicating Roosevelt, Churchill, and Stalin; *acute*, describing an angle of less than 90 degrees; *conduct*, meaning to serve as a channel; and *case*, referring to form, as in possessive case.

Connotative Meanings of Words

Words that have an emotional overtone are said to be connotative. Aside from their literal meanings, these words carry a second interpretation. For example, *celebrate* and *exultant* connote positive meanings, while *morose* and *sullen* connote negative meanings. In addition, many connotative meanings can be understood only in terms of the total context and are not usually defined as such in the dictionary. Words of this nature affect the author's meaning and should be recognizable to students in all content areas. Though science and math tend to be more objective than history or literature, connotative words are found in all content areas (for example, "fantastic discovery of radium" or "brilliantly arrived at theory of relativity").

Figurative Language

Like connotative words, figurative language is more apt to be found in history and literature than in the sciences. Figurative language is used to convey a more exact impression through the use of tropes such as metaphors, similes, and personification.

Metaphors are statements that compare two objects that are different. For example, students might read in a history book: "Roosevelt was a *tower of strength* to much of the American population during the 1930s." In English, they might read: "Mr. Foster was a *mountain of a man*."

Similes are statements that use *like* or *as* to make comparisons. An example in history is: "John F. Kennedy was *like a beacon of light* to many of the American people." An example of a simile in English is: "Toby swam *like a fish.*"

Personifications are statements that attribute human characteristics to things that are not human. For example, in history: "The *cruel* drought *drove* many families from their homes." In English, a student might read: "Dorian's portrait *spoke* to him of his sinful deeds."

Students in history and literature often need help in understanding figurative language and should be aware of how it can affect the meaning of the content.

WAYS TO INCREASE VOCABULARY SKILLS IN THE MIDDLE AND SECONDARY SCHOOL

Students' vocabulary skills may be enhanced through an increased understanding of (1) word attack skills, (2) the history of the English language, and (3) sight word skills. These vocabulary skills will be discussed under the two major headings, Word Attack Skills and Other Ways to Increase Vocabulary Skills in the Middle and Secondary School.

Word Attack Skills

The word attack skills are those five skills readers use to give meaning to and/or to pronounce printed words that they do not recognize immediately. These five strategies include illustration clues, context clues, phonic analysis, structural analysis, and dictionary skills. The following section defines and gives examples of each of these skills. Teaching suggestions and issues relating to each skill are then discussed. Further techniques for teaching each skill are given in Chapter 10.

Word Attack Skills Using Illustration Clues

Word attack skills include the use of illustrations to help readers pronounce and/or attach meaning to words that they do not recognize immediately. For example, Frank read the following sentence in *Basic Technical Drawing:*

The architect's scale, Fig. 2.1, is an all-round scale for many uses.

After reading the sentence, Frank did not know what an architect's scale was. However, he realized what it was after referring to the drawing shown in Figure 2.1.

The reader may test his use of illustration clues by looking at the term *commission government.* If the reader can give meaning to the term, then

22

he has no need for the illustration clue. If not, he may look at the picture in Figure 2.2 and then verbalize the definition of *commission government*. If the reader used Figure 2.2 to help him understand the term *commission government*, he used an illustration clue.

MECHANICAL DRAWING

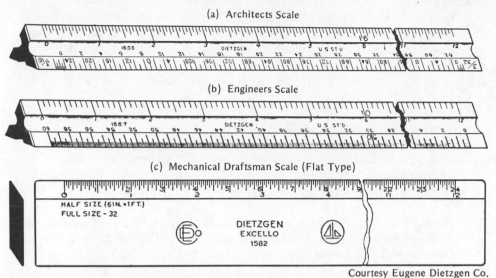

(a) Architects Scale

(b) Engineers Scale

(c) Mechanical Draftsman Scale (Flat Type)

Courtesy Eugene Dietzgen Co.

From *Basic Technical Drawing* by H.C. Spencer and J.T. Dygdon, copyright © 1974, Macmillan Publishing Co., Inc. Used with permission.

Figure 2.1 Types of Scales.

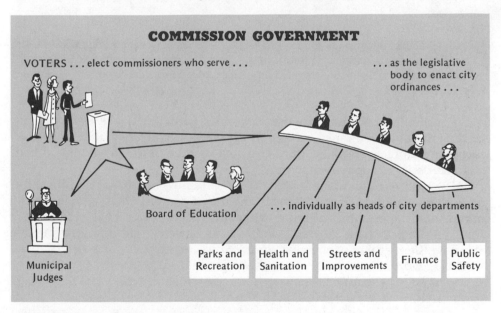

COMMISSION GOVERNMENT

VOTERS ... elect commissioners who serve ...

... as the legislative body to enact city ordinances ...

Board of Education

... individually as heads of city departments

Municipal Judges

Parks and Recreation | Health and Sanitation | Streets and Improvements | Finance | Public Safety

From *American Government,* by G. Bruntz and John Bremer, ©Copyright, 1965, by Ginn and Company (Xerox Corporation). Used with permission.

Figure 2.2 Commission Government

23

Illustration clues aid the reader in understanding the meaning of a word. In addition, they may help him pronounce the word if he knows it but simply does not recognize it in print. For example, Ada was not able to pronounce the written word *hors d'oeuvres* before she referred to an illustration of some. However, after referring to the illustration, she immediately recognized the printed word *hors d'oeuvres* as the spoken word *hors d'oeuvres.*

Illustration clues are very helpful in content areas where new words and word meanings are being taught or where new procedures that can be diagrammed are explained. Teachers in content areas such as chemistry, shop, or home economics can reinforce their students' use of illustration clues by drawing attention to explanatory figures in the textbook.

Word Attack Skills Using Context Clues

Word attack skills involve the reader's use of the words surrounding an unknown word to be able to pronounce or give meaning to it. For example, Kathy came to the following sentence in her technical drawing book:

> In the "broaching machine," a long cutting tool called a "broach," which has a series of teeth that gradually increase in size, is forced through a hole or over a surface to produce a desired shape. (Spencer and Dygdon 1974, p. 181)

Before reading the sentence, Kathy did not know the meaning of *broach* denoting *tool.* However, the context explained the meaning.

Readers may test their own use of context clues by reading the following sentence:

> For the last thirty years or more, linguistics scholars have been toying with the idea of applying the knowledge they have acquired on the development and characteristics of our spoken language to the problems of reading that language. (Aukerman 1971, p. 141)

If the reader did not know the meaning of the term *linguistics scholars* before reading the above sentence, using context clues should have made it clear that linguistics scholars are those who have a knowledge of the development and characteristics of spoken language.

Using Context Clues is the word attack skill most helpful to middle and secondary school students. Through the use of context clues, students can understand the meanings of unknown words without ever having to glance up from the paragraph they are reading. Context clues aid primarily in understanding the meaning of the new word. However, they can also help in pronouncing words if the context brings the familiar spoken word to mind.

Special Helps in Using Context Clues. Most textbooks contain various types of context clues. Several are discussed here.

1. A *definition* of the term may be directly stated; for example, "Hyracotherium are the oldest members of the genus Equidae, or horse family."

2. An *implication* of the term from the general context of the passage may suggest the meaning; for example, "Hyracotherium had a cheek teeth span of 4.3 centimeters, whereas modern-day horse has a span of 17.6 centimeters."
3. Several *examples* might illustrate the meaning; for example, "Parallel lines may take any of the following forms: ‖ ∥ = \\."
4. The use of *contrast* may provide meaning; for example, "David's speech was fanciful, unlike his usual factual presentations."
5. The *expectancy* of meaning might help the student; for example, if he were reading about conservation, he might expect to see terms such as *forest, water, mineral wealth, coal, iron, oil,* and *gas.*

Teachers in all subject areas can encourage students to use context to help them recognize words in two ways. First, the topic can be discussed prior to reading so that students will have heard many of the words before they actually read. Second, teachers can show students the different types of context clues listed above and can encourage them to look for such clues when they encounter unknown words.

Word Attack Skills Using Phonic Analysis

In this text, *phonic analysis* will refer to those skills a student uses to obtain meaning through correct pronunciation of the word. The approach used by a reader in attempting to pronounce a word usually follows this sequence: (1) the reader identifies the syllables, (2) if the word has more than one syllable, he decides which syllable is accented, (3) the reader pronounces each syllable, and (4) he blends the syllables to form the word.* For example, Palmer encountered the word *obfuscate* in his text. He had never seen the word in print before and did not recognize it. Thus, using his phonic analysis skills, he proceeded to: (1) identify the syllables (ob/fus/cate), (2) decide which syllable is accented (fus), (3) pronounce the syllables (*ob* as in *obtuse, fus* as in *fuss,* and *cate* as in *indicate*) and (4) blend the syllables to pronounce the word. Then, Palmer was able to recognize the word as he heard himself pronounce it. Therefore, he was able to gain meaning through phonic analysis.

Readers may test their own use of phonic analysis by pronouncing the word *constrainedly.*

Unless the reader recognized the word immediately, he probably went through the process of: (1) identifying the syllables (con/strain/ed/ly), (2) identifying the accented syllable (strain), (3) pronouncing each syllable (*con* as in *confuse, strain* as in *strainer, ed* as in *educate,* and *ly* as in *jelly*) and (4) blending the syllables to pronounce the word (kən–stran'–ĕd–li).

In order to use phonic analysis in this manner, students need to know the generalizations for (1) dividing words into syllables, (2) placing the accent,

*This technique is adapted from G. L. Bond and M. A. Tinker, *Reading Difficulties: Their Diagnosis and Correction,* 3rd ed. (New York: Appleton-Century-Crofts, 1973), pp. 316–318.

and (3) pronouncing syllables.

Definition of a Syllable. A syllable is a word or part of a word that is pronounced with a single, uninterrupted sounding of the voice. For each syllable, there is one and only one vowel sound. Though the word *measure* has four vowels, it has only two vowel sounds and hence consists of two syllables; namely, meas/ure, pronounced mĕzh ẽr.

1. Generalizations for Dividing Words into Syllables. There are four important generalizations for dividing words into syllables: (1) when two consonants (similar or dissimilar) occur between two vowels, the syllables divide between the two consonants (e.g., sum/mer, for/ty); (2) when a single consonant occurs between two vowels, the syllables usually divide after the first vowel (e.g., ho/tel); (3) if a consonant blend or digraph occurs between two vowels, treat the blend or digraph as a single consonant (e.g., con/stant, A/pril); and (4) a prefix or a suffix often forms a separate syllable (e.g., un/like, jump/ing). Beware of the words that have a suffix such as *jumped* and *phoned* which have only one syllable and only one vowel sound.

2. Generalizations for Accenting the Appropriate Syllables. There are two important generalizations for accenting syllables: (1) the first syllable of a word (except prefixes) is usually accented (e.g., syl'/la/ble, pre/des'/tine); (2) some syllables in multisyllabic words neither have the primary accent nor are totally lacking in accent; they have a secondary accent (e.g., ben'/e/fi'/cial).

3. Generalizations for Pronouncing Syllables. Unless a student recognizes a syllable immediately, he must relate the printed letter to the spoken sound. *Grapheme* is the term used to identify one or more printed letters that correspond to a single spoken sound, or *phoneme.* Graphemes include consonant letters such as *b, d, f*; consonant combinations such as *sh, ch, bl*; vowels such as *a, e*; and vowel combinations such as *ou* and *oi.*

The approach used by a student in attempting to pronounce a syllable usually follows this sequence: (1) the reader identifies the graphemes or grapheme groups that correspond to single phonemes, (2) the reader pronounces each phoneme, and (3) the reader blends the phonemes to form the word. For example, Marie encountered the syllable *shim*, which she had not seen in print before and did not recognize on sight. Thus she proceeded to (1) identify the graphemes, sh/i/m, (2) pronounce the phonemes, *sh* as in *shut, i* as in *it, m* as in *man*, and (3) blend the phonemes to pronounce the syllable /shim/.

To identify graphemes and pronounce phonemes, students need to know: (1) the *single consonant sounds* such as *b*at and *d*art; (2) the *consonant blends* that are formed when two or more consonants occur together and two or more sounds are heard, as in *cr*own and *spr*ing; (3) the *consonant digraphs* that are formed when two consonants occur together and only one sound, that is totally different from that of either of the consonants that form it, is heard, as in *wh*en, *sh*irt, *th*e, *ph*one, and *ch*air; (4) the *vowel diphthongs* that occur when two vowels are adjacent in one syllable and two sounds are heard, as in *oi*l, bl*ou*se, and b*oy*; (5) the *vowel digraphs* that occur when two vowels are adjacent in one syllable and only one sound is heard, as in *eat* and *boat*; (6) the *schwa sound* that occurs in unaccented syllables and has a brief *uh* sound as in reck*o*n and *a*ccount; (7) the *controlled vowels* that occur when a vowel is influenced by the consonant *r* as in g*e*rm, *l* as in *a*ll, or *w* as in y*e*w; (8) the *long and short vowels* that occur in one-syllable words or in syllables with a primary or secondary accent, as in (long) *a*te, *e*ve, h*i*, c*o*ne, *u*se and (short) c*a*t, s*e*t, s*i*t, st*o*p, and n*u*t. (Long vowels usually occur in syllables ending in a vowel as in h*i*, ending in a silent *e* as in mat*e*, and containing a vowel digraph as in m*ea*t. Short vowels occur in syllables ending with a consonant as in c*a*t.) and (9) the *silent letters*, which have no sound when the word is spoken, as in beni*g*n and mat*e*.

Limitations of Phonic Analysis. Phonic analysis will be successful only if the following two circumstances exist:

1. The student recognizes the word when it is spoken. For example, Ben came to *15 mo* in his reading. Using his phonic generalizations, he pronounced the syllable so that it rhymed with *go*. However, since he did not recognize the word when he heard himself say it, he was unable to attach meaning to the word or to tell whether his pronunciation was accurate. Another student, Harold, came to the same phrase, *15 mo*. Using his phonic generalizations, he also pronounced the word *mo* to rhyme with *go*. However, he was aware that his pronunciation was correct, since he recalled his teacher's using the word in class. He also associated appropriate meaning with it, since he knew the meaning of the spoken word.

2. The word follows the phonic generalization that should apply. For example, the underlined portions of words such as w*a*ne, ch*i*de, sm*i*te, m*u*te, del*e*te, secr*e*te, ent*i*ce, and suff*i*ce follow the generalization that the medial vowel is long in syllables that end with the letter *e*. Students who use this generalization to pronounce the word *fife* will be able to recognize it as the word they have heard their music teacher mention.

One of the major limitations to the use of phonic analysis is that many exceptions may be found to virtually all the rules, and some include more exceptions than applications. For example, the above rule concerning the silent *e* would not apply to words such as: s*o*me, c*o*me, h*e*re, fut*i*le, reg*i*me, appren*ti*ce, fest*i*ve.

Another limitation is that grapheme by grapheme analyzation is a slow process and the use of other word attack skills, such as Using Context Clues or Using Illustration Clues, usually provides a much quicker means to arrive at the meaning of a word. Therefore, students should be taught to use phonic analysis only when these other means of word attack have not proven useful. One technique that all content area teachers can use to reinforce their students' phonic skills is having them do the following: (1) divide words into syllables, (2) place the accent, (3) pronounce the syllables, and (4) blend the syllables.

Word Attack Skills Using Structural Analysis

In this text, *structural analysis* refers to an approach to word attack that relies upon dividing words so that the various meaning-bearing parts, or *morphemes*, such as root words, prefixes, and suffixes, may be used to determine word meaning. For example, Fred came to the word *acrophobia*.

He identified the prefix *acro* as meaning *high* and the root word *phobia* as meaning *a fear of.* Thus, he interpreted the meaning of the word as *a fear of heights.*

Readers may test their own use of structural analysis by analyzing the word *introspectionism.* If the reader were not familiar with the word previously, he probably went through a process such as the following to pronounce it: breaking the word into morphemes—intro/spect/ion/ism—and attaching meaning to the morphemes by interpreting (1) the prefix *intro* as *inward*, (2) the morpheme *spect* as *to look*, (3) the suffix *ion* as *state of being*, (4) the suffix *ism* as *the practice of*, and (5) the meaning of the entire word *introspectionism* as something like *the practice of looking into one's self.*

To use structural analysis the student must have a wide knowledge of the meanings of root words, prefixes, and suffixes. The following three tables list common Greek and Latin roots and affixes, common prefixes, and common suffixes.

Many English root words and affixes are derived from Greek and Latin words. Thus a knowledge of one Greek or Latin term may help the student understand several English words. Likewise, a knowledge of common prefixes and common suffixes can aid in determining word meaning.

Content teachers can reinforce their students' use of structural analysis by asking them to (1) divide the word into morphemes, (2) examine the morphemes for meaning (for example, /dogs/ is a one-syllable word that contains two meaningful units: *dog* meaning the animal, and *s* meaning more than one; on the other hand, aq/ua/ma/rine is a four-syllable word that contains two meaningful units: *aqua* meaning *water* and *marine* meaning *sea*), and (3) interpret the meaning of the word using knowledge of root words and affixes. The meaningful units *dog* and *s* must mean *more than one dog*; the meaningful units *aqua* and *marine* must refer to *sea water.*

Word Attack Skills Using the Dictionary

Word attack skills using the dictionary are the skills involved in finding an unrecognized word in a dictionary, pronouncing it according to the diacritical markings, and finding the meaning appropriate for its use.

For example, Arlen encountered the word *indicted.* He was unable to recognize it by using illustration clues, context clues, phonic analysis, or structural analysis. He, therefore, located the word in the dictionary, used diacritical markings to pronounce it, and chose the correct meaning from those listed in the dictionary.

In the following sentence, neither illustration clues, phonic analysis, nor structural analysis can help the reader if he does not already know the word. The reader may test his own use of dictionary skills by analyzing the following sentence: "The Rio Grande Valley abounds in *algarroba.*" If the reader can locate *algarroba* in the dictionary, pronounce it correctly using the diacritical markings, and identify its precise meaning, he has adequate dictionary skills.

TABLE 2.1
Common Greek and Latin Roots and Affixes

Root or Affix	Meaning	Sample Word
a	not	*a*moral
ab	away	*ab*scond
ad	to, toward	*ad*jacent
amo	love	*amo*rist
ante	in front of, prior to	*ante*chamber, *ante*bellum
anti	against	*anti*social
aqu (a)	water	*aqua*cade
audi	hear	*audi*ence
auto	self	*auto*nomic
bene	good, well	*bene*volent
bibli (o)	book	*bibli*ofilm
bio	life	*bio*synthesis
cide	destroyer	geno*cide*
circum	around	*circum*ference
con	together	*con*geal
de	down, away	*de*pose, *de*sist
dia	through, across	*dia*dem
dis	apart, opposite of	*dis*jointed, *dis*content
ex	out of	*ex*port
geo	earth	*geo*physics
graph	write	encephalo*graph*
gress	go	*gress*orial
hemi	half	*hemi*algia
inter	between, among	*inter*mediary
intra	within	*intra*molecular
magni	large	*magni*loquent
mal	bad	*mal*feasance
mis	incorrect (ly)	*mis*guided
mono	one	*mono*mania
multi	many	*multi*purpose
non	not	*non*rhetorical
ology	study of	phren*ology*
ped	foot	*ped*al
per	through	*per*meate
phobia	fear (of)	myso*phobia*
poly	many	*poly*glot
port	carry	*port*manteau
post	after	*post*erior
pre	before	*pre*marital
pro	forward	*pro*ceed
pseudo	false	*pseudo*aquatic
psych	mind	*psycho*drama
re	again, back	*re*trace
semi	half	*semi*conical
spec (t)	look (at)	*spect*acular
sub	under	*sub*committee
tele	far	*tele*cast
theo	god	*theo*centric
trans	across	*trans*om
uni	one	*uni*ted

TABLE 2.2
Common Prefixes

Prefix	Meaning	Sample Word
ad (a, ac)	to, toward	*ad*here (*a*scend, *ac*quaint)
be	about, over	*be*speckle
	thoroughly	*be*drench
	by	*be*side
com (con)	with, together	*com*mute
	very	*con*tort
de	away	*de*legate
	down	*de*pose
dis	from	*dis*miss
	opposite of	*dis*honest
en	in, into	*en*close
ex	out	*ex*animate
	from	*ex*communicate
	beyond	*ex*cel
in	in, into	*in*doors
in (ir, il, im)	not	*in*active (*ir*responsible, *il*legitimate, *im*proper)
mis	incorrect (ly)	*mis*judge
non	not	*non*fat
over	too much	*over*pay
	beyond	*over*seas
pre	prior to	*pre*historic
	in front of	*pre*axial
pro	in front of	*pro*ject
	instead of	*pro*noun
	prior to	*pro*logue
re	back	*re*cede
	again	*re*combine
sub	beneath	*sub*marine
	almost	*sub*humid
trans	across	*trans*oceanic
	not	*un*kind
	opposite of	*un*dress

Other Ways to Increase Vocabulary Skills
in the Middle and Secondary School

Another way of increasing students' vocabulary skills is to expand their conceptual backgrounds. Two means of doing this are to interest them in the history of the English language and to increase their existing sight word skills.

TABLE 2.3
Common Suffixes

Suffix	Meaning	Sample Word
able	able to	respect*able*
age	state of being	parson*age*
	process of	post*age*
al	of or pertaining to	matrimoni*al*
an, n, ian	of or pertaining to	Austr*ian*
ance, ence	state of being	perform*ance*
ant, ent	one who (which)	inform*ant*
ary	of or pertaining to	judici*ary*
	location of	infirm*ary*
ate, ite	office of	magistr*ate*
	associated with	suburban*ite*
ed	did _____	tempt*ed*
er	more _____	full*er*
	one who (which)	farm*er*
es	more than one	box*es*
est	most _____	great*est*
ful	characterized by	beauti*ful*
	as much as	spoon*ful*
ic, ical	of or pertaining to	com*ical*
ing	in the process of	jump*ing*
ion, tion, ation	act of	elec*tion*
	state of being	combin*ation*
ish	like, the nature of	boy*ish*
ity, ty	condition, state, degree of	complex*ity*
ive	tendency to	impuls*ive*
less	without	friend*less*
ly	like, the nature of	careful*ly*
ment	state or quality	amaze*ment*
	act of	induce*ment*
ness	state or degree	peaceful*ness*
or	one who (which)	guarant*or*
ous	like, full of	wondr*ous*
y	diminutive of	Bill*y*
	like	milk*y*

Understanding the History of the English Language

A brief knowledge of the history of a word can often interest students in learning it and, hence, broaden their vocabularies by putting otherwise isolated terms into new perspectives. For example, the word *knight* in the sentence "The knight was miles away from the river" does not lend itself well to decoding through context clues, structural analysis, illustration clues, or

31

phonic analysis. One way to help students put this word into their functional reading vocabularies is to provide them with a means for remembering it. Therefore, telling students that the English language comes in part from the Anglo-Saxon, and that many years ago people pronounced *knight* with the *k* sound and thus spelled it that way may help them remember the word and thus recognize *knight* when they see it.

Similarly, students can be taught characteristics of the English language such as the following.

Latin and Greek were the languages of learning for many centuries. Thus much terminology used today has developed from these languages. As a result, many of the technical terms found in the content areas are derived from Latin and Greek. For example, in history, the word *aqueduct* is derived from the Latin *aqu(a)*, denoting *water*; *capitol* is derived from the Latin *caput*, meaning *head*. In math, *monomial* comes from the Greek *mono*, meaning *one*; and *quadrant* from the Latin *quad*, meaning *four*. In biology, the term *photothermic* is derived from the Greek *phos*, denoting *light*, and *therme*, meaning *heat*. In English, the word *simile* comes from the Latin *similis*, meaning *like*; and *pseudonym* from the Greek *pseudes*, meaning *false*.

Sometimes words are borrowed almost directly from other languages rather than derived from common roots. One example from home economics is the word *pizza*. When this dish became popular with Americans in the mid-1950s, instead of developing a new term, Americans simply borrowed the Italian word naming this food. In math, the word *rectangle* comes directly from the French. In literature, the term *saga* is borrowed from the Scandinavian languages. And, in geography, the Russian word *steppe* is used.

Another characteristic of the English language is to invent new terms. This process of naming or making new words is called *coining*. Fabricating new words by joining parts or syllables of others is blending, one kind of coining. An example of a familiar nontechnical, coined word is *motel*, made from *mot*or and h*otel*. In science, the terms *altimeter* (*alti*tude, baro*meter*) and *minicam* (*mini*ature, *cam*era) are used. In history such terms as *fem lib* (*fem*inine, *lib*eration) and *Gerrymander* (*Gerry*, sala*mander*) are found.

Coining also includes the development of *acronyms*, words formed usually by joining the beginning letters of other words. Acronyms are particularly used in history where *NATO*, *UNESCO*, *UN*, *EPA*, and *HEW* often appear. In science, such acronyms as *DNA*, *RNA*, and *LSD* are commonplace.

Increasing Sight Word Skills

Sight word skills include those skills that enable the reader to recognize words immediately. For example, Michael read the following sentence in a book for his math class: "Shapes and forms make the word around us more beautiful and more pleasurable." (Van Engen et al. 1969, p. 163) Since he recognized all the words immediately he did not have to use any world attack skills and was able to rely completely on his sight word skills.

To test his own use of sight word skills, the reader may read the following sentence: "He had in mind exactly what the name implies: triangle measurement." (Vance 1969, p. 34) The reader probably read each word in the sentence accurately and immediately and, in doing so, used his sight word skills.

Most students recognize as sight words the majority of the words they encounter. This is the most rapid way to read in all subject areas and the word recognition technique most used by adult readers. The word attack skills described earlier in this chapter should be used only when a word is not recognized as a sight word.

Teachers can encourage their students to develop sight word skills by advising extensive reading and by giving their students a purpose for reading material when they assign it. Through such wide and directed reading, students will learn to recognize thousands of words.

Uses of Sight Word Skills

Identifying Weak Readers Through Diagnosing Sight Word Skills. One way to identify middle, junior, and senior high school students who are severely behind in their reading is to assess their knowledge of the most frequently used words in the English language. Various sight word lists, such as those by Dolch (1945), Stone (1956), and Fry (1957), include words that occur frequently in printed English. The first twenty-five of the six hundred words in the Fry list are *the, a, is, you, to, and, we, that, in, not, for, at, with, it, on, can, will, are, of, this, your, as, but, be,* and *have.* These words are ordinarily learned in the first grade and students who do not know them may be diagnosed as being on a first grade reading level. Though the teaching of such elementary skills to secondary and middle school students is not in the usual domain of the content area teacher, sometimes knowledge of such a word list can help the teacher determine the level of the content area material to provide for the student.

Learning Words Through Memory. Some words cannot be learned through the use of word attack skills with the exception of looking up the words in a reference book each time they are encountered. Such terms must be memorized. For example, the mathematical term p (meaning probability) and the diacritical marking " ə " (meaning schwa sound) must be memorized.

In both cases, the symbols do not lend themselves to any means of word attack. Hence they can be learned only by reference to a given definition, that is, p = probability, and ə = the schwa sound. Students who need to learn these terms would have to learn them by memory and might be encouraged to write the p on one side of a flashcard and the meaning on the other until they were thoroughly familiar with the term and it became part of their sight vocabularies.

Using a Combination of Vocabulary Skills

The vocabulary skills have been discussed in isolation in this chapter. During the reading process, they are used in combination. For example, Maurice read the following sentence in *History of a Free People:* "Throughout the North, there was opposition to the more stringent Fugitive Slave Law that was included in the Compromise of 1850." (Bragdon, McCutchen, and Cole, 1973, p. 336) Maurice recognized all the words as sight words except *stringent*. He used context clues to ascertain that *stringent* might be synonymous with rigid. Since Maurice did not recognize any historical connotations or the meaning of any morphemes, he could not use his knowledge of the history of the English language or of structural analysis. Instead he used phonic analysis to divide *stringent* into syllables, strin/gent. He used his knowledge of graphemes and phonemes, to pronounce the syllable *strin*. He could already pronounce the syllable *gent* so did not have to use his phonic analysis to pronounce it. He then blended the syllables to form the word *stringent*. Since he did not know the meaning of the spoken word, he was unable to give any additional meaning other than that which he gained through context. If he felt that it was essential that he know the exact meaning of the word, he would use his dictionary skills to define it.

The reader may test his own use of a combination of vocabulary skills by reading the following sentence. While reading, the reader should keep a mental note of the vocabulary skills he used. "Unthinkingly, he made a puerile remark." Was there any word on which the reader needed to use his word attack skills? If so, which ones did he use?

1. Using Illustration Clues
2. Using Context Clues
3. Using Phonic Analysis
4. Using Structural Analysis
5. Using Dictionary Skills
6. Expanding Background in Vocabulary
7. Using a Combination of Vocabulary Skills

Figure 2.3   Outline of the Vocabulary
Skills

References and Bibliography

Aukerman, R. C. *Approaches to Beginning Reading.* New York: Wiley, 1971.

Bond, G. L., and Tinker, M. A. *Reading Difficulties: Their Diagnosis and Correction.* New York: Appleton-Century-Crofts, 1973.

Bragdon, H. W., McCutchen, S. P., and Cole, C. W. *History of a Free People.* New York: Macmillan, 1973.

Bruntz, G. G., and Bremer, J. *American Government.* Boston: Ginn, 1965.

BSCS. *Biological Science: An Ecological Approach.* 3rd ed. Chicago: Rand McNally, 1973.

Burmeister, L. E. *Reading Strategies for Secondary School Teachers.* Reading, Mass.: Addison-Wesley, 1974.

Clymer, T. L. "The Utility of Phonetic Generalizations in the Primary Grades." *The Reading Teacher,* 16 (January 1963), 252–258.

Dolch, E. W. *A Manual for Remedial Reading.* 2nd ed. Champaign, Ill.: Garrard, 1945.

Fry, E. *Fry Instant Words.* New Brunswick, N.J.: Rutgers University Reading Center, 1957.

Fry, E. *Reading Instruction for Classroom and Clinic.* New York: McGraw-Hill, 1972.

Guth, H. P., and Schuster, Edgar H. *American English Today.* New York: McGraw-Hill, 1970.

Harris, A. J. *How to Increase Reading Ability.* 5th ed. New York: McKay, 1974.

Harris, A. J., and Jacobson, M. D. "Some Comparisons Between Basic Elementary Reading Vocabularies and Other Word Lists." *Reading Research Quarterly*, 9:1 (1973–1974), 87–109.

Heilman, A. W. *Phonics in Proper Perspective.* Columbus, Ohio: Merrill, 1968.

Karlin, R. *Teaching Reading in High School.* 2nd ed. Indianapolis, Ind.: Bobbs-Merrill, 1972.

Lamb, P. *Linguistics in Proper Perspective.* Columbus, Ohio: Merrill, 1967.

Olson, A. V., and Ames, W. S. *Teaching Reading Skills in Secondary Schools.* Scranton, Pa.: Intext Educational Publishers, 1972.

Payne, J. N., Zamboni, F. F., and Lankford, F. G., Jr. *Algebra One.* 2nd ed. New York: Harcourt Brace Jovanovich, 1972.

Robertson, J. E. "Pupil Understanding of Connectives in Reading." *Reading Research Quarterly*, 3:3 (Spring 1968), 388–417.

Rodgers, D. "Which Connectives? Signals to Enhance Comprehension." *Journal of Reading* (March 1974), 462–466.

Savage, J. F. *Linguistics for Teachers.* Chicago: SRA, 1973.

Spencer, H. C., and Dygdon, J. T. *Basic Technical Drawing.* New York: Macmillan, 1974.

Stone, C. R. "Measuring Difficulty of Primary Reading Material: A Constructive Criticism of Spache's Measure." *Elementary School Journal*, 17 (October 1956), 36–41.

Stoodt, B. D. "The Relationship Between Understanding Grammatical Conjunctions and Reading Comprehension." *Elementary English*, 49 (April 1972), 502–504.

Thomas, E. L., and Robinson, H. A. *Improving Reading in Every Class.* Boston: Allyn & Bacon, 1972.

Thomas, O. *The Structure of Language.* Indianapolis, Ind.: Bobbs-Merrill, 1967.

Thorndike, E. *The Teaching of English Suffixes.* New York: Teachers College, 1941.

Todd, L. P., and Curti, M. *Rise of the American Nation.* Vol. 2, 3rd ed. New York: Harcourt Brace Jovanovich, 1972.

Vance, E. P. *Trigonometry.* 2nd ed. Reading, Mass.: Addison-Wesley, 1969.

Van Engen, H., et al. *Mathematics—Concepts, Applications.* Glenview, Ill.: Scott, Foresman, 1969.

Zintz, M. V. *The Reading Process: The Teacher and the Learner.* Dubuque, Iowa: Brown, 1970.

Chapter 3

Identifying the Comprehension Skills

Prerequisite 3.1

Participants should have successfully completed the objectives for Chapter 1 or should have an understanding of the relationship between reading and comprehension before beginning this chapter.

Rationale 3.2

Teachers in many subject areas rely heavily upon reading materials to help students meet course objectives. To make the best use of these materials, teachers need to understand the comprehension skills. This chapter describes in detail thirteen reading comprehension skills that all secondary students should attempt to master. In addition, a three-dimensional model of the comprehension skills is introduced and shows how a teacher in any subject area might adapt instruction to his students' needs by increasing or decreasing the difficulty level. Methodology for teaching the comprehension skills is given in Chapter 10.

Objectives 3.3

On successful completion of this chapter, the participant will be able to:

1. List three comprehension skills in which he feels proficiency would be most valuable to students in the content area in which he will be teaching and give reasons for his choices.

2. Write one original question for the comprehension skills that apply to his subject area.
3. Select one comprehension skill that pertains to his area and explain how it might be adjusted in difficulty by applying the principles of the readability hierarchy, unit hierarchy, and usage hierarchy.
4. (On the lines below, add other objectives according to your instructor's directions.) _____

   _____

5. _____

   _____

6. _____

   _____

7. _____

   _____

*   *   *   *   *   *   *   *   *   *   *   *   *   *

Chapter 13, Experience 3 extends Chapter 3 with this objective:

8. During this experience, the participant will: (1) select two comprehension skills that apply to his area, (2) design questions on low, medium, and high levels of difficulty for each skill, using singly or in combination the principles of the readability hierarchy, the unit hierarchy, and the usage hierarchy, and (3) present the questions to a student.

*   *   *   *   *   *   *   *   *   *   *   *   *   *

Self Pre-Assessment 3.4

Can you complete all the activities listed in **Objectives 3.3**? Answer "yes," "no," or "not certain."

If you answered "yes" to the question, complete the enabling activities required by your instructor and take the Post-Assessment on the date assigned by him.

If you answered "no," refer to **Enabling Activities 3.5**. If you decide to do any activities that are not required, select those that best suit you as a learner. You need not complete all the optional activities or all parts of a particular optional activity. As soon as you have the information you need to complete the objectives, answer "yes" to the **Self Pre-Assessment 3.4** question and stop the activity.

If you answered "not certain" to the question, refer to **Enabling Activities**

3.5. Select the enabling activity that best suits your style of learning and peruse it. Then make a firm "yes" or "no" answer and proceed accordingly.

Enabling Activities 3.5

Complete only as many of the activities listed below as are required and which you need in order to meet the objectives.

1. *Enabling activity one* is a *reading* alternative. This is **Information Given 3.6**. It is a brief overview of a scope and organization of the comprehension skills.
2. *Enabling activity two* is another *reading* option. In this case, the material to be read is one of the textbooks used to expand the theoretical background for this course. See chart on inside front cover for keying in textbooks that may be used.
3. *Enabling activity three* is a *class session* option. Attend the class session(s) on the date(s), at the time(s), and at the place(s) announced.

_____	_____	_____
(Date)	(Time)	(Place)
_____	_____	_____
(Date)	(Time)	(Place)
_____	_____	_____
(Date)	(Time)	(Place)

4. *Enabling activity four* (These lines are left blank so that you may add other enabling activities as suggested by your instructor.)_____

   _____

   _____

   _____

5. *Enabling activity five*_____

   _____

6. *Enabling activity six*_____

   _____

Now that you have completed the appropriate number of required and/or optional learning alternatives, look back at **Self Pre-Assessment 3.4**. If you feel you can answer "yes" to all of the questions, you are ready to proceed to the Post-Assessment. This may be given to you immediately or after completion of a series of chapters.

A task force of secondary level classroom teachers had been observing middle, junior, and senior high school classes in preparation for a meeting with a newly hired reading consultant. One member of the group observed a math class in which students were being asked to solve a problem that stated, "The sum of two consecutive integers is 7; what are the two integers?" Another participant in the group visited a history class. Students there were attempting to answer the question, "What changes might occur if the presidential term of office were increased to six years?" A third teacher spent some time in a chemistry class in which students were trying to respond to the question, "Write a balanced equation for the combining of the magnesium ion and the sulfate ion." A fourth group member observed an English class in which students were endeavoring to discern Swift's purpose for writing *Gulliver's Travels*.

The task force of teachers discussed their observations and decided that even though the classes they had observed were different in content area, successfully completing each lesson had required the students to use their *reading comprehension skills*.

On completion of their discussion, the group of teachers had two questions to ask of the reading consultant: (1) What are the comprehension skills? (2) What are the components of each?

This chapter will discuss the answers to these questions.

SCOPE OF THE COMPREHENSION SKILLS

In Chapter 1, the comprehension skills are defined as those that aid the student in understanding and applying information contained within written material. They, like the vocabulary skills, are made up of many subskills. However, there is little agreement among authorities as to specifically what the comprehension subskills are. Therefore, it is not surprising that when Simons examined several major approaches to comprehension in 1971, he discovered innumerable skills lists, some containing several hundred skills. Most authorities do agree however that reading comprehension is a function of the over-all concept of comprehension as determined by one's thinking ability.

Comprehension and Thinking

The term *thinking* is ill-defined and includes many aspects. When a student reads, his eyes and his brain react to the visual stimuli of the printed word. When he comprehends what he reads, he has sorted out the words according to a thinking pattern controlled by his brain. This complexity of the thinking

39

process and the connection between thinking and reading is one reason why no single set of descriptors for the comprehension skills has ever been agreed upon.

Comprehension Descriptors

Many authorities feel that the teaching of reading comprehension can be facilitated by giving teachers an enumerated list of skills by which to assess the scope of the skills they should be teaching. Brief discussions of these types of lists—(1) unit length, (2) taxonomical, and (3) undifferentiated— are given below.

Unit Length List

Authors who present unit length lists stress teaching comprehension skills through the understanding of units of varying lengths. Teaching techniques in this approach would include teaching students to understand words first, then sentences, and then paragraphs and longer units. Representative of proponents of this kind of classification are Bond and Tinker (1973), who use it in conjunction with an *undifferentiated list.* In *Personalizing Reading Instruction in Middle, Junior, and Senior High Schools*, a unit length list is not used as a skill descriptor. Instead, sentences, paragraphs, and longer units are viewed as structures to convey thoughts that may be understood only by analyzing specific aspects contained within. This conceptualization is discussed in detail under the topic **Unit Hierarchy** in this chapter.

Taxonomical List

The taxonomical list involves dividing skills into hierarchical groups. Even though there is no differentiation in the difficulty of the skills within each, every group in the hierarchy is more difficult than the one preceding it. Therefore, each group of skills must be learned before succeeding ones can be understood. Barrett (1968) is representative of authorities who present this type of list. He delineates five categories, which in hierarchical order include the following: (1) literal comprehension—recognizing and recalling details, main ideas, sequence, comparison, cause and effect, and character traits; (2) reorganization—classifying, outlining, summarizing, synthesizing explicitly stated ideas or information; (3) inference—concluding supporting details, main ideas, sequence, comparisons, cause and effect, character traits, outcomes, and figurative language; (4) evaluation—judging reality or fantasy, fact or opinion, adequacy and validity, appropriateness and worth, desirability, and acceptability; (5) appreciation—responding emotionally to content, identifying with characters or incidents, reacting to author's use of language, and imagery.

40

In 1966, Sanders outlined seven levels of questions to be used by classroom teachers based upon a hierarchical list of educational learning objectives produced by Bloom in 1956. Sanders' categories, listed in order of increasing complexity, are memory, translation, interpretation, application, analysis, synthesis, and evaluation. Many reading authorities, including Spache and Spache (1973), Harris and Smith (1972), Fry (1972), and Burmeister (1974), have based their comprehension taxonomies on the work of Bloom and Sanders.

The purpose of the taxonomical grouping of comprehension skills is to clarify the relationships among the skills. However, such taxonomies tend to suggest precision that simply does not exist in the understanding of the comprehension skills (Clymer, 1968). Even authorities who rely upon a common theoretical background, such as those who base their classifications upon the work of Bloom (1956) and Sanders (1966) differ in their categorization of the comprehension skills. For example, Spache and Spache (1973, p. 565) classify a skill labeled as cause–effect relationship in the Sanders "memory" category, whereas Burmeister (1974) places it in the Sanders "interpretation" category.

Undifferentiated List

In this comprehension description list, skills are often presented in a simple to complex fashion, but a hierarchy through which one *must* progress in order to learn subsequent skills is not suggested. Teaching techniques do not stress a particular order for students to follow when learning the skills. Authors who present undifferentiated lists view comprehension as an aggregate of many skills. Thomas and Robinson (1972) are representative of this group and present the following skills: (1) grasping directly stated details or facts; (2) understanding main ideas; (3) grasping the sequence of time, place, ideas, events, or steps; (4) understanding and following directions; (5) grasping implied meanings and drawing inferences; (6) understanding setting and character (emotional reactions, motives, personal traits); (7) sensing relationships of time, place, cause and effect, events, and characters; (8) anticipating outcomes; (9) recognizing author's tone, mood, and intent; (10) understanding and drawing comparisons and contrasts; (11) drawing conclusions or making generalizations; (12) making evaluations.

Classification System Used in This Text

This book uses aspects of all three classification techniques. Teaching strategies involving unit length are discussed in terms of designing lessons on varying levels of difficulty. A combination of components from the taxonomical and undifferentiated lists is used as the basis for the classification system. A list of the comprehension skills as they will be discussed in this book is given in Figure 3.1.

```
1. Identifying Details
2. Identifying Main Ideas
3. Identifying Sequence
4. Following Directions
5. Identifying Cause-Effect Relationships
6. Making Inferences
7. Making Generalizations and Conclusions
8. Identifying Tone and Mood
9. Identifying Theme
10. Identifying Characterization
11. Identifying Fact, Fiction, and Opinion
12. Identifying Propaganda
13. Identifying Author's Purpose
```

Figure 3.1 Outline of the Comprehension
Skills

This classification, which includes thirteen skills almost always taught in the classroom, most closely resembles the format of the undifferentiated lists. However, in this list, the skills have been roughly sequenced into a hierarchy. That is, the first skill listed, locating details, is prerequisite to many of the remaining skills. However, not all the skills placed early on the list are needed to satisfactorily complete following skills. In other words, in order for a reader to identify propaganda (a skill placed near the end of the list), he must be able to identify details and main ideas (two skills found at the beginning of the list). However, he does not necessarily use the skill of predicting outcomes (also listed near the beginning) in order to identify propaganda. Hence identifying details and main ideas would be prerequisite skills, while predicting outcomes would not.

This list provides thirteen basic comprehension skills, but is not intended to be exhaustive or conclusive. In addition, the majority of the skills have been described initially in terms that require that the student "identify" the skill (i.e., *identify* details, *identify* main idea). However, most skills may be adapted in difficulty by changing the behavioral objectives that accompany them. For example, the behavior required to *list* a detail would be less difficult than that required to *classify* a detail. Although none of the thirteen categories includes the term *listing*, comprehension tasks requiring this level of behavior could be included under locating details (list three of Piggy's characteristics), or locating sequence (list three events that occurred before the story began). Similarly, although the term *classifying* does not appear on the list as a behavioral descriptor, it could be used with most of the comprehension skills that have been delineated; that is, a student could be asked to classify the details, outcomes, or themes. This concept is closely tied to the *usage hierarchy* discussed in a later section of this chapter.

CONTENT OF THE COMPREHENSION SKILLS

This section provides a description of each of the thirteen comprehension skills shown in Figure 3.1. Each description includes the skill name, the circumstances under which the skill would be most helpful, and an in-depth look at the skill, which might include subject area examples.

1. Identifying Details

Identifying details requires the location and recall of specifically stated facts. For example, in English, for the purpose of determining theme, details to be located and remembered might include the names of the characters and descriptions of the setting. In math, details sometimes involved are the significant numbers in story problems. In social studies, they include the names of the explorers and the lands they discovered.

Though identifying details alone requires basically concrete level concepts, it is prerequisite to higher level abstract concepts and, hence, becomes a valuable skill in its relation to others. Student assignments requiring extensive reliance upon this skill often are viewed by students as meaningless memory exercises and are soon forgotten because students don't understand the relationship between the details and the total content. A teacher who points out to students why they need to locate details and who relates the activity to the designated purpose for reading can not only facilitate his students' reading of the material but can also help to make the task more relevant to them. For example, if history students were reading to compare the present-day South with the South of fifty years ago, they should be shown that they need to locate facts that reflect characteristics of the South in each era. After understanding the reason for knowing the facts, the comprehension skill of locating relationships, requiring the higher level of thinking, becomes the reader's focus; and the facts needed to make the higher level concepts are put into their proper perspective and become important in terms of the higher-level tasks.

The ability to identify appropriate details is basic to all other skills in reading. It is impossible to formulate a main idea if the supporting facts cannot be found. For example, locating a cause-effect relationship requires finding the detail that shows cause and the one that shows effect. To identify fact and fiction requires locating items in the material that reflect fact or fiction.

Various techniques can be used to help students learn to select and recall those details that are appropriate to their purpose for reading. Primary among these is telling students *why* they are being asked to look for particulars. For example, the teacher may ask students to read a paragraph, such as the one below, being careful to look for details that will help them to describe some of the things that make the President powerful.

> Much of the President's power comes from the fact that he is head of one or the other of the two great political parties. The members of his party in Congress are under pressure to support legislation which he recommends. The presidential office has also gained strength because, as Grover Cleveland said, "The presidency is the people's office." While members of Congress represent particular states, he represents the whole country. His every action attracts nation-wide attention. No

one can rival him in his ability to appeal to public opinion—especially since the invention of radio broadcasting and television. (Bragdon, McCutchen, and Cole 1973, p. 127)

Students might pick up key details, such as "head of a political party" or "ability to appeal to public opinion," that would help them to make generalizations about the President's power. This technique is very helpful to students who feel that they have to know *all* the facts and have not yet learned to distinguish which ones are relevant to which purposes. Furthermore, *global* learning of this nature promotes better retention of facts. In other words, having a purpose for obtaining the details provides the reader with a format for putting all the details into an integrated whole. If the history teacher wants his students to learn and remember details concerning the power of the presidency, he should tell them to look for these necessary facts while reading.

2. Identifying Main Ideas

Identifying main ideas involves conceptualizing the central thought of a sentence, paragraph, chapter subsection, chapter, or an entire manuscript. Locating the main idea of a sentence may be facilitated by analyzing the grammatical structure of the sentence and the relationship between components. That is, the main idea is usually found in the portion of the sentence that contains the subject and the predicate. Consider the following sentence.

> As in other provinces, a "family compact" had come into existence, and, possessed as its members were by the outlook of the English-speaking business man, they showed little consideration for the French. (Chafe and Lower 1954, p. 242)

The clause, "they showed little consideration," contains the subject and predicate of the sentence. However, the student needs to locate the referent to the pronoun *they* in order to interpret the main idea as "members of the family compact showed little consideration."

The main idea of a paragraph may be openly stated in a topic sentence that presents the central thought and appears at the beginning, middle, or end of the paragraph. The three paragraphs opposite, in which the main idea has been italicized, illustrate this point.

In other situations, the main idea of a paragraph is not stated in a topic sentence at all and must be formulated by the reader himself. An example of a paragraph of this type follows:

> The night was unusually dark, fog lying heavy on the road ahead. I was extremely tired, and it seemed I would never reach home. The drizzling rain acted as a sedative to put my weary eyes to sleep. Then suddenly, out of the darkness appeared a stalled bus in the middle of the road. Unable to swerve around it, I slammed on my brakes, only to discover that they were gone.

44

Beginning	Middle	End
Firemen provide many important services to the community. Their most important duty, of course, is to put out any fires that may occur. They also try to prevent fires by inspecting homes and buildings to make sure that they are not firetraps and by presenting talks to schools and other community organizations to make people aware of fire causes and their prevention. Firemen are all trained life-savers and, thus, are often called upon in emergencies other than fires.	The firemen's most important duty, of course, is to put out any fires that may occur. But, *firemen provide many important services to the community.* They also try to prevent fires by inspecting homes and buildings to make sure that they are not firetraps and by presenting talks to schools and other community organizations to make people aware of fire causes and their prevention. Firemen are all trained life-savers and, thus, are often called upon in emergencies other than fires.	The firemen's most important duty, of course, is to put out any fires that may occur. They also try to prevent fires by inspecting homes and buildings to make sure that they are not firetraps and by presenting talks to schools and other community organizations to make people aware of fire causes and their prevention. Firemen are all trained life-savers and, thus, are often called upon in emergencies other than fires. It is easy to see that *firemen provide many important services to the community.*

After examining this paragraph, the reader might notice relevant details such as, *unusually dark, heavy fog, extremely tired, drizzling rain, weary eyes, stalled bus, brakes were gone,* and arrive at the main idea, *unavoidable accident.*

The main idea of a chapter subsection, chapter, or entire manuscript may be given in a summary statement that occurs at the beginning or end of the selection, or it may be found in boldface as a chapter heading or subheading. In addition, as in the case of many paragraphs, the main idea may not be directly stated at all.

One technique content area teachers can use to encourage reading for main ideas is to stress them throughout the teaching strategy. For example, when asking students to read material for the first time, the teacher might say, "Read Chapter 3 and list five of its major ideas." This exercise will accomplish two goals. First, it will tell the students what they are expected to do by making explicit their purpose for reading. Second, it will give them practice in looking for main ideas. When discussing the material, the teacher can stress main ideas. During a class session the teacher can ask questions that require students to locate or generate main ideas; for example, "What is the main point of this chapter?" "What is the main idea that the author of this paragraph is trying to convey?"

The teacher can further reinforce this skill and can help students put course work into proper perspective by setting objectives for the entire book and then making students aware of these objectives. At the end of the year, the teacher can help students to correlate all the main ideas of the book, thereby clarifying learning and making the year's study more meaningful.

3. Identifying Sequence

Identifying sequence involves aspects of both time and space. Time, or chronological, sequence involves the student's locating and recalling the order of incidents or actions explicitly stated in a selection. In reading done in history and English, a chronological sequence often prevails.

Spatial sequence involves the student's locating details as they occur from space to space, or area to area. For example, rather than telling the times at which rain began to fall, the meteorologist usually describes rainy weather as it occurred from one area of the country to the other—for instance, from the Eastern seaboard to the Gulf of Mexico. In like manner, a mathematics book may use spatial sequence to describe a geometric concept; for example, from the interior to the exterior of a triangle.

Identical techniques may be used to teach both types of sequential order. For example, although reading the map below requires that the student understand spatial relationships, he would probably follow a chronological order when using it to proceed from his home to school. In other words, he would first proceed on Elm, then turn left onto Oak, finally turn right onto Birch.

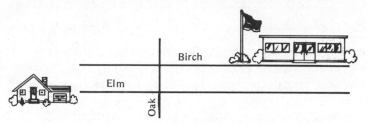

Likewise, the following instructions to a driver's education student integrate sequence of both time and space:

> Before you start the car, first check to see that your emergency brake is disengaged. Next, fasten your seat belt. Then, make certain that the car is in "park."

In this case, the student is being asked to follow the chronological order given as well as the spatial sequence from the floor of the car (brake), to the middle of the car (seat belt), to higher in the car (steering column).

Both types of sequence are important to reading comprehension in all content areas. The home economics student who puts in egg whites too soon may make a cake that does not turn out as expected; the mathematics student who calculates a square root too early in a given formula will have trouble solving the problem; and the football player who reads the spatial location of play patterns incorrectly may cause the team to forfeit the game.

46

Prerequisite skills for ascertaining sequence include finding main ideas and relevant details. Physical science students could not ascertain the progress of the shrinking of a glacier if they were unable to find the main idea (the glacier's receding) through the use of relevant details (increasing temperature, melting).

Exercises that content teachers could use to enhance their students' understanding of sequence include giving them or asking them to locate a series of facts and then to place these facts in the chronological or spatial order in which they occurred. For example, a civics teacher might give the following assignment:

> Rearrange the names of the following U.S. Presidents in the chronological order in which they were elected.
>
> Herbert Hoover
> Harry S. Truman
> George Washington
> Franklin D. Roosevelt
> Theodore Roosevelt

Other teachers might pose questions that require the use of spatial sequence, such as the following:

History: Describe the route taken by Lewis and Clark.

Literature: Describe Ichabod Crane from hat to boot.

Geography: Name the major mountain ranges of the U.S. in their order from east to west.

Mathematics: Rearrange the names of the polygons listed below in an order from simple to complex, according to their numbers of sides.
hexagon   pentagon   triangle   heptagon

4. Following Directions

Following directions requires the student to act in the manner recommended by printed instructions and is a skill used by all content areas. To make a dress, to carry out a chemistry experiment, to illustrate a computation, or to complete virtually any assignment given by a content area teacher, requires the student to follow directions.

Following directions requires well-developed skills in finding details and main ideas in sentences and also in identifying sequence. Students are seriously handicapped if they cannot find and understand important words and main ideas in written directions, such as those italicized in the sample content area directions below.

History: Trace the sequence of events that led to the War of 1812.

Spanish: Be able to *pronounce* these vocabulary words by Friday.

Science: Sketch a simple diagram of the human brain.

Home Economics: If the mixture begins to boil, *lower the heat.*

Chemistry: Add more water if the solution thickens.

The student must also be able to follow directions in a sequence.

Mathematics: Before attempting to complete this activity, read page ten.

English: After reading the story, summarize it and then go on to the next one.

Teachers in content areas can aid their students in following directions by using a two-step process. The first step involves analyzing particular activities that they will require students to perform. The second step entails isolating specific details that are important to the students' completion of the task. One way to isolate specific details is to note directions with which students have difficulty. For example, if students tend to compare and contrast when asked only to compare, or to boil when asked to simmer, these terms need clarification. During step two, these terms would be taught. The most appropriate time for such a lesson would be immediately before the term is encountered in an exercise. Thus the term *list* would be explained immediately prior to asking the students to "List events occurring between 1744 and 1760 that led to the English victory at Quebec."

5. Identifying Cause–Effect Relationships

Identifying cause-effect relationships requires students to recognize reasons for certain occurrences or reactions. When reading a particular selection, teachers can ask questions such as the following to reinforce this skill.

What caused this voting pattern? (history)

Why did this chemical reaction occur? (science)

What caused the cake to fall? (home economics)

Locating cause-effect relationships is necessary to fully understand reading material and as a background for other skills, such as making inferences and making generalizations. It is a skill dependent upon the ability to use and understand a sequence of events. Close inspection of what follows or what normally precedes a situation is often essential to determining the cause and/or effect of the action.

This skill may be reinforced by helping students recognize cause in simple situations. For example, consider the following sentence: "If one drives too fast, he may get a traffic ticket." Most youngsters would recognize "drives too fast" as the cause and "get a traffic ticket" as the effect. If students have difficulty understanding the cause-effect relationship, awareness of the clue word *because* either directly stated or implied, may help them. In the preceding example the clue word is implied, but the cause-effect relationship would be emphasized if the sentence were written, "Because one drives too fast, he may get a traffic ticket." Teachers might give students several cause-effect sentences and ask them to insert clue words such as *because* in appropriate places in the sentences. For example, the teacher might present the following sentence: "Having worked hard all day, Karl rested soundly that night." The students should be able to insert the clue word as follows: "Because he worked hard all day, Karl rested soundly that night." This should help them to identify "worked hard all day" as the cause and "rested soundly that night" as the effect.

6. Making Inferences

To make an inference, readers must select and relate relevant facts in order to synthesize unstated meaning in materials. The inference provides readers with information that the author has intended for them, even though they must uncover it for themselves. For example, inferences can be made from the following excerpts.

Literature:
"I have just returned from a visit to my landlord—the solitary neighbor that I shall be troubled with." (*Wuthering Heights* 1939, p. 1)
(Inference: The speaker is an unfriendly man who has recently moved to an isolated area.)
History:
"Thus the launching of Sputnik, the first artificial satellite, in 1957, was an immense psychological victory for the Russians, who were seen not merely to have caught up to the Americans in one kind of advanced technology, but to have surpassed them." (Bragdon, McCutchen, and Cole, 1973, p. 738–739)
(Inference: A competitive situation existed in which the Russians had previously been less progressed than the Americans in the areas of advanced technology.)
Science:
"The only excuse for these wasteful practices was that Americans had been accustomed to thinking that their natural resources were inexhaustible." (Todd and Curti 1972, p. 219)
(Inference: America's natural resources are not inexhaustible.)

To infer, the student needs to pay attention to certain details. For example, in the foregoing sentence from *Wuthering Heights*, the excerpts "solitary neighbor" and "I shall be troubled with," help the reader to make the inference that the speaker is an unfriendly man, though this is not directly stated.

Teachers can help students to make inferences through the use of questions such as the following:

1. What are the key words in the sentence?
2. Is any meaning other than that stated implied by any of the key words?
3. What inferences can be made about people or situations from descriptions of their belongings, surroundings, or actions?

7. Making Generalizations and Conclusions

To make generalizations and conclusions, students must be encouraged to establish connections and relationships among seemingly unrelated pieces of specific information.

Making a generalization requires the reader to conceptualize a relationship between facts that are both directly stated and inferred. Students generalize when they infer the similarities and differences of separate situations or events. For example, if the student were given the following passage, he would be able to fill in the blank with the correct answer (omnivores) if he generalized.

Omnivores eat meat and plants. (directly stated fact)
Dogs eat meat and cereal. (inferred fact that cereal equates with plants)
Dogs are_____. (generalization of directly stated and inferred facts)

In biology, a student might look at the following set of facts and make several generalizations.

For what is now modern-day horse, the average change in the span of cheek teeth was 4.1 cm in 20 million years (from Hyracotherium or Miohippus); was 13.1 cm in 20 million years (from Miohippus to Megahippus); and, was 3.9 cm in 10 million years (from Megahippus to Equus).

From these facts, the student could generalize that the rate of evolutionary change within the Equidae is quite variable. Likewise, the student must generalize that the direction of evolutionary change can be reversed, since the span of cheek teeth in the horse had first increased and then decreased in size.

In this text, making a conclusion refers to those tasks that require the reader to reach a generalization that is based solely on fact. In other words, the ability to make conclusions is based upon establishing valid relationships, using as bases statements that may be supported by empirical evidence. For example, the French student discovers that the plural of *chapeau* is *chapeaux*, and the plural of *bateau* is *bateaux*. From this he concludes that a French word ending in *eau* is made plural by the addition of *x*.

Some generalizations may also be considered conclusions. In the above example of the biology student, this generalization would also be considered a conclusion since the student used the facts concerning the span of cheek teeth in the horse to make conclusions about the rate of evolutionary change within the horse. He also used evidence to determine that the direction of an evolutionary change can be reversed.

50

However, if students were asked to draw a picture of the jaw of the horse as they thought it looked during the Hyracotherium era and then during the Miohippus era, they would not be making a conclusion since the task requires facts (size of cheek teeth) as well as inferences that are not necessarily factual (perception of the jawbone as similar to that of the monkey rather than of the modern-day horse).

Fraenkel (1973) suggests the following sequence of questions that teachers can use to help students make generalizations and conclusions. The teacher should ask students to study similar aspects of previously unrelated content and then should ask identical questions about content.

1. Describe the situation presented in each reading.
2. What differences do you see?
3. How do you account for these differences?
4. What does this suggest to you about the situation in general?
5. Do you know of any other situations in which differing conditions exist?

For example, the biology teacher might want students to generalize and then make conclusions about the process of evolution. He might ask them to read about how the span of the horse's cheek teeth has changed during the past 60 million years. Then he might ask them the following questions:

1. Describe the situation presented in each reading or aspect of reading. (The sizes of cheek teeth during seventeen eras are described.)
2. What differences do you see? (In each era the horse possessed cheek teeth of a different size.)
3. How do you account for these differences? (The types of food eaten affect the size of cheek teeth needed.)
4. What does this suggest about the situation in general? (Organisms that survive have adapted to meet a changing environment.)
5. Do you know of any other situations in which differing conditions exist? (The horse is different from the dog, but the same principle of adapting to environment holds true.)

It should be noted that the type of questioning strategy discussed above helps the student generalize and conclude. For example, if one student suggested that the differences in teeth size could be accounted for because horses with big teeth during the first 30 million years were the toughest fighters and, hence, survived and passed the characteristic to their descendants, the teacher could encourage the student to pursue this line of reasoning until the student is able to generate a series of alternative generalizations about how the differences in teeth size were accounted for. Each of the generalizations could be subjected to known facts (e.g., the terrain of the earth was different and this can be proven by geological survey; the fighting ability of the horse can be merely inferred since it cannot be proven in such an empirical manner). Hence the generalization that could be supported by factual evidence would become the conclusion.

8. Identifying Tone and Mood

Because tone and mood are used by the author to help convey his ideas, identifying them becomes an important skill, particularly in the content areas of literature and history. Tone is defined differently by various authors, but it is most often described as the characteristics of a writer's style by which he expresses his attitude toward his subject matter, his readers, or both. It should be emphasized that tone is not attitude itself but the quality of the author's writing style that puts forth his attitude. Tone may be described by many adjectives, including *malevolent, serious, unsympathetic, facetious, intimate, solemn, empathetic,* or *sympathetic.*

> Kennedy's years in office came to a sudden and appalling end when he was assassinated while visiting Dallas, Texas, on November 22, 1963. Throughout the world, men and women felt a sickening sense of loss. (Bragdon, McCutchen, and Cole 1973, p. 755) (Tone: tragic)

Identifying mood requires the student to assess the emotional overtones in reading material. Mood may be thought of as the atmosphere of a work; that is, the total of all the material's characteristics which create a prevalent feeling in the reader. For example, the mood of a work may be *gloom* or *cheer, sadness* or *happiness*, or *joy* or *grief*.

> Americans reacted to the tragic news with shocked disbelief, then with deeply felt anger and grief. For three days, while the body of John F. Kennedy lay in state in the rotunda of the Capitol, radio and television stations suspended regular programming. (Todd and Curti 1972, p. 557) (Mood: grief)

Determining tone and mood requires the reader to study all the elements of a work which might contribute to establishing mood and tone. Therefore the reader must be aware of general impressions gained from details, main ideas, sequence, and cause-effect relationships. Furthermore, since usually only hints regarding tone and mood are given, understanding them is dependent largely upon the ability to make generalizations from the work.

Students can be taught to recognize tone and mood most easily through the use of brief selections. A carefully chosen paragraph is often sufficient. Students can be instructed to read the selection and choose the tone and mood from a given list of possibilities, or they may be required to suggest them on their own. For example, students might consider the following sentence:

> The year 1968 saw a glorious event—Apollo 8, carrying three astronauts, voyaged around the moon and made a safe return with a phenomenally accurate splashdown in the Pacific. (Bragdon, McCutchen, and Cole 1973, p. 782)

They might then be able to assess the tone as *confident* or *successful* and the mood as *joy* or *happiness*, using the clue phrases "glorious event," and "phenomenally accurate." Students' answers could provide a basis for class discussion.

9. Identifying Theme

The theme of a work is the moral or abstract concept that the work is designed to clarify to the reader. Identifying theme requires the reader to analyze what the author is trying to say. For example, in *Macbeth*, Shakespeare demonstrates the dire aspects of an immoral quest for power. This, therefore, is the theme of the play.

Identifying theme requires a general study of the work. In nonfiction, authors may openly state their theme, or thesis. For example, an American history text could be built upon the stated theme, "America: A Product of Change." All facts presented would stress the changes through which the country has evolved during the past two hundred years. Likewise, a biology unit might be built around the theme, "Prevention Is the Best Cure." All information included would be explained in light of this theme. Although students would not have to identify the themes in such history or science texts, an awareness of the concept of theme would help them to put all facts into proper perspective and would facilitate understanding.

In fiction, however, the author often prefers not to state his theme so directly, and the reader must rely on such devices as tone and mood to determine theme. For this reason, a knowledge of main ideas, sequence, inferences, generalizations and conclusions, and tone and mood is needed if the reader is to correctly identify theme.

Students might begin studying theme by locating and reading materials identifying the themes of some of the works that they have already read. For example, if the students had read *Much Ado About Nothing*, they might read several articles that discuss its theme. Then they might attempt to identify the theme of a short selection as a group before trying to determine that of a longer selection individually.

10. Identifying Characterization

Identifying characterization requires the reader to interpret what the author has written about a personage. Seven means by which a writer indicates character to a reader are (1) the personage's thoughts, (2) the personage's speech (both what he says and how he says it), (3) the personage's appearance, (4) the personage's actions, (5) the ways in which other figures discuss the personage, (6) the actions of other figures toward the personage, and (7) the author's speech about the personage.

Many complexities might arise when the student analyzes a personage using the seven means listed above. For example, depending on the specific situation, the personage's speech, actions, or appearance may be typical or atypical for him. Also, the manner in which other figures speak about the personage may or may not be objective since comments about a personage always involve at least two characters (the character talking, the character, or personage being talked about, and sometimes the person being talked to). Thus any dialogue must be evaluated in light of the situation. This same complication arises when analyzing the actions between two characters. For example, the two might meet and be rude to one another. However, aside from this incident, the same behavior might never occur in either character. The author, speaking as a persona or describing the personage, normally states the truth. However it must be remembered that it is the truth as the author sees it.

A reader can anticipate that characters in literary works will act within the boundaries of psychological theory or will be lifelike. Thus, in *Wuthering Heights*, Heathcliff's hostile actions toward Isabella could be anticipated from his earlier actions. For Heathcliff to become suddenly thoughtful toward his bride would be beyond the limits of credibility and would leave the work open to criticism. This does not suggest that characters cannot change throughout a work, but that such change will usually be made apparent to the reader as a part of the action or by providing motives for the change.

Understanding characterization is important to the student in many subject areas, particularly literature and history. In many literary works, action is a function of character, and an understanding of character leads to a greater understanding of the action. In social studies, an understanding of the character of a historical personage may lead to a greater understanding of historical events. Understanding characterization is also a part of other content areas. For example, in science the following passage may be found.

> Charles Darwin did not set out to be a scientist. Indeed as a boy he was an unenthusiastic student who, as his father once commented, cared "for nothing but shooting, dogs, and rat-catching." But he liked to read, enjoyed travel, and collected everything he could get his hands on. (BSCS 1973, p. 607)

Science students who read this passage and understand characterization would become more familiar with Darwin from what the author and Darwin's father had to say about him.

To understand characterization, students need to locate relevant details as to words and actions and to locate cause-effect relationships. Furthermore, inferences and generalizations must be made as to whether these words and actions are in or out of character for the personage.

For example, a history teacher might ask students to formulate their own description of Truman's character by evaluating (1) Truman's own statements, appearance, and actions, (2) his peers' statements about and actions toward him, and (3) their textbook author's statement about him.

11. Identifying Fact, Fiction, and Opinion

To determine whether material is fact, opinion, or fancy, students should be aware that librarians, editors, and writers offer many clues to the factuality, opinionativeness, or fancy of materials. First, students should be taught the different locations of materials. If the librarian has classified the material as fiction, then it probably is fiction. If material is classified as nonfiction, then it is probably fact or opinion. Book editors also provide further clues to the reader by placing such clue phrases as "A novel by . . ." or "Essays on . . ."

on the cover of the book.

All three types of materials may be found in magazines. Often editors will provide clues to the reader by introducing a selection with phrases such as "A short story by . . ." or "A factual account of . . . ." Professional journals such as *Psychology Today* or *Science* contain both fact and opinion articles. Again the editor will often give clues to the reader that an article is opiniona- tive by including in its title such words as "comment" or "commentary." Authors also indicate whether their works are fact or opinion by using words which indicate personal involvement such as "I" and "my." For example, a paragraph beginning, "My favorite Christmas present when I was five was . . ." is obviously a statement of opinion, whereas one beginning, "The rats in the experimental group learned the maze in an average of forty-five seconds . . ." is probably a statement of fact.

In reading materials in the various content areas, a habit that tends to hinder in the discrimination of fact from opinion is accepting as fact (1) everything that is written down, (2) everything with which one agrees, (3) all logically developed positions, and (4) frequently repeated positions. Before forming opinions, students need to examine copyright dates, different versions of the same story, and the author's qualifications.

If students are to fully understand content area materials, they must be able to quickly distinguish fact from opinion and fact from fiction. In order to do this, students need to be able to analyze relevant details, main ideas, sequences, and relationships that might indicate the factuality of an article. Furthermore, they must be able to make inferences and generalizations.

A simple technique for alerting students to the differences between fact, fiction, and opinion is to have them compare a research article and a story on the same topic and then to classify each as fiction or nonfiction. Factors that led to the classification could then be discussed. A similar procedure could be used with fact and opinion articles. For example, a drama teacher might ask his students to decide whether the following critique of a play is fact, fancy, or opinion.

> Exhibiting a blatant lack of professionalism, the actors stumbled through their lines, with never a regard for their distinguished audience. It was as if I had been trans- ferred to an amateur drama club's rehearsal session, after paying the price of a front row seat on Broadway.

Even though they might agree with what it says, students should be able to recognize the passage as strictly an expression of opinion. Keys to this conclusion are the phrases, "never a regard for their distinguished audience" (of which the critic was a part), "price of a front row seat" (obviously dis- tasteful to the critic), "as if I had been transferred" (the suggestion of a per- sonal affront), and the author's uncomplimentary reference to amateur drama clubs. In other words, the use of terms such as *blatant*, *stumbled*, *distinguished*, and *amateur* should be pointed out to students as a clue to opinionativeness.

12. Identifying Propaganda

Identifying propaganda requires students to be aware of propaganda devices, why they are used, how they are used, what effects they have upon unwary readers, and why they may or may not be generally accepted. Seven basic types of propaganda have been identified.

1. **Name Calling**—uses an offensive name without bothering to give reasons.
   Example: "Mayor's Opponent Is Un-American"
2. **Glittering Generalities**—uses vague expressions that make it impossible to determine where he really stands.
   Example: "Candidate Promises Justice"
3. **Transfer**—uses symbols for purposes other than those for which they were intended.
   Example: "Ku Klux Klan Candidate Posts Gigantic Cross on Lawn of Campaign Headquarters"
4. **Plain Folks**—emphasizes likeness to common people.
   Example: "Councilman Shares Sandwich with Senior Citizen"
5. **Testimonial**—has famous or admired person endorse his ideas.
   Example: "Astronaut Supports Mayor's Proposal"
6. **Card Stacking**—presents only the facts that aid his cause.
   Example: "Federal Aid to Poor Doubles During President's Term"
7. **Bandwagon**—uses phrases indicating that people should support him just because others like them do.
   Example: "Blue Collar Workers Unite to Support Incumbent"

Propaganda is seen today as a device for influencing people's thinking and actions. Particularly relevant is the fact that students are often bombarded with propaganda techniques used by persuasive salespersons and advertisements. Youth today need defenses against persuasive devices and should therefore be aware of tactics for identifying the propaganda technique being used. To detect propaganda, students must be able to (1) select details that indicate propaganda techniques (name calling, for example), (2) find the main idea to determine if any major concepts are omitted, and (3) analyze generalities for accuracy.

To help students distinguish propaganda, they can be taught to (1) examine the writer's purpose, (2) examine the writer's competence, (3) consider their own background of experiences and familiarity with the subject, (4) note any propaganda techniques used, and (5) decide to accept or reject the ideas offered or to delay making a decision until more data is available.

Students need to be made aware that propaganda exists in many of their textbooks. For example, consider the following two excerpts from an American history text:

Japanese planes roared down without warning upon the United States fleet anchored in the huge American naval and air base at Pearl Harbor, in Hawaii. Victims of this surprise attack, the Americans lost almost all of their planes and eight battleships and suffered the partial destruction of several other naval units. More than 2,000 soldiers, sailors, and civilians were killed, and almost 2,000 more were wounded. (Bragdon, McCutchen, and Cole 1973, p. 453)

a solitary plane flew high over the Japanese city of Hiroshima. No alarm was sounded. Then, suddenly, the city disintegrated in a single searing atomic blast. Nearly 100,000 of the 245,000 men, women, and children in Hiroshima were killed instantly or died soon after. (Bragdon, McCutchen, and Cole 1973, p. 474)

Both passages describe surprise attacks. One attack contributes to the deaths of over 100,000 men, women, and children in Hiroshima and the other to the deaths of over 2,000 soldiers and civilians at Pearl Harbor. However the word *victim* and its implied meaning is found only in the passage discussing Pearl Harbor. Other word choices such as *roared down without warning* as opposed to *No alarm was sounded* affect the tone and mood and, hence, the interpretation of the two passages. The history teacher who asks students to read pro-Japanese versions of both incidences could illustrate to his students how elements of propaganda exist within both passages. Though propaganda may be interpreted in terms of the writer's purpose, it should also be examined in light of the writer's background.

The other previously mentioned ways in which students should examine what they read should also be utilized when teaching this concept.

13. Identifying Author's Purpose

Identifying the author's purpose requires the student to become aware of the writer's motives. Although much popular literature is written only to inform or to entertain, most writers of serious works have a more earnest aim. They are attempting to change the reader. This change might be psychological—the writer would like the reader to change his attitudes—or physical—the writer would like the reader to change his behavior. For example, in the poem *It's All Right to Cry* (Hart, et al. 1974, p. 92) Hall may be trying to change the reader psychologically, that is change his attitude about crying.

Students who realize the author's purpose are in a better position to evaluate his meaning. If the author's goal is to sell a product rather than to simply describe it, then his writing takes on a different meaning for the reader.

To determine the author's purpose, students need to be aware of pertinent details, main ideas, and cause-effect relationships. They also need to be able to make appropriate inferences and generalizations. In literature, a study of theme may encourage the reader to ascertain the author's purpose. Furthermore, students need to be able to recognize tone, mood, fact, opinion, and fiction and to detect propaganda.

Determining author's purpose is a difficult skill. Teachers may introduce students to this concept by having them compare two articles written by different authors on the same topic in order to discern each author's purpose. For example, in a lesson on current events in local government, the social studies teacher might present two articles on rezoning, one written by a councilman who favors it and the other by one who opposes it. In order to ascertain each author's purpose, the student might ask the following questions: "Is the author reporting in a factual manner?" "Is the author asserting opinion?" "Does the author use any propaganda techniques to persuade his readers?"

COMPREHENSION SKILLS AND LEVELS OF LEARNING

Thirteen important comprehension skills have been described in an order from simple to complex in the previous section of this chapter. The next section will analyze three ways in which the difficulty of each skill can be adjusted: (1) usage, (2) readability level of the material, and (3) length of unit.

These three hierarchies are shown in Figure 3.2. The Usage Hierarchy is shown in the in-depth plane; the Readability Hierarchy is shown in the vertical plane; and the Unit Hierarchy is shown in the horizontal plane.

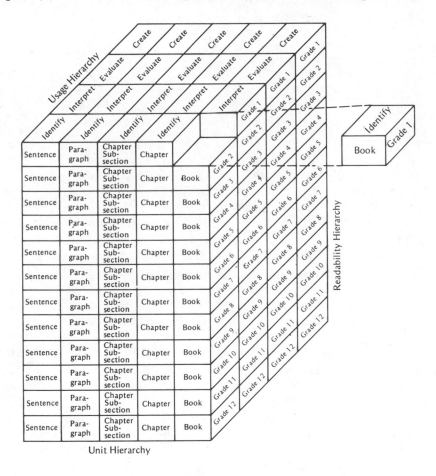

Figure 3.2   Comprehension Skill Hierarchy for Each Skill

Usage Hierarchy

Close inspection of Figure 3.2 reveals a four-step usage hierarchy: (1) Identify, (2) Interpret, (3) Evaluate, (4) Create. The skills included under *Identify* are based on facts. They require the reader to recall facts or to restate them in his own words. This level includes such tasks as listing, recalling, naming, identifying, locating, and labeling. The *Interpret* level requires greater emphasis on thoughtful reading or thinking along with the information given in the printed material. When practicing these skills, students must exercise judgment in selecting and relating relevant facts, and they must do this in such a way that a conclusion is produced. This level includes tasks such as classifying, outlining, summarizing, solving problems based on given information, inferring, and comparing and contrasting. The *Evaluate* level requires the reader to pass personal judgment on the truthfulness and accuracy of what is read. It involves asking questions such as, "Is the material factual?" and "Is the material verifiable?" This level includes determining adequacy, validity, appropriateness, worth, or acceptability of a piece of writing. The *Create* level includes going beyond the message of the author to form an extended message. Tasks required of students in this category include exploring problems similar to those posed by the author, looking for similarities in unrelated selections, finding contrasts in similar descriptions, suggesting new solutions to replace the author's, examining consequences that may arise other than those stated, and using new ideas for application. Every comprehension skill may be used in each of these four ways and may vary in difficulty according to the way it is used. Usually, the *Identify* level is the easiest, followed in succession by the *Interpret, Evaluate*, and *Create* levels. For example, to *identify* a main idea that is openly stated in a paragraph is usually easier than to *interpret* one that is not directly stated, to *evaluate* one, or to *create* a selection with a given main idea. Similarly, at the lowest level, students can locate a sequence given by the author (identify); or, at a higher level, outline a sequence that is not stated by the author (interpret); or, at a still higher level, determine the adequacy of the sequence (evaluate); or, at the highest level, produce a sequence of their own on a related topic (create).

In planning instruction in a content area, a teacher might use the concept of Usage Hierarchy in the following manner. (Note that although this could be done with any skill, Locating Details is used in this example.)

> *Example:* Frank Jackson is aware of the fact that his students' abilities to comprehend vary greatly.

Thus he might give his literature students who are having difficulty comprehending *Lord of the Flies* an assignment such as, "List five physical characteristics of the island."

The students would be working with the *Identify* skills. Those students whose comprehension skills were somewhat better might be given a question drawing on the *Interpret* skills such as, "Compare the physical characteristics of the island with those of Piggy's home." Students whose comprehension skills were superior might perform skills on the *Evaluate* level such as, "Do the physical characteristics of the island make it a good place to live?" Students capable of working with the most difficult level of comprehension skills (*Create*) could respond to the problem, "Give the island entirely new physical traits and then discuss how the 'new' island would have caused the plot to change."

A second way in which the usage hierarchy could be used is shown below.

Example: Cheryl Scott noted that her students were having difficulty locating details needed to answer science questions. Thus for a short while, she used questions that required only identification skills.

Examples of the *Identify* level questions that she used included:

> List the steps needed to create hydrosulfuric acid.
>
> Name five dangers involved in heating a beaker over a Bunsen burner.
>
> Identify the single most important detail in determining which components in an unknown mixture are water soluble.

After the youngsters learned these skills, she introduced questions on the *Interpret* level. These required more thought than the identification questions. For example, she asked:

> If you remove water from a mixture and the volume is reduced more than expected, what has occurred? (making an inference)

With more practice, students were able to deal with *Evaluate* level questions. A question of this type included:

> Given five possible commercial uses for hydrogen sulfide, evaluate the ones that would be least abusive to our environment.

Eventually students became adroit enough to manage questions on the *Create* level. A question from this level might require the student to make up an original experiment to determine what water soluble chemical exists in an unknown mixture.

Sol Lentz, the social studies teacher, used the Usage Hierarchy in a different way. He taught a skill on one level and, as he taught it on higher levels, he made sure that the skill was reviewed at the lower level.

Example: Mr. Lentz taught the skill of identifying details by having his students list the characteristics of the Old South that helped to cause the Civil War. Later he reinforced the skill of looking for details with the interpretation skill of summarizing the characteristics of the Old South that helped cause the war. After additional practice, he asked his students to evaluate General Grant's actions in terms of what was right for the country as opposed to what was right for the Old South. In order to do this, they had to read for details of Grant's actions as well as for details denoting the country's needs at that time. The final step, the use of a *Create* skill, required the students to make up a characteristic of the Old South and discuss how they thought the outcome of the Civil War would have been altered if that characteristic had been actual. Again, the skill of locating details was reinforced.

Susan Mathew, the mathematics teacher, used the Usage Hierarchy in a fourth way. Although the students in one of her math classes were adequate readers, she found herself asking many questions from the two easiest comprehension levels, *Identify* and *Interpret*. She used the Usage Hierarchy to make sure that she asked some questions that required more thought on the part of the student. She used many questions from the *Identify* level such as, "Write the formula for finding the hypotenuse of a triangle" or "List the steps needed to derive the formula for the area of an eight-sided figure." Interpretation questions included, "Given the formula, determine the area of the given triangle" and "Compare the area of the given triangle with the area of the given square." In addition she tried to include evaluation questions such as, "If Mr. Jones had two drafting tools, a triangle and a square, which of the following formulas could he best use to determine the area of an eight-sided figure?" and "Make up a formula for determining the area of a nine-sided figure."

Readability Hierarchy

Printed materials vary in reading difficulty, or *readability*. Content, word length, sentence length, structure, complexity, and the ratio of abstract and concrete terms are all aspects that affect the degree of reading difficulty. Readability is often expressed in terms of grade level. Thus a book on a grade seven readability level would be easier than one on a grade ten level. Methods for determining the readability level of a book are given in Chapter 6. It is interesting to note at this point that a skill may be taught using material at any grade level (readability level). As the reading material becomes increasingly difficult from level to level, the skill also becomes more complex. For example, an adolescent reading on third grade level might learn the skill of predicting outcomes through exercises in which the teacher shows a picture story whose conclusion is missing. The student would then be encouraged to make up and discuss his own final picture for the story. The teacher accepts all imagined endings and encourages divergent thinking. A student reading on eighth grade level might be asked to predict outcomes of more complex situations. For example, Piggy in *Lord of the Flies* is an overweight child with asthma and glasses. The teacher might ask, "How do you think the other children felt about Piggy?" "Which type of children would be most likely to be his friends? His tormentors?" A youngster reading at the twelfth grade level might be asked to predict outcomes of the current energy crisis.

Unit Hierarchy

The comprehension skills vary in difficulty also according to the length of the unit to which they apply. It is easier to find the main idea of a sentence than of a paragraph, chapter subsection, chapter, or book.

Skills may be taught in relation to any of the units to which they apply. Ascertaining sequence may be taught in relation to a sentence, paragraph, chapter subsection, chapter, or book. As the unit becomes longer, the skill becomes more complex.

Frank Jackson used the concept of Unit Hierarchy in the following manner. When attempting to teach the concept of determining tone and mood to his literature students, he began by having them find the tone and mood in sentences, then in paragraphs, chapter subsections, chapters, and books.

The Relationship Between Usage Hierarchy, Readability Hierarchy, and Unit Hierarchy

In planning instruction in reading in the middle and secondary school, the three hierarchies give teachers several options. They can adapt instruction for students by adjusting the difficulty level of the skill (Usage Hierarchy), by adjusting the difficulty of the reading material (Readability Hierarchy), or by adjusting the length of the selection to which the skills apply (Unit Hierarchy). Furthermore, teachers may use more than one of these factors at the same time. For example, Frank Jackson felt that it was important that his students read *Hamlet*. However he knew that this play would be difficult for them to read and, therefore, he asked them questions based on identification skills. In contrast, knowing that *Gulliver's Travels* would be easier, he asked interpretation, evaluation, and creation questions. Frank Jackson employed the Usage Hierarchy to adjust his instruction.

Philip Edwall felt it was important that his driver's education students pass the written exam for their driver's licenses. However, many of them struggled with the text that was normally read. Therefore he allowed his students to study a book, covering the same material but written on a lower readability level. Mr. Edwall used the Readability Hierarchy to adjust reading material for his students.

Sol Lentz found that his junior high students encountered difficulty in answering questions that were based on given chapters of the history text. Thus, he tried basing questions on each subsection of the text. When adapting instruction in this manner, he was using the Unit Hierarchy.

Cheryl Scott, the science teacher, used a combination of hierarchy adjustments with two of her classes. With her class of high-achieving students, she used books on high readability levels and asked many interpretation, evaluation, and creation questions covering material at least a chapter in length. However, with her class of low-achieving students, she used textbooks that covered the same concepts as the grade level text but that were several readability levels below it. Furthermore, she used identification questions on short units such as paragraphs or chapter subsections.

References and Bibliography

Abrams, M. H. *A Glossary of Literary Terms*. New York: Holt, Rinehart & Winston, 1961.

Barrett, T. C. "Taxonomy of Cognitive and Affective Dimensions of Reading Comprehension." Discussed by Clymer, T. in "What is reading?: Some Current Concepts." Pp. 1–30 in Helen M. Robinson, ed., *Innovation and Change in Reading Instruction*. 67th Yearbook, National Society for Study in Education. Part II. Chicago: University of Chicago Press, 1968.

Beach, R. "Conceiving of Characters." *Journal of Reading*, 17:7 (April 1974), 546–551.

Berg, P. C., and Rentel, V. M. "Guide to Creativity in Reading." *Journal of Reading*, 10 (January 1967), 219–230.

Bloom, B., ed. *Taxonomy of Educational Objectives: Handbook 1, Cognitive Domain*. New York: McKay, 1956.

Bond, G. L., and Tinker, M. A. *Reading Difficulties: Their Diagnosis and Correction*. 3rd ed. New York: Appleton-Century-Crofts, 1973.

Bragdon, H. W., McCutchen, S. P., and Cole, C. W. *History of a Free People*. New York: Macmillan, 1973.

Bronte, E. *Wuthering Heights*. New York: Washington Square Press, 1939.

BSCS. *Biological Science: An Ecological Approach*. 3rd ed. Chicago: Rand McNally, 1973.

Burmeister, L. E. *Reading Strategies for Secondary School Teachers*. Reading, Mass.: Addison-Wesley, 1974.

Chafe, J. W., and Lower, A. R. M. *Canada—A Nation*. New York: McKay, 1954.

Clymer, T. "What Is Reading? Some Current Concepts." Pp. 7–30 in Helen M. Robinson, ed., *Innovation and Change in Reading Instruction*. 67th Yearbook, National Society for Study in Education. Part II. Chicago: University of Chicago Press, 1968.

Dickens, C. *Oliver Twist*. Edited by J. Hillis Miller. New York: Holt, Rinehart & Winston, 1962.

Fraenkel, J. R. *Helping Students Think and Value: Strategies for Teaching the Social Studies*. Englewood Cliffs, N. J.: Prentice-Hall, 1973.

Fry, E. *Reading Instruction for Classroom and Clinic*. New York: McGraw-Hill, 1972.

Giroux, J. A., and Williston, G. R. *Recognizing Tone*. Providence, R. I.: Jamestown, 1974.

Golding, W. *Lord of the Flies*. Edited by James R. Baker and Arthur P. Siegler. New York: Putnam, 1964.

Harris, L. A., and Smith, C. B. *Reading Instruction Through Diagnostic Teaching*. New York: Holt, Rinehart & Winston, 1972.

Hart, C., et al. (eds.) *Free to Be . . . You and Me*. New York: McGraw-Hill, 1974.

Institute for Propaganda Analysis. *Guide to the Analysis of Propaganda*. New York: Institute for Propaganda Analysis, 1937.

Karlin, R. *Teaching Reading in High School*. 2nd ed. Indianapolis, Ind.: Bobbs-Merrill, 1972.

Olson, A. V., and Ames, W. S. *Teaching Reading Skills in Secondary Schools*. Scranton, Pa.: Intext Educational Publishers, 1972.

Putnam, L. R. "Don't Tell Them to Do It . . . Show Them How." *Journal of Reading*, 18:1 (October 1974), 41–43.

Roberts, E. V. *Writing Themes About Literature*. Englewood Cliffs, N.J.: Prentice-Hall, 1964.

Sanders, N. *Classroom Questions: What Kinds?* New York: Harper & Row, 1966.

Simons, H. D. "Reading Comprehension: The Need for a New Perspective." *Reading Research Quarterly*, 6:3 (Spring 1971), 338–363.

Spache, G. D., and Spache, E. B. *Reading in the Elementary School.* 3rd ed. Boston: Allyn & Bacon, 1973.

Stauffer, R. G. *Directing Reading Maturity as a Cognitive Process.* New York: Harper & Row, 1969.

Steinmann, M., and Willen, G. *Literature for Writing.* 2nd ed. Belmont, Calif.: Wadsworth Publishing, 1967.

Stowe, H. B. *Uncle Tom's Cabin.* New York: Books, Inc.

Swift, J. *Gulliver's Travels.* Edited by John F. Ross. New York: Holt, Rinehart & Winston, 1948.

Thomas, E. L., and Robinson, H. A. *Improving Reading in Every Class.* Boston: Allyn & Bacon, 1972.

Todd, L. P., and Curti, M. *Rise of the American Nation.* 3rd ed. New York: Harcourt Brace Jovanovich, 1972.

Trezise, R. L. "The Hilda Taba Teaching Strategies in English and Reading Classes." *English Journal,* (April 1972), 577–593.

The Works of William Shakespeare. New York: Walter J. Black, 1937.

Chapter 4

Identifying the Study Skills

Prerequisite 4.1

Participants should have successfully completed the objectives for Chapter 1 or should have an understanding of the relationship between reading and the study skills before beginning this chapter.

Rationale 4.2

If students are to learn successfully, they must have well-developed skills in using the instructional resources available to them. Before teachers will be able to encourage students to develop these skills, they themselves must first understand the study skills. This chapter describes in detail fourteen study skills that all secondary students should master. Methodology for teaching the study skills is given in Chapter 10.

Objectives 4.3

Upon successful completion of this chapter, the participant will be able to:

1. Name, describe, and differentiate among the fourteen study skills described in Chapter 4.
2. Describe one teaching technique for each of the fourteen study skills described.
3. List the study skills in which proficiency would be most valuable

to students in his specific subject area and give reasons for his choices.

4. (On the lines below, add other objectives according to your instructor's directions.)_____

_____

5. _____

_____

6. _____

_____

7. _____

_____

_____

* * * * * * * * * * * * * *

Chapter 13, Experience 4 extends Chapter 4 with this performance/consequence objective:

8. During this experience, the participant will: (1) select those study skills that apply to his area, (2) design questions that will ascertain the extent to which the student has mastered each skill, and (3) present the questions to a student.

* * * * * * * * * * * * * *

Self Pre-Assessment 4.4

Can you complete all the activities listed in **Objectives 4.3**? Answer "yes," "no," or "not certain."

If you answered "yes" to the question, complete the enabling activities required by your instructor and take the Post-Assessment on the date assigned by him.

If you answered "no," refer to **Enabling Activities 4.5**. If you decide to do any activities that are not required, select those that best suit you as a learner. You need not complete all the optional activities or all parts of a particular optional activity. As soon as you have the information you need to complete the objectives, answer "yes" to the **Self Pre-Assessment 4.4** question and stop the activity.

If you answered "not certain" to the question, refer to **Enabling Activities 4.5**. Select the enabling activity that best suits your style of learning and peruse it. Then make a firm "yes" or "no" answer and proceed accordingly.

Enabling Activities 4.5

Complete only as many of the activities listed below as are required and which you need in order to meet the objectives.

1. *Enabling activity one* is a *reading* alternative. This is **Information Given 4.6.** It is a brief overview of fourteen study skills that all secondary students should master.
2. *Enabling activity two* is another *reading* option. In this case, the material to be read is one of the textbooks used to expand the theoretical background for this course. See chart on inside front cover for keying in textbooks that may be used.
3. *Enabling activity three* is a *class session* option. Attend the class session(s) on the date(s), at the time(s), and at the place(s) announced.

(Date)	(Time)	(Place)
(Date)	(Time)	(Place)
(Date)	(Time)	(Place)

4. *Enabling activity four* (These lines are left blank so that you may add other enabling activities as suggested by your instructor.)_____

5. *Enabling activity five*_____

6. *Enabling activity six*_____

Now that you have completed the appropriate number of required and/or optional learning alternatives, look back at **Self Pre-Assessment 4.4.** If you feel you can answer "yes" to all of the questions, you are ready to proceed to the Post-Assessment. This may be given to you immediately or after completion of a series of chapters.

Miss Millard had been evaluating her class carefully. Some of her students had excellent vocabulary and comprehension skills and spent adequate time studying. However these students failed to do well on class assignments and tests. On the other hand, one of her students, John, whose vocabulary and comprehension skills were not as good as many students', always made higher scores in class and on his tests. Miss Millard determined that although the other students had vocabulary and comprehension skills better than John's, their study skills were not as well developed. A major contributor to John's academic success was his mastery of the reading-related skills known as the study skills. This chapter will categorize, define, and describe these skills.

SCOPE OF THE STUDY SKILLS

The study skills were defined in Chapter 1 as those skills that help readers make the best use of their vocabulary and comprehension skills. There is no one exact delineation of study skills. These skills are categorized and defined by various authors in different ways. For example, Burmeister (1974) discussed several strategies for reading textbooks, including previewing and reviewing, reading speed, and using library resources, although she does not use the label *study skills*. However, Burmeister does not stress other study skills, such as summarizing. Olson and Ames (1972) do not include this label either but do discuss previewing, reviewing, and rate of reading.

Personalizing Reading Instruction in Middle, Junior, and Senior High Schools provides the teacher with an enumerated list of study skills. The fourteen study skills presented in this text include those most often needed

1. Scheduling Time
2. Setting Purposes
3. Using a Study Technique
4. Using Locational Aids in the Library
5. Recording References
6. Using the Library Call System
7. Using Locational Aids Within Books
8. Using Footnotes
9. Using Glossaries
10. Using Maps, Graphs, and Tables
11. Matching Materials with Purposes
12. Understanding the Organization of Paragraphs
13. Organizing Information
14. Adjusting Rate to Purpose

Figure 4.1 Outline of Study Skills

by middle, junior, and senior high school students. This list is not intended to be exhaustive or conclusive. The study skills may be presented in any sequence as long as the student has adequate vocabulary and comprehension skills to complete the tasks involved.

The fourteen study skills will be discussed later in this chapter under nine headings: Scheduling Time; Setting Purposes; Using a Study Technique; Locating Information in the Library (including using locational aids in the library, recording references, using the library call system); Locating Information Within Books (including using locational aids within books, using footnotes, using glossaries, using maps, graphs, and tables); Matching Materials with Purposes; Understanding the Organization of Paragraphs; Organizing Information; and Adjusting Rate to Purpose. Despite the lack of agreement over the names and classification of components within the study skill categories, major authorities appear to agree that these skills are of primary importance in helping students to read with greatest efficiency. A study done by McClusky (1934) divided 118 college students into two equal groups. One group was shown how to skim over headings and summaries and the other was not. When these two groups were given a selection to read, the trained group read 24 per cent faster and just as accurately as the control group. In a study involving several thousand high school students (Spitzer 1939), it was shown that only 20 per cent of what was known immediately after an initial reading was remembered two weeks later and that a test-type review after the reading reduced the forgetting from 80 per cent to only 20 per cent. Robinson (1961) points out that average and superior students in high school and college excel in grades mostly because of differences in intellectual ability rather than because of better reading and study methods. In other words, although academically talented students succeed, they could improve their grades with proper guidance in the study skills. Therefore all students, regardless of intellectual ability, should profit from instruction in the reading study skills; and study skills should be an integral part of the teaching of all the content areas. But, although these skills are of paramount importance to the student, they are seldom part of the formal curriculum. One reason may be that these particular skills cut across all subject areas so that the responsibility for teaching them is vague (Heilman 1972). Therefore all teachers should take the responsibility for developing reading study skills in their areas of expertise.

Students probably will not learn these important study-type reading methods through teacher presentation alone. If an instructor wishes a student to acquire these skills, he must prepare study skill exercises and then provide supervised practice during which students are required to follow the proper procedures (Fry 1972). Research studies by Stordahl and Christensen (1956) point out that simple explanation of better techniques is not sufficient to bring about better skills. With supervised practice, there is a definite gain in skills to levels far beyond those attained with self-help methods. Furthermore, even if the material to be read is written in such a manner as to lend itself easily to study strategies, the student will not utilize these aids without specific instruction. Robinson (1961, p. 196) points out that "students may not be able to read better when they are given well-organized and facilitative material unless they are given special instruction." Hence, the remainder of this chapter will discuss the study skills and one way in which content area teachers may introduce each of these skills to their students.

CONTENT OF THE STUDY SKILLS

This section provides a description of each of the study skills shown in Figure 4.1.

Scheduling Time

Scheduling time involves learning that adhering to a regularly scheduled time basis for each subject area is an efficient way to study. For example, a student might schedule 45 minutes on Monday, Wednesday, and Saturday for the study of Latin. Obviously if a major biology test were scheduled for Thursday, the student might wish to move his usual time for studying Latin to a new time slot so that he could devote all his efforts to biology on Wednesday.

The classroom teacher can help students in making a study schedule by conducting an open discussion in which both the teacher and the students clarify their tasks in a particular content area. For example, the teacher of German explains to students that he will assign a given number of words to be learned as well as a given number of passages to be translated each day. It is the students' responsibility to keep current the words they have learned the preceding month.

One way to encourage students to specifically plan their study time is to require them to hand in a schedule of the time periods in which they do study a particular topic. For example, the German teacher in the class just mentioned might require students to outline the day and time in which they studied their German words and to hand in their outlines every Friday for a month.

Setting Purposes

It is important that students know their purpose for reading because this will inform them of the kinds of information that they are supposed to be acquainted with. For example, Bill was assigned to read Chapter 30 in his American history book for the purpose of identifying the major events of the Truman era and the dates on which they occurred. Bill read with this purpose in mind and was able to perform successfully on the quiz that was subsequently given in class and that required the sequencing of Truman-era events.

A study conducted by Smith (1961) indicates that good readers do attempt to adjust their reading techniques to the purpose for which they are reading. However, the same study supports the contention that most students have had little, if any, direct guidance in reading for different purposes. Thus, students need to be taught to approach a written selection in light of their purpose for reading.

The teachers' task of building purposes for reading can be facilitated through close inspection of their purposes for having their students read the material

70

and then informing their students of these purposes. For example, Bill's history teacher might have believed that it was important that his students be able to answer the following questions regarding the Truman era:

1. What were the major events of Truman's presidency and when did each occur? (identifying details)
2. What was the general opinion of Truman in 1945? (identifying details)
3. What is likely to be history's evaluation of Truman's presidency? (making generalizations)
4. Do you consider the Truman administration to have been a success? (making conclusions)

The teacher could have communicated these purposes to his students by first asking them to read the chapter to identify and sequence the major events of the Truman era. Following discussion of this topic, the teacher could have shown the students how to reread the chapter with the purposes of determining people's opinions of Truman in 1945 and history's likely opinion of Truman. Students could then be asked to reread the chapter a third time to determine their own opinions of Truman.

Using a Study Technique

This skill requires students to have an organized strategy for their reading. For example, a student in a science class might first skim over the materials in boldface, then read the questions at the end of the chapter, and finally go back and begin to actually read the material. A number of such strategies have been designed by reading authorities. Most of these are activities that direct the student to follow a series of steps in order to approach study-type reading tasks in an organized manner. In most cases, the strategies include instructions to survey the material to be read and to formulate questions concerning the data before actually reading the material. Then students are shown how to assess their understanding of the content after reading the material. Often these series of steps are given labels arranged in the form of an acronym that provides the student with a mnemonic device for remembering the steps and their order. The forerunner of most of the study techniques was the SQ3R method (survey, question, read, recite, and review) developed by Robinson in 1946. Others include Spache and Berg's (1966) PQRST (preview, question, read, summarize, and test) and Pauk's (1974) OK4R (overview, key ideas, read, recall, reflect, and review). The procedures, practices, and repetition that are built into study systems like these lend themselves to the theoretical support of many of the sound principles of learning psychology.

The SQ3R method can be used to illustrate the strategy behind most of the other techniques. It also demonstrates how the student may use the strategy in cases where the teacher has not set specific purposes for reading the chapter. Students who are taught to use the SQ3R method are encouraged to follow these steps.

1. *Survey*—Take five to ten minutes to overview the chapter about to be read. Read introductory material, words in italics, words in large type, headings of various sizes that show the subordination and organization of ideas, and the final summary. Note: By providing them with "advance organizers" (Ausubel 1960), this step helps students to understand the author's format and main points. Gestalt psychology views surveying as a procedure that facilitates the selection of relevant stimuli, making reading a process of integrating the relevant parts into a new whole.

2. *Question*—Look through the text again and formulate questions concerning what is to be read. Change subheadings and topic sentences into questions. For example, the heading "The Effect of Valences on the Writing of Formulas" can be changed into the question, "How do valences affect the writing of formulas?" Note: This step helps students to focus and add specific purpose to their reading by aiding them in selecting relevant stimuli, as does the survey step (Gestalt).

3. *Read*—Complete this step immediately after the questions are formulated and before going on to another section. Read thoroughly to find the answers to the questions and record the answers. Note: Recording may be in any form that allows students to review the answers to their questions without being able to see the answer when they read the question. For instance, students may divide their notebook page lengthwise and write the question on one side and the answer on the other. Or they may write the question on one side of an index card and the answer on the opposite side. Some students find underlining the answer in the text or making marginal notes sufficient.

4. *Recite*—Immediately after reading a chapter, go back to your questions and try to answer them. Look away from the answer and try to respond correctly to the question. If the answer is incomplete, reread appropriate sections of the chapter. Note: Skinnerian psychologists explain the worth of the recitation in terms of reward caused by immediate feedback. However, the amount of recitation needed will depend on the nature of the material read. If the material is not meaningfully involved (e.g., foreign language vocabulary), almost all of the study time needs to be spent on recitation. If the material is well organized and storylike (e.g., a literature selection), much less time needs to be spent on recitation.

5. *Review*—Take a second look at the chapter at a later time in order to gain new insights into the material. Self-test a few times between the first recitation and the final review for the examination. Possibly skim over the headings in the book to reformulate the outline of each chapter and then attempt to answer the questions. Reread the answers to be sure that nothing has been forgotten. All the material to be covered on the examination should be gone over during the final pre-examination review.

Ideally these strategies should be an integral part of the teaching of all content areas and should be presented to the students along with a specific purpose for reading. For example, the biology teacher might determine that his purpose for asking students to read a chapter in the biology book is to answer the question, "Why are viruses difficult to control?"

Then the teacher might show his students the SQ3R study strategy by doing the following:

1. Teach the students to *survey* the chapter, looking for italics, headings, boldface, and other typographical clues that would assist them in locating sections concerning viruses.
2. Show students how to transform typographical clues into *questions* that are related to their purpose of determining why viruses are difficult to control. For example, the title "Experiments Show the Role of Viral Nucleic Acids" might be made into the question "How does the role of viral nucleic acids make viruses difficult to control?"
3. Teach students how to go back and *read* the identified sections with their questions in mind and how to record their answers.
4. Instruct students to pause after reading all the material on viruses and try to *recite* the answers to all the questions they formulated as well as to the original question. If they cannot, tell them to reread appropriate sections.
5. Teach students to *review* by repeating steps 1 through 4 if necessary and by surveying key points, reciting their answers, and rereading to judge their accuracy immediately prior to the examination.

Locating Information in the Library

Locating information in the library includes three reading skills: (1) using locational aids in the library, (2) recording references, and (3) using the library call system.

Joe was a student writing a term paper on personality tests. To locate information on the topic, he selected key topics related to his subject—such as personality tests, tests, personality, and psychology—and looked for them in the subject index of the card catalog because he knew neither an author's name nor a title of a work to look for. When he found appropriate references, Joe also noted useful additional topics found at the back of each classification.

Although he had found many helpful references in the card catalog, Joe knew that it contained neither references to articles in periodicals nor the most recent library materials on the topic. So Joe located the *Reader's Guide to Periodical Literature*. Again he looked under several appropriate topics and used any cross-references that were provided. Joe familiarized himself with the unusual format of the *Reader's Guide* and read its key so that he would be able to interpret the abbreviations. Joe then looked in the specialized *Psychology Index* to find more periodical references to his topic.

If Joe had been looking for information on a different topic, he could have used another of the specialized indexes, such as the *Who's Who in Amer-*

ica, which gives bibliographic information on well-known Americans; dictionaries, which are very helpful in literature because they note changes in the meanings of words; *Roget's International Thesaurus*, which lists synonyms by topic; and the *World Almanac*, which gives a variety of statistics.

Joe also used the encyclopedia to locate information on his topic. He looked under a variety of subject headings and also used the encyclopedia's index and cross-references to find scattered references on the topic. To locate each, he used the guide words that label each volume. The encyclopedia provided Joe with a summary of the topic; through each entry's bibliography, he located additional references.

While consulting the card catalog, *Reader's Guide*, specialized indexes, and encyclopedias, Joe noted appropriate information, including call numbers that give directions to the location of the references. Furthermore, he was careful to note the references in the form that he would later use to write his paper's list of references and bibliography.

Having checked several sources, Joe used the classification chart in the library to find the books and periodicals that he believed would be useful to him. Although he was able to find the materials by use of the chart alone, Joe's knowledge of the Library of Congress System for classifying materials, which his library used, was also helpful. Unlike the Dewey Decimal System, which allows for only ten classifications, the Library of Congress system allows for twenty-one classifications.

Students need direct instruction in the use of the library and this instruction should be given in the context of meaningful assignments. For example, a Spanish teacher might wish each of her students to write a short paper on the geography of a Latin American country. If her students were not familiar with the library, she might have the librarian explain the subject index, the location of the materials, and a format for writing reference cards. The teacher might then ask each student to locate at least three references, to write a card for each, and then to find the books and write his paper. If students were more advanced, the librarian might explain the use of the *Reader's Guide* or one of the specialized indexes.

Locating Information Within Books

Locating information within books involves four skills: (1) using locational aids within books such as indexes, tables of contents, and chapter headings and subheadings, (2) using footnotes, (3) using glossaries, and, (4) using maps, graphs, and tables.

An index may be used to locate information on a given topic. If students are to use an index successfully, they must be able to select key words that may be listed, locate the index, find the key words in the index, and then locate them as headings or information in the text. For example, Linda was writing a term paper on the Shakespearean theater and was using a book on Shakespeare as a reference. She located information by finding the index and then looking for key entries, such as *theater* and *stage*.

Tables of contents and chapter headings and subheadings may also be used to ascertain the location of textual information. For example, Bette was interested in ecology. The table of contents in her biology book indicated that a chapter was devoted to the biosphere. So Bette turned to this chapter and used its subheadings to locate information on ecosystems.

Footnotes and glossaries may be used to explain concepts not presented within the text. For example, Alan was reading and came to the term *Scotland Yard*. Since he did not know the meaning of this term, he consulted footnotes at the bottom of the page and the glossary in the back of the book to find its meaning.

Illustrations may be found in any subject area. For example, a unit in career education includes a *map* of the United States showing where heavy industry is located, a *chart* showing incomes for various vocations in heavy industry, and a *graph* showing the amount of unemployment in heavy industry over the period 1965–1975. Therefore, like the career education teacher, teachers of all subject areas should be aware that maps, graphs, tables, and other illustrations such as pictures, figures, and charts require students to possess many skills. Maps, for example, involve an understanding of projections, distortions, distance, directions, longitude and latitude, and reading a key. Graphs require an understanding of how numbers can be pictured and that they may be shown in bar, circle, line, or picture concepts. The student must be familiar with many kinds of tables such as timetables and those used in making forecasts.

One method for teaching how to use indexes, tables of contents, and subheadings in any subject area is to have students locate a book on a topic of their choice. Then have them attempt to find their specific topic in the book's index. If they are unable to do so, they might use the table of contents or chapter headings or subheadings. Following this activity, the teacher and the students should discuss any problems encountered.

Footnotes and glossaries are usually included in high school textbooks and, thus, are readily accessible. A lesson devoted to using them could include a teacher-led discussion of the purposes of footnotes and glossaries, followed by the students' locating information in them.

There are many ways in which teachers may provide instruction in reading maps, graphs, and tables. For example, a lesson devoted to reading tables could include a teacher-led discussion on the nature of headings and subheadings and vertical and horizontal columns. After the discussion, students could be asked to locate in their textbook a table that includes subheadings or columns.

Matching Materials with Purposes

Once students have located material relevant to a topic, they need to determine whether it is suitable for their purposes. Evaluating appropriateness of material includes two aspects: (1) Does the material fit the needs of the reader? (2) In what respects is the writer an authority?

Walter was planning a speech entitled "School Grading Systems Are Archaic and Unnecessary." By using the card catalog, the *Reader's Guide*, and the *Ed-*

ucation Index, he located five books and four articles on the topic *grades*. After examining their indexes, tables of contents, and subheadings, he found that two of the books contained pertinent information. By reading the introductory materials and summaries of each of the articles, he discovered that two of them contained information on school grading practices. However, because one of the articles was written twenty-five years ago, he realized that its value would be mainly in historical interest.

When Walter had completed examining the materials for appropriate content, he evaluated the authority of the writers. According to the prefaces and other information given, one author was the principal of an open-area high school, another was a college professor whose major field was evaluation, and the third was a parent. Walter realized that each author's viewpoint had its strengths. The school principal would have knowledge of grading practices in open-area schools, the professor would have theoretical background, and the parent would have gained an understanding of the topic by having had children in school.

One technique content teachers can use to encourage their students to judge the appropriateness of materials would be to have students locate one reference on a given topic. The suitability of each could then be discussed by asking the questions: (1) Does the book contain appropriate information? (Discuss index, table of contents, heading, and subheading.) (2) What is the expertise of the writer? (Assess the writer's competence.)

Understanding the Organization of Paragraphs

Understanding the organization of paragraphs requires students to determine the author's organization so that they may more easily locate and understand what they read. Several types of paragraph organization have been described by a variety of authors. The four most common patterns include cause-effect, comparison-contrast, enumerative, and chronological. The paragraphs below illustrate these patterns and key words for each pattern are enumerated.

The following paragraph illustrates cause-effect organization.

> If the reserve requirements were lowered from, say, 15 per cent to 10 per cent, this would mean that a larger volume of deposits could be supported by a given volume of reserves—in fact 10 times as many instead of 6.67 times as many. Thus, banks could expand their lending and investing activities and increase the money supply. (Calderwood and Fersh 1974, p. 219)

The key words in this paragraph which indicate a cause-effect organization are *if* and *thus*. Other key terms that signal a cause-effect paragraph are *as a result, therefore, hence, for this reason,* and *consequently*.

The following paragraph illustrates a comparison-contrast format.

> The principal difference between direct investments and portfolio investments is that, in the case of the former, Americans maintain control over the use of the capital in the foreign country, whereas in the case of the latter, control over American capital is handed over to foreigners. For example, if General Motors builds an automobile plant in Germany, its management controls this foreign operation. But

76

if an American citizen or insurance company buys bonds issued by the Province of Quebec in Canada, it is the Canadians who control the use of the money. (Calderwood and Fersh 1974, p. 270)

Key terms in this paragraph type are *like, although, however, but, on the other hand,* and *whereas.*

A third paragraph type is enumerative.

The United States is divided into 12 Federal Reserve Districts, each with its own Federal Reserve Bank. These banks hold the reserves of the member banks and act as agents for the federal government in such matters as issuing or redeeming government bonds and providing checking accounts for the government. The Federal Reserve Banks also supervise and examine member banks to make sure they are observing the banking laws. The Federal Reserve Banks are run not for profit but as public services. (Calderwood and Fersh 1974, p. 215)

Although this one is not, sometimes paragraphs with enumerative formats are signaled by key words such as: *additionally, also, besides,* and *another.*

A fourth common paragraph structure is chronological.

In the meanwhile the Assyrians were slowly gaining strength in the upper valley of the Tigris River. By the ninth century B.C. they had built a powerful army that enabled them to begin a series of conquests. It was the most efficient military power that had ever existed in the area. Eventually, by the seventh century B.C., the Assyrian Empire included all of the Fertile Crescent and stretched as far west as the Nile Valley of Upper Egypt . . . . (Tachau 1970, p. 62)

Key signals in this format are *in the meanwhile, by, eventually, when, next, after,* and *finally.*

Other paragraph structures that have been described include Karlin's transitional (1972), Pauk's problem-effect-solution (1974), and Smith's substantiated fact (1961).

One way to teach students to understand the organization of paragraphs is to locate paragraphs that provide examples of the formats described above. After reading the paragraphs in class, the students can analyze their structural formats. For example, after giving introductory instruction, the career education teacher might present a paragraph such as the following:

There are plenty of places a student can go for advice once he has conceived a serious interest in archeology. Museum officials are an obvious choice. So are university professors—who, according to Professor Dyson, are usually willing to help the perplexed inquirer. Then there are the professional associations like the Archeological Institute of America in New York City, which can be reached at 100 Washington Square East. Dr. Claireve Grandjouan, the institute's general secretary, recommends that students mention the branch of archeology they are interested in when writing for assistance. (Footlick 1970, p. 15)

After reading the paragraph, students should be able to (1) evaluate its format (enumerative), (2) tell what is enumerated (places to go for advice), and

(3) list the enumerated items (museum officials, university professors, professional associations).

Organizing Information

The skill of organizing information requires students to select an appropriate method of recording information that is pertinent to their purpose. For example, if students wanted to know how electrons work and had located a paragraph that described the process in detail, they might *outline* that paragraph. If they were to retell the short story "Young Goodman Brown," they might *take notes* on it first. If they wanted to find out which fabrics are natural and which are man-made, they might *classify* the information. If they were interested in only the main points of the settlement of the West between 1870 and 1900, they might *summarize* the information. If they wished to compare Huck Finn's and the widow's views on smoking, they might use *comparison and contrast.*

Outlining is used when the reader wishes to note main points and details, and to organize the order and relationships among them. For example, students providing a broad outline of a book might list the chapter headings and perhaps one or two main topics under each heading. If they were outlining a chapter, they might list the chapter subheadings and one or two important points under each. To outline a paragraph, they might state the main idea and the details. Sample outlines of each type are shown in Figure 4.2.

Note-taking is used to record pertinent facts without necessarily attempting to order them. The format of the notes should vary according to the purpose for which they are being taken. For example, if the student's purpose were to list details, the notes might appear as follows.

Distinct groups in Mid-East

1. own areas of towns and cities
2. follow certain jobs
3. own community organizations and customs; that is, religion, dress
4. each speaks own language
5. own religious denomination

Classifying requires the reader to find items of information that can be placed into appropriate categories. For example, a consumer education student might read the following grocery ads and classify pertinent information as shown in the "Least Expensive Dairy Products" chart.

GROCERY ADS

```
Grand Opening Specials              Buddingham's
    Connerly's Mkt.                  Weekly Bargains


Cottage Cheese  .59/pt.         Ice Cream   1.99/½ gal
Ground Beef  .68/lb.            Detergent  1.69/king size
Yogurt 3 oz. cartons  5/1.00    Grade "A" Large Eggs  .59/dz
Bread  .30                      Ground Round  .80/lb.
Sponges  .05                    Cottage Cheese  .80/qt
Ice Cream  1.59/½ gal           Longhorn Cheese  1.09/lb
Grade "A" Lrg. Eggs  .64/dz.    Paper Towels  3/1.00
Donuts  .94/dz.                 Yogurt 3 oz/.15
Milk  1.09/gal.                 Sweet Rolls  .59/½ dz
Longhorn Cheese  .89/lb.        Milk  .89/½ gal.
```

CLASSIFICATION

```
            Least Expensive Dairy Products

    Connerly's                    Buddingham's

    ice cream                     cottage cheese
    milk                          yogurt
    longhorn cheese               eggs
```

Summarizing, like note-taking and outlining, requires the selection of main points. The final product of summarizing is better not recorded as sentence fragments, but rather as a complete sentence or as a paragraph made up of complete sentences. After reading the paragraph given below, a student might summarize it as shown.

> But, of course, the Plains Indians were no more free of duties and responsibilities than any other men. They had tribal hunting territories to defend. They had families. They had property in the form of horses, weapons, household goods, and the tipis which sheltered them and their belongings. (Marriott 1968, p. 139)
>
> *Summary:* The Indians were not totally "free" because they had to care for families, property, and territories.

Comparison and contrast is used by students when their purpose for reading is to note similarities (compare) and differences (contrast). Thus a chemistry student might read the following paragraphs and then produce notes like those given on page 81.

Book

"The Scope of World Economics"

I. Individual's role

  A. Producer
  B. Consumer

II. Policies and goals

  A. Personal
  B. Social
  C. Economic
  D. Conflicting

III. Trade

  A. Policies
  B. Barriers

IV. Finance

  A. International investments
  B. Foreign aid

Chapter

"Economic Growth in the United States"

I. Elements of economic growth

  A. Higher living standards
  B. Full employment
  C. International competition
  D. Communism
  E. Developing countries

II. Measurement of economic growth

  A. Gross national product
  B. Real per capita gross national product
  C. Index of industrial production
  D. Increase of leisure time

III. Economic growth of the United States

  A. Long-run economic growth
  B. Recent economic growth
  C. Unevenness of economic growth

Paragraph

"The Unevenness of Economic Growth"

I. Unequal growth rate

  A. Eastern Kentucky and West Virginia
  B. Rural areas and city slums
  C. Older people and minorities

II. Unsteady growth rate

  A. Standstill 1969–1970
  B. Rapid advance 1962–1966, 1972–1973

Figure 4.2 Sample Outlines

Carbon monoxide is a very toxic gas that has no color and no odor. Although it is obtained by the dehydration of formic acid, it is not considered to be its anhydride because the gas is insoluble in water. Carbon monoxide is used commercially in the preparation of pure nickel. Because it interrupts normal oxygen transport, it is a serious factor in air pollution.

Carbon dioxide is a dense gas with no color. It is used to carbonate beverages. Its taste in a water solution is attributed to the weak acid properties of the solution. This stable compound is invaluable to man because of its involvement in photosynthesis.

The notes might appear as follows.

	Form	Color	Odor	Water Soluble	Commercial Value	Worth to Humans
CO	gas	none	none	yes	yes, pure nickel	harmful
CO_2	gas	none	none	no	yes, beverages	beneficial

One method by which teachers might introduce the skill of organizing information to their students is to carefully select paragraphs that lend themselves to one of the above types of organizing information. Then, the teacher could discuss the paragraph structure with the class and together they could develop a set of notes. For example a biology teacher used the following paragraphs to instruct his students in comparing and contrasting.

The phylum bryophyta includes plants usually found in moist places. They are small and nonvascular. The bryophytes do not have true leaves, stems, or roots. Examples of bryophytes are mosses, liverworts, and hornworts.

The plants in the phylum tracheophyta all have vessels for conducting food and water. All ferns, woody plants, and trees are tracheophytes. Therefore, they range in size from small to very large.

The notes might appear as follows.

Bryophyta	Tracheophyta
environment moist	environment not necessarily moist
small	small to very big
nonvascular	vascular
no true roots, stems, leaves	true roots, stems, leaves
mosses, liverworts, hornworts	ferns, woody plants, trees

Adjusting Rate to Purpose

An efficient reader can read at a variety of speeds and can use rate flexibly, according to the demands of the reading situation. Depending on the nature of the material and the reader's purpose, he may use a rate varying from under 50 words per minute to over 1,000 words per minute.

The rate at which students read will depend on two main factors. The first of these is the *purposes* for which they are reading. For example, if they are reading an algebra problem for full understanding, they will probably read at a *slow careful rate* because each detail presented requires thoughtful consideration. A more rapid rate, the *textbook reading rate*, is used when the student is reading continuous running material such as a history or biology book. This rate is slow enough so that the reader can pay attention to the main points and details and can retain much of what has been read. Students might use this rate when they are completing the *read* step of the SQ3R study technique. If students are reading the newspaper to get a general idea of what is happening in their town, they might read at a *rapid reading rate*. This rate can be used to read textbook material that is very easy and does not require a recollection of many facts. For example, the material in an algebra book that presents the biography of a *mathematician* at a low readability level could probably be read at this rate. Also, much recreational reading is done at this speed.

The next more rapid reading rate might be referred to as *skimming*. Skimming is used when the reader wishes to glance over material to get the gist of what it contains and usually involves reading titles in heavy print, other subheadings, italicized words, initial sentences in paragraphs, and other occasional sentences. If a student is using an index to locate the number of the page on which the Federal Reserve System is discussed, he would use the skimming rate. One faster reading rate is often used. This speed, known as *scanning*, is used when a single fact is being looked for or when the answer to a specific question is being located.

The second main factor in determining a student's reading rate is the difficulty of the material. For example, Fred's purpose for reading was to gain a thorough understanding of the behavior of gases. He located two textbooks that discussed this topic. One used uncomplicated sentence structures, common words, and copious examples. The other was written in a less readable manner. Thus Fred should have been able to obtain the information at a much more rapid rate from the first textbook than from the second.

Students should be made aware of the various reading rates and the appropriate times to use them. They should also be taught that a reader sometimes must adjust his rate as he reads. For example, if he is reading a novel at a rapid reading rate, he may want to slow down to read a section that is especially humorous. Conversely, if he is reading a required book at a textbook reading rate and he comes to a section that is already familiar to him, he can increase his rate accordingly.

One method of teaching students about reading rates and the advantages of using them appropriately is to present students with hypothetical situations and then have them discuss the appropriate reading rate. A hypothetical situation might read:

> You are to read the chapter on the life of the Sioux Indians in your social studies book. Your purpose for reading is to obtain an overview of Indian life, not specific facts.

Assuming that the social studies text was very readable, students would probably read at a rapid rate because no retention of facts was required. Students might then be asked to read short selections from their textbooks for a variety of purposes and to discuss the rates at which they read each selection.

References and Bibliography

Ausubel, D. P. "The Use of Advance Organizers in the Learning and Retention of Meaningful Verbal Material." *Journal of Educational Psychology*, **51** (1960), 267–272.

Bamman, H. A., Dawson, M. A., and McGovern, J. J. *Fundamentals of Basic Reading Instruction*. 3rd ed. New York: McKay, 1973.

Burmeister, L. E. *Reading Strategies for Secondary School Teachers*. Reading, Mass.: Addison-Wesley, 1974.

Burron, A., and Claybaugh, A. L. *Using Reading to Teach Subject Matter: Fundamentals for Content Teachers*. Columbus, Ohio: Merrill, 1974.

Calderwood, J. D., and Fersh, G. L. *Economics for Decision-Making*. New York: Macmillan, 1974.

Dallmann, M., et al. *The Teaching of Reading*. 4th ed. New York: Holt, Rinehart & Winston, 1974.

Footlick, J. K., ed. *Careers for the Seventies*. Princeton, N. J.: Dow Jones, 1970.

Fry, E. E. *Reading Instruction for Classroom and Clinic*. New York: McGraw-Hill, 1972.

Guth, H. P., and Schuster, E. H. *American English Today*. New York: McGraw-Hill, 1970.

Harris, L. A., and Smith, C. B. *Reading Instruction Through Diagnostic Teaching*. New York: Holt, Rinehart & Winston, 1972.

Heilman, W. *Principles and Practices of Teaching Reading*. 3rd ed. Columbus, Ohio: Merrill, 1972.

Jones, D. M. *Teaching Children to Read*. New York: Harper & Row, 1971.

Karlin, R. *Teaching Reading in High School*. 2nd ed. Indianapolis, Ind.: Bobbs-Merrill, 1972.

Marriott, A. *Kiowa Years: A Study in Culture Impact*. New York: Macmillan, 1968.

McClusky, H. Y. "An Experiment on the Influence of Preliminary Skimming on Reading." *Journal of Educational Psychology*, **25** (1934), 521–529.

Olson, A. V., and Ames, W. S. *Teaching Reading Skills in Secondary Schools*. Scranton, Pa.: Intext Educational Publishers, 1972.

Pauk, W. *How to Study in College*. 2nd ed. Boston: Houghton Mifflin, 1974.

Pauk, W. *A Skill at a Time Series: Perceiving Structure*. Providence, R. I.: Jamestown, 1975.

Robinson, F. P. "Study Skills for Superior Students in Secondary School." *The Reading Teacher*, **15** (September 1961), 29–33, 37.

Robinson, F. P. *Effective Study*. 4th ed. New York: Harper & Row, 1970.

Robinson, H. M. "Developing Critical Readers." *Dimensions of Critical Reading*, **11** (1974), 1–11. Edited by Russel G. Stauffer. Proceedings of Annual Education and Reading Conferences. Newark, Del.: University of Delaware.

Smith, H. K. "Research in Reading for Different Purposes." *Changing Concepts of Reading Instruction*, **6** (1961), 119–122. Edited by J. Allen Figuul. Proceedings of the International Reading Association. New York: Scholastic Magazines.

Spache, G. D., and Berg, P. C. *The Art of Efficient Reading*. New York: Macmillan, 1966.

Spache, G. D., and Spache, E. B. *Reading in the Elementary School.* 3rd ed. Boston: Allyn & Bacon, 1973.

Spitzer, H. F. "Studies in Retention." *Journal of Educational Psychology,* **30** (1939), 641–656.

Stordahl, K. E., and Christensen, C. M. "The Effect of Study Techniques on Comprehension and Retention." *Journal of Educational Research,* **46** (1956), 561–570.

Tachau, F. *The Middle East.* New York: Macmillan, 1970.

Thomas, E. L., and Robinson, H. A. *Improving Reading in Every Class.* Boston: Allyn & Bacon, 1972.

Zintz, M. V. *The Reading Process: The Teacher and the Learner.* Dubuque, Iowa: Brown, 1970.

Part Two

Matching Reading Needs to Classroom Materials

Chapter 5

Determining Student's Reading Ability

Prerequisite 5.1

Before beginning this chapter participants should have successfully completed the objectives for Chapters 1 through 4 or should have some knowledge of the skills involved in learning to read.

Rationale 5.2

Because the reading achievement levels of middle and secondary school students differ widely, the teacher should have a means to assess reading levels in the classroom. This chapter briefly overviews several ways, both formal and informal, by which the teacher may do this.

Objectives 5.3

On successful completion of this chapter, the participant will be able to:

1. State why the reading achievement levels of middle and secondary school students should be assessed.
2. Describe at least six ways other than formal testing, by which a student's reading achievement level may be estimated.
3. Describe, distinguish among, and give at least one example of the three types of tests that may be used to specifically measure reading achievement.
4. Define *standardized* reading test.

5. Describe, distinguish among, and give at least one example of the following types of standardized reading tests: (1) survey tests, (2) analytic tests, (3) diagnostic tests, and (4) special tests.
6. Describe at least four ways in which the standardized test may be useful to the classroom teacher or administrator.
7. Describe at least three advantages and at least three limitations of a standardized reading test.
8. State at least three criteria that should be used in the selection of a standardized reading test.
9. Identify at least two references that may be used to assist in the selection of standardized reading tests.
10. Define informal reading inventory (IRI) and describe how one may be constructed, administered, and interpreted.
11. Describe and differentiate between group and individual administration of an IRI.
12. Describe and give examples of at least three different uses for an IRI.
13. Describe at least two advantages and two limitations of an IRI.
14. Accurately score a reading of the oral portion of an IRI and a set of answers to the questions following the silent reading selections.
15. Given a set of scores on both oral and silent portions of an IRI, state (1) instructional level, (2) independent level, (3) any noticeable strengths or weaknesses.
16. Given the years in school and the I.Q. score of a middle or secondary school student, identify reading expectancy.
17. (On the lines below, add other objectives according to your instructor's directions.)_____

_____

18. _____

_____

19. _____

_____

20. _____

_____

*   *   *   *   *   *   *   *   *   *   *   *   *   *

Chapter 13, Experience 5 extends Chapter 5 with these performance/consequence objectives:

21. Evaluate a standardized reading test according to a checklist given in Chapter 13; and/or

22. Administer, score, and interpret the results of an informal reading inventory.

* * * * * * * * * * * * * *

Self Pre-Assessment 5.4

Can you complete all the activities listed in **Objectives 5.3**? Answer "yes," "no," or "not certain."

If you answered "yes" to the question, complete the enabling activities required by your instructor and take the Post-Assessment on the date assigned by him.

If you answered "no," refer to **Enabling Activities 5.5.** If you decide to do any activities that are not required, select those that best suit you as a learner. You need not complete all the optional activities or all parts of a particular optional activity. As soon as you have the information you need to complete the objectives, answer "yes" to the **Self Pre-Assessment 5.4** question and stop the activity.

If you answered "not certain" to the question, refer to **Enabling Activities 5.5.** Select the enabling activity that best suits your style of learning and peruse it. Then make a firm "yes" or "no" answer and proceed accordingly.

Enabling Activities 5.5

Complete only as many of the activities listed below as are required and which you need in order to meet the objectives.

1. *Enabling activity one* is a *reading* alternative. This is **Information Given 5.6.** It is a brief overview of formal and informal ways to assess reading achievement level.

2. *Enabling activity two* is another *reading* option. In this case, the material to be read is one of the textbooks used to expand the theoretical background for this course. See chart on inside front cover for keying in textbooks that may be used.

3. *Enabling activity three* is a *class session* option. Attend the class session(s) on the date(s), at the time(s), and at the place(s) announced.

(Date)	(Time)	(Place)

(Date)	(Time)	(Place)

(Date)	(Time)	(Place)

4. *Enabling activity four* (These lines are left blank so that you may add other enabling activities as suggested by your instructor.)_____

_____

_____

5. *Enabling activity five*_____

_____

6. *Enabling activity six*_____

_____

Now that you have completed the appropriate number of required and/or optional learning alternatives, look back at **Self Pre-Assessment 5.4.** If you feel you can answer "yes" to all of the questions, you are ready to proceed to the Post-Assessment. This may be given to you immediately or after completion of a series of chapters.

Information Given 5.6
Determining Student's Reading Ability

During the first week in September, Mr. Cilak discovered that the reading achievement of the students in his ninth grade English class varied widely. He had asked his students to read the first chapter in *Huckleberry Finn*. Although this chapter is only three pages long, some of his students were unable to complete it after almost forty-five minutes. On the other hand, several of the students not only finished this chapter but also read further into the book. At the next class session, one student revealed that he had continued reading in the evening and had finished the book.

VARIANCE IN READING ACHIEVEMENT LEVELS

Students' reading abilities vary widely. At any grade level, the student who has the best developed reading skills will read significantly better than the student who has the least developed reading skills. Examples of ranges in reading achievement are shown in Figures 1.1 and Table 1.1 of Chapter 1.

Because of the range in reading abilities, teachers who wish their students to have maximum reading growth must use materials that are on a variety of reading levels. Teachers greatly decrease their chances for success when they use materials that are inappropriate to the student's reading level, particularly when the materials are above the student's reading level. Obviously, if a student reading on fourth grade level were being instructed from a book on ninth grade level, the materials would simply be too difficult for the student to read.

When material is used that is below a student's reading level, he is being deprived of the opportunity to learn new skills, although he might enjoy the content. Therefore it is imperative that teachers determine students' reading levels so they may select materials that encourage progress in developing reading skills.

METHODS FOR EVALUATING READING ACHIEVEMENT

There are several ways to evaluate a student's reading achievement. These include (1) teacher observation; (2) teacher records; (3) permanent school records; (4) interviews with parents or students; (5) discussions with other teachers, the counselor, or the school nurse; (6) self-appraisal by the student through interview, essay, or questionnaire; and (7) teacher analysis through interview, essay, or questionnaire.

In addition, tests constructed specifically to measure reading achievement may be used. Tests of this type include placement tests, standardized reading achievement tests, and informal reading inventories.

Placement Tests

Placement tests are designed by the publishers of commercially produced instructional materials in reading to help the teacher determine which of their materials are on the reading level appropriate for a given youngster. Though publishers' tests vary in content and format, they usually all contain items that correspond to the content of the correlated instructional materials. For example, the placement test that accompanies *EDL Word Clues*, a programmed text in vocabulary development published by Educational Development Laboratories, measures the level of the book in which students should begin their work on context clues. The test that accompanies *Tactics I*, published by Scott, Foresman and Company, is more comprehensive in nature and measures ten subskills, all of which correlate with the instructional materials into which the student may be placed. Other examples of placement tests include materials that accompany all the basal reading series and the kits produced by Educational Development Laboratory as well as Science Research Associates. (See Chapter 11 for further description of these materials.)

Standardized Reading Achievement Tests

Gronlund (1976) defines a standardized test as one that has a fixed set of test items, that has specific directions for administration and scoring and that has been given to representative groups of individuals for the purpose of establishing norms. Norms are the average scores made by members of representative groups at various age and grade levels that make it possible to compare one person's test score with those of other individuals whose characteristics are known. Thus it is possible to administer a standardized reading test to a student in the ninth grade and to compare his or her performance with that of a typical ninth grader in the norm population.

Mavrogenes et al. (1974) describes standardized reading tests in terms of four categories: (1) survey tests, (2) analytic tests, (3) diagnostic tests, and (4) special tests.

Survey Tests. Survey tests are designed to give an overview of the general reading ability of the student. They are usually administered in a group situation and take about one class session (that is, forty-five to fifty minutes) to complete. Results are ordinarily given in terms of two or three subskills, which include measures of vocabulary, comprehension, and study skills, and sometimes rate. However some of these tests give only one score. For example, the *Stanford Achievement Test: Advanced Paragraph Meaning* gives only a comprehension score.

The classroom teacher uses survey tests to determine reading achievement level, to identify students who may have reading problems and who should be further diagnosed, and to measure student progress. School administrators may also use these tests to assess effectiveness of instruction, to evaluate new programs or different methods of teaching, and to designate pupils for special classes or for intra- or interschool comparisons of reading achievement levels.

Analytic Tests. Analytic tests are actually survey tests with diagnostic features. They are usually administered in group situations and take somewhat longer to give than the typical survey test. Though they may yield more than five subscores, the three basic subscores are measures of vocabulary skills, comprehension skills, and rate. Some of the tests, such as the *Iowa Silent Reading Test*, also yield a score for such areas as locating information and skimming and scanning.

Classroom teachers usually use these tests to obtain a more detailed profile of the student's reading achievement. Often this test is administered in lieu of a survey test to youngsters with suspected reading problems.

Diagnostic Tests. Diagnostic tests are usually individually administered and are somewhat more difficult to give than survey or analytic tests. They ordinarily yield very specific information about certain reading skills. For example, the *Gray Oral Reading Test* measures only a student's ability in oral reading, and though comprehension questions accompany each passage, the student's responses to the questions do not enter into the scoring.

Content area teachers usually do not administer diagnostic tests because special training is often required. For example, in order to interpret the *Gray Oral* discussed in the preceding paragraph, knowledge of a coded recording system is required. In most cases, this type of test is used by a reading clinician or a classroom teacher who has had some background in reading and is teaching reading as a subject.

Special Tests. Special tests are described by Mavrogenes et al. (1974) as those that cover only one aspect or some unusual aspect of reading. These tests may be used by classroom teachers for specific purposes. Many of these are group tests and are easy to administer and interpret. For example, the *Survey of Study Habits and Attitudes* published by the Psychological Corporation, is a group test that measures aspects not usually assessed by standardized tests, such as efficiency, promptness, and attitudes toward teachers. Results of this test may be used by classroom teachers who are interested in improving the study habits of their students.

A chart written by Mavrogenes et al., which may be used as a concise guide to standardized reading tests, is included in Appendix B of this text. This chart gives an overview of more than fifty standardized secondary reading achievement tests according to the four categories that have been discussed previously.

Uses for Standardized Tests

The classroom teacher and administrator can find the standardized test useful in a number of ways. Lennon (1967) discussed several functions of a standardized test. It provides (1) a measure of status in particular skills or content areas for a pupil, a class, or a school; (2) a measure of growth, development, or progress toward desirable educational goals; (3) a measure of differential status; (4) analytic or diagnostic information, which permits sharper definition of learning difficulties; (5) inventories of skills; and (6) one source of data essential for continuing evaluation of the total instructional program.

Strang (1964) suggests that the standardized test may be used in a number of more specific ways: (1) analyzing by section, subtest, or item in order to diagnose the student's reading performance in a specific skill and to note patterns of consistency or inconsistency; (2) giving the teacher an idea of the range of reading ability in a given class and thus providing a better basis of grouping for instruction; and (3) identifying students in need of special reading instruction.

Obviously, standardized tests may also be used by the classroom teacher to help formulate recommendations for such things as needed materials, facilities, personnel, and courses.

Advantages and Limitations of a Standardized Reading Test

Advantages of standardized tests are: (1) They allow teachers to compare, through national norms, the achievement levels of their students with other students of the same age and/or grade level. They may compare each of their students not only with the norm groups but also with other students in the same school or the same class. (2) Standardized tests are designed to be objective. The teacher's personal feelings toward a youngster are not reflected in the test score. (3) The development, administration, and interpretation of the tests are such that teachers may benefit from the research and do not have to rely upon their own skills to design and interpret a test.

Limitations of standardized tests include the following: (1) The tests reflect only the *author's* viewpoint toward the aspect of reading that should be measured and, as such, may not include aspects that the teacher feels important. (2) Many tests indicate the type of errors made but do not indicate the cause of the error. Sometimes the reasons for particular errors can easily be inferred from the type of error made, but frequently the causes of deficiencies

93

are multiple and interrelated in a complex manner. Hence the teacher needs to be aware that the scores obtained may not be due entirely to a reading deficiency. For example, intelligence, vision, hearing, general physical condition, and emotional state also need to be considered. (3) The number of items measuring each type of error should be closely inspected because tests with relatively few items tend to have low reliability. Hence findings regarding specific strengths and weaknesses for a particular pupil should be regarded only as clues to be verified by other objective evidence and by regular classroom observation (Gronlund 1976). (4) Grade level norms are generally an indication of the pupil's frustration level since standardized tests tend to overrate the pupil's ability when compared with scores from informal reading inventories. Hence the teacher who assumes that a grade level score of 9.0 on a standardized test means that the student can easily read a grade nine book will be giving the youngster materials that he can read only with great effort. Generally students should be given instructional materials a year or two below the grade level score reported on a standardized test.

Criteria for Selection of a Standardized Test

Because there are a great many standardized tests that measure reading, test selection may be a complex task. There is obviously a wide variation in the completeness and quality of test materials as well as in the purpose for which the test was designed. The following criteria may be helpful to teachers in deciding which test to use with their students.

Purpose of the Test. The test should measure what the teacher wants to measure. If the teacher needs a test that briefly overviews the general reading skills of his students rather than one which specifically diagnoses word attack skills, then he should select a survey test rather than a diagnostic word attack test.

Appropriateness of Test to Population. The grade range for which the test is intended should encompass the grade level tested—that is, if ninth grade students are taking the test, ideally the range of the test should be from grades seven through eleven. Scores on tests written for grades five through nine or for grades nine through thirteen tend to be less accurate because the ninth grade norms are the extremes of the test ranges. If a test whose range sandwiches the grade level is not available, then the teacher will have to determine which test form (e.g., grades five through nine or grades nine through thirteen) is more appropriate for his students. He must then interpret test results in terms of which extreme includes the students in his class.

Technical Quality of the Test. The test items should have been developed by someone well trained in test construction. In addition, each item should have been tried out experimentally, and selected on the basis of difficulty, discriminating power, and relationship to a rigid set of specifications.

Furthermore, the test should be reliable (producing a consistency of results) and should be valid (measuring what it purports to measure). In other words, students should make approximately the same scores on Monday as they would on Tuesday if there were no instruction between test administrations. Consistent results of this kind are found with tests that are reliable. Likewise,

94

if students are taking a test that purports to measure comprehension skills, the test should measure comprehension and not word attack. A test that measures what it is supposed to measure is said to be valid.

Comparable forms of the test should be available, as should information concerning the degree to which the forms are equivalent. For example, the teacher should have the choice of using Form A or Form B and should also be informed as to how closely these forms measure the same skills. Occasionally one form may be more reliable or more consistent than the other. The teacher needs to be aware of this type of information in order to assess or compare growth. Having two forms allows the teacher to retest or use the test in a pretest-posttest situation.

Though the test should be technically sound, it should be simple enough to be administered, scored, and interpreted by a classroom teacher without special training in test procedures.

Informative Test Manual. The test manual should be understandable to the teacher and should give complete directions for administering, scoring, and interpreting the test. The background of the students on which the norms have been based should be clearly stated. The norm group should be representative of a cross section of the population or similar to that of the students who will be taking the test.

Ease of Administration. Directions for administering and scoring should be precisely stated so that the procedures are standardized for all users of the test. Directions for the students to follow should be clear and concise. The format should be uncluttered, logical in arrangement, and have print that is easy to read. Answer sheets should be separate from test booklets and should be machine-scorable for reasons of convenience, speed, and economy. Hand scoring should also be possible so that teachers may hand check if they prefer or recheck individual tests in detail.

If the test is too long to be administered within one class period, then it should be designed so that it can be administered in two. For example, it might be divided into sections, several of which could be given the first day, while the rest could be given the second day. If the test exceeds two class periods, it may disrupt program schedules or fatigue students and teachers.

Group tests usually require less teacher time and effort than do individual tests. If both a group test and an individual test measure the same skill equally well, the group test would be considered most efficient.

Ease of Interpretation. Performance profiles should be provided with the test materials. Test results should be reported in a manner which is easily interpreted by the classroom teacher.

Types of Score Results Reported. Scores may be reported to the teacher in many forms. One of the simplest is grade level score. In this form, a score of 9.0 would indicate that the student read at a level equal to that read by the average ninth grade student in the norm population.

Another widely used means of reporting is percentile rank. This indicates a pupil's score relative to the percentage of students scoring higher and lower. Thus if a student has a percentile rank of 75, this means that 75 per cent of the students in the norm group scored lower than he did.

Another form for reporting results is in stanines. As its name indicates, this system of reporting divides the distribution of raw scores into nine parts (standard nine). Stanine 5 is located precisely in the center of the distribution and includes all cases within one fourth of a standard deviation on either side of the mean. The remaining stanines are evenly distributed above and below stanine 5. Each stanine—with the exception of 1 and 9, which cover the extremes of the distribution—includes a band of raw scores the width of one half of a standard deviation unit. Thus for all practical purposes, stanines present test norms on a nine-point scale of equal units.

Figure 5.1 illustrates percentile scores as well as stanine scores.

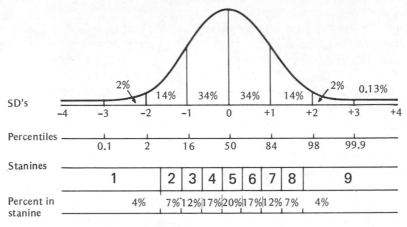

Adapted from Gronlund, 1976, p. 406.

Figure 5.1   Corresponding Standard Scores and Percentiles in a
Normal Distribution

References to Aid in Test Selection

Since means of evaluating the qualities of standardized tests may be difficult and/or time consuming, references that help in the selection of these tests may be used by the classroom teacher. Three such references are the following:

Blanton, W., Farr, R., and Tuinman, J. J., eds. *Reading Tests for Secondary Grades: A Review and Evaluation.* Newark, Del.: International Reading Association, 1972. (reviews 14 tests)

Buros, O. K., ed. *Reading Tests and Reviews.* Highland Park, N. J.: Gryphon Press, 1968.

Mavrogenes, N., Hanson, E., Winkley, C. K., and Vacca, R. T. "Concise Guide to Standardized Secondary and College Reading Tests." *Journal of Reading*, 18:1 (October 1974), 12-22.

Informal Reading Inventories

A third instrument specifically designed to assess reading skills is the informal reading inventory (IRI). This instrument is based on the premise that

96

in order to determine the grade level at which youngsters read, it is necessary to try them out on several different reading levels in materials that are similar to those they will be asked to read in school. Hence these inventories consist of a series of graded passages ranging from grade levels one through twelve. Students are asked to read passages on progressively higher levels until their reading errors exceed an amount determined as a cutoff point. The specific format, construction, and administration of informal reading inventories vary widely, but all have in common the series of graded passages that students are asked to read.

Construction of an Informal Reading Inventory

Informal reading inventories are usually constructed by teachers or other school personnel from materials used in classroom instruction.

Obtaining Appropriate Passages. One way to construct an informal reading inventory is to accumulate passages written at different grade levels until samples from grade levels one through twelve have been collected. The content of all passages should be appropriate to the interests of adolescents. A first grade passage written for a first grade student would not reflect the interest of a ninth grade student who reads at the first grade level.

Although there are several ways in which a teacher may obtain materials written on a variety of grade levels, the simplest way is to locate materials that have already been identified by grade and interest level. Reference lists, such as those suggested in Chapter 11 of this text, are excellent sources for locating materials. The teacher who has trouble locating materials written at the lower end of the spectrum might find George Spache's *Good Reading for Poor Readers* quite helpful. This text contains a large list of books written on various reading levels and geared to adolescent interests.

Commercially produced materials containing a series spanning many grade levels may also prove helpful. For example, *Reading Skill Builders*, published by the *Reader's Digest* (discussed in Chapter 11), may be a source of passages because the series consists of a sequence of carefully graded materials ranging in reading level from grades one through nine.

A third method of obtaining test passages is to use a readability formula (such as the Fry one, discussed in Chapter 6 of this text) to determine the reading level of various books.

Selection of Test Passages. Materials, on varying reading levels, that reflect the type of reading to be done in the content area should be used as the basis for selection of test passages. Students may differ considerably in their abilities to read dissimilar content areas. For example, a seventh grade student who enjoys science might read widely in this area. If he disliked history, he might have consistently avoided any literature that tended to be historical. Hence he would be likely to be more familiar with terms and concepts technical to science than he would be with those technical to history. As such, it is feasible that he could score on the sixth grade level on history passages and at the tenth grade level on science passages.

Passages selected should be anywhere from 100 to 175 words in length.

However, some may slightly exceed 175 words in order to provide enough material for a good comprehension check or to avoid having the selection end in the middle of a paragraph.

Furthermore, the specific passage selected should be typical of the type of reading done in the content area represented and should contain enough ideas to lend itself to the construction of various well constructed comprehension questions measuring different types of reading skills. The variety of comprehension questions that may be asked are described in the following section.

Development of Comprehension Questions. Once suitable passages representing all grade levels have been selected, the teacher should construct ten comprehension questions on *one* of the passages at each grade level. (Only the silent reading passage is accompanied by comprehension questions; the oral reading passage is not.) Some authorities suggest that test questions should assess the comprehension areas of details and inferences as well as some vocabulary skills. Other authors, such as Valmont (1972), believe that specific questions concerning the comprehension areas of main idea, details, inferences, conclusions, sequence, cause and effect, as well as some of the vocabulary skills should be included. Each teacher should decide on the type of comprehension questions that he feels are most important to his course and should then use such questions.

In addition to the content of each question, teachers should be careful of the type of questions they construct. For example, they might ask a student, "Is the name of the horse in the passage Rondo, Wimpy, or Spooks?" This type of question aids the student in remembering the correct answer. It is better for the teacher to reword the question and simply ask the student, "What is the name of the horse?" To respond correctly, students must recall the answer from their reading. Many errors of this type occur in test construction. Both Valmont (1972) and Gronlund (1976) suggest several guidelines to follow in order to construct good questions. Their guidelines include the following:

1. Design questions that can be answered only by reading the passage and that cannot be answered from past experience.
2. Adapt the language of the questions to the level of the materials. If the passage is on the third grade readability level, the readability level of the questions should be no more difficult than third grade level.
3. Ask the questions in the sequential order in which the information upon which the questions are based appears in the passage.
4. Check the sequence of questions to see if a later question is not answered by an earlier one.
5. Check to make certain that two or more questions do not call for the same response.
6. Make the questions as brief and simple as possible. Do not say in ten words what could be said in four.
7. Generally state questions so that they start with who, what, when, where, why, and how.

8. Avoid asking negative questions. That is, say, "What are Brian's most important physical traits," not "What are not Brian's most important physical traits."
9. Avoid making the question so general that the student has difficulty responding with the specific answer that is desired.
10. Ask a pupil to define rather than recall a word.
11. Avoid questions on which the student has a fifty-fifty chance of being correct, such as those using either-or or yes-no questions.

Administration and Interpretation of an IRI

An informal reading inventory is usually administered by asking a student to read the first selection to himself. After he has read the silent reading selection, the youngster is asked to answer the comprehension questions that follow. This procedure is repeated until the level that is appropriate for the student can be determined from his responses.

Oral Reading Score. The student's oral reading score is considered to be the same as the grade level of the most difficult passage on which the student pronounces at least 95 per cent of the words correctly. For example, if a student mispronounced four out of a hundred words on an eighth grade passage, five out of a hundred on a ninth grade passage, and six out of a hundred on a tenth grade passage, his oral reading score would be grade nine.

Silent Reading Score. The student's silent reading score is considered to be the same as the grade level of the most difficult passage on which he answers correctly at least 70 per cent of the comprehension questions. For example, if he misses one out of ten questions at the fifth grade level, three out of ten at the sixth grade level, and four out of ten at the seventh grade level, his silent reading level would be grade six.

Assessment of Reading Levels

The highest level at which the student is able to pronounce at least 95 per cent of the words correctly with at least 70 per cent comprehension is termed the student's *instructional level.* If the scores are not the same, the lower of these two scores—the oral reading score or the silent reading comprehension score—represents the reading level of materials in which the youngster should be instructed. For example, if the oral reading score were grade nine and the silent reading score were grade six, the student should be instructed from material written at the grade six level. If he were given materials written at the grade nine level, he might be able to pronounce all the words correctly, but he probably could not understand the meaning of all the words and hence would not correctly comprehend the content of the assigned materials.

When students are assigned classroom material on their instructional level, the material should be difficult enough to be challenging but not so difficult that the student becomes frustrated.

There are three other levels in addition to the instructional level that may be used by the teacher to aid in selecting suitable instructional materials for each youngster. The *independent level* is the level at which youngsters can read fluently without aid. They should have few if any problems with the vocabulary or sentence structure, and their comprehension should be close to 100 per cent. Usually this level begins about one year below the level assessed as instructional. If students are assigned material at this level, they may read it without aid. However, if the teacher gives them material that is more than one year below instructional level, it may bore them. Hence material for supplementary and independent reading should probably be close to one year below the students' instructional level.

Materials written on a more difficult level than the instructional level may be considered to be on the students' *frustration level.* Their pronunciation is less than 95 per cent and/or their comprehension is less than 70 per cent. Usually the frustration level begins about one year above the level assessed as instructional. If students are assigned material at the frustration level, their reading skills cannot improve unless the teacher adapts the material or helps students read it through the use of aids such as the guided reading sheets discussed in Chapter 8 of this text.

Reading *capacity level* is the highest level at which students can understand material that is read aloud to them. This level is ascertained by reading the silent reading passages aloud to the students and asking them to respond to the questions. The teacher should begin with the last silent passage on which the student was able to answer 70 per cent correctly and then continue with progressively more difficult passages until the student's comprehension of the material drops below 70 per cent. Instructional materials written at this level may be used if adapted to an auditory format. This level is sometimes considered as the student's "potential" reading level as the student knows all the words and concepts, but is unable to recognize them in print. Figure 5.2, adapted from Betts (1946), illustrates the relationship between these four levels.

Varying the Administration of an IRI

Because the informal reading inventory is not a standardized test, there is much room for variation in administration. In addition, though it is labeled as an individual test, some of the administration may be done in a group situation. Means for both a group administration and an individual administration are described below.

Group Administration of an IRI. Oral Reading. In the oral reading situation, the teacher often gives the class an assignment that frees him for the entire period. Then he asks students to come to the teacher's desk individually and read the grade level passage aloud. As each student reads, the teacher tallies all errors. If the student is able to read the passage successfully, the teacher asks him to read progressively more difficult passages until he reaches the level where he makes more than 5 per cent oral errors. Conversely, if the student is unable to read the grade level selection successfully, the teacher asks him to read progressively less difficult selections until one is found where he makes fewer than 5 per cent error.

Independent:	Few if any oral errors. Comprehension close to 100 per cent. No head movements, finger pointing, or vocalization. Good phrasing. Usually begins about one year below level assessed as instructional. Material read which is more than one year below may be boring to the reader. Thus about one level below is usually the level for recreational reading.
Instructional:	Highest level on which reader pronounces at least 95 per cent of the words correctly with at least 70 per cent comprehension. No head movements, finger pointing. Good phrasing. No vocalization. Conversational tone. If possible, this is the level on which most of the instructional materials should be written.
Frustration:	Below 95 per cent pronunciation and/or 70 per cent comprehension. Inability to anticipate meaning. Head movements, finger pointing, tension, withdrawal, slow word-by-word reading, vocalization, substitutions, repetitions, insertions. Usually begins about one year above level assessed as instructional. Thus material assigned at frustration level must be adapted or supplemented with reading aids.
Capacity:	Highest level on which listener is able to achieve at least 70 per cent comprehension. Student must be able to understand selection and express himself accurately. No vocalization. Accurate pronunciation in retelling what is heard. Precise use of words to describe facts or experiences. Answers using language similar to selection. Can supply additional facts from background of experience. Instructional materials at this level may be used if adapted to an auditory format. This level is sometimes called the potential reading level.

*Adapted from Betts, 1946.

Figure 5.2 Levels of Reading*

Silent Reading. After the teacher has located the oral reading level of all the students, he duplicates the silent reading selections and gives each student the level passage correlated with the highest level reading passage at which the student made less than 5 per cent oral error—that is, if the student's oral reading level were grade seven, he is asked to read a grade seven passage and then answer the questions that follow. If the student is able to answer the questions successfully, then the teacher gives him more difficult selections until he reaches the point where he is unable to answer 70 per cent of the questions successfully. Conversely, if the student is unable to answer 70 per cent of the comprehension questions accurately, then the teacher gives him selections and questions on progressively easier grade levels until the student reaches the level on which he can answer 70 per cent of the comprehension questions successfully.

Individual Administration of an IRI. Oral Reading. The administration of the IRI to individuals is very similar to administering it to groups. However the teacher often starts at a level about two grades below the one on which the student is expected to function or the one on which the teacher thinks the student has a reasonable chance for success. Then the teacher gives the student progressively harder passages until the student reaches the level on which he makes more than the allowable number of errors. For example, if the student were a ninth grader who appeared to be on grade level, the teacher would begin him with the seventh grade level passage. If the student were a ninth grader who appeared to be on the fifth grade level, the teacher would begin him with the third grade level passage.

101

Silent Reading. The student is first given the silent reading passage that is one level below the highest level oral passage that he read successfully. Then the teacher gives the student progressively easier or harder passages until the teacher can determine the highest level at which the student makes more than the allowable number of errors.

Aids to Efficient Use of the IRI

Informal reading inventories can be constructed by teachers in any content area. However, to help illustrate the design of an informal reading inventory, one particularly appropriate to a reading class or an English class has been included in Appendix A of this text. Before the IRI in Appendix A may be used with a youngster, it needs some adaptation. Directions for doing so are given in Appendix A immediately preceding the test itself.

Detailed suggestions for administering, scoring, and interpreting the results of this test will be given in the following section in the context of one of Mr. Cilak's ninth grade English classes.

Mr. Cilak's Testing Procedure

Mr. Cilak was a ninth grade teacher who taught courses in both English and reading. He was concerned about the reading levels of the students in his classes and wanted to make certain they could read the instructional materials he would be giving them throughout the school year.

Preparation of Test Materials for Oral Reading. Since Mr. Cilak was an English teacher as well as a reading teacher, the IRI in the appendix of this text was similar to the type of materials read in his content area; therefore he decided to use this already constructed instrument rather than to develop his own.

First, Mr. Cilak located the IRI found in the appendix and prepared it for student use according to the guidelines mentioned there.

Administration of the Oral Reading Selections. Mr. Cilak brought each ninth grader to a quiet place in the classroom and asked him to read aloud. He used any information he had, such as the student's age, grade placement, or school history, to decide the level on which to begin testing. The first student Mr. Cilak tested was David. He knew only that David was in grade nine and, from classroom observation, that he appeared to be an average student. Mr. Cilak asked David to read the grade nine selection first. Second, Mr. Cilak tested Peter. From a perusal of school records and from having worked with him for the last three weeks, Mr. Cilak was aware that Peter was a weak reader. He asked Peter to begin with the seventh grade selection. Dan was the third youngster whom Mr. Cilak tested. From observation and school records, Mr. Cilak believed that Dan was an above average student. He had Dan begin reading on a tenth grade level.

As each student read, Mr. Cilak listened very carefully to determine whether he omitted, added, or mispronounced any words because these were all considered errors. Mr. Cilak did not count as errors spontaneous corrections in which the reader corrected himself immediately, mispronunciations of proper nouns or very rare words, or words that the student pronounced differently because of speech or dialect differences. If a reader could not say a word, Mr. Cilak told him the word and, of course, counted the word as an error. If a youngster missed the same word several times, Mr. Cilak scored this as only one error.

When David read, he made 4 per cent error on the first selection (grade nine level) that he was asked to read. Because this was less than the 5 per cent error allowed, Mr. Cilak then tested him on the next most difficult selection—that equal in difficulty to material considered as grade ten. On this selection, David made 6 per cent error—more than the allowed five per cent. Thus Mr. Cilak was led to believe that, on the basis of this test, David's oral reading score was grade nine. Table 5.1 shows David's oral reading score and the scores of the others tested.

Mr. Cilak then tested Peter. When he asked Peter to read the grade seven selection, Peter made 10 per cent error. Therefore Mr. Cilak tested him on the grade six level, where he made 8 per cent error. Mr. Cilak finally asked Peter to read the selection on the grade five level. Here, Peter was successful. He made only 5 per cent error.

As Mr. Cilak tested all the students in his class, he found that he could speed up the testing process in several ways. With some of the youngsters who were reading orally to him, it quickly became apparent that the reader was going to make fewer or many more than the 5 per cent error allowed. Therefore Mr. Cilak did not have them read the entire selection. For example, after Dan had read the first few sentences of the grade ten selection, it was obvious that he was going to make fewer than 5 per cent error. Mr. Cilak simply marked his score "OK" and did not have him read the entire selection. On the grade eleven selection, Dan made 6 per cent error. Hence he passed the oral reading portion of the test at the grade ten level. Conversely, Jane needed help on three out of the first six words on the grade seven selection, so Mr. Cilak simply marked her score as "not OK" on that level. Jane proceeded to have extreme difficulty with the grade six selections; and again Mr. Cilak had her read only a portion of this selection. On the grade five selection, Jane made 4 per cent error and therefore passed the oral reading portion of the test on the grade five level.

Mr. Cilak also found that he could reduce the time required to administer the oral portions by not testing each youngster on every level but by skipping levels on which he was sure that they would be successful or not successful. For example, after Mr. Cilak had tested Ronnie at the grade nine level and had found his reading to be very weak, Mr. Cilak skipped down to the grade six level on which Ronnie did better but still made eight errors. On the fifth grade level Ronnie made only 4 per cent error.

Another shortcut Mr. Cilak had used when he was too busy to spend the entire class period in individual testing was to ask each student to read into a tape recorder. Since he wanted to obtain a quick estimate of which students could and could not read on grade level, he asked them to read only the ninth grade passage. After listening to the tape, Mr. Cilak proceeded to ascertain the exact reading levels of all the students through individual testing. He be-

TABLE 5.1
Informal Reading Inventory—Oral Reading Scores for a Portion of Mr. Cilak's Grade Nine Class

Name	Grade 11 oral	Grade 11 silent	Grade 10 oral	Grade 10 silent	Grade 9 oral	Grade 9 silent	Grade 8 oral	Grade 8 silent	Grade 7 oral	Grade 7 silent	Grade 6 oral	Grade 6 silent	Grade 5 oral	Grade 5 silent	Grade 4 oral	Grade 4 silent
David			6		(4)											
Peter									10		8		(5)			
Dan	6		(ok)													
Jane									not ok		not ok		(4)			
Ronnie					not ok						8		(4)			

Note:

Column marked *oral* is for recording errors in oral reading.

Column marked *silent* is for recording errors in silent reading comprehension.

Circle in oral reading column indicates oral reading score; that is, highest level on which youngster made 5 per cent or fewer errors.

gan with those students who could not read the grade level materials because he felt they were most in need of immediate help and would not be able to learn the subject matter until materials that they could read were made available to them.

Preparation of Test Materials for Silent Reading Comprehension. Mr. Cilak was then ready to test his class on the silent reading comprehension portion of the test. He prepared the student's copy of the IRI found in Appendix A in the manner suggested by direction given in the same appendix. Mr. Cilak made enough copies of each sheet in order that the students in the class could each have three sets of silent reading selections and the accompanying comprehension questions—one that was the level above their oral reading score, one that was the same as the level of their oral reading score, and one that was the level immediately below their oral reading score. For example, David's oral reading score was grade nine. Mr. Cilak, therefore, made copies for David of the selections on the grade ten, nine, and eight silent reading levels. Likewise, Peter's score was level five. Mr. Cilak made copies for Peter of the selections on the fourth, fifth, and sixth grade levels.

By giving students three passages instead of just the one that was on the student's oral reading level, Mr. Cilak was able to reduce the time needed to diagnose each student's silent reading level. Hence he utilized shortcut techniques when administering the silent reading selections in much the same manner as he did when administering the oral reading passages.

Administration of the Silent Reading Comprehension Selections. Mr. Cilak simultaneously gave each person in his class the three silent reading passages that he deemed appropriate. He instructed his students to first read the story carefully, then to turn the sheet so that only the questions showed, and finally to answer the questions without looking back at the selection. Mr. Cilak told the youngsters that upon finishing the first selection and set of questions, they should proceed in the same manner with the second and third sets of selections and questions.

Mr. Cilak graded the papers, counting as errors any answers that he would consider incorrect if the student made that response in a classroom assignment. He then recorded the number of errors each youngster made on the score sheet that contained their oral reading scores. Table 5.2 shows the errors made in oral reading and in silent reading comprehension.

Interpreting the Results of the Test. Mr. Cilak then proceeded to interpret the test results. From the data in Table 5.2, it appeared that the highest level on which David passed both the oral and silent reading portions of the test was grade nine. Thus David should be instructed from a grade nine book. Peter showed a different pattern. He made only 3 per cent error on the most difficult set of silent reading comprehension tests that Mr. Cilak gave him. It was possible that Peter could comprehend on a level higher than grade six. Mr. Cilak made a note to test him using the silent reading selections on progressively higher levels until he identified the highest level on which Peter could answer 70 per cent of the comprehension questions accurately. Tentatively he placed him at a grade five level, aware of the fact that Peter's ability to pronounce the words was weaker than his ability to understand them. Dan showed a problem that was the reverse of Peter's. Although he could pro-

TABLE 5.2
Informal Reading Inventory—Oral Reading and Silent Reading Comprehension Scores for a Portion of Mr. Cilak's Grade Nine Class

Name	Grade 11		Grade 10		Grade 9		Grade 8		Grade 7		Grade 6		Grade 5		Grade 4	
	oral	silent	oral	silent	oral	silent	oral	silent	oral	silent	oral	silent	oral	silent	oral	silent
David			6	5	[4]	([3])										
Peter								0	10		8	3	[5]	([2])		
Dan	6	8	(ok)	5		[3]										
Jane					not ok				not ok		not ok	8	4	7		
Ronnie										5	8	(3)	([4])	([3])	[3]	2

Note:

Rectangle indicates level on which youngster should be instructed.

Circle in *silent* reading column indicates highest level on which youngster scored 70 per cent or better on comprehension questions.

nounce the words accurately on the grade ten level, he could pass the silent reading comprehension test on only the grade nine level. Mr. Cilak, aware of the fact that Dan's oral reading was superior to his ability to understand what he had read, placed Dan on a grade nine level. Mr. Cilak proceeded to analyze the remainder of his class in the same manner, tentatively assigning each youngster to a level for instruction, noting those cases in which students needed further testing, and recording the particular strength or weakness in either oral reading or silent reading comprehension.

Uses of the IRI

The IRI may be used in many of the same ways as the standardized test, but in addition it may provide the teacher with a measure of the level of instructional materials that would be most appropriate for each student. That is, the teacher can readily determine whether a tenth grade biology book is too difficult for his students by examining their performance on a passage from that text as well as from other science materials.

Another important use of the IRI is to provide a measure by which the teacher may identify symptoms that reflect difficulty in reading for a specific youngster. This may be done by close inspection of the type of errors made by the student. (See also Gray 1963.)

If a teacher has enough copies of the oral reading portion of the test to record each student's oral reading errors, he may use the following marking system:

1. Repetition—student repeats a word; draw a wavy line under word (heavy).

2. Insertion—student inserts word that does not belong; write in the

    red

    inserted word above place where it occurred (big balloon).

3. Omission—student omits word; draw a circle around the word (staff).

4. Substitution—student substitutes one word for another; draw a

    consistent

    line through intended word and add substitute word (constituent).

5. Gross mispronunciation—student pronounces a word that only slightly resembles the intended word; try to write the mispronun-

    barrety

    ciation above the intended word (battery).

6. Aid—student asks teacher to pronounce word for him; put word in parentheses ((covert)).

107

7. Reversal—student says word like *was* for *saw*; draw a wavy line through word to show changed letter order (w\a/s).

8. Pause of over ten seconds; write a *P* over the word (gaunt).

The following group of sentences further illustrates this marking system:

        moved
Peter ~~shifted~~ direction (away) from the others and proceeded to where the just

        emit
perceptible path led him into the eminent jungle. Towering trunks bore (unexpectedly)
pale flowers.

    Analyzing these oral errors can enable the teacher to make several educated guesses about some of the reading problems this reader had. The reader probably knew how to use context clues since he substituted a word that was very similar in meaning to *shifted*, and his omission of the word *away* did not affect the meaning. The fact that he repeated the word *just*, a basic sight word, probably indicated that he was having trouble with the next word, *perceptible*. The gross mispronunciation of the word *eminent* most likely indicated that he might need to learn how to divide a word into syllables. The fact that the teacher had to pronounce the word *unexpectedly* for him may have further indicated that he relied primarily upon context clues and that when the context of the sentence did not give him the exact meaning of the word, he did not try to use structural or phonic analysis to figure it out.

    Other patterns to students' mispronunciations, such as certain types of vowel errors or error principally in word endings, should be noted in words they mispronounced in reading the oral passages. If they consistently made the same type of errors, this reading weakness can be fairly accurately diagnosed.

    In a like manner, answers to the questions on the silent passage may be used to interpret each youngster's comprehension skills. For example, if the youngster always misses questions that dealt with inferences, he probably needs to work on this skill.

Advantages and Limitations of the IRI

    Advantages. The IRI usually reflects the type of materials to be used by the student, may be administered and interpreted by the classroom teacher with little special training, may be administered within a short time span, and may give the teacher an opportunity to determine the youngster's attitude toward the reading task.

    If the IRI were constructed by the classroom teacher from available content area materials, he would be able to assess the materials he had on hand to use with the youngster. A teacher-made test is inexpensive, and one-to-one administration of the oral passage helps the teacher assess the students' attitude toward reading while developing some rapport with them. At the same time, the students' reactions to the IRI can help the teacher determine something about their interests and can prove useful in locating materials that they might like to read.

Limitations. The IRI is limited by aspects that have been mentioned previously. The skills of the teacher in constructing and administering the test can affect the quality of the IRI. For example, this would be true if the teacher used an IRI that had poorly written comprehension questions, or if the teacher miscounted the number of oral errors made by the student, or if the teacher selected a passage that had been mismarked by grade level or that was not representative of the remainder of the material from which it was selected. Another limitation is that the teacher may not be able to easily locate material at all grade levels.

READING EXPECTANCY

The term *reading expectancy* indicates the highest level at which a student can be expected to be able to read. This level may be arrived at through several means. One such means is the following formula: (Bond and Tinker 1967)

$$\text{reading expectancy } = \frac{\text{years in school} \times \text{I.Q.}}{100} + 1$$

For example, a youngster with an I.Q. of 100 who was in the seventh grade in September could be expected to read at seventh grade level. That is, his reading expectancy would be seventh grade.

$$\text{reading expectancy } = \frac{6.0 \text{ (years in school)} \times 100 \text{ (I.Q.)}}{100} + 1 = \text{7th grade}$$

Likewise, a youngster in the ninth grade in November with an I.Q. of 130 would have a reading expectancy of

$$\frac{8.3 \times 130}{100} + 1 = 11.8.$$

The youngster in the seventh grade in February with an I.Q. of 80 would have a reading expectancy of

$$\frac{6.6 \times 80}{100} + 1 = 6.3.$$

In this text, a remedial reader is referred to as one who reads two or more years below his potential reading level. Hence the ninth grader with an I.Q. of 130 who read on ninth grade level would be a remedial reader; the seventh grader with an I.Q. of 80 who read on sixth grade level would not be a remedial reader.

Before a teacher begins to plan improvement for a student in reading instruction, that teacher should have some idea of what to expect from the student in terms of potential reading capacity. Since most classroom teachers do not have access to I.Q. scores in order to determine reading expectancy, the use of this formula is basically geared to the needs of the reading specialist. However, the classroom teacher can arrive at some estimate of a student's reading potential by using the concept of capacity level described earlier in this chapter.

References and Bibliography

Aukerman, R. C. *Reading in the Secondary Classroom.* New York: McGraw-Hill, 1972.

Betts, E. A. *Foundations of Reading Instruction.* New York: American Book, 1946.

Blanton, W., Farr, R., and Tuinman, J. J., eds. *Reading Tests for Secondary Grades: A Review and Evaluation.* Newark, Del.: International Reading Association, 1972.

Bond, G. L., and Tinker, M. A. *Reading Difficulties: Their Diagnosis and Correction.* 2nd ed. New York: Appleton-Century-Crofts, 1967.

Burmeister, L. E. *Reading Strategies for Secondary School Teachers.* Reading, Mass.: Addison-Wesley, 1974.

Buros, O. K., ed. *Reading Tests and Reviews.* Highland Park, N. J.: Gryphon, 1968.

Burron, A., and Claybaugh, A. *Using Reading to Teach Subject Matter: Fundamentals for Content Teachers.* Columbus, Ohio: Merrill, 1974.

Cushenbery, D. *Remedial Reading in the Secondary School.* West Nyack, N. Y.: Parker, 1972.

Fry, E. *Reading Instruction for Classroom and Clinic.* New York: McGraw-Hill, 1972.

Gray, W. S. *Gray Oral Reading Test.* Indianapolis, Ind.: Bobbs-Merrill, 1963.

Gronlund, N. E. *Measurement and Evaluation in Teaching.* New York: Macmillan, 1976.

Karlin, R. *Teaching Reading in High School.* 2nd ed. Indianapolis, Ind.: Bobbs-Merrill, 1972.

Lennon, R. T. "Selection and Provision of Testing Material." *Test Service Bulletin,* Number 99. New York: Harcourt Brace Jovanovich, 1967.

Mavrogenes, N. A., et al. "Concise Guide to Standardized Secondary and College Reading Tests." *Journal of Reading* (October 1974), 12–22.

New Advanced Reading Skill Builders. Pleasantville, N. Y.: Reader's Digest Services, Educational Division, 1973.

Niles, O., Bracken, D. K., Dougherty, M. A., and Kinder, R. F. *Tactics in Reading I.* Chicago: Scott, Foresman, 1961.

Olson, A., and Ames, W. *Teaching Reading Skills in Secondary Schools.* Scranton, Pa.: Intext Educational Publishers, 1972.

Reading Laboratory Kits 3b,4a. Chicago: Science Research Associates.

Robinson, H. *Teaching Reading and Study Strategies: The Content Areas.* Boston: Allyn & Bacon, 1975.

Spache, G. D. *Good Reading for Poor Readers.* rev. ed. Champaign, Ill.: Garrard, 1972.

Strang, R. *Diagnostic Teaching of Reading.* New York: McGraw-Hill, 1964.

Survey of Study Habits and Attitudes. New York: Psychological Corporation, 1967.

Taylor, S., et al. *EDL Word Clues.* Huntington, N. Y.: Educational Laboratories, 1963.

Thomas, E., and Robinson, H. *Improving Reading in Every Class: A Source Book for Teachers.* Boston: Allyn & Bacon, 1972.

Thurstone, T. G. *Reading For Understanding.* Chicago: Science Research Associates, 1958.

Valmont, W. J. "Creating Questions for Informal Reading Inventories." *The Reading Teacher* (March 1972), 509–512.

Chapter 6

Identifying Reading Problems with Textbooks

Prerequisite 6.1

Before beginning this chapter, participants should have successfully completed the objectives for Part One of this text and should have some understanding of the nature of reading and the reading skills.

Rationale 6.2

Because the content area textbook is the major instructional tool in so many middle and secondary school classrooms, the participant needs to be familiar with the reading problems that often occur while using textbooks. This chapter will make the participant aware of such problems so that their solutions, given in Chapters 7 and 8, may be more clearly understood.

Objectives 6.3

On successful completion of this chapter, the participant will be able to:

1. Describe four major factors that cause students difficulty when instruction is given through content area textbooks.
2. State a technique for overcoming at least one problem, caused by factors inherent to the student, that may be encountered in reading a textbook.
3. Identify and discuss three variables used in assessing the probable reading difficulty of textbooks.

4. Using a readability formula, assess the probable difficulty of a specific textbook.

5. Describe at least one reason why the teacher should not rely solely upon a readability formula to assess the level of difficulty of a textbook.

6. Describe how various levels of abstraction affect the readability of a given textbook.

7. Identify at least one reading skill particularly needed in a specific content area and discuss:

    (1) Why is it particularly important to that specific content area?
    (2) How do most of the other content areas also use that same reading skill?

8. Identify at least three available textbook aids that may be used by the teacher to facilitate instruction.

9. (On the lines below, add other objectives according to your instructor's directions.) _____

    _____

10. _____

    _____

11. _____

    _____

12. _____

    _____

* * * * * * * * * * * * * *

Chapter 13, Experience 6 extends Chapter 6 with this performance/consequence objective:

13. Administer and interpret a questionnaire that assesses some of the factors that make a textbook difficult for a student.

* * * * * * * * * * * * * *

Self Pre-Assessment 6.4

Can you complete all the activities listed in **Objectives 6.3**? Answer "yes," "no," or "not certain."

If you answered "yes" to the question, complete the enabling activities required by your instructor and take the Post-Assessment on the date assigned by him.

If you answered "no," refer to **Enabling Activities 6.5**. If you decide to do any activities that are not required, select those that best suit you as a learner. You need not complete all the optional activities or all parts of a particular optional activity. As soon as you have the information you need to complete the objectives, answer "yes" to the **Self Pre-Assessment 6.4** question and stop the activity.

If you answered "not certain" to the question, refer to **Enabling Activities 6.5**. Select the enabling activity that best suits your style of learning and peruse it. Then make a firm "yes" or "no" answer and proceed accordingly.

Enabling Activities 6.5

Complete only as many of the activities listed below as are required and which you need in order to meet the objectives.

1. *Enabling activity one* is a *reading* alternative. This is **Information Given 6.6**. It is a brief overview of the problems students encounter when reading content area textbooks.
2. *Enabling activity two* is another *reading* option. In this case, the material to be read is one of the textbooks used to expand the theoretical background for this course. See chart on inside front cover for keying in textbooks that may be used.
3. *Enabling activity three* is a *class session* option. Attend the class session(s), on the date(s), at the time(s), and at the place(s) announced.

| _____ | _____ | _____ |
| (Date) | (Time) | (Place) |

| _____ | _____ | _____ |
| (Date) | (Time) | (Place) |

| _____ | _____ | _____ |
| (Date) | (Time) | (Place) |

4. *Enabling activity four* (These lines are left blank so that you may add other enabling activities as suggested by your instructor.) _____
   _____
5. *Enabling activity five* _____
   _____
6. *Enabling activity six* _____
   _____

Now that you have completed the appropriate number of required and/or optional learning alternatives, look back at **Self Pre-Assessment 6.4.** If you feel you can answer "yes" to all of the questions, you are ready to proceed to the Post-Assessment. This may be given to you immediately or after completion of a series of chapters.

Information Given 6.6
Identifying Reading Problems
with Textbooks

Miss Downing was conducting a mathematics lesson on functions. She placed the transparency shown in Figure 6.1 on the overhead projector. Then

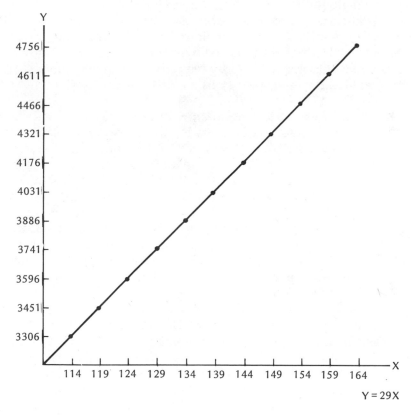

Average calorie needs for a fifteen-year-old boy based on information adapted from Lyght (1966, p. 1736).

Figure 6.1   Calories Consumed Versus Weight in Pounds for
Fifteen-Year-Old Boy — 5'9" Tall

she asked the class to use the graph to determine the number of calories that a 5'9", fifteen-year-old boy should consume if he wanted to weigh 139 pounds. She showed them that the correct answer would be 4031 calories and explained that weight is a function of number of calories consumed. In other words, for the average fifteen-year-old, 5'9" boy, it takes 29 calories per pound to maintain a given weight. Therefore the x-axis (horizontal) equaled the weight in pounds and the y-axis (vertical) equaled the weight times 29.

She then gave the class other charts containing information about the number of calories required to maintain the weight of various sized fifteen-year-old boys and girls. Each student was asked to use this information to graph the function of his own weight. A few boys interested in auto mechanics asked Miss Downing if they could graph the relationship between carburetor size and engine power rather than between calories and weight. Miss Downing accepted this as an alternative assignment.

The next day, after the class had completed their graphs, there was more discussion on the definition of the word *function* and the various types of functional relationships that occur in everyday life. Miss Downing told her class that she would give extra credit to anyone who would bring in examples of functions from current newspapers or magazines.

Close inspection of the class lesson described in the preceding paragraphs reveals various difficulties encountered by students while learning subject matter, and methods that may be used by teachers to overcome them. These problems and Miss Downing's solutions are delineated below:

1. *Factors inherent to the student.* The topic of functions was not exciting to the students. Miss Downing overcame this problem by using topics (calories, carburetors) interesting to adolescents.
2. *Readability level of the textbook.* The textbook that presented functions was much too difficult for most of the students. Therefore, Miss Downing presented the concept using another vehicle (graphs).
3. *Instructional focus of the teacher.* Miss Downing's main responsibility was to teach mathematics content. However, her instructional focus was to include reading skills that would encourage her students' grasp of the content. Therefore she taught the meaning of the word *function*.
4. *Inadequate use of available textbook aids.* Many teachers fail to utilize available textbook aids. However Miss Downing consulted the manual accompanying her textbook and found the suggestion for relating the lesson on functions to the topic of calories.

These four areas will be discussed further in the remaining sections of this chapter.

FACTORS INHERENT TO THE STUDENT

Many aspects that are very difficult to measure are involved in a student's ability to cope with a particular textbook. Aukerman (1965) discusses a dozen or so variables which contribute to the difficulty of understanding literature. Most of these aspects also apply to the other content areas. Among those Aukerman mentions are (1) the reader's interest in the topic, (2) the reader's past experience with the topic, (3) intrinsic motivation of the reader, (4) extrinsic motivation provided by the teacher, and (5) the relevancy of the time in which the materials were written in terms of the times in which they are read.

As illustrated by Miss Downing's lesson, material presented by the content area teacher can be adapted so that it is more relevant to the students. When Miss Downing pointed out the relationship between weight and calories, she was hoping to make the topic of functions relevant by capitalizing on the adolescents' acute awareness of their physical appearances. Since she knew that relevancy and motivation are based on individual needs, she allowed the boys interested in mechanics to graph the functions of "carburetors versus power" rather than "weight versus calories."

When she told the class members she would give them extra credit for presenting examples of common functional relationships, she was taking advantage of current interests as well as providing extrinsic motivation for the students.

TEXTBOOK READABILITY

Readability refers to the ease with which a book can most likely be read by a particular population. For example, a book labeled as *grade seven* would be read comfortably by someone with an instructional reading level of grade seven. The same book would be extremely difficult for someone with an instructional reading level of grade three and extremely easy for someone with an instructional reading level of grade twelve. Klare (1974–1975) discusses several ways in which readability may be assessed. One way is to construct a comprehension test covering the material in order to find out how well it has been understood by persons of varying ages and reading abilities. This technique is discussed in Chapter 5. A second possible means is to use a readability formula. A third technique is for writers and teachers to make estimates of readability based on the ease with which former students have read the material to be assigned.

Assessment Through Readability Formulas

A readability formula measures some of the language variables in a piece of writing in order to estimate the probable readability level. These language variables include assessments of the difficulty of words and sentences. Several readability formulas have been developed including those by Fry (1972), Flesch (1948), and Dale and Chall (1948). Fry's graph has been validated on both primary and secondary materials, and the scores derived from it correlate highly with those from several well-known formulas. This graph will be explained in detail in the next section.

Use of Fry Readability Formula

In order to use Fry's graph, four basic steps should be completed. First, three passages, each one hundred words long, are randomly selected from near the beginning, middle, and end of the book. All proper nouns are skipped and do not enter into the calculation.

Second, the sentences in each one hundred-word passage are counted, estimating to the nearest tenth of a sentence; that is, one hundred words that contained six sentences and one third of a seventh sentence would be counted as 6.3 sentences. The average number of sentences per one hundred words is then determined for the three samples.

Third, the total number of syllables in each one hundred-word sample are counted and the average of the total number of syllables for the three samples is computed.

Last, the average number of sentences per one hundred words and the average number of syllables per one hundred words are plotted on the graph.

Three one hundred-word passages, randomly selected from a high school American history book, are shown in Figures 6.2, 6.3, and 6.4. The syllables per one hundred words, the number of sentences, and the approximate grade levels have been calculated.

Number of Sentences:	5.9
Number of Syllables:	150
Approximate Grade Level:	9th grade

In Rhode Island and North Carolina, state paper money was worth almost nothing because so much was printed. This was a result of pressure from debt-ridden farmers. With the closing of the usual markets in the West Indies and Britain, farmers were often unable to pay off their debts and faced the loss of their lands and homes. If the currency could be inflated, however, they could pay their creditors with cheap or worthless paper money. Getting control of both the North Carolina and Rhode Island legislatures, the debtors simply ran the printing presses. In Rhode Island, the legislature passed laws forcing creditors to accept the valueless currency in the payment of/*all debts.

From *History of a Free People* by H. W. Bragdon, S. P. McCutchen, and C. W. Cole, p. 89. Copyright © 1973, Macmillan Publishing Co., Inc. Used with permission.

Figure 6.2 American History Excerpt

*Slash indicates the end, and in some cases the beginning, of the 100-word passage.

Number of Sentences:	5.8
Number of Syllables:	167
Approximate Grade Level:	12th

(5) *A mobile labor supply* / European capitalists often had difficulty recruiting labor for new industries because workingmen had been brought up to traditional occupations and hated to leave their home villages. In the United States, labor was more mobile. The American tradition was to "keep moving." Laborers came to new jobs in new cities the way pioneers moved into new lands. Furthermore, the flood of immigration continued; the newcomers, already uprooted from their homes and traditions, supplied much of the "floating" labor force that industry demanded. The native American workers were noted for the ease with which they learned new processes, and the immigrants such as English textile workers, Welsh miners, and/Italian farmers often brought with them important skills.

From *History of a Free People* by H. W. Bragdon, S. P. McCutchen, and C. W. Cole, p. 388. Copyright ©1973, Macmillan Publishing Co., Inc. Used with permission.

Figure 6.3 American History Excerpt

Number of Sentences:	4.6
Number of Syllables:	174
Approximate Grade Level:	College

Nader resembled the "muckrakers" of the progressive period (see pp. 529–530) in his ability to ferret out facts, his willingness to name names, his sensationalism, but his activities were wider in scope. He was interested not merely in better products and services but in the whole relationship between corporations, government, and the general public. He attacked corporations for placing profits ahead of the common good and campaigned for representation of the public on boards of directors. He put the heat on federal regulatory agencies such as the Interstate Commerce Commission by exposing ways in which they favored interests they were supposed to control.

Nader was more than a/ "one-man gang." He enlisted hundreds of young men and women ("Nader's Raiders"), most of them lawyers or law students, to work long hours for low pay to investigate ways in which the public was cheated. He inspired many others, so the consumer movement became nationwide, forcing federal, state, and municipal officials as well as private enterprise to act in protection of ordinary citizens.

From *History of a Free People* by H. W. Bragdon, S. P. McCutchen, and C. W. Cole, p. 785. Copyright ©1973, Macmillan Publishing Co., Inc. Used with permission.

Figure 6.4 American History Excerpt

The estimated readability level of the book based on the average of the three calculations is plotted on the graph in Figure 6.5.

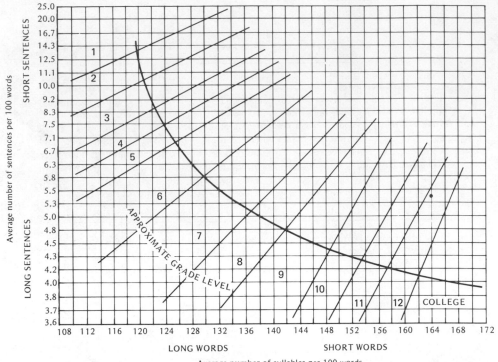

Example:

	Syllables	Sentences
1st Hundred Words	150	5.9
2nd Hundred Words	167	5.8
3rd Hundred Words	174	4.6
AVERAGE	164	5.4

Readability 12th Grade (see dot plotted on graph)

From Fry (1972), p. 232.

Figure 6.5 Fry's Readability Graph

Assessment of Readability by the Teacher

Readability formulas are useful tools for assessing readability, but they do have limitations. For instance, not all factors related to word and sentence variables are taken into consideration in any one formula. In addition, other factors, such as the number of abstract concepts contained in a text, are not easily subjected to objective measurement through a readability formula. Therefore, in addition to information gleaned from formulas, teachers must use their own knowledge of the content area and of the difficulties students encountered in order to assess readability. These aspects will be considered under the topics, *use of readability formulas by the teacher* and *levels of abstraction.*

120

Fry's formula uses number of syllables and number of sentences per one hundred words as a basis. Two other measures that are commonly used in other readability formulas are the familiarity of the words to the reader and the complexity of the sentence.

Familiarity of Words. Word Lists. A word list is probably the most common means for determining whether or not a word is likely to be familiar to a reader. The Dale list, one of the most widely used, was compiled in 1948 and contains the 3,000 words known to 80 per cent of fourth grade children in the 1940s (Klare 1974–1975, p. 71). Though words may vary from one readability formula to another, most lists contain a common core of the same words and are based on studies that identify the most frequently used words in the English language (Spache 1972, p. 34). Obviously words specific to a content area and considered *technical words*, such as *embryo* (technical to science), would not appear on any of the lists of frequently used words.

It is interesting to note inconsistencies between word measurement by syllabication as used by Fry and word measurement by reference to a word list. By assessing readability through syllabication, *umbra* with two syllables would be considered more readable than *satisfactory* with five syllables. By assessing readability through a word list, the word *satisfactory*, which is on the Dale list, would be considered easier than the word *umbra* (technical to science), which is not on the Dale list.

Flexible Use of Word Lists. Some content area specialists believe that readability formulas that are based on word lists often misrepresent the readability of the content area textbook. For example, one study cited by Andersen (1969) was done by Brown (1965). Brown used the Dale-Chall formula to check the reading level of a science book published in 1961. Though an 11 to 12 grade reading level was calculated, reviews by students seemed to indicate that the book was easily read by most seventh and eighth grade students. Andersen contended that this was primarily due to the fact that many words considered technical to science in 1948 should no longer be considered technical and would be on the Dale list if the list were redone today. Some of the words in the science text that are absent from the Dale list are mission, spacecraft, helicopter, location, photographic, television, jet, battery, and camera. Andersen believes that the current emphasis on science in both the school and society enables many children to develop a core vocabulary containing a large number of science words before they ever begin formal instruction in school.

Some recent studies have attempted to update word lists to include content area vocabulary that researchers consider to be familiar to the average student (Brown 1965; Stocker 1971–1972). Other content area specialists have chosen to use readability formulas that do not rely upon word lists such as the one by Fry discussed earlier.

Technical Words. Many of the words that are new to students have been formulated from familiar word forms through borrowing, coining, or shortening. For example, the word *logarithmic* in mathematics has been borrowed from the Greek; the word *gerrymandering* in social studies has been coined to identify a special type of political activity; the acronym RADAR in science is an abbreviation of the term *radio detecting and ranging.*

Words such as the ones listed here for the content areas of mathematics, science, language arts, and social studies might be considered new to readers unfamiliar with the subject matter.

Mathematics—logarithmic, mantissa, nappe, and sine

Science—moraine, umbra, albate, taconite, RADAR, SNAFU, and SONAR

Language Arts—syntax, gerund, paralinguistic, epithalamion, cacophony, onomatopoeia, and simile

Social Studies—gerrymandering, ombudsman, filibuster, mandamus, monetarist, NATO, SALT, OAS, and CED

Technical Symbols. In addition to technical words, most content areas include technical symbols as part of their basic vocabulary. Examples from mathematics and science include:

Mathematics	Science
$<$	$C_6H_2O_6$ (S)
$>$	
$=$	$V_1 = \dfrac{P_1 V_1}{P_2}$
$\sqrt{}$	
$\div$	H
$\neq$	H C H————COOH
β	H

Specialized Meanings of Common Words. To add to the difficulty, many words that may initially appear familiar to the student have different connotations as used in the content areas. In some cases, the content area words have entirely different meanings from the general ones the students are accustomed to; in other cases the content area words contain the same general idea but have a more precise meaning. The words listed here are of both types.

Mathematics—function, vector, domain, range, coordinate, meter

Science—vector, base, casting, property, stress, tension

Language Arts—conceit, nominal, object, foot, meter, novel, refrain, scene, setting, stress, tension, abstract, tragedy

Social Studies—inflation, recession, depression, ghetto, logrolling, rider, featherbedding

Sentence Complexity. Another variable to consider in assessing readability is sentence structure. Klare (1974–1975, p. 97) believes that "the sentence variable, though not as predictive of difficulty as the word variable, does have an important contribution to make to formulas."

There are formulas available that measure the complexity of sentence structure. However, this type of sentence structure analyzation takes time and many authorities feel that measures of this sort are not needed in order to determine readability. Klare states

> Though sentences can be evaluated in several ways, a simple count of length is generally sufficient either by hand or by machine. Sentence complexity is probably the real causal factor in difficulty, but length correlates very highly with complexity and is much easier to count. (1974–1975, p. 97)

Levels of Abstraction

In addition to often complex vocabulary and sentence structure, the frequent need for the reader to understand high level abstract concepts adds to the difficulty of the content area textbook. Though certain words and sentences may add to the abstractness of written matter, quantifying through any means, including a readability formula, is difficult and sometimes impossible. Therefore degree of abstractness must be assessed basically by teachers in terms of their students' reactions to the content area. Fraenkel (1973) distinguishes between facts and concepts by suggesting that unlike facts, concepts are mental constructions devised by humans to enable them to organize in some systematic manner a wide variety of individual and separate pieces of information. Concepts vary in degree of abstractness and complexity. Low-level abstractions are made concerning concepts that can be pointed to or experienced directly. High-level abstractions are made concerning concepts whose characteristics cannot be experienced directly. For example, Fido as *dog* is a very low-level abstraction; Fido as *man's best friend* involves dimensions of trustworthiness, honesty, and loyalty and concerns high-level abstractions. Fido as a dog can be touched, but the traits of trustworthiness, honesty, and loyalty can be illustrated only through actions that reflect those characteristics.

The excerpts from mathematics, science, language arts, and social studies (see Figures 6.6, 6.7, 6.8, and 6.9) serve to illustrate the use of high-level abstract concepts. In addition, the readability of each passage is calculated by the Fry formula, using the number of syllables and the number of sentences. It should be pointed out that the readability level assessed can be interpreted only as a measurement of the specific passage represented. A larger sampling from each text would be necessary to state the readability of the total textbook.

In calculating readability of the mathematics excerpt illustrated here, Arabic numbers were counted as words (e.g., 1956 would be counted as a five-syllable word).

123

In the example in display 7 the domain is the set of first components of the ordered pairs. This is the set of real numbers from 0 through 4. The range is the set of second components, which is the set of real numbers from 0 through 16. The graph provides the rule for pairing each member of the domain with a member of the range.

The result of this pairing is a set of ordered pairs. We sometimes say that a function is a set of ordered pairs in which no two pairs have the same first component.

For/ each graph give the missing numerals in the table and use exercises A through D.

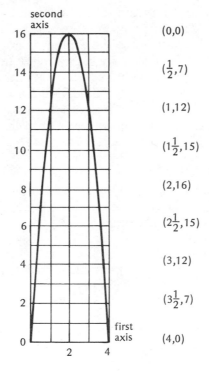

(0,0)

$(\frac{1}{2},7)$

(1,12)

$(1\frac{1}{2},15)$

(2,16)

$(2\frac{1}{2},15)$

(3,12)

$(3\frac{1}{2},7)$

(4,0)

From H. Van Engen et al., *Mathematics Concepts Application* (Glenview, Ill.: Scott, Foresman, 1969), p. 283.

Figure 6.6   Math Excerpt

The number of sentences in the one hundred-word passage in Figure 6.6 is 6.1 and the number of syllables is 131. On the Fry scale this passage would be considered as *grade six*. The task involved in this passage requires that the student understand the relationship between the numbers in a function. A graph is provided to help picture the concept, but the intended learning occurs when the student can visualize the concept himself and can relate its principle to all similar types of paired numbers. Mathematics by nature consists of a massive number of high-level abstract concepts. Some of the more common ones are

1. Visualizing the derivation of pi.
2. Differentiating between the need for computations in base five, six, seven, and eight.
3. Identifying steps to take in solving a multiple-step word problem.
4. Discussing the rationale behind repeating decimals.
5. Defining powers and exponents.
6. Computing per cent, ratio, and simple interest.
7. Utilizing logarithms for addition, subtraction, multiplication, and division of whole and rational numbers.
8. Computing fractions from decimals and vice versa.
9. Defining the reciprocal of a number.

The science excerpt (Figure 6.7) is from a biology text.

Number of Sentences:	4.0
Number of Syllables:	151
Approximate Grade Level:	10th

Here, then, is a new idea: To detect the basic structure of an organism, we may have to study not only its adult form but its embryonic states as well. On the basis of such a study, zoologists group all the animals we have been studying into a single **phylum, the** chordates. Although they differ greatly, all the animals in this phylum share at some stage of their development (1) a notochord, (2) pharyngeal pouches, and (3) a *dorsal* nerve cord—that is, one that is near the upper side of the **body./**

From BSCS, *Biological Science: An Ecological Approach*, 3rd ed. (New York: Rand McNally, 1973), p. 103.

Figure 6.7   Science Excerpt

The number of sentences in the passage in Figure 6.7 is 4.0 and the number of syllables is 151. On the Fry scale this passage would be considered as *grade ten*. In order to understand this passage the student must be able to visualize that the basic structure of an organism may be reflected in its embryonic development. Examples of common high-level abstractions required in the study of science include the following:

1. Visualizing the concept of energy.
2. Identifying the causes of common chemical reactions.
3. Describing solutions in equilibrium.

125

4. Discussing the evolution of Earth's terrain.
5. Comparing the potential and kinetic climates of the planet Earth.
6. Describing the concept of motion.

The language arts excerpt is taken from Faulkner's novel, *Light in August* (1959).

Number of Sentences:	3.6
Number of Syllables:	134
Approximate Grade Level:	9th

It is as though they had merely waited until he could find something to pant with, to be reaffirmed in triumph and desire with, with this last left of honor and pride and life. He hears above his heart the thunder increase, myriad and drumming. Like a long sighing of wind in trees it begins, then they sweep into sight, borne now upon a cloud of phantom dust. They rush past, forwardleaning in the saddles, with brandished arms, beneath whipping ribbons from slanted and eager lances; with tumult and soundless yelling they sweep past like a tide whose crest is jagged/ with the wild heads of horses and the brandished arms of men like the crater of the world in explosion. They rush past, are gone; the dust swirls skyward sucking, fades away into the night which has fully come. Yet, leaning forward in the window, his bandaged head huge and without depth upon the twin blobs of his hands upon the ledge, it seems to him that he still hears them: the wild bugles and the clashing sabres and the dying thunder of hooves.

From W. Faulkner, *Light in August* (New York: Random House, 1959), pp. 466–467.

Figure 6.8   Literature Excerpt

In the passage in Figure 6.8 the number of sentences is 3.6 and the number of syllables is 134. On the Fry scale, this excerpt would be considered as *grade nine.* As is typical of much literature studied in middle, junior, and senior high school curricula, this excerpt may be interpreted upon many different levels, giving it a variety of levels of abstraction. To understand this passage, the reader needs first to grasp the literal message. Then he must analyze the word choice and sentence structure to determine the intended messages of the author. For example, when studying this particular passage, English teachers might want their students to inspect closely the use of the carefully controlled grammar and specific sentence patterns to convey the intended message, the use of alliteration as in "He hears above his heart . . .," and the use of special word combinations such as "phantom dust" and "soundless yelling."

In addition to those skills needed to interpret the excerpt in Figure 6.8, other tasks requiring that the student understand difficult concepts that teachers may assign include the following:

1. Distinguish between factual honesty and stylistic honesty.
2. Analyze logistic and attitudinal points of view in conveying a message.
3. Discriminate between alternative possibilities of meaning and tone that depend upon rhetorical, syntactical, and lexical distinction.

126

4. Identify characteristics of Romanticism within a particular literary work.
5. Define the terms *humanism, expressionism, primitivism,* and *internationalism* in relation to literature.

The social studies excerpt in Figure 6.9 is taken from a book ordinarily used at the eleventh grade level. It should be noted that words such as "Republican," "Democrat," "New Deal," "Dixiecrat," "Negro," and "Communist" were considered as technical words and not proper nouns. Hence they were included in the word count.

Number of Sentences:	5.2
Number of Syllables:	160
Approximate Grade Level:	11th

The election was so close that the result was uncertain until the day after the polls closed. Although he lost four southern states to Thurmond and a million northern votes to Wallace, Truman was returned to office. Among the explanations for this amazing upset were Republican overconfidence; successful Democratic efforts to get voters to the polls; and the continuing strength of the New Deal, especially in major agricultural states. The three-way Democratic split that looked ruinous may have been a blessing in disguise. The Dixiecrat rebellion helped Truman's cause with Negro voters in the North; Wallace's campaign blunted efforts to pin the Communist/ label on the President. The professional pollsters were caught off base because they failed to note a last-minute swing of undecided voters toward the Democratic column. In any case, the result was an immense personal triumph for Truman: his whistle-stop campaign had turned the tide.

From *History of a Free People* by H. W. Bragdon, S. P. McCutchen, and C. W. Cole, p. 700. Copyright ©1973, Macmillan Publishing Co., Inc. Used with permission.

Figure 6.9 Social Studies Excerpt

The number of sentences is 5.2 and the number of syllables is 160. On the Fry scale this excerpt would be considered as *grade eleven.* It is interesting to note that this passage contains several words that are unique to social studies and that require that students understand the origin of the words in order to understand the implied concepts. For example, *Dixiecrat* implies much more than just the literal message; students need to be aware that the ideologies of the Southern Democrats were so different from those of the Truman Democrats that the Southerners formed their own political party. Hence *Dixiecrat* connotes much more than *Southern Democrat.* It reflects the political attitudes of a large portion of the Southern United States during the Truman era. In addition, an awareness of the general reaction of Americans in Truman's time to words such as *Communism* enhances the students' understanding of the country's attitude at that time and subsequently aids in understanding the topic as a whole. Other tasks requiring high-level abstract concepts often used in social studies include being asked to

1. Describe the effect of democracy upon a nation.
2. Discuss how the reconstruction of the South after the Civil War affected its contemporary political views.

3. Identify the influence of environmental protection on the present economy.
4. Compare trends toward isolationism in the past with those of today.
5. Differentiate between power structures of various governments and their effects upon the government's efficiency.

INSTRUCTIONAL FOCUS

Since the function of the content area teacher in the past has been primarily to teach students the content of a particular subject area, it is not surprising that the teacher's focus would be upon the content of the subject matter and not the means by which students could most effectively read the material. However, the learning of facts and concepts can be enhanced if the teacher presents the subject matter with consideration of the specific reading skills needed to understand it.

Direct Teaching of Word Recognition and Comprehension Skills

Although there is not necessarily a transfer of reading skills from general instruction in reading improvement to specific content area reading (Gray 1960), research indicates that there is a need for specific instruction in reading dealing with the concepts found in each content area (Serra 1953; Johnson 1952). As discussed earlier in this chapter, each discipline has its own language (technical vocabulary) and concepts. These components tend to emphasize the need for certain reading skills. For example, the subject matter of mathematics puts youngsters into contact with numerical concepts that are expressed by new sets of symbols.

Comprehension in mathematics depends heavily upon sequential understanding of basic concepts. If a student enters an algebra class in the middle of the semester, his chances of understanding the content are less than if he were entering an American history class at midterm. If a student does not know the underlying mathematics concept, his understanding of all else based on that concept is affected. Mathematics content is so specialized that the general background information possessed by most American youngsters that would enable them to catch up in American history usually would not provide them with any background of algebraic concepts.

In science, the knowledge explosion and the rapid development of technology have caused almost constant creation of new vocabulary. Frequently these new words are based on Latin or Greek roots, and the teachers who recognize the effectiveness of structural analysis in providing students with skills for attacking unknown science words have lessened the burden of understanding the technical vocabulary encountered by their students. The skill of following directions is also particularly important in the science content. A student who does not follow the steps in the lab manual in the correct order may cause a chemical explosion in the classroom.

128

Reading in social studies requires that the student learn how to read maps, charts, diagrams, and graphs. Many of the vocabulary words reflect high-level abstract concepts—for example, democracy, feudalism, and chauvinism. The interpretation of relationships, especially cause-effect, can create difficulty in comprehending the content materials. Ascertaining sequence, specifically chronological, can help students identify the cause-effect relationship by helping them to determine which events caused others. For example, the student who does not know that Franklin D. Roosevelt preceded Harry S. Truman, will not be able to interpret the cause-effect relationships between the unknown who stepped into the presidential office and the existing political situations that necessitated immediate major decisions.

Reading in language arts encompasses a variety of skills. Literature requires the interpreting of figurative language, locating imagery, assessing tone and mood, and determining theme. Most of the other content areas do not rely so heavily upon these aspects. While it is important for the student to be able to identify tone and mood in order to determine the validity of historical material, chemistry experiments and the derivation of pi are usually written in denotative language and do not require this skill.

Aspects of the language arts other than literature require different reading skills. For example, the study of grammar might require that the student be particularly aware of ascertaining sequence and locating cause-effect relationships. A feasible assignment in grammar might be to identify the relationship of word order to meaning in the sentences, "John bit the apple" and "The apple bit John."

Likewise, understanding each of the other content areas in the middle and secondary school curriculum also emphasizes the use of certain reading skills.

Though the various disciplines require certain reading skills that more closely identify with them than with others, reading ability requires the synthesis of all reading skills. For example, although *following directions* may be a skill that is particularly needed in science, it is also used in reading all the other subject areas. Likewise, though *sensory imagery* involved in the comprehension skill of identifying tone and mood may usually be associated with literature, other content areas also require students to use their sensory organs—for example, in science, "bitter taste occurs on the end of the tongue" (taste); in mathematics, "move the bead on the abacus and count out the number of apples" (haptic).

Content area teachers who are aware of the reading skills generally needed in their content areas can help their students understand the content area material more easily. For example, if a teacher is aware of the fact that history usually requires the ability to locate cause-effect relationships, he can do much to facilitate understanding of the chapter by pointing out to the students key words such as *because* and *if*, (which help the student locate the cause-effect relationships). In addition, the students should look closely at the same material and determine what reading skills may be needed in terms of their specific assignment on that lesson. For example, if the teacher asks the students to write a paragraph concerning what they think historians will think of Truman in fifty years, the reading skill of predicting outcomes would also be important. Therefore, in that specific lesson, the teacher should not only point out ways in which cause-effect relationships are important but also should review ways in which outcomes may be predicted.

Direct Teaching of Study Skills

Burron (1974) states that there are two main kinds of subject matter learnings—the learning of specific facts or concepts and the learning of specific study skills related to the study of subject matter. Knowing the skills related to finding specific information is perhaps more important than retaining specific items of information. This seems to be an especially logical conclusion when one considers the vast quantity of information that confronts the contemporary learner. It would seem reasonable to recommend that selected study skills be taught by the subject matter teacher, and that discussion activities and assignments in subject matter classes include student responses that call for application of those selected study skills. This approach does not intend to ignore the importance of subject matter content because fruitful study is impossible without some mastery of content. However, both content and accompanying study skills are essential components of successful subject matter teaching and learning.

For example, in mathematics students should be told that the language is extremely concise. As such, they need to read and reread sections carefully before proceeding to solve any problems. Students should be encouraged to read a problem slowly and carefully, first for the general essence, second for specific directions on what they are supposed to do with the problem, and third to locate important information that can help them solve the problem.

Likewise, in science, students should be shown how to use the format of the textbook to distinguish between facts of varying importance. Because so many new facts are presented, only the most important ones can be retained. By pointing out such aspects as the typographical clues to important words and graphic aids, the teacher can give the students guidelines for distinguishing between facts that are supportive and facts that are essential. Students should also be shown how to use the *scientific method* in their approach to reading science—that is, form a hypothesis, collect data, organize data, form conclusions, and test conclusions. Furthermore, because the scientific method is an essential scientific concept as well as a process, students should be guided toward interpreting what they read in light of this concept.

In social studies, the student can be helped to retain and identify essential concepts by learning to take notes based on the organizational pattern of the textbook. For example, if the text reflects chronological order, students can construct a time line as a base for tying together all the facts that otherwise may overwhelm them.

In language arts, particularly in literature, the student should know that many levels of interpretation can be made and that a single word can have a variety of meanings at each level of interpretation. In some cases, particularly in poetry, signaling devices are especially important to understanding the in-

130

tended meaning. In the poem, "next to of course god america i" by e. e. cummings, the poet's lack of capitalization of all the words in the title is a typographical clue to meaning. The fact that the words are written in lower case in the poem is a signaling device to the author's special meaning. Because of the various levels of interpretation, students should be made aware that they may have to reread the same piece of literature several times in order to understand it completely. However, they should be shown how to skim it rapidly for the main idea, read it slowly and carefully to locate details, or scan it quickly to identify signaling devices. In all cases, they need to be shown the study skill of adjusting rate to purpose for reading.

There are many other study strategies that are particularly important to each content area. Teachers who closely examine their content areas to identify needed study skills and then pass this information on to their students are helping them learn both the subject matter and the method of assimilating the subject matter most efficiently.

INADEQUATE USE OF AVAILABLE TEXTBOOK AIDS

Though contemporary educators seem to support an eclectic curriculum that uses a plethora of materials in an integrated content area approach, many middle and secondary school curricula still rely upon textbooks as the major instructional tool. These textbooks come with a variety of aids, which can produce a well-rounded program.

The format of the textbook itself can be one of the most important aids. Words in italics, bold print, or colored type are typographical aids that have been used by the authors to help the reader identify words that are new, difficult, or especially important. Many textbooks have glossaries or lists of important terms at the end of each chapter, which help teach the technical vocabulary. The size of type is a clue to the organization of the textbook and the importance of various topics in relation to others. Most books contain pictorial aids such as maps, graphs, charts, line drawings, or photographs.

The teacher's edition may be written in a variety of ways. It may be a separate volume containing objectives and suggested procedures for teaching the content area, or it may be the same textbook used by the student but overlaid with special instructions to the teacher. In some cases, teacher's editions point out only objectives and teaching strategies for the content area concepts. In other cases, the teacher's editions also point out reading problems that students may have with the content and the means the teacher can use to overcome the problems. Tests to accompany the material are usually available for purchases, can save the teacher time, and can be effective determiners of the student's ability to read the material.

Many publishing companies also have supplementary materials available to accompany their textbooks. These aids include film, sound recordings, and slide tapes to expand or reinforce ideas presented in the textbook; colorful posters to illustrate important events, people, and formulas; workbooks for practicing application of principles; and reference lists to additional reading.

The checklist following is designed to help the teacher evaluate a textbook on these terms. It asks the teacher to look at the content and format of the student's text and the teacher's guide in order to see what has been done to facilitate the students' learning of the content area material.

Checklist for Evaluating Textbook Materials

Name of Book _____ Age of Intended

Publisher_____ Audience _____

Author/Editor_____ Readability
                                                 Level _____

Teacher's Edition

1. Identifies age level of intended audience?

    yes_____ no_____ If no, how did you find it?_____

2. Identifies the reading level of text?

    yes_____no_____If no, how did you find it?_____

3. Contains procedures for teaching each unit?

    yes_____ no_____

4. Gives more than a minimum of suggestions for teaching each unit so that a teacher might have several readily available teaching alternatives?

    yes_____ no_____

5. Easy to follow and understand?

    yes_____ no_____ Why or why not?_____

    _____

6. List supplementary materials and activities?

    yes_____ no_____

7. Discusses provisions for students who are unable to read and/or understand the text?

    yes_____ no_____

8. Contains objectives for teaching each unit?

    yes_____ no_____

9. Gives more than a minimum number of objectives so that, if a teacher wishes, he might have readily available objectives for advanced students?

    yes_____ no_____

10. Points out vocabulary or concepts that might be particularly difficult for the students?

    yes_____ no_____

11. Gives aids to the teacher for teaching technical vocabulary or special concepts?

    yes_____ no_____

Student's Edition

12. Contains typographical aids to students so that they are helped to learn vocabulary or concepts that might be difficult? (e.g., italicized words, colored print)

    yes_____ no_____ .

13. Contains special aids in format so that the student may be helped to learn vocabulary or concepts that might be difficult? (e.g., glossary, technical words reinforced or taught with aid of context clues)

    yes_____ no_____

14. Contains a great many visual aids? (e.g., maps, graphs, line drawings, photographs)

    yes_____ no_____

15. Provides transitional paragraphs in the text that help the student realize the relationships between previous paragraphs, sections, and chapters?

    yes_____ no_____

16. Provides summaries for each chapter, either by concluding paragraphs or by summaries?

    yes_____ no_____

17. Contains motivating introductory sections to each chapter and section?

    yes_____ no_____

18. Contains questions at the end of the chapter that require several different levels of comprehension?

    yes_____ no_____

19. Contains questions at the end of the chapter that relate to the purpose for which the teacher wants the students to read the chapter?

    yes_____ no_____

20. Contains suggested activities related to the purpose for which the teacher wants the students to read the chapter?

    yes_____ no_____

21. Contains a list of reference materials that students may use to expand or revise their knowledge of the content?

    yes_____ no_____

134

22. Contains suggestions to the students for reading the material?

yes_____ no_____

23. Contains provisions for learners of varying reading skills and academic abilities?

yes_____ no_____

24. Contains attractive illustrations, appropriate type size, and is constructed of durable material?

yes_____ no_____

25. Contains chapters that are organized systematically? (e.g., thematic order, geographical or place order)

yes_____ no_____

Materials

26. Are any of the following types of aids available from the publishers?

   a. Visual aids such as pictures, maps, models?

   yes_____ no_____

   b. Tests to accompany text?

   yes_____ no_____

   c. Students' workbooks and accompanying teacher's manual?

   yes_____ no_____

   d. Games?

   yes_____ no_____

   e. Film strips, recordings, films?

   yes_____ no_____

   f. Skill laboratories?

   yes_____ no_____

   g. Supplementary reading materials to expand or reinforce the basic text?

   yes_____ no_____

   h. Supplementary reading materials for students of varying reading abilities?

   yes_____ no_____

   i. Other materials?

   yes_____ no_____ If yes, what are they?_____

135

References and Bibliography

Andersen, H., ed. *Readings in Science Education for the Secondary Schools.* New York: Macmillan, 1969.

Aukerman, R. C. "Readability of Secondary School Literature Textbooks: A Final Report." *English Journal* (1965), 533–540.

Bamman, H., Dawson, M., and McGovern, J. *Fundamentals of Basic Reading Instruction.* 3rd ed. New York: McKay, 1973.

Bragdon, H. W., McCutchen, S. P., and Cole, C. W. *History of a Free People.* New York: Macmillan, 1973.

Brown, W. R. "Science Textbook Selection and the Dale-Chall Formula." *School Science and Mathematics* (1965), 164–168.

Burmeister, L. E. *Reading Strategies for Secondary School Teachers.* Reading, Mass.: Addison-Wesley, 1974.

Burron, A., and Claybaugh, A. *Using Reading to Teach Subject Matter: Fundamentals for Content Teachers.* Columbus, Ohio: Merrill, 1974.

BSCS. *Biological Science: An Ecological Approach.* 3rd ed. New York: Rand McNally, 1973.

Cummings, E. E. *Poems 1923–1954.* New York: Harcourt Brace Jovanovich, 1954.

Cushenbery, D. *Remedial Reading in the Secondary School.* West Nyack, N. Y.: Parker, 1972.

Dale, E., and Chall, J. S. "A Formula for Predicting Readability." *Educational Research Bulletin* 27 (21 January 1948), 11-20 and (15 February 1948), 37–54.

Dawkins, J. *Syntax and Readability.* Newark, Del.: International Reading Association, 1975.

Faulkner, W. *Light in August.* rev. ed. New York: Random House, 1959.

Flesch, R. "A New Readability Yardstick." *Journal of Applied Psychology* (1948), 221-233.

Fraenkel, J. R. *Helping Students Think and Value: Strategies for Teaching the Social Studies.* Englewood Cliffs, N. J.: Prentice-Hall, 1973.

Fry, E. *Reading Instruction for Classroom and Clinic.* New York: McGraw-Hill, 1972.

Gray, W. S. "Reading." Page 1,092 in Chester W. Harris, ed. *Encyclopedia of Educational Research.* 3rd ed. New York: Macmillan, 1960.

Herber, H. *Teaching Reading in Content Areas.* Englewood Cliffs, N. J.: Prentice-Hall, 1970.

Johnson, M. E. "The Vocabulary Difficulty in Content Subject in Grade Five." *Elementary English* (1952), 29, 277–280.

Karlin, R. *Teaching Reading in High School.* 2nd ed. Indianapolis, Ind.: Bobbs-Merrill, 1972.

Karlin, R. *Teaching Reading in High School: Selected Articles.* Indianapolis, Ind.: Bobbs-Merrill, 1969.

Klare, G. R. "Assessing Readability." *Reading Research Quarterly* (1974-1975), 62–102.

Lyght, C. E., ed. *The Merck Manual of Diagnosis and Therapy.* 11th ed. Rahway, N. J.: Merck Sharp and Dohme Research Laboratories, 1966.

Olson, A., and Ames, W. *Teaching Reading Skills in Secondary Schools.* Scranton, Pa.: Intext Educational Publishers, 1972.

Olson, A., and Ames, W. *Teaching Reading Skills in Secondary Schools: Readings.* Scranton, Pa.: Intext Educational Publishers, 1970.

Robinson, H., and Thomas E., eds. *Fusing Reading Skills and Content.* Newark, Del.: International Reading Association, 1969.

Robinson, H. *Teaching Reading and Study Strategies: The Content Areas.* Boston: Allyn & Bacon, 1975.

Serra, M. C. "The Concept Burden of Instructional Materials." *Elementary School Journal* (1953), 53, 508–512.

Spache, G. D. *Good Reading for Poor Readers.* rev. ed. Champaign, Ill.: Garrard, 1972.

Stocker, L. P. "Increasing the Precision of the Dale-Chall Readability Formula." *Reading Improvement* (1971–1972), 887–889.

Thomas, E., and Robinson, H. *Improving Reading in Every Class: A Source Book for Teachers.* Boston: Allyn & Bacon, 1972.

Van Engen, H., et al. *Mathematics Concepts Application.* Glenview, Ill.: Scott, Foresman, 1969.

Chapter 7

Planning Reading Instruction in the Content Area Classroom

Prerequisite 7.1

Before beginning this chapter participants should have successfully completed the objectives for Chapter 6 or should have some knowledge of the reading skills that are needed in a particular content area.

Rationale 7.2

In order to plan lessons in a manner that will be most helpful to students, teachers must know which reading skills are needed for understanding a content area and how to plan a lesson so that both the needed reading skills and the content area objectives are learned. This chapter describes in detail procedures that the teacher may use to do this.

Objectives 7.3

On successful completion of this chapter, the participant will be able to:

1. Describe the purpose and composition of each of the following components of a five-step lesson plan: behavioral objectives, pre-assessment, materials, procedures, and post-assessment.
2. Describe at least two benefits of careful lesson planning.
3. Describe and differentiate between the composition of each of the following components of a five-step directed reading lesson: preparation, silent reading, oral reading and discussion, follow-up, and extension activities.

4. Differentiate between a five-step directed reading lesson and a five-step daily lesson plan.

5. (On the lines below, add other objectives according to your instructor's directions.)_____
_____

6. _____
_____

7. _____
_____

8. _____
_____

*   *   *   *   *   *   *   *   *   *   *   *   *   *

Chapter 13, Experience 7 extends Chapter 7 with this performance/consequence objective:

9. Design and teach at least one step of a directed reading lesson using a format that includes a behavioral objective, a pre-assessment, a list of materials, a description of procedure, and a post-assessment.

*   *   *   *   *   *   *   *   *   *   *   *   *   *

Self Pre-Assessment 7.4

Can you complete all the activities listed in **Objectives 7.3**? Answer "yes," "no," or "not certain."

If you answered "yes" to the question, complete the enabling activities required by your instructor and take the Post-Assessment on the date assigned by him.

If you answered "no," refer to **Enabling Activities 7.5**. If you decide to do any activities that are not required, select those enabling activities that best suit you as a learner. You need not complete all the optional activities or all parts of a particular optional activity. As soon as you have the information you need to complete the objectives, answer "yes" to the **Self Pre-Assessment 7.4** question and stop the activity.

If you answered "not certain" to the question, refer to **Enabling Activities 7.4**. Select the enabling activity that best suits your style of learning and peruse it. Then make a firm "yes" or "no" answer and proceed accordingly.

Enabling Activities 7.5

Complete only as many of the activities listed below as are required and which you need in order to meet the objectives.

1. *Enabling activity one* is a *reading* alternative. This is **Information Given 7.6**. It is a brief overview of the components within and the differences between a five-step directed reading lesson and a five-step daily lesson plan.
2. *Enabling activity two* is another *reading* option. In this case, the material to be read is one of the textbooks used to expand the theoretical background for this course. See chart on inside front cover for keying in textbooks that may be used.
3. *Enabling activity three* is a *class session* option. Attend the class session(s) on the date(s), at the time(s), and at the place(s) announced.

| (Date) | (Time) | (Place) |

| (Date) | (Time) | (Place) |

| (Date) | (Time) | (Place) |

4. *Enabling activity four* (These lines are left blank so that you may add other enabling activities as suggested by your instructor.) _____

_____

5. *Enabling activity five* _____

_____

6. *Enabling activity six* _____

_____

Now that you have completed the appropriate number of required and/or optional learning alternatives, look back at **Self Pre-Assessment 7.4**. If you feel you can answer "yes" to all of the questions, you are ready to proceed to the Post-Assessment. This may be given to you immediately or after completion of a series of chapters.

Information Given 7.6
Planning Reading Instruction
in the Content Area Classroom

Lisa Stone, a first year teacher had made arrangements to observe a biology class conducted by Miss Scott, who had been teaching for several years. After introducing themselves to each other, the two teachers began discussing Miss Scott's lesson plan for that day. The biology teacher opened her planning book and showed Lisa the following outline.

```
10 min. — slides
15 min. — I lead discussion
20 min. — reading period
```

LESSON PLANNING

It became apparent to Lisa that Miss Scott had done several things poorly when constructing her lesson plan. For instance, most of the content was not stated in terms specific enough to be understood. Therefore the beginning teacher could not determine what type of slides were involved, what the topic of discussion was to be, or what was to be read during the reading period. Furthermore, the topic of *slides* and *reading period* were not stated in behavioral terms; that is, neither the activities nor their purposes were clearly stated. Perhaps Miss Scott wanted her students to view 35 mm slides for the purpose of illustrating animals from different phyla; or it was just as feasible that she wanted her students to prepare slide plates for growing yeast cultures.

Components of Lesson Plans

Miss Scott's lesson plan could have easily been improved to be more useful to both Miss Scott and Lisa. Though the teacher's editions and/or curriculum guides are usually quite helpful in delineating contents and procedures for teaching each topic, students in each classroom are different. Teachers must adapt their lessons to suit the particular needs of their students. One means to facilitate planning instruction for a specific class is for the teacher to use the five-step lesson plan containing: (1) a behavioral objective, (2) a pre-assessment, (3) a list of materials, (4) a description of procedures, and (5) a post-assessment.

Behavioral Objectives

This component describes what the students should be able to do after they complete the lesson. It forces teachers to pinpoint the purpose for having students complete the activity. The only component in Miss Scott's lesson that was described in behavioral terms was "I lead discussion." However, the focus of the behavioral objective was upon Miss Scott's behavior rather than the students' behavior. This step should have focused upon the learner and not the teacher because behavioral objectives describe outcomes or performances that the *students* should accomplish as a result of their participation in

141

the lesson. Teaching lessons based upon objectives helps teachers clarify their thinking about desired student learning, plan instruction to bring about this learning, and determine to what extent students have learned the designated tasks. When writing objectives, the teacher must describe outcomes in terms of observable acts to be completed by students. An objective might be written, "the student will describe ten characteristics of . . .," not "the teacher will ask about ten characteristics of . . . ." Examples of some verbs that can help the teacher in planning lessons based on observable behavior are *recite*, *identify*, *differentiate*, *solve*, *compare*, *contrast*, *predict*, *design*, *teach*, *remake*, *describe*, *define*, *analyze*, *select*, *demonstrate*, and *present*. Examples of some verbs that are not helpful because they are not specific enough are (1) *know*— How does the teacher measure *know*? If students list, define, or predict, they show the teacher what they must do in order to prove that they *know*. (2) *appreciate*—What must they do to show the teacher that they *appreciate*? If students analyze a story or write a book report, they show the teacher what they can do to demonstrate *appreciation*. (3) *enjoy*—How does the teacher know the students *enjoy*? If they request additional books, smile when given the books, and enthusiastically ask specific questions about the books, the teacher may determine that they have *enjoyed* what they read.

Pre-Assessment

Pre-assessment identifies the students who already know the subject matter to be taught. If the student can do the task involved in the lesson, he should be given another. This new task may be completely different, or it may simply extend the original one to a more sophisticated level. One legitimate task for a student who already knows the content matter would be to act as a resource person for the students who have not yet learned the subject matter. Pre-assessments may be of various types. Though teachers often use more formal assessments, such as objective tests or asking students to respond in essay format, many times informal responses in class discussion can be used by the teacher to assess an individual's knowledge of the lesson's objectives.

Materials

The third step includes a listing of materials—textbooks, supplementary readings, audiovisual equipment—to be used in the lesson. Listing of such items helps remind teachers that if they are going to use transparencies, they need to reserve the overhead projector; or if they are going to use mimeo worksheets, they need to make sure they have duplicated enough for all the students.

Procedures

In the fourth step, teachers summarize what they are going to do in order to teach the lesson. It may include such aspects as whether they intend to use

142

large-group discussion, small-group discussion, lecture, or student-led discussion. Beginning teachers often write down almost verbatim what they are going to say to their classes. As teachers become more experienced they usually write less about their procedures. The important aspect of this step is that enough information should be written down so that if someone not familiar with the lesson reads it, he can understand what the teacher intended to do that day. Miss Scott's lesson plan was too sketchy and did not contain enough description to be helpful to someone else reading it. Had Miss Scott had a substitute teacher that day, it is doubtful that the lesson she intended would have been taught.

Post-Assessment

The fifth step delineates how teachers measure their students to see if their objectives have been achieved. This step may well be the most important step in all the lesson planning. It forces teachers to evaluate whether or not their teaching has been successful. If the students meet the teacher's objectives, then they can proceed to new materials; if students do not, the teacher should reteach the material.

The format used for the post-assessment can parallel the format used for the pre-assessment—that is, objective tests or informal observation are both valid measures for assessing whether a student has met the objectives. As long as the post-assessment measures the behavior delineated in the objectives, the format is acceptable.

Benefits of Careful Lesson Planning

One of the obvious benefits of careful lesson planning is that it allows the teacher to individualize instruction. For example, if all but one student pass the pre-assessment, the teacher may decide to go on to another lesson with the class. The student who was unable to pass the pre-assessment needs to learn the objectives. Therefore, by adapting the lesson so that it may be taught for the student who needs it, the teacher is able to individualize instruction. Possible ways in which the teacher could adapt a comprehension lesson for a variety of students was discussed in a prior chapter of this text. (See Chapter 3 for ways to adapt a comprehension lesson to meet individual needs.)

Another benefit of carefully planning lessons in the above format is that it gives help to the teacher when teaching the same content at a later time. Reviewing her lesson after a few months, Miss Scott might not be able to recall what she had done or whether it worked well. If she had carefully written out her lesson, she probably could remember whether the slide on the phyla needed to be replaced and whether the content needed to be expanded with handouts. In a like manner the whole lesson can be improved and reused without rethinking the entire planning process. In addition, writing out a procedure before one teaches enables the new teacher to ask a colleague to make suggestions for possible improvement in the classroom situation.

THE FIVE–STEP, DIRECTED READING LESSON

Once students enter middle and secondary schools, they spend more time reading (or trying to read) content area material than they spend in formal reading instruction. Reading is the major self-study tool used in learning. If the assignments are given properly, students can learn the content through reading and at the same time develop their reading skills. Because of the difficulties encountered by students in understanding the content area lessons, teachers can help by including direct instruction in the reading of the content area. Since reading is a skill and not a content, the teacher is actually doing two things: (1) teaching students the content and (2) teaching students how to most effectively read the content. The five-step reading lesson that can be used efficiently by teachers of any content area includes (1) preparation, (2) silent reading, (3) oral reading and discussion, (4) follow-up, and (5) extension activities.

Step 1—Preparation

Step 1 includes (1) motivating the student, (2) setting purposes for reading, (3) developing concepts involved, (4) identifying problem words, and (5) creating an awareness of the reading skills needed.

Motivating the Student

Motivating the student may be done in a number of ways. One of the simplest is to make the subject matter as relevant to the needs and interests of the students as possible. If the students have expressed an interest in how the human being is related to the ape, this relationship could be discussed in light of taxonomical groups before the topic of *biological classification* was assigned.

Setting Purposes for Reading

Setting purposes for reading is essential in helping the students gain from the material what the teacher intended them to gain. The teacher should inform the students of exactly what they will be expected to do with the material after they finish. For example, in biology, if they are going to be asked to identify at least two representatives of any five species placed in the subphylum vertebrata, then they should be told that before they read. In this way, they can read the material with that purpose in mind. In addition, it facilitates both motivation and understanding if the students are told *why* they are being asked to read the materials.

Developing Concepts Involved

Developing concepts involved may be facilitated by relating students' background experiences with unfamiliar concepts they will be encountering in the subject matter. For example, the concept of *biological classification* could be related to classification of food items in a grocery store—that is, not only are canned goods separated from produce, but all the canned fruits are separated from the canned vegetables. This system of classification makes it easier to locate types of food quickly.

Identifying Problem Words

Identifying problem words can be a big help to the reader. Sometimes even though the authors of a textbook have placed words in italics, given definitions in bold print, or reinforced a technical word through use in context, students fail to use these aids efficiently. By reminding the students of words that do exist and that they might not know, the teacher can help the students read the material in an easier manner. In addition, the teacher should constantly remind the students that most of the problem words the teacher has identified for the student have already been identified in the textbook. The teacher should show them again and again how to use the textbook aids to decode any words they do not know.

Creating an Awareness of Reading Skills

Creating an awareness of the reading skills involved gives the student more options for successful understanding of the material contained in the textbook. In the case of biological classification, the student could be reminded that structural analysis might be used to detect the meanings of many of the scientific words used in the classification system. By reviewing the meanings of Greek and Latin roots, many of the scientific words and classifications become more meaningful to students. For example, the word *edenta* comes from two Latin words, *ex* meaning *away* and *dens* meaning *tooth*. In science, the term *edenta* refers to an order of animals that do not have front teeth. To learn traits of members of this order, the student can remember the root word *dens* (as in dentist) and think of animals without teeth.

Step 2—Silent Reading

Step 2 includes more than just asking the students to read the chapter. They should be reminded of all the aspects touched upon in step 1—that is, they should be asked to read for a specific purpose and told what specific task, if any, they will be required to perform after they finish their reading. In addition, they should be encouraged to apply the reading skills that they were made aware of during the preparation step.

Step 3—Oral Reading and Discussion

Oral reading and discussion is a follow-up to the silent reading to assess whether or not the pupils understand the new words, concepts, and ideas presented in the material they just read. This step includes both oral and silent reading of material in order to answer specific questions related to the purpose for reading the chapter. Oral reading does not mean round robin reading in which each student reads a paragraph according to his sequence in the classroom seating arrangement. Oral reading refers to the practice of asking students to locate answers to specific questions and reading them aloud for the benefit of the teacher and the remainder of the class. In this manner, the teacher is giving the student a chance to prove he knows the answer and the teacher is also giving the other students a chance to see how the student arrived at the right answer. This procedure has the advantage of allowing the student who did not get the answer the first time to locate the answer and mark the passage in the textbook when another student reads the passage aloud. Sometimes students need to read it themselves and slowly cogitate over it privately before they understand the concepts involved. Oral reading of this sort expands the options for those who learn best in this manner.

In addition, some students have never been shown how to deal with reading skills at the higher usage levels and could benefit by seeing other students do so. For example, by asking students to locate passages that help them to evaluate why one animal might be considered more sophisticated than another, those who do not know how to evaluate why details are placed in particular sequential order will be able to observe how a peer accomplishes this task.

Suggested procedures for conducting the discussion include reminding the students of their purpose for reading. This gives purpose to the oral reading and helps the youngsters remember that reading means gaining meaning from the printed page and not just parroting isolated sets of facts.

As many students as possible should be involved in the oral reading. If the same students always locate the correct sentence or paragraph, and the teacher is concerned that the others are not getting to read orally or to participate because they are poor readers, he can ask nonparticipating students to reread specific sentences. For example, Miss Scott was discussing the chapter with the students, building on questions she asked them prior to the silent reading. John said *taxonomic group* refers to a group in which an organism *belongs*. Mary said that no organism *belongs* in a taxonomic group, but that an organism is *placed* in a taxonomic group on the basis of a set of characteristics specified by someone making a classification. Miss Scott told the two to read the part in the chapter that proved their points. The other students actively tried to find the part in the text where the author discussed this issue. After Mary read the correct paragraph aloud, the teacher asked Sue, a less able reader, to silently reread the same sentences and discuss why this viewpoint on the issue was expressed before the remainder of the material in the chapter was presented. (Note: The teacher did *not* ask Sue to read aloud as Sue might be embarrassed by stumbling over words in front of her peers. Because Mary had just read the sentence, the teacher assumed that Sue was able to follow along in print and understand the meaning of the sentence enough that she could give a correct response in class.) Almost all the questions concerning chapter contents can be used in this manner to create purpose and increase participation during oral reading and discussion.

Step 4—Follow-up

Step 4 includes all the individual tasks students need to do after they have finished their reading and discussion. Some students who read above the content area level might be working on sophisticated expansion of skills; other students, for whom the content area text is appropriate, may be expanding the skills learned in the lesson of the day; and still other youngsters who are reading below grade level may be doing lessons to help them catch up in the skills in which they are the least proficient. This step encompasses both teaching a new reading skill and practicing a reading skill already taught.

Teaching a New Reading Skill

The teacher looked at the material to be assigned and determined that her students needed to know the answers to the following questions: "Why do organisms with annelid bodies always lack skeletons?" "How does lacking a skeleton affect their position in the hierarchy that is implicit in the biological classification system?" It became apparent to the teacher that in order to answer these questions, the students were going to have to detect the cause-effect relationships between annelid bodies and lack of skeletons and the annelids' level of development in the biological hierarchy. Therefore she spent some time with the class showing them how to look for cause-effect relationships of this type.

Practicing a Reading Skill Already Taught

While some youngsters went on to learn about cause-effect relationships, others who did not understand structural analysis well enough to use it to decode scientific words were given additional exercises in which they were asked to locate and use Latin and Greek roots related to the vocabulary in the chapter.

Both learning a new reading skill and practicing an old one may be done in this step. The teacher first reviewed with the students the many Latin and Greek roots of scientific words before she introduced the idea of cause and effect. She let the students get some feeling of confidence in their use of structural analysis before they went on to a new skill.

Step 5—Extension Activities

Step 5 includes many activities designed to reinforce skills already taught. There is a definite difference between teaching a reading skill and reinforcing a reading skill. For example, youngsters can be asked to complete a project that reinforces the cause-effect skills needed in the study of biological classification, but they probably can not learn to identify cause-effect relationships by completion of the project alone. They must first be *taught* that animals are arranged in a hierarchical level according to structural characteristics that make them increasingly more sophisticated than animals on a lower level of the hierarchy. After students understand this cause-effect relationship, they can *reinforce* the skill through the completion of an extension activity. For example, after they have learned what is meant by cause-effect relationships, they might be asked to make a scrapbook by locating pictures of representatives of the classes amphibia, reptilia, aves, or mammalia. They could then delineate traits that caused each animal to be placed in its particular class and perhaps be asked to determine the cause-effect relationship of why possessing a particular trait made them more advanced in the hierarchy.

In short, step 5 includes all those activities designed to reinforce and extend the reading skills previously taught. These activities include supplementary reading, dramatization, rereading for a different purpose, games, and creative activities. Each of these components will be discussed.

Supplementary Reading

Supplementary reading could be reading for pleasure. It could also consist of readings assigned to enrich the students' knowledge of a topic—for example, one student might like to read an article about animals in a nature magazine and then write a short summary of the article or merely relate the essence of the article to the other class members.

Dramatization

Dramatization involves taking a topic just read and presenting it dramatically to the class. For example, science students might be asked to conduct a panel discussion on the worth of the various biological classification systems. Other science students, after reading *Inherit the Wind*, might wish to dramatize some of the issues touched upon in the Scopes trial and then discuss some of these issues in terms of evolution and levels of development within the taxonomic system. Math students might be asked to present a symposium on the worth of changing the current U.S. measurement system to the metric system; social studies students might be asked to dramatize part of the play *Give 'Em Hell, Harry* or participate in a mock political caucus. Language arts students might be asked to dramatize scenes from *Huckleberry Finn*.

Rereading for a Different Purpose

Though the students may have understood the basic concepts the first time they read the material, they may be asked to read it again to determine specifics such as whether some of the animals in subphylum vertebrata might be reclassified into a new order. Likewise, in English, the student may be asked to read parts of *Huckleberry Finn* again to determine what sort of background music would be appropriate for the dramatization mentioned above. If the student is a very poor reader, he might have to reread the material to understand the idea because he read it the first time just to decode the unknown words.

Games

Some teachers, even at the senior high level, like to use games to reinforce skills or expand certain concepts. For example, to reinforce the skill of cause-effect, biology students might be asked to play a bingo game in which the director called out the names of specific animals instead of numbers. The players would be asked to look at their bingo boards and cover up the trait that caused that animal to be placed in a certain class. The first person to cover up a straight column by correctly identifying traits would be the winner.

Likewise, the biology teacher could extend the concept of evolution by presenting the class with a simulation activity in which the students would pretend to be living in the year 9000 B.C. Their task would be to look over a list of animals in Homo sapiens' evolutionary progression and to decide for themselves which ones to eliminate or to have become extinct. They could then discuss how their decision would affect the characteristics of modern humans.

Social studies students could simulate current economic situations such as *building your own society*, *being in court*, *going on strike*, and *selecting a candidate for President*.

There are various games that add to the pleasure of mathematics. Many teachers like to use word puzzles that require mathematical logic to solve. One suggested by Johnson and Rising is given here:

> Phillip and his wife, Mary, both work at night. Phillip is off duty every ninth evening; his wife is off duty every sixth evening. Phillip is off duty on this Sunday evening; Mary is off duty the following Monday evening. When (if ever) will they be off duty the same evening? (1972, p. 249)

Language arts students seem to enjoy activities such as using a map of the Mississippi River as a game board. After answering questions about *Huckleberry Finn* correctly, they move down the river. The first to reach Illinois wins the game. (See Chapter 11 for more information about teacher-made games and Chapter 10 for more specific suggestions about games that might be used.)

Creative Activities

Creative activities, including artistic, musical, or verbal composition, are often used as extension activities. Science students could think up new names for animals that are combinations of existing orders and farther along in the evolutionary process. They could make up a song about environmental pollution or collect advertisements about ecology and the environment. Mathematics students might be asked to do curve stitching to illustrate how curves may be formed from straight lines. Mathematics students might also enjoy making up word puzzles such as the one discussed above. Language arts students might be asked to do the following: "Draw a picture that reflects the background when Huck was talking with Jim." "Make a collage that reflects how Huck and Jim felt as they watched the tarring and feathering of the Duke and the King." "Write a creative story showing how the ending would have been different if one of the major characters had lived ten years before he did." Social studies students might be asked to create a relief map of a certain geographical area, or collect newspaper and magazine pictures that reflect the clothing, hair style, or the music predominant during Truman's presidency.

COMPARISON OF LESSON PLANS
AND A DIRECTED READING LESSON

The five steps of a directed reading lesson and the five steps of a lesson plan are not the same. The teacher may have five different lesson plans, each one containing only one step of a directed reading lesson; or the teacher may have one lesson plan containing all five steps of the directed reading lesson. For example, the teacher might make a lesson plan in which the entire day is spent in motivating the students to want to read a particular science or mathematics lesson. Thus the preparation step of the directed reading lesson would take up all five steps of the daily lesson plan—that is, the teacher would have a *behavioral objective* that concerned motivating the students, a *pre-assessment* that assessed whether or not they were already motivated, a list of *materials* designed to create motivation, a *procedure* that used the materials to help motivate the class, and a *post-assessment* that assessed whether or not the students had become motivated as a result of the lesson.

In addition, when including a directed reading lesson within a lesson plan, the teacher is actually concerned with two types of behavioral objectives. The first deals with the content of the lesson; the second deals with the reading skill emphasized. Therefore if the teacher wanted the students to read about taxonomy but at the same time wanted them to learn how to use structural analysis when encountering unfamiliar words, he might have the following two behavioral objectives in the five-step lesson plan: (1) The student will be able to list members of at least two different subphyla in the phylum chordata. (2) The student will be able to identify the meanings of the Greek and Latin roots in at least eight out of ten given scientific words.

The sample lesson plans that follow will serve to illustrate these distinctions as well as to clarify the steps in both the lesson planning and the directed reading lesson. An important rule of thumb in each lesson plan is not to plan more objectives than can be evaluated in a lesson.

150

SAMPLE LESSON PLANS

Sample Lesson Plan 1—Mathematics

The following lesson plan includes an entire five-step directed reading lesson within the context of one day's lesson plan. Figure 7.1 illustrates schematically the relationship between the lesson plan format and the directed reading plan format.

(One day only on topic of functions)
Behavioral Objective: Using graphs
Pre-Assessment: Graphs drawn on mimeo
Materials: Overhead projector, transparencies, charts, textbooks
Procedure:
    Step 1—Preparation: (teacher shows entire class how to use graphs; explains functions)
    Step 2—Silent Reading: (in textbook on functions)
    Step 3—Oral Reading and Discussion: (discuss textbook assignment)
    Step 4—Follow-Up: (small group work for those who need extra help; all reread assignment to verify their solutions to the function problems)
    Step 5—Extension: (locate everyday functional relationships, e.g., carburetor size versus amount gas used)
Post-Assessment: Graphs drawn on mimeo

Lesson Plan Format	Directed Reading Lesson Format
Behavioral Objective	Step 1—Preparation
Pre-Assessment	Step 2—Silent Reading
Materials	Step 3—Oral Reading and Discussion
Procedure	Step 4—Follow-Up
Post-Assessment	Step 5—Extension Activities

Figure 7.1   Sample Lesson Plan—Mathematics

The lesson plan itself follows.

Behavioral Objectives: At the completion of this lesson, the student will be able to

1. Read graphs (reading objective).
2. Differentiate between graphs that show functions and graphs that do not show functions (content area objective).

Pre-Assessment: Hand each student a mimeographed sheet with four graphs drawn on it. Two of the graphs should show functions and two of the graphs should not. Those students who can correctly differentiate between the graphs showing functions and those which do not should go on to another lesson.

Materials: Overhead projector, color transparencies of graphs containing functions, charts on desirable weights for fifteen-year-olds, mathematics books.

Procedure

Step 1—Preparation
Place transparencies on the overhead and ask if anyone sees the relationship be-

151

tween body weight and amount of calories consumed. Ask students if they remember how to read graphs from past lessons. Ask one of the students to review techniques involved in reading graphs. Then ask students to use the graph on the transparency to locate the amount of calories needed to maintain a given weight (motivate and create awareness of needed reading skills).

Question students about their attempts to gain or lose weight. Elicit the information that weight versus calories consumed is a functional relationship because each individual's weight corresponds to a specific number of calories consumed (develop concepts involved).

Point out the words *function, domain,* and *range* and ask the class if they know the general meanings of the words. Ask them if they know the meanings of the words in relation to mathematics (identify problem words).

Tell the students that they are going to be reading a chapter on functions and that after reading their assignment, they should be able to differentiate between graphs that show functions and those that do not (set purposes for reading).

Step 2—Silent Reading

Remind the students of their purpose for reading and show them the problems they will be expected to solve after they finish their reading. Tell them that their main purpose in reading this time will be to differentiate between paired numbers that represent functions and paired numbers that do not. They will have to use that information to solve the problems at the end of the chapter.

Step 3—Oral Reading and Discussion

After the class has read the required pages, ask them what steps they think they need to take in order to answer the questions. Ask them if anyone located the definition of a function. Ask one student to read the passage containing the definition. Ask other students to react to the passage. Do they agree with the passage? Do they understand functions? Discuss best methods for solving the problems. Show them that drawing graphs can help them to visualize the concepts. Suggest that they draw graphs to answer the questions.

Step 4—Follow-up

Allow the students time to work the problems on functions. If some students seem to be having problems with the concepts, formulate a small group and discuss functions with them in more detail. Those who seem comfortable with the concept can continue with the original assignment. Those who finish early might be encouraged to look in magazines for examples of *functions* in everyday life. Have all students reread the chapter to determine whether their solutions to the problems are correct.

Step 5—Extension Activities

Ask students to choose a project related to functions and develop it. Suggest topics such as constructing a collage out of newspaper clippings of activities related to functions. Examples of clippings might be a modern-day car with a huge engine surrounded by various types of carburetors. A statement such as "the size of the carburetor affects the power of the engine" could be in big bold letters across the top. Others could be asked to construct or participate in a game in which situations concerning ordered pairs are written on index cards. For each situation correctly identified as a function, the student would receive a point. The student with the most points at the end of the game would be considered the winner.

Post-Assessment: Pass out mimeographed sheets containing four graphs, two of which are not functions. Those students who correctly differentiate between the graphs that contain functions and those that do not have met the objectives.

Sample Lesson Plan 2—Science

The relationship between three lesson plans on the topic of *biological classification* and the directed reading lesson is illustrated graphically in Figure 7.2.

(Day 1 of three-day lesson on topic of biological classification system)
Behavioral Objectives: Identifying details; categorizing
Pre-Assessment: Paragraphs written by students
Materials: Pictures and written descriptions of various animals
Procedure:
    Step 1—Preparation: (teacher motivation; students move through stations and then
      devise a classification system)
Post-Assessment: Development of feasible classification system by each group

(Day 2 of three-day lesson on same topic)
Behavioral Objective: Identifying Greek and Latin roots
Pre-Assessment: List of words containing Greek and Latin roots
Materials: Mimeo, textbook, chalkboard
    Step 1—Preparation: (teacher presentation on roots)
    Step 2—Silent Reading: (looking for roots in textbook)
    Step 3—Oral Reading and Discussion: (discuss lesson in text)
Post-Assessment: List of words containing Greek and Latin roots

(Day 3 of three-day lesson on same topic)
Behavioral Objective: Identifying point of view
Pre-Assessment: List of statements reflecting points of view
Materials: Textbook, mimeo
Procedure:
    Step 4—Follow-Up: (review of roots; class discussion on point of view of various
      authors on same topic)
    Step 5—Extension: (reread text to find point of view; select topics for projects to be
      completed at later date)
Post-Assessment: List of statements reflecting points of view

---

Lesson Plan Format	Directed Reading Lesson Format
Behavioral Objectives	Step 1—Preparation
Pre-Assessment	Step 2—Silent Reading
Materials	Step 3—Oral Reading and Discussion
Procedure	Step 4—Follow-Up
Post-Assessment	Step 5—Extension Activities

Figure 7.2 Sample Lesson Plan—Science

The following lesson plan is the first in a series of three on the same topic. It contains only one step of the directed reading lesson, Step 1—Preparation.

Behavioral Objectives: On completion of this lesson, the student will be able to

1. Identify relevant details and group them into categories (reading objective).
2. Establish at least four criteria that might be used to delineate a biological classification system.

Pre-Assessment: Ask the students to write a paragraph in which they describe at least four criteria for a biological classification system. Those students who are able to correctly describe at least four characteristics should go on to another lesson.

Materials: Pictures and written descriptions of animals from a variety of phyla.

Procedure

Step 1—Preparation

Ask the students how human beings and apes are the same. As they state characteristics, write these characteristics on the blackboard. Such aspects as the following should come out of the discussion: *skin structure* (do both have hair, feathers, or scales?), *appendages* (do both have legs, fins, or wings?), *skeletons* (do both have bones or cartilage?), *teeth* (do both have teeth?), *jaws* (do both possess a jaw?), *diet* (do both eat similar things?). Tell the students that these are the traits by which most animals can be grouped, and that their task for the day will be to distinguish between types of animals that possess each trait and subsequent classification systems that might be used (motivation and concept development).

Place the students into groups of two or three and assign each group to a station. Each station contains several short written descriptions accompanied by pictures of animals that belong in the same biological order (i.e., order rodentia at one table, order primate at a second table). The students are to construct a checklist of characteristics of the animals at each station. Every few minutes, ask the students to move to a new station. After all students have gone through all stations, give each group a few minutes to devise a classification system so that all the animals at each station may be classified into a specific order.

Post-Assessment: Collect the classification systems devised by each group. Then ask each group to discuss the classification system they developed. If at least four feasible criteria have been established by each group, the students have met the objectives.

Lesson Plan 3—Science

Lesson 3 takes place one day after Lesson 2. It encompasses three steps of a directed reading lesson: Step 1—Preparation, Step 2—Silent Reading, and Step 3—Oral Reading and Discussion. Though the lessons are correlated, the teacher has delineated new objectives for the day.

Behavioral Objectives: At the completion of this lesson the students will be able to

1. Identify the meanings of at least eight out of ten given Latin and Greek roots (reading objective).
2. Delineate at least one classification system used by an expert in the field of biological classification (content area objective).

Pre-Assessment: Give the students a list of ten words that have Greek and Latin roots used in the classification system. Ask the students to identify the meanings of the roots and then to discuss how these words are used by experts in the field of biological classification in order to delineate a classification system. Those students who know the meanings of eight out of ten of the Greek and Latin roots, and who are able to correctly discuss an expert's delineation of a biological classification system have met the objectives and should go on to another lesson.

Materials: Mimeographed sheet containing list of Latin and Greek roots and their meanings, biology textbook, chalkboard.

Procedure

Step 1 — Preparation

Point out to the students words such as *insectivora,* and *tubulidentata.* Show them that though science words are technical many of them may be learned by the use of structural analysis. Hand out a list that contains the following:

> *Carnivora* = Latin—*carnis,* flesh + *vorare,* to eat
> *examples* = seal, striped hyena, cheetah
>
> *Rodentia* = Latin—*rodere,* to gnaw
> *examples* = woodchuck, squirrel
>
> *Insectivora* = Latin—*insectum,* insect + *vorare,* to eat
> *examples* = mole, shrew
>
> *Tubulidentata* = Latin—*tubulus,* small tube + *dens,* tooth
> *example* = aardvark
>
> *Chiroptera* = Greek—*cheir,* hand + *pteron,* wing
> *example* = vampire bat
>
> *Dermoptera* = Greek—*derma,* skin + *pteron,* wing
> *example* = colugo

Point out to the students that each of these names is a label given to orders of animals in the subphylum vertebrata. If the students closely examine the root words, they should discover clues to the traits that caused the animals to be placed in a particular biological order. For example, members of order carnivora eat meat, members of order insectivora eat insects, members of order rodentia have chisel-like teeth that enable them to gnaw, and adult members of order tubulidentata have only a few teeth. Likewise the wings of members of order chiroptera are formed of webs of skin between the fingers, while the wings of order dermoptera are formed of webs of skin that almost surround the entire animal.

Have them look at the list of traits from the previous day and note if the classification systems they used took into consideration the types of teeth or food eaten by various types of animals that they grouped together. Ask the students to read the chapter to determine what traits were used by the scientist who devised the classification system delineated in their textbook.

Step 2—Silent Reading

Direct the students to read the assigned portion of the textbook. Remind them that after they finish reading they will be asked to discuss the classification system delineated by the author of the textbook.

Step 3—Oral Reading and Discussion

After the students have finished their reading, elicit comments about the traits the author used to place animals into the classification system. Discuss other ways in which animals could be classified. Compare the classification systems devised by the students the previous day with the system that was used by the author of the textbook. Ask the students to read specific passages from the text that discuss the rationale behind the author's classification system. Ask students to look for passages in which the author discusses other classification systems that could also be used.

Post-Assessment: Give the students a copy of the same words given to them as a pre-assessment and ask them to define them. If they can tell the meanings of eight of the ten Latin and Greek roots and correctly discuss at least one expert's delineation of a classification system, they have met the objectives.

Sample Lesson Plan 4—Science

Lesson plan 4 is the third in a series of three on the same material. It contains Step 4—Follow-up and Step 5—Extension Activities. Again it should be noted that although this lesson is correlated closely with the previous two, it contains different behavioral objectives.

Behavioral Objectives: At the completion of this lesson the student should be able to

1. Determine the point of view of at least two experts in the field of scientific taxonomy (reading objective).
2. Identify at least one reason why equally experienced scientific taxonomists may differ with one another about the classification of a particular species.

Pre-Assessment: Give the students a list of ten statements concerning various taxonomic classifications. Those students who are able to correctly identify the taxonomic point of view reflected in eight of the ten statements should go on to another lesson.

Materials: Textbook, mimeographed sheet containing Latin and Greek roots from previous day.

Procedure

Step 4—Follow-up

Ask the students to take out the list of Latin and Greek roots they were given the day before. Ask a few of the students to orally review the meanings of some of the roots in relation to the traits of the animal it represents. Remind the class of the importance of the skill of structural analysis in learning the meanings of scientific words. Ask the class if they know how to determine an author's point of view. Discuss how their own points of view were reflected in the classification systems they devised while at their group stations two days before. Ask one of the students to review techniques involved in determining an author's point of view. Show the class other ways by which an author's point of view can be determined. Have individuals read aloud from the text some of the passages located the previous day that indicate that more than one classification system for scientific taxonomy exists. Discuss what animals would be classified into different species or orders if a point of view other than the author's had been emphasized in the textbook.

Step 5—Extension Activities

Have the students reread the same chapter for a new purpose. Tell them they should locate as many different points of view on biological classification as they can. After they locate several, have a large group discussion to synthesize the students' findings.

Obtain several college biology textbooks and have the students compare the types of classification systems used. Discuss the idea of survival of the fittest and ask each student to select an animal and trace its development. Relate it to animals of higher and lower orders and try to determine its chance of survival. Discuss what needs to be done if the animal is to survive. Try to discover characteristics of animals that live in the city, such as the rat, and discover or determine what enables them to survive and/or thrive in that environment. Let the students select projects in which they obtain pictures or slides of animals from almost all the phyla. Let them present their pictures as a collage for the bulletin board. Some of the species could be reclassified into new species with the statement "points of view vary from classification system to classification system."

Post-Assessment: Give the students the same list of ten statements that they were given as a pre-assessment. Those who are able to correctly identify the taxonomic point of view reflected in eight out of ten statements have met the objectives.

Sample Lesson Plan 5—Language Arts

The relationship between two lesson plans on the topic of Faulkner and the directed reading lesson is illustrated schematically in Figure 7.3.

This lesson plan contains the first three steps of a directed reading lesson: Step 1—Preparation, Step 2—Silent Reading, and Step 3—Oral Reading and Discussion.

157

```
(Day 1 in a two-day lesson plan on topic of Faulkner)
Behavioral Objective: Identifying tone and mood
Pre-Assessment: Checklist containing traits that characterize an author's style
Materials: tape player, tape recordings, passages from Faulkner
Procedure:
    Step 1—Preparation: (teacher-led discussion; play tape recording of excerpt; students
        write paragraphs and discuss them in small groups)
    Step 2—Silent Reading: (in Chapter 20 of Light in August)
    Step 3—Oral Reading and Discussion: (discuss reading assignment)
Post-Assessment: Not to be completed until day 2

(Day 2 in two-day lesson on topic of Faulkner)
Behavioral Objective: Identifying tone and mood
Pre-Assessment: Given on day 1
Materials: Themes written by students for homework
Procedure:
    Step 4—Follow-Up: (discuss and rewrite themes in small groups; large-group sharing
        follows)
    Step 5—Extension Activities: (select topics for projects to be completed at a later
        date; e.g., rewrite Faulkner passage in different style to reflect different tone
        and mood)
Post-Assessment: Theme handed in by students at end of class period
```

Lesson Plan Format	Directed Reading Lesson Format
Behavioral Objectives Pre-Assessment Materials Procedure Post-Assessment	Step 1—Preparation Step 2—Silent Reading Step 3—Oral Reading and Discussion Step 4—Follow-Up Step 5—Extension Activities

Figure 7.3   Sample Lesson Plan—Language Arts

Behavioral Objectives: At the completion of this lesson the student will be able to

1. Identify tone and mood (reading objective).
2. List at least three traits that characterize the writing of Faulkner (content objective).

Pre-Assessment: Give the students a list of twenty traits that may characterize an author's style. Ask the students to put check marks by those that characterize Faulkner. Those students who mark at least ten of the twelve Faulkner characteristics correctly may go on to another lesson.

Materials: Several passages from Faulkner, tape recordings of each passage, and tape player.

Procedure

Step 1—Preparation

Ask the students what they would be thinking about if they knew they had only a few moments to live. Have them write one-word images of what they would think would be flashing through their minds. Ask them to exchange papers with a neighbor and see how they differed from one another. Tell them that the selection they will be reading contains a passage that deals with the thoughts of a main character who is dying.

Play a tape recording of an excerpt from *Light in August* (see excerpt on page 126 of Chapter 6). Explain to the students that Faulkner used words to convey much more than just a literal meaning. Discuss the precise use of words and the implied meanings of phrases such as *phantom dust, whipping ribbons, eager lances, soundless yelling,* and *skyward sucking* (identify problem words).

Discuss with the students how different authors use different types of words and sentence structures to convey their meanings. Ask each student to write a short paragraph integrating all the words they used to describe their last thoughts. Break the class into small groups and ask them to select one passage from each group to read to the remainder of the class. Compare the difference in word usage and sentence structure. Use the blackboard to list traits that appear (e.g., short words, long words, compound sentences, simple sentences, figurative language). Discuss the effect of each of these devices upon the audience. Ask the authors why they chose the words they did (develop concepts involved).

Tell the students that they are to read Chapter 20 of William Faulkner's *Light in August* and analyze his prose style. Tell them that after they have read it, they will be expected to write a theme summarizing their analysis (set a purpose for reading).

Discuss with the students what types of word choice and sentence choice affect mood and tone in a passage. Review connotative language and the use of similes and metaphors. Tell the students that unless they are able to identify imagery used to develop tone and mood, they will be unable to fully describe traits reflective of William Faulkner's style of writing (create awareness of needed reading skills).

Step 2—Silent Reading

After restating their purpose for reading Chapter 20, allow the students time to read their book. Remind them that they will be asked to write a theme on traits found in Faulkner's style after they finish their reading.

Step 3—Oral Reading and Discussion

Refer to the traits previously listed on the blackboard and ask the students if anyone can find an example of any of them in Chapter 20. Call upon several volunteers to read aloud sentences that reflect those traits. Ask other students to react to the oral reading of the sentences and the interpretation as intended by Faulkner. Discuss what reactions these traits cause the reader to have.

Post-Assessment: This is a two-day lesson plan and will not be post-assessed until the next day.

Sample Lesson Plan 6—Language Arts

Sample lesson plan 6 is the second lesson in a series of two. Step 4—Follow-up and Step 5—Extension Activities are included. The lesson plan is designed to be completed in two days. Therefore, in this case, the behavioral objectives, pre-assessment, and post-assessment are the same for both days.

Behavioral Objectives: The same as the previous day.

Pre-Assessment: The same as the previous day.

Materials: Themes written by students.

Procedure

Step 4—Follow-up

Assemble the class members into groups of four or five and let them read each others' themes. After twenty minutes, ask for feedback from each group. As one person from each group reports, place the traits concerning Faulkner's writing style on the blackboard. Discuss in a large group the composite list of the traits of Faulkner's style. Allow students time, if they so wish, to rewrite their themes before they hand them in.

Step 5—Extension Activities

Let the students choose which project they would like to do: (1) Read a book by Faulkner and verify traits identified in the theme. (2) Rewrite Chapter 20 in a completely different style and see how the meaning is affected. (3) Continue the chapter using a style imitating Faulkner's in order to extend the idea of what happens to the main characters after death. (4) Make a tape recording of several key passages in *Light in August* in order to use oral interpretation to reflect many different levels of meaning.

Post-Assessment: If the theme written by the student correctly identifies at least three traits used by Faulkner, the objectives have been successfully met.

Sample Lesson Plan 7—Social Studies

This lesson plan is the first in a series of three. It contains the first step in a directed reading lesson, Step 1—Preparation. Step 2—Silent Reading is to be done by the students at home. The relationship between three lesson plans on the topic of the Truman era and the directed reading lesson is illustrated graphically in Figure 7.4 at the top of page 161.

Behavioral Objectives: At the completion of this lesson, students will be able to

1. Predict outcomes (reading objective).
2. Describe at least three projections that they think will be made about Truman in 1985 (content objective).

Pre-Assessment: Ask the students to write a paragraph estimating what the United States will think of Harry Truman in 1985. Those that are able to cite specific details from 1945 to make believable predictions may go on to another lesson.

```
(Day 1 in three-day lesson on topic of Truman era)
Behavioral Objective:  Predicting outcomes
Pre-Assessment:  Paragraph written by students
Materials:  Film, textbook, magazine articles
Procedure:
    Step 1—Preparation: (show film on Truman; teacher-led discussion on predicting
        outcomes)
    Step 2—Silent Reading: (in textbooks on Truman era)
Post-Assessment:  Not given until third day

(Day 2 in three-day lesson on same topic)
Behavioral Objective:  Predicting outcomes
Pre-Assessment:  Given on day 1
Materials:  Same as on day 1
Procedure:
    Step 3—Oral Reading and Discussion: (entire class discussion on outcomes predicted
        from reading assignment on the Truman era)
    Step 4—Follow-Up: (students construct projects that predict what history will think
        of Truman in 1985)
Post-Assessment:  Not given until day 3

(Day 3 in three-day lesson on same topic)
Behavioral Objective:  Predicting outcomes
Pre-Assessment:  Given on day 1
Materials:  Same as on day 1
Procedure:
    Step 4—Follow-Up: (students show their projects to the class)
    Step 5—Extension Activities: (class discussion comparing Truman to other Presidents;
        debate and/or panel discussion on McCarthy's tactics during Truman era and
        charges against CIA in 1975)
Post-Assessment:  Project completed by students
```

Lesson Plan Format	Directed Reading Lesson Format
Behavioral Objective Pre-Assessment Materials Procedure Post-Assessment	Step 1—Preparation Step 2—Silent Reading Step 3—Oral Reading and Discussion Step 4—Follow-Up Step 5—Extension Activities

Figure 7.4 Sample Lesson Plan—Social Studies

Materials: Film, current magazine articles on the play *Give 'Em Hell, Harry,* textbook.

Procedure

Step 1—Preparation

Throughout the classroom, display pictures showing James Whitmore in the play *Give 'Em Hell, Harry.* Ask the students if anyone has seen the play. Discuss why it is so popular (motivate).

Show film on Truman. Discuss how his decisions in 1945 affected what is happening today (develop concepts).

Point out the jargon in the chapter. Discuss the connotation of words such as *Dixiecrats* and *Communism.* Make certain that all students understand the concepts behind the term *cold war* (identify problem words).
Tell the students that after they read the chapter, they will be asked to write a statement predicting the view that the United States will have of Truman in 1985. Tell them that they can use any means possible to make this statement (e.g., collages, posters, essays, films, slides) but that it must be supported through the use of factual evidence concerning Truman (set purposes for reading).

Discuss the ways to predict outcomes. Select an action of Truman's and illustrate the consequences of that event in current world policies. Point out factors that could have been used to predict that the historical outcome would have been what it turned out to be. Together, discuss what future consequences of that same act will probably evolve (create awareness of reading skills involved).

Step 2—Silent Reading

Remind the students of their purpose for reading the chapter and, if there is time, allow them to start on their reading. They are to have the chapter read before they return to class the next day.

Post-Assessment: Post-assessment will be accomplished by successful completion of the project on the third day of the series of three lessons.

Sample Lesson Plan 8—Social Studies

This lesson is the second in a series of three. It contains steps three and four. In this case, the behavioral objectives, pre-assessment, materials, and post-assessment are the same for all three days.

Behavioral Objectives: Same as the previous day.

Pre-Assessment: Same as the previous day.

Materials: Same as the previous day.

Procedure

Step 3—Oral Reading and Discussion

Ask the students to point out events in recent history that could have been predicted from events that occurred in 1945. Have them read aloud the passages that deal with those past events. Let other students react to whether or not they think the current event could be predicted from the past event and why they think so.

Step 4—Follow-up

Allow the students time to construct essays, collages, or projects that predict what the United States will think of Truman in 1985.

Post-Assessment: Post-assessment will be accomplished by successful completion of the project on the third day.

Sample Lesson Plan 9—Social Studies

This lesson is the third in a series of three. It contains steps four and five of a directed reading lesson. In this case, the behavioral objectives, pre-assessment, materials, and post-assessment are the same for all three days.

Behavioral Objectives: Same as day one.

Pre-Assessment: Same as day one.

Materials: Same as day one.

Procedure

Step 4—Follow-up

The students show their projects to other members of the class.

Step 5—Extension Activities

Ask the students to compare some of the modern Presidents with Truman and attempt to predict what the United States will think of other Presidents forty years after their administration. Point out that during Truman's era, Senator Joseph McCarthy attempted to purge members of the American Communist party. Organize a debate on the issue of McCarthy or let the students organize a panel discussion on the relationships between tactics used by McCarthy and charges against the CIA in 1975.

Post-Assessment: If the projects completed by the students reflect enough specific details from 1945 to make their predictions believable, they have met the objectives.

References and Bibliography

Aukerman, R. C. *Reading in the Secondary School Classroom.* New York: McGraw-Hill, 1972.

Bamman, H., Dawson, M., and McGovern, J. *Fundamentals of Basic Reading Instruction.* 3rd ed. New York: McKay, 1973.

Bragdon, H. W., McCutchen, S. P., and Cole, C. W. *History of a Free People.* New York: Macmillan, 1973.

BSCS. *Biological Science: An Ecological Approach.* 3rd ed. New York: Rand McNally, 1973.

Burmeister, L. E. *Reading Strategies for Secondary School Teachers.* Reading, Mass.: Addison-Wesley, 1974.

Burron, A., and Claybaugh, A. *Using Reading to Teach Subject Matter: Fundamentals for Content Teachers.* Columbus, Ohio: Merrill, 1974.

Clemens, S. L. *Adventures of Huckleberry Finn.* New York: Grosset, 1948.

Cushenbery, D. *Remedial Reading in the Secondary School.* West Nyack, N.Y.: Parker, 1972.

Dickens, C. *A Tale of Two Cities.* St. Louis, Mo.: Webster, 1954.

Faulkner, W. *Light in August.* rev. ed. New York: Random House, 1959.

Fleay, D. "Strange Animals of Australia." *National Geographic* (September 1963), 388–411.

Gallu, S. *Give 'Em Hell, Harry.* New York: Viking Press, 1975.

Herber, H. *Teaching Reading in Content Areas.* Englewood Cliffs, N. J.: Prentice-Hall, 1970.

Johnson, D. A., and Rising, G. R. *Guidelines for Teaching Mathematics.* 2nd ed. Belmont, Calif.: Wadsworth, 1972.

Karlin, R. *Teaching Reading in High School.* 2nd ed. Indianapolis, Ind.: Bobbs-Merrill, 1972.

Lawrence, J., and Lee, R. E. *Inherit the Wind.* New York: Bantam, 1969.

Olson, A., and Ames, W. *Teaching Reading Skills in Secondary Schools.* Scranton, Pa.: Intext Educational Publishers, 1972.

Olson, A., and Ames, W. *Teaching Reading Skills in Secondary Schools: Readings.* Scranton, Pa.: Intext Educational Publishers, 1970.

Robinson, H., and Thomas, E., eds. *Fusing Reading Skills and Content.* Newark, Del.: International Reading Association, 1969.

Robinson, H. *Teaching Reading and Study Strategies: The Content Areas.* Boston: Allyn & Bacon, 1975.

Thomas, E., and Robinson, H. *Improving Reading in Every Class: A Source Book for Teachers.* Boston: Allyn & Bacon, 1972.

Van Engen, H., et al. *Mathematics Concepts Application.* Glenview, Ill.: Scott, Foresman, 1969.

Chapter 8

Adapting Content Area Materials to Student's Reading Ability

Participants should have successfully completed the objectives for Chapters 6 and 7 or should have an understanding of the reading problems inherent to the content areas before beginning this chapter.

Rationale 8.2

Because there is a wide diversity among students' reading abilities in all content areas, special provisions should be made for the student who reads above or below grade level. The purpose of this chapter is to acquaint the reader with several strategies for adapting content area instruction to meet the reading needs of individual students.

Objectives 8.3

On successful completion of this chapter, the participant will be able to:

1. Describe how a content area informal reading inventory can be constructed, administered, and interpreted.
2. Describe how the following components involved in lesson planning help the teacher design content area lessons that meet the reading needs of various students: (1) a designated purpose, (2) the use of appropriate materials, and (3) the guidance of student's reading.

3. Discuss the following ways in which content area materials may be differentiated to meet the reading needs of various students: (1) single materials approach, (2) multilevel, single materials approach, and (3) multilevel, multiple materials approach.

4. Discuss the relationship between a teacher's conceptual framework in designing a lesson and the types of materials selected for instructional purposes.

5. Identify at least two methods for locating various content area materials on a variety of reading levels.

6. Utilize a checklist to help match instructional materials with the specific purposes for their use.

7. Discuss the purpose and construction of a guided reading sheet.

8. Given a description of a specific student in a specific content area, discuss how to design content area instruction appropriate to his reading level.

9. Given a description of a specific content area reading program, evaluate it according to issues discussed in this chapter.

10. (On the lines below, add other objectives according to your instructor's directions.)_____

_____

11. _____

_____

12. _____

_____

13. _____

_____

* * * * * * * * * * * * * *

Chapter 13, Experience 8 extends Chapter 8 with these performance/consequence objectives:

14. Construct, administer, score, and interpret an informal inventory based on a content area textbook.

and/or

15. Design and use three guided reading sheets according to the following criteria:

a. Select a specific content area lesson and identify one reading skill particularly needed to understand the lesson.

b. Construct a lesson plan that uses at least one step of a directed reading lesson in a format that includes a behavioral objective, a pre-assessment, a list of materials, a description of procedure, and a post-assessment.

c. Include in the procedure section of the lesson plan three guided reading sheets—one for the below grade level reader, one for the grade level reader, and one for the above grade level reader.

* * * * * * * * * * * * * *

Self Pre-Assessment 8.4

Can you complete all the activities listed in **Objectives 8.3**? Answer "yes," "no," or "not certain."

If you answered "yes" to the question, complete the enabling activities required by your instructor and take the Post-Assessment on the date assigned by him.

If you answered "no," refer to **Enabling Activities 8.5.** If you decide to do any activities that are not required, select those that best suit you as a learner. You need not complete all the optional activities or all parts of a particular optional activity. As soon as you have the information you need to complete the objectives, answer "yes" to the **Self Pre-Assessment 8.4** question and stop the activity.

If you answered "not certain" to the question, refer to **Enabling Activities 8.5.** Select the enabling activity that best suits your style of learning and peruse it. Then make a firm "yes" or "no" answer and proceed accordingly.

Enabling Activities 8.5

Complete only as many of the activities listed below as are required and which you need in order to meet the objectives.

1. *Enabling activity one* is a *reading* alternative. This is **Information Given 8.6.** It is a brief overview of various strategies that may be used to differentiate instruction by reading levels in the content area classroom.
2. *Enabling activity two* is another *reading* option. In this case, the material to be read is one of the textbooks used to expand the theoretical background for this course. See chart on inside front cover for keying in textbooks that may be used.
3. *Enabling activity three* is a *class session* option. Attend the class session(s) on the date(s), at the time(s), and at the place(s) announced.

| _____ | _____ | _____ |
| (Date) | (Time) | (Place) |

| _____ | _____ | _____ |
| (Date) | (Time) | (Place) |

| _____ | _____ | _____ |
| (Date) | (Time) | (Place) |

4. *Enabling activity four* (These lines are left blank so that you may add other enabling activities as suggested by your instructor.)_____

_____

_____

5. *Enabling activity five*_____

_____

6. *Enabling activity six* _____

_____

Now that you have completed the appropriate number of required and/or optional learning alternatives, look back at **Self Pre-Assessment 8.4.** If you feel you can answer "yes" to all of the questions, you are ready to proceed to the Post-Assessment. This may be given to you immediately or after completion of a series of chapters.

Information Given 8.6
Adapting Content Area Materials
to Student's Reading Ability

Mr. Lentz's eleventh grade American history class was involved in a myriad of simultaneous activities. Joe and Sally were listening to a tape recorder and following along in their textbooks. Randy was sketching a 1945 Chevrolet, using an advertisement in a 1945 newspaper to accompany a research project on transportation which he was completing. Mr. Lentz and Lorraine were discussing material concerning Truman that Mr. Lentz had copied from a fifth grade American history book and placed in a manila folder (so that Lorraine would not know the material's source). The remainder of the class was reading a variety of materials according to Mr. Lentz's directions.

By having his American history students perform all these activities, Mr. Lentz was differentiating instruction for them. His instructional strategies included the following procedures:

1. *Diagnose Before Instruction.* In order to determine the materials he could use to help teach his content area, Mr. Lentz spent the

first few days of the school year assessing his students' reading levels.

2. *Design Instructional Strategies.* Once he had determined each student's reading level, he did the following:

    (a) *Designated a Purpose for Reading*—Every student in the previously described classroom setting had been directed to read with the purpose of identifying at least three of Truman's actions in 1945 that affect current United States political policy.

    (b) *Used Appropriate Materials*—Though the students were reading for the same purpose, they were using a variety of instructional tools. Joe and Sally were listening to a tape recorder while following along in the grade level text; Randy was using a 1945 newspaper; and Lorraine was reading material from a fifth grade history book. Likewise, the other class members were reading a variety of materials, all of which focused upon Truman as President.

    (c) *Guided Students' Reading*—All the students in class had been given verbal or written instructions designed to help them locate the material on Truman that they had been asked to read. Not all the students were given guidance in the same manner. Each method of guidance had been determined by Mr. Lentz according to the reading needs of the individual. For example, since Lorraine read at the fifth grade level, her instructions and reading tasks were geared to fifth grade reading skills. Likewise, since Randy read at the eleventh grade level, his instructional and reading tasks were appropriate for eleventh grade reading skills.

3. *Diagnose After Instruction.* After all the students had completed their assignments in the manner designated as appropriate by him, Mr. Lentz diagnosed the youngsters to see whether they had learned the material as intended.

Each of the above steps used by Mr. Lentz will be discussed in more detail in the remainder of this chapter.

DIAGNOSING BEFORE INSTRUCTION

Mr. Lentz had been teaching for several years and he knew that each of his classes would include students whose abilities spanned a wide range. Therefore, at the outset of each school year, Mr. Lentz assessed his students' reading levels. He wanted to determine the exact grade levels of the materials that he would need to obtain for those students who could not read the basic class materials. His two main instruments for determining reading level were standardized reading tests made available to him by the school and a content area IRI that he had constructed himself.

Standardized Tests

The school had purchased several standardized tests; but Mr. Lentz knew that many selections used to assess reading level are literary and, therefore, do not adequately assess a student's competence with other content areas. However some of the tests do use selections from a variety of content fields, and teachers who are careful to use this kind of test increase their chances of diagnosing their students' reading level in a specific content area. Even tests that do include reading selections from many content areas seldom break reading skills down into interpretable separate scores; that is, if the grade level score for a student is given as fifth grade, it might be that the reading level on the history section was actually seventh grade level, and that the total of all the other content selections lowered the average score. If teachers closely examine the test items, they can usually identify the specific items that assess skills in their own content area and, therefore, arrive at a better estimate of the student's competence in that area of reading (see Chapter 5 for more information on this topic).

Content Area IRI

A great many hard to isolate factors influence a student's ability to understand textbooks. An assessment of a student's ability to read the materials he or she is actually going to be asked to use is probably a better way to estimate the reading level of the content area material that can be read independently by the students. Also, since different content areas emphasize different reading skills and experiential backgrounds, many students who do well in one content area can hardly read another. Teachers who use an IRI based on their content areas have the best chance of identifying the students who cannot read the instructional materials to be used in their classroom.

Construction of a Content Area IRI

Mr. Lentz used the following plan to construct his content area IRI. He tried to select material from the texts that he would actually be using. Since his topic in September was the Truman era, he tried to find material on a variety of reading levels that supported that topic. He then checked reading level by applying a readability formula to the material or by relying upon information given by the publishers of the material. Once he determined that he had books about Truman ranging from first to twelfth grade reading level, he used excerpts from each to determine the students' abilities to cope with the material. He selected two passages of about one hundred words each from the history textbooks. Then he constructed ten comprehension questions to accompany one of the passages at each level.

The administration of the IRI helped Mr. Lentz to locate each student's instructional reading level. His procedure for doing this was very similar to the administration of the IRI described in Chapter 5 of this text. If the youngsters could answer seven out of ten questions on the silent reading and could correctly pronounce ninety-five out of one hundred words on the oral reading, he assumed that they could read the content area text. If they could not answer the questions and pronounce the words, he felt that they might have trouble with the text, and that he needed more information about their reading skills as soon as possible. He proceeded to administer the other IRI silent and oral reading passages exactly as discussed in Chapter 5 of this text, until he was able to determine the *instructional* level of each of the problem readers.

In addition to helping him determine whether or not the student could read the content area materials to be used in the classroom, the IRI also helped Mr. Lentz identify each student's *capacity* level, or the level at which the student could understand materials read to him. Mr. Lentz's procedure in determining student listening capacity with the textbook was relatively simple. He read a passage aloud to the student and then asked him questions about it. If the student could answer seven out of ten questions correctly, Mr. Lentz determined that he could understand the material, although he could not read it. If the student comprehended less than seven out of ten questions, Mr. Lentz determined that factors other than mere visual decoding of print were involved. But the outcome was the same: the student could not use the grade level text in either written or oral format.

Ascertaining Instructional Needs

Mr. Lentz decided not to use a standardized reading test and instead used a content area IRI to diagnose the instructional reading level of every student in his class. In addition, he diagnosed the capacity reading level of those students who could not read the content area text at an instructional level. He tried to view each score as an estimate of reading level; and he knew that he should use it only as a flexible guideline for designing instruction.

In addition, he knew he needed to consider the four major readability factors discussed in Chapter 6 of this text before he made any judgments about which materials and media to assign each student. These factors are (1) factors inherent to the student, such as interest in the topic, background with the topic, and relevancy of the times to the topic; (2) factors inherent to the textbook, which include vocabulary difficulty, sentence complexity, and high-level abstract concepts; (3) instructional focus in which the teacher ignores the reading skills needed to understand the content area; and (4) inadequate use of textbook aids caused by ineffective teacher use of the textbook.

After examining all the factors involved in readability, as well as the students' instructional and capacity levels on the content area IRI, Mr. Lentz made the following assumptions about several of the students in his class.

Joe's instructional reading level was grade four, but his capacity reading level was well above grade level. Mr. Lentz felt that Joe might be able to read the sixth grade level text when the class studied Viet Nam because his brother had been in the service there, and Joe talked a great deal about the war and the country. However, most of Joe's instructional reading assignments in history would probably have to be done with fourth grade material. Because Joe's capacity level was high enough to understand the regular textbook, Mr. Lentz had read the chapter on Truman into a tape recorder and asked Joe to follow along in the text while listening to the tape.

Sally did extremely well on both portions of the IRI. However she disliked reading and frequently did not complete her textbook reading assignments. In addition, she seemed to learn best in listening situations. Therefore, though she did well on the test material, Mr. Lentz told her she had a choice of learning alternatives: she could either read her text or listen to it on a tape. Hence the audiotape that had been prepared for Joe became a motivational device as well as an effective means of learning required course objectives for Sally.

Randy did very well on the IRI; but from conversations with other teachers, Mr. Lentz knew that Randy was academically unmotivated and was thinking about quitting school to work full time as an auto mechanic. He had talked to Mr. Lentz about enrolling in the vocational education program so that he could go to school part time while learning a vocation. Mr. Lentz informed him that he would have to make good grades to stay in the program. This provided some extrinsic motivation, and Randy seemed to be doing all his assignments. In addition, Mr. Lentz tried to capitalize on Randy's interest in cars by trying to make assignments from the text deal with the topic of cars whenever possible. Therefore Randy had been assigned an extension activity to research transportation during the Truman era. As part of his assignment, he was sketching a 1945 Chevrolet to put up on the bulletin board for the rest of the class.

Lorraine's capacity level and instructional reading level were grade five. Mr. Lentz located Truman-related material for Lorraine in a fifth grade text. Although Lorraine was able to read the material independently, Mr. Lentz usually tried to sit and talk with her after her reading in order to fill in any details that were considered important in the eleventh grade text but that were not supplied by the fifth grade text.

Gene's reading ability was well above grade level on both portions of the IRI. In addition, he was an extremely motivated student who enjoyed history, was quite knowledgeable about the Truman administration, and had already read the material concerning Truman in the grade level textbook. Mr. Lentz obtained a short paperback book that extended topics discussed in the classroom textbook. Gene read the paperback according to directions on a guided reading sheet given to him by Mr. Lentz.

Most of the other students in Mr. Lentz's class were diagnosed by him in much the same way. Not all the students worked in small groups or with special aids. The majority worked with the grade level text according to directions given to them by Mr. Lentz.

The situations just described not only illustrate how instruction may be differentiated but also reflect techniques that the classroom teacher may use to lessen the negative effect of peer pressure upon students who do not read as well as others. Mr. Lentz knew that adolescents are acutely aware of the opinions of their peers. He tried to be very careful when he differentiated instruction so that he did not cause any of the youngsters to be the object of teasing by their peers. When dealing with youngsters who read below grade level, he made certain that the books he selected for their use did not appear to be babyish. For example, the fifth grade history textbook material that he used with Lorraine was obviously geared to a fifth grade child. Therefore, Mr. Lentz copied the material from the textbook and placed it in a manila folder so that it would not be so easily identifiable as fifth grade material. In some cases he was able to locate material written especially for eleventh grade students who read on a fifth grade level, and no effort to disguise reading level had to be made.

He gave students of all reading levels a variety of means for learning the course content. Because most students had occasionally listened to audio-taped materials, had been assigned materials handed to them in manila folders, and had read paperback books instead of the regular classroom textbook, the weak readers who could not be assigned the grade level textbook looked less obvious to their peers. In addition, by having good readers, such as Sally, listen to audiotapes with poor readers, like Joe, Mr. Lentz was lessening the effect of the stigma that learning by listening is an activity just for poor readers.

DESIGNING INSTRUCTIONAL STRATEGIES

Once Mr. Lentz had determined the best way to help expose each of the youngsters to the materials he had available, he began to design his instructional strategies. The three main components of his instructional strategies were (1) designate the purpose for gaining the information discussed in the materials, (2) use appropriate materials to meet the purpose and the needs of the students, (3) develop methods of guiding the students' reading in order to meet the designated purpose.

Designate Purpose

Before assigning any materials, Mr. Lentz carefully looked over his lesson plans, the curriculum guide, and the materials he had available to determine exactly what he wanted the students to know after they had finished reading the unit. Once he determined, for example, that he wanted them to read the material about Truman in order to identify several of Truman's actions that have had a great effect upon the world today, he could ask students to read specifically for that purpose.

173

Use Appropriate Materials

Mr. Lentz tried to take the needs of *all* the students into account when designing instruction. He knew that in order to do this effectively he had to organize his classroom so that he could efficiently use materials appropriate to a variety of students' listening and reading levels. He felt that he needed some sort of instructional focus around which to design the instruction within the organizational pattern. The discussion that follows entails his organization, his conceptual framework for using the materials, and his methods for locating the appropriate materials.

Three Approaches for Organizing Materials

Mr. Lentz relied upon three major approaches for organizing his materials in the content area: (1) the single materials approach, (2) the multilevel, single materials approach, and (3) the multilevel, multiple materials approach.

Single Materials Approach. In this approach, Mr. Lentz used the American history book supplied by the school as his basic teaching resource. After he determined his purpose for asking the students to read the text, he reviewed his diagnosis of the reading abilities of the students in the class and tried to vary instruction accordingly.

The youngsters who could not read the textbook but were diagnosed at grade level reading capacity were given the information contained in a variety of ways. He usually used at least one or more of the following alternatives in one way or another throughout the year, but did not do each with every lesson.

1. He would read the textbook to the group of students who could not read the text, while the rest of the youngsters were doing silent reading. Though Mr. Lentz was doing the reading aloud, the youngsters were asked to follow along in their books. He felt this helped them increase their reading skills by allowing them to see the words in print when he pronounced them. In addition, since they were listening for a specific purpose, they were able to locate many of the answers to questions related to that purpose when they heard the appropriate portions of the chapter. These students were included in any follow-up discussion in much the same manner as those who read the material independently.

2. Since the oral reading method took up much of his teaching time, Mr. Lentz audiotaped his own summary of some of the chapters and allowed small groups to listen to this material while he was working with other groups. Because he had used the same textbook several times, he made a point to audiotape several lessons a year so that eventually he would have the entire book summarized on audiotape.

3. In addition, he had talked with the drama teacher, whose students needed more practice in oral interpretation. Mr. Lentz and the drama teacher arranged for a group of drama students to audiotape some of the content area chapters. In that way, several of the members of the drama class received needed practice with oral reading.

174

4. Another strategy used by Mr. Lentz was to pair his own students and have the better reader read to the weaker one. This had some social implications because some parents did not like their children always being helped by other children, and some youngsters resented being given help. Therefore, he established a routine in which every youngster helped every other youngster in some way. (See end of this chapter for more ideas on ways in which peers can be shown how to help each other.)

Multilevel, Single Materials Approach. The techniques described above would only be appropriate to the students who could understand the materials when they were put into audiomedia. For those students who could not understand the material in an auditory format, Mr. Lentz knew that he would have to gather materials written on easier levels. IIe had several options for doing this. Some of the commercial publishers had the same books available at several different readability levels. For example, the novel *A Tale of Two Cities* by Charles Dickens is available on a fourth grade level, a seventh grade level, and a tenth grade level. Mr. Lentz could also use the same history textbook with all his students, but some would get the third grade version of the text, others the fifth grade version, and so forth.

Since the same text was not readily available on more than one level, Mr. Lentz used his classroom textbook as his basic instructional tool by adapting the book to an easier reading level. In order to do this, Mr. Lentz looked at one of the readability formulas (see Chapter 6) and noted that word and sentence complexity were the two factors primarily used to calculate difficulty. He used this knowledge to adapt Passage One to the simpler form of Passage Two as shown in Figure 8.1.

It can be seen that Mr. Lentz simply shortened the sentences and substituted simpler words for some of the more complex terms. Hence, he was able to reduce the original tenth grade reading level of the passage to fifth grade reading level (as calculated by the Fry Readability Graph discussed in Chapter 6 of this text).

It is interesting to note that when the passage is rewritten, the concepts become less abstract and, hence, easier to understand. For example, "Republican overconfidence" was changed to read, "the Republicans were very sure they would win. Therefore, they did not campaign as much as they should have." Much less is left to inference in the rewritten example. The student does not have to picture *overconfidence* in his mind, but is given tangible examples of *overconfidence*.

Multilevel, Multiple Materials Approach. When teachers use several editions of the same textbook, each written on a different reading level, they are using a multilevel, single materials approach. However, when they use a variety of textbooks, each written on a different reading level, they are using a multilevel, multiple materials approach. For example, the English teacher who obtains and uses a third grade version, a fifth grade version, and a ninth grade version of *Huckleberry Finn* is using the multilevel, single materials approach. The teacher who obtains and uses a third grade book about the life of Mark Twain by author A, a fifth grade book about the life of Mark Twain by author B, and a ninth grade book about the life of Mark Twain by author C is using a multilevel, multiple materials approach. Though the topic is the same, each author

175

may present Mark Twain in a different manner; therefore the material is different as well as multilevel.

Passage One — Tenth Grade Level*

The election was so close that the result was uncertain until the day after the polls closed. Although he lost four southern states to Thurmond and a million northern votes to Wallace, Truman was returned to office. Among the explanations for this amazing upset were Republican overconfidence; successful Democratic efforts to get voters to the polls; and the continuing strength of the New Deal, especially in major agricultural states. The three-way Democratic split that looked ruinous may have been a blessing in disguise. The Dixiecrat rebellion helped Truman's cause with Negro voters in the North; Wallace's campaign blunted efforts to pin the Communist label on the President. The professional pollsters were caught off base because they failed to note a last-minute swing of undecided voters toward the Democratic column. In any case, the result was an immense personal triumph for Truman: his whistle-stop campaign had turned the tide.

*From *History of a Free People* by H.W. Bragdon, S.P. McCutchen, and C.W. Cole, p. 700. Copyright © 1973, Macmillan Publishing Co., Inc. Used with permission.

Passage Two — Adapted to Fifth Grade Level

The election was close. The results could not be guessed. No one was sure who won until the day after the election. Truman lost four southern states to Thurmond. He lost a million votes to Wallace. However, Truman did win the election. People gave several reasons for Truman's surprise victory. One was that the Republicans were very sure they would win. Therefore, they did not campaign as much as they should have. A second reason was that the Democrats did much campaigning. As a result, many Democrats voted. A third reason was that Truman supported the "New Deal" policies. These policies contained some measures to speed up the recovery of the farming industry. The people in the major farming states approved this. They voted for Truman in the election.

Figure 8.1

The distinction between these approaches is made because, just as it is possible to use one textbook on only one reading level, it is also possible to use many different textbooks that are all on basically one reading level. In other words, the use of a variety of materials does not necessarily indicate that a variety of reading levels is also available to the students.

Though Mr. Lentz could see worth in having all the students read the same textbook, either as it existed or in a simpler format, he discovered that there were not many textbooks available that were written on exactly the same topic but on varying readability levels. He also discovered that it was quite time-consuming to rewrite the existing textbook. Using such resources as the curriculum guide and the textbook, he ascertained the objectives for that particular aspect of the eleventh grade social studies program. Because he felt that his main task was to teach the students certain concepts, the *purpose* he had delineated for reading the textbook was related to those concepts, and not to all the material that happened to be in the textbook; he knew he could use a variety of multilevel materials in order to help the students meet the instructional objectives in materials that were compatible with each student's reading level.

176

Once Mr. Lentz had determined that there were many instructional materials at various reading levels, he began to plan his strategies for using these materials. Before he obtained any of the materials, he looked again very closely at his objectives and then planned his use of the materials accordingly.

Topic Focus. One of Mr. Lentz's purposes in having the student read the text was to "identify acts initiated and supported by Truman which have an effect upon the world today." In order to do this, he made an audiotape of the eleventh grade text for Joe, he assigned Lorraine material from the fifth grade American history text, he rewrote a chapter of the text for Paul, and he found a paperback book written on the fifth grade level but geared to senior high interests for Sylvia. Each student read his own materials and was given the same basic objective for reading. During the large-group session with the whole class, each student gave his viewpoint on important acts initiated by Truman.

Thematic Focus. Another approach Mr. Lentz sometimes used was a "thematic approach" to teaching his content area. Theme may be thought of as an idea—usually a moral or abstract concept—dominant throughout a unit of study. The thematic approach may be applied to a single textbook, a single content area using multiple materials, or a group of content areas taught together in an integrated teaching approach.

Thematic Focus in a Single Content Area: The history book Mr. Lentz used presented factors primarily in chronological order. Events were related in reference to their temporal order of occurrence. Had Mr. Lentz wanted to use a thematic approach, he could have revised his lesson plans to reflect some abstract concept. Hence, the topic "Truman" could have been adapted to be included in a broad theme, such as "Truman, A Product of Change." Most studying done in connection with this unit would focus on the characteristics of Truman as he dealt with change. Lesson plans would still have objectives, but those objectives would support the theme of change. Hence the objective concerning Truman's unexpected election in 1948 might be rewritten as follows: "After the completion of this unit of study, the student will be able to identify at least three factors reflective of the changing economy in 1948 which caused Truman to be re-elected."

Thematic Focus—Several Content Areas: On occasion, Mr. Lentz participated in team teaching with several of the other content area teachers. They combined objectives for algebra, chemistry, literature, and history. In such instances, the objectives broadened. Instead of asking youngsters in history only to identify three factors reflective of the change in the economy in 1948 that caused Truman to be re-elected, the students were asked to examine the theme of change in Truman's era in the other three content areas as well.

The algebra teacher asked the students to work problems concerning change in population, types of jobs, and women in the medical profession from 1945 to present. In addition, the algebra teacher had students study the growth of inflation and to compare in terms of buying power, the worth of money in 1945 to its worth in the present. Both the algebra teacher and Mr. Lentz worked together to show the students how wartime economy affects buying power, unemployment, and international trade.

177

The chemistry teacher presented material on the nucleus of the atom, the changes that take place inside it, and the energy that accompanies these changes. Much discussion ensued about the history of the development of the atom bomb and the effect of radiation upon the people of Japan from 1945 to the present.

The literature teacher assigned prose and poetry written during that time and focused class discussion on events of the late 1940s that caused the authors to write about the things they did. Since the theme of change was to be emphasized, the class talked about how literature before the 1940s was different from that after the 1940s. Comparisons of literary style, content, and genre that predominated between 1945 and the present were examined.

Methods for Locating Multilevel Materials

The social studies curriculum in the average American school system follows a cyclic pattern. The rationale behind the cycle is that students should be introduced to the various areas of the social studies in the elementary school years and then have the basic concepts reinforced and expanded during the middle, junior, and senior high school years. Mr. Lentz's task of locating material on Truman began with the knowledge that United States history is usually taught in the fifth grade, the eighth grade, and the eleventh grade (Clark, Klein, and Burks 1972). Therefore the first thing he did when he discovered that Lorraine read on the fifth grade level was to locate fifth grade American history books by a variety of publishers to see if they contained material about Truman that Lorraine could read. After he had located several different texts, he checked with Lorraine to see if she had read any of them. Though Lorraine was familiar with one of the texts, she had not read three others that were quite similar.

Another tool useful to Mr. Lentz in locating materials on various reading levels was the resource lists put out by some professional organizations. One strong point about materials recommended by several of these lists was that they designated not only reading level but interest level as well. For example, a book about Truman written at the third grade level for third grade interests would probably not be useful to the students in the eleventh grade because senior high students would be bored with it. Many publishers have taken into account the needs of underachievers and have adapted books to meet these needs. Thus it is possible to obtain a book about Truman written on a third grade reading level but geared for eleventh grade interest (see Chapter 11 for more information about these resources).

In addition to various reference lists available to the classroom teacher, a look at current catalogs from some of the major publishers of secondary textbooks can be helpful. Many publishing companies are coming out with multilevel materials so rapidly that the best way for a teacher to keep current on the materials is to contact a publisher and ask for catalogs of promotional information on the materials. It is feasible to find, in just the content area of American history, the following types of books available from a single publisher.

1. A text designed to help the average seventh or eighth grader understand the "traditional values, ideals, and spirit of America."
2. A text designed to help the average seventh or eighth grader in an interdisciplinary manner. The content involves anthropology, sociology, geography, and other social sciences. Focus is on all ethnic groups and the values that have shaped the nation.
3. A text designed to help the junior high school student whose reading abilities are below grade level expectancy. Special emphasis is placed on the importance and contributions of minority groups in America.

Senior High Level — Designed to Be Used As Basic Text

1. A text, designed for the junior year in high school, that presents American history in basically chronological order, though one or more major themes are interpreted within a broad chronological setting (e.g., theme of change from 1776 to present).
2. A textbook, designed for the junior year in high school, that uses a case study approach.
3. An American history text, designed for senior high students with reading disabilities, that presents America as a multiethnic, multicultural society. Focus is on outstanding men and women in American history.
4. An American history text that focuses on minority groups in America. Several different textbooks that focus on minority groups are included.

Junior and Senior High Level — Designed to Be Used As Supplementary Material

1. Biographies of famous Americans, written on various reading levels.
2. Articles on Americans by foreign observers.
3. Guided reading books that parallel the contents of one of the basic books and extend certain facets.
4. Collections of original source materials for the high school history course.
5. Slide systems supplementing basic textbooks.

A close look at material available from publishers also reveals that some material already based on a thematic focus is available. For example, one such American history textbook is centered on the theme of *values*. The focus is on a variety of famous Americans and the values that shaped the nation. Though the main events are portrayed chronologically, the approach is a casebook in which Americans representing a variety of ethnic backgrounds are discussed and the student is required to analyze events and draw conclusions about the course of history and the shape of values based on the evidence presented. In this textbook, Truman's values might be inferred and discussed from his actions. His famous statement, "the buck stops here," could be used as a focal point for assessing his values.

In addition, some publishing companies also have available multilevel, multiple materials organized into units whose components focus on a particular theme. For example, one publisher's unit on values allows each student to read a book written at his own reading level. One student might read *Hiroshima*, another student might read a book about McCarthy, and still another student might read a biography of Truman. Although students read different books, all activities—including large-group discussions, small-group discussions, and individual assignments—would center around the values reflected in each student's reading matter.

Match Materials with Purpose

Though readability of a textbook and the reading levels of the students who will be using it should always be considered before a textbook is selected, even more fundamental is the purpose for which the textbook is to be used. Before teachers use any textbook, they should evaluate their purpose for asking students to read it. One aid to identifying purpose is to use a checklist that points out the major roles the textbook might play in the unit being studied. The checklist below, adapted from materials discussed by Burron and Claybaugh (1974), can be of use to teachers.

Directions: Place a check by the appropriate purpose for which this textbook is to be used during this unit of study.

	All Students	Most Students	Some Students
1. Introductory Material			
2. Fundamental Source of Information			
3. Supplementary Information			
4. Alternative Source of Information			
5. Reference Source			
6. Review Source			

Introductory material refers to the text as a motivating device or a step into a deeper unit of study. Some teachers like to use the textbook at the beginning of a unit primarily to provide the students a basis for study. After the unit of study begins, the teacher provides a wide range of other materials that support the scope and sequence of the text.

Fundamental source of information indicates that the teacher intends to use the textbook as the primary resource tool for his students.

Supplementary information refers to the use of a textbook to fill in any concepts and/or subject matter not provided elsewhere. It may be supplementary to another textbook used as a "fundamental source" but which doesn't cover some concept adequately. It may be supplementary and used to fill in the scope and sequence of content to be studied as provided by another textbook used as "introductory material," or as provided by some other guide to scope and sequence of content, such as a teacher-made outline.

Alternative source of information indicates that the teacher has more than one source of information for the students and is able to help them select the learning alternatives most comfortable to them. Hence if a student cannot read the grade level text, an easier text on the same topic might provide an alternative source of information. Likewise, even if the student is able to read but doesn't like to, some media other than print might provide an alternative for learning.

Reference source refers to the text intended primarily for consultation rather than consecutive reading.

A *review source* might be a textbook written especially for review purposes. For example, a teacher conducting a second-year French course might ask his students to use a book that reviewed first-year French grammar and vocabulary during the first few weeks of school. Books written especially for review purposes are not meant to be used as fundamental sources of information. For example, if the students had not already had a first-year course in French, the review book would not be very helpful to them. Most review books present background information and concepts in as brief a manner as possible; the authors assume that the reader already knows the basics but needs a brief overview of the more important topics.

Textbooks that were written to be used as fundamental sources of information can also be used for review purposes. Some teachers like to use the textbook primarily as a summarizing tool to pull everything together for the students at the end of a unit of study. These teachers rely upon a wide range of other materials to introduce and expand the basic concepts and content to be presented.

In addition, some teachers prefer that students review topics by using textbooks different from the ones used to supply the fundamental course information. These teachers may ask the student to compare the perspectives of textbooks published by different companies, or they may just want the student to have a fresh means of reviewing a topic that might otherwise be a stale task because the material had been reread many times before.

Guide Student's Reading

Donald Durrell (1956) recommends that teachers make reading and reasoning guides to help readers of different abilities to do their assignments. He suggests that differences in students' needs for study guides on different levels is greater than differences in students' needs for materials written on different reading levels. If the teacher can provide the right kind of help, materials of the same reading level can be used for the entire class. Herber (1970) has written an entire textbook in which his thrust is based upon Durrell's concept. In the following section, Mr. Lentz has modeled his lessons after those suggested by Herber in his text, *Teaching Reading in the Content Areas.*

When Mr. Lentz looked over the next chapter in the American history textbook, he read the accompanying teacher's manual and the follow-up questions designed for students. Nine questions were located under a section marked "For Mastery and Review." One of the questions asked the students to discuss the factors that explain Truman's unexpected re-election in 1948 (Bragdon, McCutchen, and Cole 1973). Mr. Lentz knew that his poorest readers would have great difficulty in answering this question. In addition, he knew that the reading skill of "locating cause-effect relationships" was particularly important in this assignment. Therefore he did several things. When he introduced the chapter, he reviewed the skill of cause and effect with the students, and he gave them a guided reading sheet before they read the assignment. Since he knew the importance of purpose for reading in the understanding of content, each guided reading sheet gave the student his purpose for reading the assignment. The poorest readers needed the most guidance, so Mr. Lentz gave them a specific description of political conditions existing in 1948 and a list of possible effects. Then he asked the students to match the conditions with the effects. The average readers needed less guidance and so were given only a list of effects and the page numbers on which they were found. They were to use their textbooks to locate the causes of all the effects that were listed. The superior readers needed the least guidance. They could have been given the original question in the text and asked to answer it. However, Mr. Lentz chose not to use it. Instead, he gave them a task that he felt accomplished the same purpose, but made them focus more upon cause–effect relationships. Excerpts from the assignment sheets for the different students follow.

Excerpt from Assignment Sheet for Poor Readers

Purpose: To determine the effect that political conditions in 1948 had upon Truman's re-election.

Directions: Given below are some descriptions of the political situation in the United States in 1948 as found in your textbook on page 700. In each case, the first event caused a second event to take place. Draw a line from each cause to its effect. You should check with Chapter 30, page 700, in order to match the effect correctly.

Event 1 (cause)	*Event 2 (effect)*
1. The Republican candidate for President, Thomas Dewey, was certain he would win.	1. Democrats renominated Truman.

2. General Eisenhower would not be a presidential candidate for the Democrats.

3. Southern Democrats resented Truman's racial policies.

4. Dixiecrats nominated Strom Thurmond for President.

5. Henry Wallace ran for President under Progressive party label and campaigned for better relations with Russia.

6. Truman traveled 22,000 miles in whistle-stop campaigning.

2. Undecided voters who heard Truman voted for him.

3. Blunted efforts of opponents to pin Communist label to Truman.

4. Helped Truman's cause with Negro voters in the North.

5. A separate states' rights party nicknamed Dixiecrats formed.

6. Dewey avoided discussion of issues in his campaign.

Excerpt from Assignment Sheet for Average Readers

Purpose: To determine the effect the political conditions in 1948 had upon Truman's re-election.

Directions: In each of the following sentences about the 1948 re-election of Truman, the incident described has been caused by another incident that took place first. Look in your textbook on page 700 to find the event that caused the second event to occur. The first one has been done for you.

Event 1 (cause)	*Event 2 (effect)*
1. The Republican candidate for President, Thomas Dewey, was certain he would win the election.	1. Dewey avoided discussion of issues in his campaign.
	2. The Democratic party nominated Truman for President.
	3. A separate states' rights party nicknamed Dixiecrats was formed.
	4. Helped Truman's cause with Negro voters in the North.
	5. Blunted efforts of opponents to pin Communist label to Truman.
	6. Undecided voters who heard Truman voted for him.

Purpose: To determine the effects the political conditions in the United States in 1948 had upon Truman's re-election.

Directions: In real life, certain events happen that cause other events to occur. Look in your textbook on page 700 and locate at least six events concerning political conditions in the United States in 1948 that caused Truman to win the election. Put the first event in the first column (cause) and the resulting event in the second column (effect) as shown below. The first one has been done for you.

Event 1 (cause)	*Event 2 (effect)*
1. The Republican candidate for President, Thomas Dewey, was certain he would win the election.	1. Dewey avoided discussion of issues in his campaign.

LESSON PLANS AND GUIDED READING SHEETS

A guided reading sheet is one of the instructional tools used to help differentiate instruction. As such, it would be listed in the materials section of a five-step lesson plan and may also be an aid to help the student learn in a five-step directed reading lesson.

When Mr. Lentz used the three guided reading sheets shown earlier, he did not just pass them out and ask students to complete them. Rather he used them in the total context of his daily lesson planning. His lesson plan for the day is shown below.

Behavioral Objective: At the completion of this lesson the student will be able to identify at least three cause-effect relationships of Truman's term as President.

Materials: History textbook, guided reading sheets on differentiated reading levels, photograph of Truman.

Pre-Assessment: Ask the students to write a short paragraph in which they discuss at least three cause-effect relationships between the political conditions in the United States in 1948 and the re-election of Truman. Those who respond with at least three correct cause-effect relationships have met the objective and may go on to another lesson.

Procedure: Use directed reading lesson format to teach the skill of identifying cause-effect relationships using the textbook as the main instructional tool. The following steps will be taken.

Step 1—Preparation

Show the class a photograph of Truman holding a newspaper with the headline "Dewey Defeats Truman." Ask the class to tell why the newspaper had that headline. Discuss the relationship between political opinion polls and predictions for election victories. Demonstrate to the class how the opinion poll made the newspaper publishers think that Truman would lose and hence publish the headline. Discuss other cause-effect relationships. Tell the class to read the part of Chapter 30 that deals with the election of 1948. Give each student one of the three guided reading sheets shown earlier in this chapter.

Step 2—Silent Reading

Allow class members time to read the assignment using their guided reading sheets to help them locate cause-effect relationships.

Step 3—Oral Reading and Discussion

After the section has been read, hold a discussion about the materials. Point out cause-effect relationships found in the section on Truman's 1948 election. Ask some students to read aloud specific passages they located that show a cause-effect relationship.

Step 4—Follow-up

If all the students are able to complete their guided reading sheets on the section of the text dealing with Truman's election, extend the skill identifying cause-effect relationships into the rest of the chapter. The guided reading sheets below extend this skill.

Excerpt from Assignment Sheet for Poor Readers

Purpose: To show the cause-effect relationship in the gap between Truman's Fair Deal proposals and what was enacted into law.

Directions: Attached is a photostat of page 701 in your textbook. Many cause-effect relationships exist in this section. The *effect* half of the relationship has been underlined with a straight line for you. Locate the *cause* half of the same relationship and underline it with a wavy line. The first one has been done for you. (See Figure 8.2 for students' attached assignment.)

Excerpt from Assignment Sheet for Average Readers

Purpose: To show cause-effect relationships in the gap between Truman's Fair Deal proposals and what was enacted into law.

Directions: Attached is a photostat of page 701 in your textbook. Many cause-effect relationships exist in this section. You are to locate at least five of them. Underline the cause with a wavy line and the effect with a straight line in each relationship you find. The first one has been done for you. (See Figure 8.3 for students' attached assignment.)

medical insurance, aid to agriculture, and higher minimum wages. But although the new Congress was Democratic, it was generally controlled by an unofficial coalition of Republicans and conservative southern Democrats. Hence only part of the Fair Deal program became law. Farmers were promised subsidies if the market prices of major farm products fell below certain fixed parity prices, based upon a cost-of-living index. Federal funds were voted for slum clearance. A Minimum Wage Act raised the minimum hourly wage for businesses engaged in interstate commerce from 40 to 75 cents. Social security benefits were extended to new groups, including teachers and the self-employed.

In 1949 there was a halt in postwar prosperity. Heavy industry slackened off; unemployment rolls increased. But the situation was never as bad as in any year during the 1930's. There was no panic, nor serious need for large-scale relief. In contrast to the situation before the New Deal, there were now various "built-in stabilizers" that operated almost automatically against a downward plunge in the economy. These included price supports for agricultural products, unemployment insurance, increased social security benefits, and minimum wage laws. The Full Employment Act also helped to create confidence because the federal government was now committed to action to stop a catastrophic drop like that of 1929–1932. Private enterprise contributed to economic stability by such measures as company pension plans.

The Korean War, beginning in 1950, changed the economic picture sharply, as a rearmament program competed with the demand for consumer goods.

The "Truman Scandals"

During the latter years of Truman's presidency it was revealed that there was corruption in high places. Men close to him had received valuable presents in return for political influence with government bureaus. Members of the Reconstruction Finance Corporation, the Department of Justice, and the Internal Revenue Service took bribes in return for favors. Democratic city machines were shown to have close ties with gangsters. While the President was not personally involved and misdoing was on no such scale as under the Grant and Harding administrations, the "Truman scandals" provided the Republicans with a ready-made issue for the 1952 presidential election.

OPENING OF THE COLD WAR

Overshadowing all domestic problems during the Truman administration was the opening of the Cold War between the United States and the rest of the free world on the one hand, and Russia with her satellites and China on the other. This struggle could be foreseen even before World War II came to an end, when Stalin violated the Yalta agreement concerning free elections in Poland. The Cold War was fully joined when Truman helped Greece and Turkey to resist Communist aggression in 1947, and it has not stopped since. It is a strife like none other in which Americans have been engaged. Only twice, in Korea and in Vietnam, has it involved putting armies into combat. It has meant, however, a state of constant military preparedness, and military support for enemies or possible victims of communism all over the globe. It has been fought in the economic sphere, as both sides attempted to "buy" allies with gifts, ranging from foodstuffs to steel plants. Above all, it has become a struggle for the minds of men. This has produced propaganda of every sort—posters, broadcasts, overseas libraries, student exchanges. Ultimately, the Cold War involves the question of which system *deserves* to survive by offering the most opportunities for good lives.

From *History of a Free People* by H.W. Bragdon, S.P. McCutchen, and C.W. Cole, p.701. Copyright ©1973, Macmillan Publishing Co., Inc. Used with permission.

Figure 8.2 Excerpt from Assignment for Poor Readers

medical insurance, aid to agriculture, and higher minimum wages. But although the new Congress was Democratic, it was generally controlled by an unofficial coalition of Republicans and conservative southern Democrats. Hence only part of the Fair Deal program became law. Farmers were promised subsidies if the market prices of major farm products fell below certain fixed parity prices, based upon a cost-of-living index. Federal funds were voted for slum clearance. A Minimum Wage Act raised the minimum hourly wage for businesses engaged in interstate commerce from 40 to 75 cents. Social security benefits were extended to new groups, including teachers and the self-employed.

In 1949 there was a halt in postwar prosperity. Heavy industry slackened off; unemployment rolls increased. But the situation was never as bad as in any year during the 1930's. There was no panic, nor serious need for large-scale relief. In contrast to the situation before the New Deal, there were now various "built-in stabilizers" that operated almost automatically against a downward plunge in the economy. These included price supports for agricultural products, unemployment insurance, increased social security benefits, and minimum wage laws. The Full Employment Act also helped to create confidence because the federal government was now committed to action to stop a catastrophic drop like that of 1929–1932. Private enterprise contributed to economic stability by such measures as company pension plans.

The Korean War, beginning in 1950, changed the economic picture sharply, as a rearmament program competed with the demand for consumer goods.

The "Truman Scandals"

During the latter years of Truman's presidency it was revealed that there was corruption in high places. Men close to him had received valuable presents in return for political influence with government bureaus. Members of the Reconstruction Finance Corporation, the Department of Justice, and the Internal Revenue Service took bribes in return for favors. Democratic city machines were shown to have close ties with gangsters. While the President was not personally involved and misdoing was on no such scale as under the Grant and Harding administrations, the "Truman scandals" provided the Republicans with a ready-made issue for the 1952 presidential election.

OPENING OF THE COLD WAR

Overshadowing all domestic problems during the Truman administration was the opening of the Cold War between the United States and the rest of the free world on the one hand, and Russia with her satellites and China on the other. This struggle could be foreseen even before World War II came to an end, when Stalin violated the Yalta agreement concerning free elections in Poland. The Cold War was fully joined when Truman helped Greece and Turkey to resist Communist aggression in 1947, and it has not stopped since. It is a strife like none other in which Americans have been engaged. Only twice, in Korea and in Vietnam, has it involved putting armies into combat. It has meant, however, a state of constant military preparedness, and military support for enemies or possible victims of communism all over the globe. It has been fought in the economic sphere, as both sides attempted to "buy" allies with gifts, ranging from foodstuffs to steel plants. Above all, it has become a struggle for the minds of men. This has produced propaganda of every sort—posters, broadcasts, overseas libraries, student exchanges. Ultimately, the Cold War involves the question of which system *deserves* to survive by offering the most opportunities for good lives.

From *History of a Free People* by H.W. Bragdon, S.P. McCutchen, and C.W. Cole, p. 701. Copyright ©1973, Macmillan Publishing Co., Inc. Used with permission.

Figure 8.3 Excerpt from Assignment for Average Readers

Purpose: To show the cause-effect relationship in the gap between Truman's Fair Deal proposals and what was enacted into law.

Directions: Read page 701 in your textbook and locate at least five cause-effect relationships. After you locate them, discuss how you think the effect would have been different if another cause had been present. An example has been done for you.

EXAMPLE

Effect: Truman was able to get only a part of his Fair Deal legislation passed.

Cause: The new Congress was controlled by an unofficial coalition of Republicans and conservative Democrats.

Discussion: If a more liberal Congress or a Congress more favorable to Truman had been in power, then it would have supported his ideas on slum clearance and subsidies for public schools.

Step 5—Extension Activities

After the class has finished the second set of guided reading sheets, assign the following extension activities. Give students options as to which activities they may select, but they must select at least one. (1) Organize a debate or panel discussion on the merits of political opinion polls. (2) Write a paper in which you compare the ideological bases of Dixiecrats and Northern Democrats in 1948. (3) Read the play *Give 'Em Hell, Harry* and make a report on it to class. (4) Collect at least six reviews of the play *Give 'Em Hell, Harry* and make a bulletin board for the class.

Post-Assessment: Ask the class members to write a paragraph in which they identify at least three cause-effect relationships that affected Truman's term in office as President. If they can do so, they have met the objective and may go on to the next lesson. If not, they need more help on the skill of identifying cause-effect relationships.

DIAGNOSING AFTER INSTRUCTION

Mr. Lentz diagnosed how well the students had met the objectives of each lesson through use of the post-assessment format in his lesson plan. However he also gave periodic reading assessments to the students in his class to ascertain whether they could be given more difficult materials. He usually gave the more comprehensive reading assessment when he gave the students the unit exam over various chapters in the text. Hence he was able to reassess his students' growth in reading in an over-all manner about every six weeks.

Gradual Development of Resources

The task of making out differentiated assignment sheets for each student was a massive one which Mr. Lentz completed over a period of years. The first year he taught, he made differentiated assignment sheets only for the poorest readers because he felt they needed the most help. The following years, he built up assignment sheets for other students. In addition, he allowed his students to help him. For example, the assignment sheet prepared for the superior students, discussed earlier, could become a guide sheet by the next group of average students. Likewise, the assignment sheet completed by the average students could become the basis for a guide sheet for the poor readers.

Peer Helpers

Mr. Lentz frequently used peers to help each other, but was very careful about how he asked students to work together. When using peer helpers, he followed two basic premises: (1) All students must be given some sort of preparation before giving or receiving help. (2) All students must be able to be helpers as well as helpees (those receiving help). Mr. Lentz believed that these two aspects of pupil aid to one another could not be overemphasized. The students in most classes have a wide enough range of reading levels, skill needs, and interests so that teachers may give every student an opportunity to both give and receive help.

His strategy for meeting his two basic premises included the following: Before asking any youngsters to work with others, he gathered a group of helpers together in a small-group seminar format and discussed the following issues through inductive questioning techniques: "How would you like to receive help? Do you like it when someone is bossy with you? How can you tell someone they are wrong without making fun of them?" Furthermore he included a role-playing situation in which one of the youngsters was bossy with another. All the helpers watched or participated in the role playing and then discussed how they could do it better.

Then (the *key* to the success of his program) he held a seminar for those who were to receive help. In this seminar, a role-playing situation similar to one held by the helpers was conducted. However the emphasis was switched from "How can you give help" to "How can you be helpful by receiving help?" Mr. Lentz did *not* emphasize how to receive help but rather how to give help by receiving help. Past experience had shown him that it was somehow easier for the youngster to give help than to receive it. In other words, most youngsters enjoyed helping other youngsters, but no one liked to be the student who needed the help. His seminar with the helpees consisted of questions such as: "Would you like to help someone who acted like that? How can you tell the helper that he is not being very nice when he helps you, without getting him mad at you? Could he help you at all if you wouldn't let him? How does it make him feel when he has helped you? Do you like to make people feel good? Can you help them feel good by letting them help you?" All the helpees participated in the role playing and then discussed how help could be given to the peer teacher in a better manner.

Mr. Lentz didn't hold all the seminars the same day. He found it most useful to ease into the peer-teaching situation. He worked with the peer helpers when they were to teach the first time; and likewise with the peer helpees when they were to receive help for the first time. Since his basic premises were to prepare all youngsters before they gave or received help and to make certain all youngsters got to both give and receive help, he gradually managed to have all the students in his class participate in both a helper and helpee seminar. He continued to hold seminars on the issues of giving and receiving help at various intervals throughout the year. While he did not plan a definite schedule for follow-up helper and helpee seminars, he watched his peer teachers closely and formulated seminars whenever he felt someone was forgetting how to help.

Some teachers have extended the techniques used by Mr. Lentz into "cross-age tutoring" situations. This procedure takes advantage of the fact that many of the weakest readers in the upper grades are in need of reading skills presented at the lower grades. For example, a ninth grade teacher might make plans for the weakest readers in the class to teach reading skills to the weakest readers in the seventh grade. If planned carefully, the low-achieving ninth graders could be asked to give help in reading skills that they needed themselves. One of the traits of adolescents is to admire and/or imitate youngsters who are a year or two older. Hence the attitude of younger adolescents toward older ones seems to improve the older student's attitude toward academic work in general. Often older students will research and learn reading skills that the person they are tutoring needs but that they would not practice otherwise. In addition, the one tutored also gains reading skills through the tutoring session.

References and Bibliography

Aukerman, R. C. *Reading in the Secondary School Classroom.* New York: McGraw-Hill, 1972.

Bamman, H., Dawson, M., and McGovern, J. *Fundamentals of Basic Reading Instruction.* 3rd ed. New York: McKay, 1973.

Bragdon, H. W., McCutchen, S. P., and Cole, C. W. *History of a Free People.* New York: Macmillan, 1973.

Burmeister, L. E. *Reading Strategies for Secondary School Teachers.* Reading, Mass.: Addison-Wesley, 1974.

Burron, A., and Claybaugh, A. *Using Reading to Teach Subject Matter: Fundamentals for Content Teachers.* Columbus, Ohio: Merrill, 1974.

Clark, L. H., Klein, R. L., and Burks, J. B. *The American Secondary School Curriculum.* 2nd ed. New York: Macmillan, 1972.

Clemens, S. L. *Adventures of Huckleberry Finn.* New York: Grosset, 1948.

Cushenbery, D. *Remedial Reading in the Secondary School.* West Nyack, N.Y.: Parker, 1972.

Dickens, C. *A Tale of Two Cities.* St. Louis, Mo.: Webster, 1954.

Durrell, D. *Improving Reading Instruction.* Yonkers-on-Hudson, N.Y.: World Book Co., 1956.

Gallu, S. *Give 'Em Hell, Harry.* New York: Viking, 1975.

Herber, H. *Teaching Reading in Content Areas.* Englewood Cliffs, N. J.: Prentice-Hall, 1970.

Hershey, J. *Hiroshima.* New York: Bantam, 1946.

Karlin, R. *Teaching Reading in High School.* 2nd ed. Indianapolis, Ind.: Bobbs-Merrill, 1972.

Karlin, R. *Teaching Reading in High School: Selected Articles.* Indianapolis, Ind.: Bobbs-Merrill, 1969.

Olson, A., and Ames, W. *Teaching Reading Skills in Secondary Schools.* Scranton, Pa.: Intext Educational Publishers, 1972.

Olson, A., and Ames, W. *Teaching Reading Skills in Secondary Schools: Readings.* Scranton, Pa.: Intext Educational Publishers, 1970.

Robinson, H., and Thomas, E., eds. *Fusing Reading Skills and Content.* Newark, Del.: International Reading Association, 1969.

Robinson, H. *Teaching Reading and Study Strategies: The Content Areas.* Boston: Allyn & Bacon, 1975.

Thomas, E., and Robinson, H. *Improving Reading in Every Class: A Source Book for Teachers.* Boston: Allyn & Bacon, 1972.

Part Three

Planning
Diagnostic-Prescriptive
Instruction

Chapter 9

Using Diagnostic-Prescriptive Techniques

Prerequisite 9.1

Before beginning this chapter, participants should have successfully completed the objectives for Chapters 1 through 8 or should have a broad knowledge of reading skills, reading problems in instructional materials, ascertaining instructional levels, lesson planning, and instructional strategies.

Rationale 9.2

Diagnostic-prescriptive instruction may be used to aid the student in mastering the reading skills in an efficient systematic manner. The purpose of this chapter is to introduce the concept of diagnostic-prescriptive instruction and to aid the participant in establishing such a program. Components include selecting a scope and sequence of reading skills, forming assessments, keeping records, planning lessons, and scheduling instruction.

Objectives 9.3

Upon successful completion of this chapter, the participant will be able to:

1. State the advantages which a diagnostic-prescriptive approach lends to the skills program.
2. Tell his method for choosing specific skills for his scope and sequence of skills.

3. List three possible sources for designing assessment items to be used to discern which skills a student has or has not mastered.
4. State the criteria for a formal assessment.
5. When given an objective and a sample assessment, state whether the assessment has the characteristics of a formal one.
6. State the conditions under which an informal assessment may be used.
7. State the reason for pre-assessing only a few objectives at one time.
8. Describe a record-keeping system.
9. Describe his preferred method for scheduling diagnostic-prescriptive instruction. Description should include the amount of time that would elapse between pre-assessment and initial teaching lesson, initial teaching lesson and first reinforcement lesson, reinforcement lessons, and the last reinforcement lesson and the post-assessment.
10. (On the lines below, add other objectives according to your instructor's directions.) _____

_____

11. _____

_____

12. _____

_____

13. _____

_____

* * * * * * * * * * * * * *

Chapter 13, Experience 9 extends Chapter 9 with this objective:

14. The participant will describe a diagnostic-prescriptive reading program that he has observed.

* * * * * * * * * * * * * *

Self Pre-Assessment 9.4

Can you complete all the activities listed in **Objectives 9.3**? Answer "yes," "no," or "not certain."

If you answered "yes" to the question, complete the enabling activities required by your instructor and take the Post-Assessment on the date assigned by him.

If you answered "no," refer to **Enabling Activities 9.5**. If you decide to do any activities that are not required, select those that best suit you as a learner.

You need not complete all the optional activities or all parts of a particular optional activity. As soon as you have the information you need to complete the objectives, answer "yes" to the **Self Pre-Assessment 9.4** question and stop the activity.

If you answered "not certain" to the question, refer to **Enabling Activities 9.5.** Select the enabling activity that best suits your style of learning and peruse it. Then make a firm "yes" or "no" answer and proceed accordingly.

Enabling Activities 9.5

Complete only as many of the activities listed below as are required and which you need in order to meet the objectives.

1. *Enabling activity one* is a *reading* alternative. This is **Information Given 9.6.** It is an introduction to a diagnostic-prescriptive skills program.
2. *Enabling activity two* is a *class session* option. Attend the class session(s) on the date(s), at the time(s), and at the place(s) announced.

_____	_____	_____
(Date)	(Time)	(Place)
_____	_____	_____
(Date)	(Time)	(Place)
_____	_____	_____
(Date)	(Time)	(Place)

3. *Enabling activity three* (These lines are left blank so that you may add other enabling activities as suggested by your instructor.)_____

4. *Enabling activity four*_____

5. *Enabling activity five* _____

Now that you have completed the appropriate number of required and/or optional learning alternatives, look back at **Self Pre-Assessment 9.4.** If you feel you can answer "yes" to all of the questions, you are ready to proceed to the Post-Assessment. This may be given to you immediately or after completion of a series of chapters.

A group of classroom teachers were gathered for a workshop on reading instruction in the middle and secondary school. A content area teacher and a reading teacher had been asked to describe how they taught and reinforced reading skills in their classes.

The reading teacher, Miss Hyde, explained her method for diagnosing her students' reading levels as well as their individual skill needs. She further described how she assigned each student's instructional materials according to the appropriate reading level and the specific skill needs. She completed her talk with the following statement: "The reading program seems to be working very well. However I am somewhat overwhelmed by the amount of coordination needed to locate and assign materials that are appropriate to each student. Furthermore I am certain that I sometimes assign new skills before some adolescents have mastered the one currently being taught and that I include some skills that many students have already mastered. Also I frequently run out of materials needed to teach a skill to a specific student and don't have time to look for more or to make up additional lessons on my own."

Mr. Hudson, a chemistry teacher, then told the group how he emphasized reading skills needed in his content area. His strategy included diagnosing the reading level of each adolescent, determining the readability level of the chemistry books, and planning lessons so that they incorporated the five-step reading lesson plan. He concluded his presentation by stating, "I am concerned about the reading skills needed in chemistry. I try to identify the reading skills required and then attempt to teach the skills that my students need to complete their assignments. However I believe that I am not selecting and teaching to all my students the skills needed to read chemistry content materials effectively."

The consultant for the workshop then made the following comment. "Both Miss Hyde and Mr. Hudson seem to be having a problem in the same area—that of individualizing the reading skills program to meet the needs of the students. A diagnostic-prescriptive skills program that provides orderly instruction in vocabulary, comprehension, and study skills might be the solution for both of them. Miss Hyde and Mr. Hudson are already using several aspects of diagnostic-prescriptive instruction. First, when Miss Hyde assigned instructional materials based on each student's achievement level and skill need, she was using instruction based on a diagnostic-prescriptive premise. Second, the five-step lesson plan Mr. Hyde has been using is diagnostic-prescriptive in nature. Students are diagnosed prior to the start of the lesson and, if they can already meet the objective, they are not required to perform the activities in the lesson. Furthermore, if they are not able to pass the post-assessment at the end of the lesson, then they receive additional instruction.

However Mr. Hudson and Miss Hyde could use a more extensive diagnostic-prescriptive approach to add the following elements to their existing reading programs: (1) A scope and sequence of skills should be developed early in the semester in order to determine the skills that the teacher wishes to include. Necessary skills are then neither omitted nor duplicated. (2) Further formalization of the pre-assessment and the post-assessment provides a means to identify the skills that have been learned and facilitates the reteaching of only those skills in which students show a need for further instruction. (3) An efficient record-keeping system helps coordinate all needed skills and allows the teacher to readily visualize the skills that have been learned. (4) Instructional strategies should be designed so that they follow a sequence of instruction that includes a pre-assessment, an initial teaching lesson, several reinforcement activities, and a post-assessment. (5) The steps in each lesson should be scheduled at regular intervals in order to help the teacher allow adequate time in class for lessons to be taught and learned. (6) Instruction should be differentiated so that each student is taught only the skills he does not know and in a manner conducive to his specific learning style."

The remainder of this chapter is divided into two sections. The first part, *Teacher Tasks in a Diagnostic-Prescriptive Skills Program*, describes the organization and management of a diagnostic-prescriptive program. The second section, *Use of a Diagnostic-Prescriptive Program*, gives several examples of various content area teachers using diagnostic-prescriptive techniques to help students read and understand their subject matter assignments.

TEACHER TASKS IN A DIAGNOSTIC-PRESCRIPTIVE SKILLS PROGRAM

When conducting a diagnostic-prescriptive skills program in reading, the teacher has six main tasks. These tasks are:

Task 1—*Designing a Scope and Sequence of Skills.* The teacher needs to have a listing of the reading skills that are appropriate to the specific content area and the skills should be listed in the order (if any) in which they should be taught. (scope and sequence of skills)

Task 2—*Diagnosing Before and After Instruction.* The teacher needs to assess the student's competence in a skill before instruction is given. (pre-assessment) The teacher also needs to assess the student's ability to use a skill following instruction. (post-assessment)

Task 3—*Keeping Records.* The teacher needs to record the skills that students have and have not mastered.

Task 4—*Designing Instructional Strategies.* For those skills that students have not mastered, the teacher needs to plan instruction. Such instruction should include an initial teaching lesson and reinforcement lessons.

Task 5—*Scheduling Instruction.* The teacher needs to schedule assessments and teaching procedures.

Task 6—*Differentiating Instruction.* The teacher needs to plan appropriate instruction for all students so that the best use is made of their time.

A discussion of these six tasks follows.

Task 1—Designing a Scope and Sequence of Skills

To design a scope and sequence of skills, teachers need to: (1) find one or more general lists of reading skills for secondary students (scope and sequence of skills), (2) select from those lists the skills appropriate to the specific content area course being taught.

Lists of Reading Skills for Middle and Secondary School Students

A discussion of the availability and criteria of lists of reading skills for middle and secondary school students follows.

Availability. Reading skill outlines may be found as part of instructional materials in reading designed to be used by middle and secondary school students, as part of a curriculum packet designed for a total school reading program, and in reading methodology texts written to be used by teachers.

Examples of middle and secondary reading materials that include skill lists are *Houghton Mifflin Readers*, the *Reader's Digest New Advanced Reading Skill Builders*, and the *Scott, Foresman Tactics in Reading*.

Though not all curriculum packets designed for a total school reading program are diagnostic-prescriptive, many do include listings of skills as well as diagnostic information and instructional strategies. An example of a diagnostic-prescriptive reading program is the *Fountain Valley Reading System* (Sanches, et al. 1975), which includes a complete list of skills and correlated assessments for secondary school students.

Several professional books on reading instruction include skill lists. The compilation of skills described in Otto and Smith, *Administering the School Reading Program* (1970) is representative of lists often found in professional texts.

Criteria. In selecting a list of reading skills upon which to base the improvement of content area instruction, teachers should use the following criteria.

1. The list should be comprehensive, including vocabulary, comprehension, and study skills. If the skill chart listed vocabulary and comprehension skills, but omitted study skills, teachers might not be as aware of the study skills as they should be. For example, they might instruct their students in the vocabulary skill, Using Context Clues, and in the comprehension skill, Following Directions, but omit the study skill, Using a Study Technique. Although their students would profit from the vocabulary and comprehension skill instruction, they would be missing instruction in the study skills.

2. Each skill should be stated as a *behavioral objective*, which, if possible, includes the *condition* under which the objective is to be performed. This format has the advantage of specifying the exact nature of the skills to be mastered and of simplifying the teacher's task of developing objectives for each lesson. For example, the following objective gives considerable guidance to the teacher: "Given a selection in a content area text from which a cause-effect relationship may be made (condition), the student will be able to identify the relationship." In contrast, without a stated objective, the simple skill descriptor, Cause-Effect Relationship, is open to many interpretations, includ-

ing Evaluating Cause-Effect Relationships, Justifying Cause-Effect Relationships, and Comparing Cause-Effect Relationships. Each interpretation requires a different behavior by the student. Furthermore the *condition* such as "given a selection in his content area text" tells the classroom teacher that the objective is not limited to performance in a workbook designed to teach reading, but should be performed by the students in order to effectively read their classroom assignments in all subject areas. However, topic skill descriptors identified by a short phrase, such as Identifying Characterization, are useful for presenting the skills in a concise fashion so that an overview of all the skills involved in reading as well as the relationship among them may be visualized simultaneously.

3. The skill list should include some indication of the areas in which the skill would most often be used. For example, the skill Identifying Theme is important in literature and history, but is not particularly important to the study of math.

Scope and Sequence of Skills

A sample list of reading skills to which a teacher might refer to select those to be included in a personal scope and sequence of skills is given in Chapter 10 of this text. This list is divided into the areas of vocabulary, comprehension, and study skills and is presented in Figure 10.1. Figure 9.1 shows the comprehension portion of the scope and sequence of reading skills.

```
 8. Identifying Details
 9. Identifying Main Ideas
10. Identifying Sequence
11. Following Directions
12. Identifying Cause-Effect Relationships
13. Making Inferences
14. Making Generalizations and Conclusions
15. Identifying Tone and Mood
16. Identifying Theme
17. Identifying Characterization
18. Identifying Fact, Fiction, and Opinion
19. Identifying Propaganda
20. Identifying Author's Purpose
```

Figure 9.1   Portion of Scope and Sequence of Skills
Comprehension Skills

Annotated Scope and Sequence of Skills. In addition to the simple listing of skills as illustrated in Figure 9.1, Chapter 10 also presents an annotated scope and sequence of skills listing. This expanded description of the basic list of skills includes in each section (1) the subject areas in which the skill would be most used, (2) the objective(s), (3) the criterion level, (4) a pre-assessment strategy, (5) several generic teaching strategies, (6) a post-assessment strategy, and (7) correlated instructional materials. Figure 9.2 shows a typical entry from the annotated scope and sequence of skills.

Description: Identifying Propaganda   **Skill Number** 19

Subject Areas: This skill is required by any subject area—for example, history, literature, and science—in which the ability to recognize propaganda is needed.

Objective: Given a selection on his instructional level, the student will be able to identify the propaganda statements.

Criterion Level: _____

Pre-Assessment: Locate material that contains propaganda and which students might be required to read as part of their course work. Ask students to identify the propaganda in the selection. Give credit for accurate identification.

Sample Generic Teaching Strategy

Initial Teaching Procedure

To introduce this concept, use copies of newspaper advertisements to demonstrate to students examples of those propaganda techniques that might occur in your field of study. (See *Identifying Propaganda* in Chapter 3 for a list of the types of propaganda.) Next, give examples of propaganda statements from course-related materials (texts, articles, supplementary readings). Divide the class into groups of two or three and have the students find examples of propaganda in advertisements and course-related materials. List the following five questions that students should ask themselves when attempting to detect propaganda.

1. What is the writer's purpose?
2. How competent is the writer on this topic?
3. How familiar am I with the topic?
4. Do any propaganda techniques appear to be used?
5. Should I accept, reject, or delay my opinion of this source?

Reinforcement Procedures

1. Have students locate two pieces of writing (e.g., books, articles, speeches, editorials) on the same course-related subject and answer questions one through five above in regard to them.
2. Have students locate one piece of course-related material and accept or reject it on the basis of their answers to the five questions listed above.

Post-Assessment: Same as pre-assessment.

Correlated Materials
Professional Texts Written for Teacher Use:
   Burmeister (1974) pp. 207–211
Instructional Material Written for Student Use:
   (Attach sheet.)

Figure 9.2   Sample Entry from Annotated Scope and Sequence of Skills

Designing a Personal Scope and Sequence of Skills

Once teachers have chosen one or more skill lists from which to work, they need to select and sequence those skills that will be most helpful to students in their subject areas. Criteria that may be used to select skills include:

1. *The nature of the subject matter.* For example, an English course might require the skill Identifying Propaganda, whereas a mathematics course probably would not.

202

2. *The course requirements.* For example, if a modern language course required library research, the skills Using Locational Aids in the Library, Recording References, and Using the Library Call System should be taught. However, if library research were not required, these skills would not be needed.
3. *The teacher's personal priorities in determining what students should know.* For example, a mathematics teacher may feel that the skill Locating Details is particularly important to the students in his content area. Therefore, he would include this skill in his scope and sequence of skills.
4. *The time allotment.* For example, a home economics teacher who met with a class only one time per week, might select fewer objectives for concentration than an instructor who met with a class five times per week.
5. *The students' reading achievement.* For example, an English teacher who had a class of students with average or above average reading ability, might include such skills as Identifying Theme and Identifying Characterization. However, if he had a class whose reading skills were below average for their grade level, he might include more basic skills such as Identifying Details and Identifying Main Ideas.

After considering the criteria discussed above, teachers may find that the skill lists from which they are choosing do not specify some skills which they feel are important to their courses. Many lists, such as Figure 10.1 are meant to concisely summarize the reading skills. Hence, some which teachers think are particularly important to their subject areas might not be listed specifically, as the teachers desire. In perusing the list in this text, teachers might decide that unlisted skills would probably be subskills of the skills listed. In such cases, they might feel that these subskills should be specifically listed and might add them to the personal scope and sequence of skills (e.g., Predicting Outcomes added as a subskill of Making Generalizations and Conclusions).

Teachers should also list the skills needed in their course areas in the order in which they intend to teach the skills. For example, if the first lesson in mathematics required students to identify details and the second required students to identify sequence, the teacher should present the skills in that order rather than in the order in which they were found on the skill list used as a reference. Figure 9.3 shows the scope and sequence for the comprehension skills listed in this book and then illustrates those selected for use by a mathematics instructor. This list is included for illustration purposes only and is not intended as a guide for all mathematics teachers.

Task 2—Diagnosing Before and After Instruction

The teacher needs to perform three types of assessments for each student. First, each adolescent's instructional level needs to be assessed. The procedure for finding instructional level in a diagnostic-prescriptive program is identical to that of finding reading levels in any other program. This procedure is given in Chapter 5.

Scope and Sequence of Comprehension Skills Listed in This Book	Skills Selected for Use in a Math Class (Showing Scope)	Skills Selected for Use in a Math Class (Showing Scope and Sequence)
8. Identifying Details	8. Identifying Details	11. Following Directions
9. Identifying Main Ideas	10. Identifying Sequence	8. Identifying Details
10. Identifying Sequence	11. Following Directions	10. Identifying Sequence
11. Following Directions	12. Identifying Cause-Effect Relationships	13. Making Inferences
12. Identifying Cause-Effect Relationships	13. Making Inferences	12. Identifying Cause-Effect Relationships
13. Making Inferences	14. Making Generalizations and Conclusions	14. Making Generalizations and Conclusions
14. Making Generalizations and Conclusions	14.1 Predicting Outcomes (sub-skill of skill number 14)	14.1 Predicting Outcomes (sub-skill of skill number 14)
15. Identifying Tone and Mood		
16. Identifying Theme		
17. Identifying Characterization		
18. Identifying Fact, Fiction, and Opinion		
19. Identifying Propaganda		
20. Identifying Author's Purpose		

Figure 9.3 Comparison of a Portion of a Scope and Sequence of Skills and a Portion of a Scope and Sequence of Skills for Use in a Mathematics Class

Second, the teacher needs to assess the student's competence in each skill listed on the scope and sequence chart in order to determine whether the student needs instruction (pre-assessment).

Third, the teacher needs to assess the student's competence in the skills in which instruction has been given in order to determine whether the student has mastered each skill (post-assessment).

Pre- and Post-Assessing

Pre-assessments differ from post-assessments in time of administration. While pre-assessments are administered prior to instruction to determine whether such instruction is required, post-assessments are administered after instruction to determine whether the skill has been mastered or if further instruction is necessary.

Pre-assessments are similar to post-assessments in content and format. A pre-assessment for any objective may also be used as the post-assessment; or the post-assessment may be parallel in format but with content different from that of the pre-assessment. Because post-assessments should closely parallel pre-assessments, the material contained in the following sections pertaining to procedures for constructing and conducting assessments may apply equally well to either pre- or post-assessments.

Informal Assessments

A student does not have to be formally assessed on each skill. Many assessments may be performed through classroom observation. For example, Miss Horton included Identifying Details on the list of reading skills she believed her students needed to understand science. However, she knew through previous experience and standardized tests, that all the students in her fifth-hour class had mastered this skill. Therefore she did not need to further assess these students on that skill. In addition, she soon realized from student responses in class that all these students had also mastered the skill Following Directions. Therefore Miss Horton did not need to administer a formal pre-assessment for either of these skills.

Criteria for Formal Assessments

In many cases, the teacher cannot adequately assess the needs of the class through informal means and must design a more explicit way to determine needed reading skills. Formal assessments should exactly match the objectives they are designed to measure, should contain more than two questions for each objective being assessed, and should be on the reading level of the students being tested. The following is a discussion of each of these characteristics.

1. The assessment must exactly match the objective it is designed to measure. For example, if the objective reads "Given ten unknown words with Greek or Latin roots, the student will be able to discern the meaning of each of the words by using his knowledge of Greek and Latin roots," the assessment should contain ten words whose meanings may be determined through their Greek or Latin roots. Words that do not contain Greek or Latin roots or whose meanings cannot be identified by using their Greek or Latin roots should not be included in the assessment.

2. More than one or two questions should be used to assess a student's skill on an objective. For example, for the objective, "Given a paragraph from content area materials, the student will be able to find the main idea," the student should be given at least three content area paragraphs and asked to find the main idea for each. Similarly, if the objective required a history student to interpret the meanings of metaphors, then at least three metaphors from history material should be presented.

3. The difficulty level of the material should be appropriate to the student's reading level. For example, if the objective reads "Given a selection on his instructional level that contains a generalization, the student will be able to identify the generalization," then the selection must be on the student's instructional level. If the selection is on a level more difficult than the student's instructional level, the instructor will not know whether the student's error is due to a lack of skill in identifying generalizations or due to the difficulty level of the material.

Unless a published diagnostic-prescriptive program that includes an assessment, such as the *Fountain Valley Reading System* (Sanches, et al. 1975), is being used, it is the teacher's responsibility to design assessment items to aid in determining whether a student has mastered a given skill. A teacher can ordinarily do this by using a knowledge of reading skills to make up questions that assess these skills. However, already developed materials from student textbooks, teacher's manuals, or professional reading texts may also be used to evaluate a student's competence in a specific skill.

For example, questions provided in student textbooks can often be used as assessment items with little or no adaptation. The history textbook question, "List the economic reasons for American interest in a canal through Central America," is an item appropriate for assessing the skill Identifying Details.

Many professional texts in reading provide exercises for reinforcing specific skills. These reinforcement activities may often be used as assessments. For example, if a teacher wanted to determine whether a student could use structural analysis to identify meaningful units in words, the students might be asked to underline each morpheme in the words following.*

rampage	floccule	hardy	plaintiff
Egypt	paranoid	leisure	frigate
cycle	poodle	maple	temple

In addition, the teacher might use the suggestions for assessing each skill presented in the annotated scope and sequence of skills in Chapter 10 of this text.

Number of Students to Pre-Assess Simultaneously

Assessments may be administered with any of the following teacher/pupil ratios: one teacher/one student, one teacher/small group of students, or one teacher/large group of students. Single-student assessments are often used for objectives that require students to answer orally to the teacher. For example, if a French teacher were concerned about the manner in which a student pronounced vocabulary words, she might have the youngster meet with her individually to pronounce the words. Small-group assessments are used when each student's performance must be observed, but the teacher is able to assess several students at one time. For example, the objective, "The student will be able to use guide words to locate given words in the dictionary," lends itself well to small-group assessment. The teacher may simply ask the students to locate the words *beluga, lieve, suttee* and then note which students use guide words to do this. Large-group assessments are most often used when responses can be written by individual students. For example, the objective,

*From Lou E. Burmeister, *Reading Strategies for Secondary School Teachers* (Reading, Mass.: Addison-Wesley, 1974), pp. 140–141.

"The student will be able to identify the cause-effect relationship," would lend itself to large-group assessment if the teacher administered a paper-pencil test in which students were asked to individually identify a given number of cause-effect relationships.

Single-student, large-group, and small-group assessments may each give precise measures of students' reading skills. However, individual assessments are extremely time-consuming for teachers. Though small-group and large-group assessments represent a more efficient use of teacher time, they are not as personal. Likewise, when only a portion of the class needs to be assessed, small-group assessment would be more appropriate than large-group assessment. Hence when teachers design their pre-assessments, they need to take into consideration the number of students they are going to assess, the use of teacher time, and their need for rapport with their students.

The assessment strategies suggested in Chapter 10 usually describe large-group procedures. Only when large-group assessments are not adequate are assessments for other group sizes described. Obviously the teacher could use any of the techniques for large-group assessments in a small-group or single-student situation if there were reason for believing that an individual assessment would be more appropriate.

Selection of Skills for Assessment

Pre-assessment of a series of objectives should be administered over a period of time. For example, a mathematics teacher had seven reading objectives, which he hoped his students would be able to master before the end of the semester. He tested the students on only the three skills that he felt they needed to know in order to understand their current mathematics lessons. Once the students had mastered these three skills, the teacher did further assessing on the additional objectives. Performing assessments in this manner assures a current diagnosis. On the other hand, when all objectives are tested at one time, the results may be outdated by the time instruction has begun. For example, Nancy's teacher had tested her on all the skills on a skill list in September. At that time, Nancy showed difficulty with many skills, including Locating Words in the Dictionary. However, before instruction in this skill began, Nancy had already learned to locate words in the dictionary. Thus her diagnosis was outdated before instruction even started.

Number of Post-Assessments

Teachers may administer a single post-assessment after the completion of several correlated lessons or at the end of an entire unit. However, teachers may administer more than one post-assessment on a skill. They might give the first post-assessment at the end of each lesson on a specific skill and then post-assess again a week or so later. Furthermore most teachers like to space the timing on their final post-assessments in a manner that they personally believe measures learning most effectively. For example, some teachers prefer to post-assess one day after the last lesson, while other teachers like to wait a week or two before post-assessing to assure themselves that the student has learned the skill and still remembers how to use it.

Task 3—Keeping Records

A diagnostic-prescriptive skills program requires records of skills that have been mastered and skills that need to be mastered. One form for record-keeping is illustrated in Figure 9.4. The form includes a listing of reading skills and students' names as well as a means for keeping track of whether the student has mastered the skills according to the pre- and post-assessments. A key used to indicate each youngster's performance on a given skill is located at the bottom of the checklist in Figure 9.4.

Inspection of Figure 9.4 shows that all the students passed the pre-assessment on skill 8, Identifying Details. All the students except two, Betty and John, passed the pre-assessment on skill 9, Identifying Main Ideas. Therefore Betty and John need instruction on skill 9. None of the students were able to satisfactorily pass the pre-assessment on skill 10, Identifying Sequence. However all received instruction and were then able to pass the post-assessment. On skill 11, Following Directions, five of the students passed the pre-assessment, four passed the post-assessment after they had received instruction, and two are still in need of instruction.

Teachers' checklists in the format shown in Figure 9.4, which correlate with the reading skills outlined in this book, are shown in Chapter 10. Figure 10.2 outlines the vocabulary skills; Figure 10.3 outlines the comprehension skills; and Figure 10.4 outlines the study skills.

Many skills on the scope and sequence of skills listed in Chapter 10 have subskills that have not been specifically delineated but that a teacher might feel important enough to list as separate skills on the personal scope and sequence of skills. For example, Using Structural Analysis includes the subskill of Identifying Greek and Latin Roots. In cases such as this, a separate chart listing each subskill might be kept. Figure 9.5 indicates which Greek and Latin roots each student has and has not mastered.

Task 4—Designing Instructional Strategies

Components in a Diagnostic-Prescriptive Format

The procedure for teaching each skill in a diagnostic-prescriptive program includes an initial teaching lesson and several reinforcement lessons. For each objective, there should be an initial teaching lesson that provides for explanation and demonstration of the skill. This lesson is usually teacher-directed. The initial teaching lesson is then followed by sufficient reinforcement lessons to ensure mastery of the skill. Usually two or three reinforcement lessons are sufficient for this purpose, although any number could be used if necessary. Reinforcement lessons may include explanation and demonstra-

Skill Descriptor	Skill Number	Betty	John	Rhonda	Robert	Steven	Renee	Rosa	Theresa	Otis	Carl	Charles
Identifying Details	8	√	√	√	√	√	√	√	√	√	√	√
Identifying Main Ideas	9	O	O	√	√	√	√	√	√	√	√	√
Identifying Sequence	10	⊘	⊘	⊘	⊘	⊘	⊘	⊘	⊘	⊘	⊘	⊘
Following Directions	11	√	√	⊘	⊘	⊘	O	O	⊘	√	√	√
Identifying Cause-Effect Relationships	12											
Making Inferences	13											
Making Generalizations and Conclusions	14											
Identifying Tone and Mood	15											
Identifying Theme	16											
Identifying Characterization	17											
Identifying Fact, Fiction, and Opinion	18											
Identifying Propaganda	19											
Identifying Author's Purpose	20											

Suggested Key: Blank Space — Not Assessed

√ — Passed Pre-Assessment

O — Did Not Pass Pre-Assessment; Needs Instruction

⊘ — Did Not Pass Pre-Assessment; Has Received Instruction and Passed Post-Assessment

Figure 9.4 Teacher's Checklist of Skills—Comprehension

Greek and Latin Roots	Betty	John	Rhonda	Robert	Steven	Renee	Rosa	Theresa	Otis	Carl	Charles
anti	Ⓥ	Ⓥ	○	Ⓥ	○	Ⓥ	Ⓥ	○	Ⓥ	○	○
aqua	Ⓥ	Ⓥ	Ⓥ	○	Ⓥ	Ⓥ	Ⓥ	Ⓥ	○	Ⓥ	Ⓥ
audi	○	Ⓥ	○	○	○	Ⓥ	Ⓥ	○	○	Ⓥ	○
dis	Ⓥ	Ⓥ	Ⓥ	Ⓥ	Ⓥ	Ⓥ	○	Ⓥ	Ⓥ	○	Ⓥ
hemi	Ⓥ	Ⓥ	Ⓥ	○	Ⓥ	Ⓥ	Ⓥ	○	○	Ⓥ	Ⓥ
inter	Ⓥ	Ⓥ	○	○	○	Ⓥ	○	○	○	Ⓥ	○
multi	Ⓥ	Ⓥ	Ⓥ	○	○	Ⓥ	Ⓥ	Ⓥ	Ⓥ	○	Ⓥ
mono	Ⓥ	Ⓥ	○	Ⓥ	Ⓥ	Ⓥ	Ⓥ	Ⓥ	○	Ⓥ	○
ology	○	Ⓥ	Ⓥ	○	Ⓥ	Ⓥ	Ⓥ	Ⓥ	○	Ⓥ	Ⓥ
ped	Ⓥ	Ⓥ	○	○	○	○	Ⓥ	Ⓥ	Ⓥ	○	○

Suggested Key: Blank Space — Not Assessed

√ — Passed Pre-Assessment

○ — Did Not Pass Pre-Assessment; Needs Instruction

Ⓥ — Did Not Pass Pre-Assessment; Has Received Instruction and Passed Post-Assessment

Figure 9.5   Teacher's Checklist of Subskill — Identifying Greek and Latin Roots

tion or may simply provide practice in the skill to be mastered. As such, reinforcement lessons may be teacher- or student-directed. Group and individual reading games and activities may be profitably used as reinforcement lessons.

Lesson planning in a diagnostic-prescriptive program is much the same as lesson planning in other teaching strategies, as described in Chapter 7. Therefore, each diagnostic-prescriptive lesson plan includes a behavioral objective, pre-assessment, materials, procedure, and post-assessment. The procedure section may include all or just part of the five steps that make up the directed reading lesson (i.e., step 1—preparation; step 2—silent reading; step 3—oral reading and discussion; step 4—follow-up; and step 5—extension activities). Figures 9.10, 9.12, 9.13, and 9.14 presented later in this chapter, schematically illustrate the relationship among the diagnostic-prescriptive technique, the lesson plan format, and the five-step directed reading lesson.

Resources for Designing Skill Lessons

Ideas for teaching each of the reading skills on any scope and sequence of skills chart are available from a variety of resources.

The annotated scope and sequence of skills located in Chapter 10 of this text describes three such resources. The first resource is the major portion of each section of the annotated scope and sequence of skills that delineates specific ways in which all the skills introduced in this textbook may be taught. For each reading skill, suggestions for one initial teaching lesson and two reinforcement activities are presented. The second resource is the portion entitled "Professional Texts Written for Teacher Use," which lists other professional textbooks in reading methodology for secondary school teachers. The third resource is titled "Instructional Materials Written for Student Use." In this section the classroom teacher is shown how to develop a systematic means for coordinating instructional materials written for students with the teaching suggestions presented. For example, a science teacher may decide to teach the skill Following Directions. He could use the specific teaching suggestions found in Chapter 10 to teach this skill, or the teaching suggestions found in other professional texts designed for teacher use, or he might already have available several copies of a workbook designed to help students follow directions in the science laboratory. In the latter case, he could correlate this workbook with the skill Following Directions by including a portion of the workbook as a reinforcement activity.

Task 5—Scheduling Instruction

When using a diagnostic-prescriptive program, the teacher needs to schedule a time for the pre-assessment, the initial teaching lesson, the reinforcement lessons, and the post-assessment. The amount of time that elapses between each step is at the discretion of the teacher. For example, Mr. Eby administered pre-assessments for five reading skills the week prior to the start of instruction on a skill to allow himself time to plan any needed lessons. He planned the reinforcement lessons so that they followed the initial teaching lesson at three-day intervals. Then he administered the post-assessment one week after the last reinforcement lesson. Thus his calendar appeared as shown in Figure 9.6.

	Monday	Tuesday	Wednesday	Thursday	Friday
Week 1				8 (Pre) 9 (Pre) 10 (Pre) 11 (Pre) 12 (Pre)	
Week 2	8 (In)	9 (In)	10 (In)	11 (In) 8 (1st)	12 (In) 9 (1st)
Week 3	10 (1st)	11 (1st) 8 (2nd)	12 (1st) 9 (2nd)	10 (2nd)	11 (2nd)
Week 4	12 (2nd)	8 (Post)	9 (Post)	10 (Post)	11 (Post)
Week 5	12 (Post)				

Key:

		Numbers represent skills:	
Pre	—Pre-Assessment	8	—Identifying Details
In	—Initial Teaching Lesson	9	—Identifying Main Ideas
1st	—First Reinforcement Lesson	10	—Identifying Sequence
2nd	—Second Reinforcement Lesson	11	—Following Directions
Post	—Post-Assessment	12	—Identifying Cause-Effect Relationships

Figure 9.6   Mr. Eby's Schedule for Diagnostic-Prescriptive Reading Instruction

	Monday	Tuesday	Wednesday	Thursday	Friday
Week 1				8 (Pre)	
Week 2	8 (In)	8 (1st)	8 (2nd)	8 (3rd) 9 (Pre)	8 (Post)
Week 3	9 (In)	9 (1st)	9 (2nd)	9 (3rd) 10 (Pre)	9 (Post)
Week 4	10 (In)	10 (1st)	10 (2nd)	10 (3rd) 11 (Pre)	10 (Post)
Week 5	11 (In)	11 (1st)	11 (2nd)	11 (3rd) 12 (Pre)	11 (Post)

Key:

		Numbers represent skills:	
Pre	—Pre-Assessment	8	—Identifying Details
In	—Initial Teaching Lesson	9	—Identifying Main Ideas
1st	—First Reinforcement Lesson	10	—Identifying Sequence
2nd	—Second Reinforcement Lesson	11	—Following Directions
Post	—Post-Assessment	12	—Identifying Cause-Effect Relationships

Figure 9.7   Mrs. Moore's Schedule for Diagnostic-Prescriptive Instruction

Mrs. Moore also pre-assessed the week prior to beginning instruction on a skill, but she selected only one skill. She then concentrated on teaching that skill during the following week through the presentation of an initial teaching lesson, three reinforcement lessons, and a post-assessment on that skill. Her schedule is shown in Figure 9.7.

Task 6 — Differentiating Instruction

When youngsters pass the pre-assessment on a given skill, there is no reason for them to complete the lessons on that skill, and the teacher has several options for alternative instruction for these students.

Because the diagnostic-prescriptive program is used in conjunction with the ongoing classroom program, the teacher can allow students who are competent on the reading skill to simply proceed with the content objective. Or the teacher can allow the adolescent to engage in enrichment activities related to course content or to the content of the reading skill. For example, biology students participating in enrichment activities related to course content might create a model of a cell; or they might do further reading for review purposes. Biology students involved in enrichment activities related to the content of the reading skill might, if the skill were Using Greek and Latin Roots and Affixes create new biological terms. An example of such a term is "poly-pseudopedology." A knowledge of Greek and Latin roots and affixes would be used by other students to reveal the meaning of the word, "the study of many false feet." (Bergman, 1976)

USE OF A DIAGNOSTIC–PRESCRIPTIVE PROGRAM

Teachers who teach reading as a subject as well as teachers who teach other content areas may use diagnostic-prescriptive techniques in order to teach their students the reading skills needed to understand content area assignments. Examples of content area teachers applying all the tasks needed in a diagnostic-prescriptive program are described in this section of the text.

To illustrate how lessons may be adapted from traditional to diagnostic-prescriptive techniques, each of the lessons described in Chapter 7 will be adapted for use in a diagnostic-prescriptive program. The adapted program in mathematics illustrates how a teacher used diagnostic-prescriptive instruction to teach a needed reading skill prior to a content lesson that required that skill. The adapted program in science describes how a teacher used diagnostic-prescriptive instruction to omit those skills that his students had mastered or to stress those skills that they had not. The adapted lesson plan in language arts shows how a teacher used a diagnostic-prescriptive approach to determine whether instruction was necessary; and the adapted lesson plan in social studies shows how a teacher differentiated instruction on the basis of his diagnosis.

Adapted Program 1—Mathematics

When Miss Downing became a diagnostic-prescriptive teacher, her first step was to list the reading skills that students would need to know for her particular program. Her list of skills, in the order in which she intended to teach them, is shown in Figure 9.8. This list is a sample only and is not intended as a guide for other mathematics teachers. Miss Downing's checklist of skills appears in Figure 9.9.

---

*Teaching
Order:*

First: Identifying Details (8)*
Second: Identifying Main Ideas (9)
Third: Identifying Sequence (10)
Fourth: Following Directions (11)
Fifth: Using Graphs (30.1, subskill of 30, Using Maps, Graphs, and Tables)
Sixth: Identifying Cause-Effect Relationships (12)
Seventh: Making Inferences (13)
Eighth: Making Generalizations and Conclusions (14)
Ninth: Using Tables (30.2, subskill of 30, Using Maps, Graphs, and Tables)
Tenth: Using Illustration Clues (1)

---

*Number of the skill as found in the scope and sequence of skills described in this text.

**Figure 9.8   Scope and Sequence of Reading Skills for Miss Downing's
Grade Nine Mathematics Class**

Having taught the first four skills, she began prerequisite work on a lesson on functions. She knew that her students should be able to use graphs before the lesson. Although using graphs was her reading objective, she knew that she would not have time to do more than review this concept, and this review would be insufficient for those students who were seriously deficient in this area. Therefore, she diagnosed her students on reading graphs by using appropriate pre-assessment suggestions from the annotated scope and sequence of skills for skill number 30, Using Maps, Graphs, and Tables, in Chapter 10 of this book. All but five of her students were able to pass the pre-assessment. So, while the remainder of the class proceeded with their regular lesson, she gave these five students an initial teaching lesson, and then she had them complete two reinforcement activities and a post-assessment. All five students passed the post-assessment and were ready to go on to the lesson on functions as described in Chapter 7. However, since students had already completed the pre-assessment on using graphs, this aspect was deleted from the lesson.

Miss Downing's schedule and lesson on functions appear in Figure 9.10.

Adapted Program 2—Science

When Miss Scott became a diagnostic-prescriptive teacher, she designed a

214

Teaching Order	Skill Descriptor	Skill Number*	Caryn	Irma	Rosemary	Jake	Margaret	Mickey	George	Edward	Ricardo	Tony	Dixie	Jeanine	Murray	Melissa	Gayle	Kevin	Patrice	Mary Lynn	Beth	Sharon	Anna	Lee
1.	Identifying Details	8	√	√	√	√	√	√	√	√	√	√	√	√	√	√	√	√	√	√	√	√	√	√
2.	Identifying Main Ideas	9	○	Ⓥ	√	√	Ⓥ	√	√	√	Ⓥ	√	○	○	√	Ⓥ	√	Ⓥ	√	√	√	√	Ⓥ	√
3.	Identifying Sequence	10	√	√	√	Ⓥ	√	√	√	Ⓥ	√	√	Ⓥ	√	√	Ⓥ	√	√	√	Ⓥ	√	√	√	√
4.	Following Directions	11	Ⓥ	Ⓥ	Ⓥ	Ⓥ	Ⓥ	Ⓥ	Ⓥ	Ⓥ	Ⓥ	Ⓥ	Ⓥ	Ⓥ	Ⓥ	Ⓥ	Ⓥ	Ⓥ	Ⓥ	Ⓥ	Ⓥ	Ⓥ	Ⓥ	Ⓥ
5.	Using Graphs	30.1	Ⓥ	√	Ⓥ	√	√	Ⓥ	√	√	Ⓥ	√	√	Ⓥ	√	√	√	√	√	√	√	√	√	√
6.	Identifying Cause-Effect Relationships	12																						
7.	Making Inferences	13																						
8.	Making Generalizations and Conclusions	14																						
9.	Using Tables	30.2																						
10.	Using Illustration Clues	1																						

Suggested Key: Blank Space — Not Assessed

√ — Passed Pre-Assessment

○ — Did Not Pass Pre-Assessment; Needs Instruction

Ⓥ — Did Not Pass Pre-Assessment; Has Received Instruction and Passed Post-Assessment

*As designated in the scope and sequence of skills described in this text.

Figure 9.9   Checklist of Skills for Miss Downing's Grade Nine Mathematics Class

Schedule for Teaching the Skill, Using Graphs

	Monday	Tuesday	Wednesday	Thursday	Friday
Week 1	30.1*(Pre)		30.1 (In)		
Week 2	30.1 (1st)		30.1 (2nd)		
Week 3	30.1 (Post)				
Week 4	Lesson on functions scheduled (See lesson below)				

Key:

Pre —Pre-Assessment   2nd —Second Reinforcement Lesson
In —Initial Teaching Lesson   Post —Post-Assessment
1st —First Reinforcement Lesson

*30.1 is the skill of Using Graphs and is a subskill of skill 30, Using Maps, Graphs, and Tables.

Lesson on Functions †

(One day only on topic of functions)
Behavioral Objective: Using graphs
Pre-Assessment: Graphs drawn on mimeo
Materials: Overhead projector, transparencies, charts, textbooks
Procedure:
    Step 1—Preparation (teacher shows entire class how to use graphs; explains functions)
    Step 2—Silent Reading (in textbook on functions)
    Step 3—Oral Reading and Discussion (discuss textbook assignment)
    Step 4—Follow-Up (small-group work for those who need extra help, all reread assignment to verify their solutions to the function problems)
    Step 5—Extension (locate everyday functional relationships; e.g., carburetor size versus amount gas used)
Post-Assessment: Graphs drawn on mimeo

Pre-assessment scheduled twenty-one days prior to lesson on functions
† Abstract of mathematics lesson found in Chapter 7.

**Figure 9.10 Miss Downing's Schedule and Lesson on Functions in a
Diagnostic-Prescriptive Program**

scope and sequence of reading skills to be used with each of her classes. Four of the skills on her scope and sequence of skills list were number 8, Identifying Details; number 33.1, Categorizing, a subskill of skill number 33, Organizing Information; number 4.1, Using Greek and Latin Roots, a subskill of skill number 4, Using Structural Analysis; and number 20.1, Determining Point of View, a subskill of skill number 20, Identifying Author's Purpose.

Although the skills, Categorizing, Using Greek and Latin Roots, and Determining Point of View were not listed as major categories on the scope and sequence of skills described in this text, Miss Scott believed that these specific skills were particularly important to biology and should be isolated; therefore, she included them on her skills list. Although Miss Scott could have assigned any numerals to them, she felt they were actually subskills of two other skills already on the chart. Hence she labeled Categorizing as skill number 33.1, a subskill of skill number 33, Organizing Information; and labeled Determining Point of View as skill number 20.1, a subskill of skill number 20, Identifying Author's Purpose.

Miss Scott designed more precise pre-assessments and scheduled them differently than she had before she became a diagnostic-prescriptive teacher. To design the assessments for these four objectives, she adapted the suggestions in the annotated scope and sequence of skills found in Chapter 10 of this book. Furthermore, she scheduled the pre-assessments for administration several days prior to teaching the skills. The results of Miss Scott's testing are found in Figure 9.11.

All the students passed the pre-assessment for Identifying Details (8) and Categorizing (33.1); and no students passed the pre-assessment for Using Greek and Latin Roots (4.1) and Determining Point of View (20.1). Therefore Miss Scott did not need to give instruction in Identifying Details (8) and Categorizing (33.1), although she did teach a lesson on biological classification that required these skills. (See Figure 9.12, day one.) Miss Scott taught lessons that stressed Using Greek and Latin Roots (4.1) and Determining Point of View (20.1) to all students. (See Figure 9.12, days two and three.)

Miss Scott's initial teaching lesson on Greek and Latin roots was a teacher-directed lesson in which she pointed out how structural analysis (including using Greek and Latin roots) can be used to find the meanings of science words. At the end of this class session, Miss Scott administered a post-assessment on Greek and Latin roots to gauge her students' progress. At the next class session, she directed the first reinforcement activity in which she asked students to orally review the meanings of some of the roots and reminded them of the importance of structural analysis in learning the meanings of science words. Miss Scott planned to do an additional reinforcement activity based on the suggestions given for Using Greek and Latin Roots, skill 4 in the annotated scope and sequence of skills in Chapter 10, before administering her final post-assessment a week later.

Similarly, Miss Scott presented an initial teaching lesson on determining point of view in which she conducted a teacher-led discussion. The first reinforcement activity was completed the same day when students reread the assignment to determine the author's point of view. The second reinforcement activity was completed a week later, when students presented the results of projects based on describing a different biological classification system. In another week's time, Miss Scott administered the final post-assessment, which she designed to supplement the post-assessment she used at the end of the third daily lesson.

Miss Scott's schedule and lesson plans for teaching these reading skills appear in Figure 9.12.

Adapted Program 3—Language Arts

When Mr. Jackson became a diagnostic-prescriptive teacher, one of the skills that he wished his students to master was Identifying Tone and Mood. When he pre-assessed his class, he found that none of the students had mastered this skill. He then worked through an initial teaching lesson and several reinforce-

Teaching Order	Skill Descriptor	Skill Number	Donna	Edward	Kimberley	Ben	Mack	Sheila	Pat	Colby	Kelly	Oscar	Al	Mae	Nell	Bobby	Dennis	Donald	Danny	Alan	Velia	Felix	Juanita	Minnie
1.	Identifying Details	8*	√	√	√	√	√	√	√	√	√	√	√	√	√	√	√	√	√	√	√	√	√	√
2.	Categorizing	33.1†	√	√	√	√	√	√	√	√	√	√	√	√	√	√	√	√	√	√	√	√	√	√
3.	Using Greek and Latin Roots	4.1†	○	○	○	○	○	○	○	○	○	○	○	○	○	○	○	○	○	○	○	○	○	○
4.	Determining Point of View	20.1†	○	○	○	○	○	○	○	○	○	○	○	○	○	○	○	○	○	○	○	○	○	○

Suggested Key: Blank Space — Not Assessed

√ — Passed Pre-Assessment

○ — Did Not Pass Pre-Assessment; Needs Instruction

Ⓥ — Did Not Pass Pre-Assessment; Has Received Instruction and Passed Post-Assessment

*As designated in the scope and sequence of skills described in this text.
†Subskills to those listed in the scope and sequence of skills described in this text.

Figure 9.11 Partial Checklist of Skills for Miss Scott's Science Class

Schedule for Teaching the Skills, Identifying Details, Categorizing,
Using Greek and Latin Roots, and Determining Point of View

	Monday	Tuesday	Wednesday	Thursday	Friday
Week 1					8* (Pre) 33.1 (Pre) 4.1 (Pre) 20.1 (Pre)
Week 2	Lesson on classification systems (See day 1 below)	4.1 (In) (See day 2 below)	4.1 (1st) 20.1 (In) 20.1 (1st) (See day 3 below)	4.1 (2nd)	
Week 3			20.1 (2nd)	4.1 (Post)	
Week 4			20.1 (Post)		

*Numbers represent skills:

  8 —Identifying Details
33.1 —Categorizing, a subskill of skill 33, Organizing Information
 4.1 —Using Greek and Latin roots, a subskill of skill 4, Using Structural Analysis
20.1 —Determining Point of View, a subskill of skill 20, Identifying Author's Purpose

Lesson on Biological Classification Systems †

(Day 1 of three-day lesson on topic of biological classification systems)
Behavioral Objectives: Identifying details; categorizing
Pre-Assessment: Paragraphs written by students
Materials: Pictures and written descriptions of various animals
Procedure:
    Step 1—Preparation (teacher motivation; students move through stations and then
        devise a classification system)
Post-Assessment: Development of feasible classification system by each group

---

Pre-assessment scheduled three days prior to day 1

(Day 2 of three-day lesson on same topic)
Behavioral Objective: Identifying Greek and Latin roots
Pre-Assessment: List of words containing Greek and Latin roots
Materials: Mimeo, textbook, chalkboard
    Step 1—Preparation (teacher presentation on roots)
    Step 2—Silent Reading (look for roots in textbook)
    Step 3—Oral Reading and Discussion (discuss lesson in text)
Post-Assessment: List of words containing Greek and Latin roots

---

Pre-assessment scheduled four days prior to day 2

(Day 3 of three-day lesson on same topic)
Behavioral Objective: Determining point of view
Pre-Assessment: List of statements reflecting points of view
Materials: Textbook, mimeo
    Step 4—Follow-Up (review of roots; class discussion on point of view of various
        authors on same topic)
    Step 5—Extension (reread text to find point of view; select topics for projects to be
        completed at later date)
Post-Assessment: List of statements reflecting points of view

---

Pre-assessment scheduled five days prior to day 3

† Abstract of science lesson found in Chapter 7.

**Figure 9.12 Miss Scott's Schedule and Lesson in Science in a
Diagnostic-Prescriptive Program**

ment lessons on this skill based on ideas given in his student's textbook. None of the students were able to pass the post-assessment following these activities.

Two weeks later, Mr. Jackson attempted to teach the concepts again. Using the two-day lesson plan shown in Figure 9.13 he pre-assessed before he presented the second set of lessons in case some students had learned the skill on their own during the lag between the two teaching approaches. He determined that no students in his class had learned the skill. He began with an initial teaching lesson in which he presented a teacher-led discussion on tone and mood and an audiotape of a passage from William Faulkner's *Light in August*. In addition, the students wrote one-paragraph themes and then met in small groups to compare the tone and mood of each. The first reinforcement activity took place the same day that the students read and discussed Chapter 20 of *Light in August*. The second and third reinforcement activities took place the next day when Mr. Jackson asked students to react to themes written by peers and to begin individual projects. Mr. Jackson gauged his students' progress by the themes that were completed in the second lesson. However, his final post-assessment took place five days later, after students had completed their projects.

Most of the students were able to pass this post-assessment. Those who did not, appeared to be having only minor problems with the concept. Therefore Mr. Jackson gave each of these students individual help until all were able to meet the objective.

Before checking students off on his checksheet as having mastered tone and mood, Mr. Jackson planned to design another lesson on this skill based on a prose selection which would be assigned in a few weeks. Those students who could pass the pre-assessment would be given credit for the skill Identifying Tone and Mood, and would be asked to apply the skill when reading the prose selection. Those students who were unable to pass the pre-assessment would be given further lessons on the skill in the content of the prose selection. In the third approach, Mr. Jackson planned to use the suggestions and materials referenced under Identifying Tone and Mood, skill 15 in the annotated scope and sequence of skills in Chapter 10 of this text for more ideas on instructing his students.

Figure 9.13 shows Mr. Jackson's schedule for teaching the skill Identifying Tone and Mood and the lesson plans for Approach 2.

Adapted Program 4—Social Studies

When Mr. Lentz became a diagnostic-prescriptive teacher, he placed the skill Predicting Outcomes on the scope and sequence of skills that he had designed for his classes. Although this skill is not on the scope and sequence of skills described in this text, Mr. Lentz believed it to be a skill particularly important to history and, therefore, included it on his skills list. Mr. Lentz located course-related sentences and short paragraphs from whose beginnings, the endings might be anticipated. He pre-assessed his students on predicting outcomes by showing students the beginnings of selections and asking them

Schedule for Teaching the Skill, Identifying Tone and Mood

	Monday	Tuesday	Wednesday	Thursday	Friday
Week 1		15 (Pre) Approach 1		15 (In) Approach 1	
Week 2	15 (1st) Approach 1	15 (2nd) Approach 1			
Week 3		15 (Post) Approach 1			
Week 4					
Week 5	15 (Pre) Approach 2	15 (In) 15 (1st) Approach 2	15 (2nd) 15 (3rd) Approach 2		
Week 6	15 (Post) Approach 2				
Week 7					
Week 8	15 (Pre) Approach 3		15 (In) Approach 3		15 (1st) Approach 3
Week 9		15 (2nd) Approach 3			
Week 10		15 (Post) Approach 3			

Note: 15 is the skill of Identifying Tone and Mood

Lesson on Faulkner's Style—Approach 2 to Identifying Tone and Mood*

(Day 1 in a two-day lesson plan on topic of Faulkner)
Behavioral Objective: Identifying tone and mood
Pre-Assessment: Checklist containing traits that characterize an author's style
Materials: Tape player, tape recordings, passages from Faulkner
Procedure:
    Step 1—Preparation (teacher-led discussion, play tape recording of excerpt, students
        write paragraphs and discuss them in small groups)
    Step 2—Silent Reading (in Chapter 20 of *Light in August*)
    Step 3—Oral Reading and Discussion (discuss reading assignment)
Post-Assessment: Not to be completed until day 2

Pre-assessment scheduled one day prior to day 1

(Day 2 in two-day lesson on topic of Faulkner)
Behavioral Objective: Identifying tone and mood
Pre-Assessment: Given on day 1
Materials: Themes written by students for homework
Procedure:
    Step 4—Follow-Up (discuss and rewrite themes in small groups; large-group sharing
        follows)
    Step 5—Extension Activities (select topics for projects to be completed at a later
        date; e.g., rewrite Faulkner passage in different style to reflect different tone and
        mood)
Post-Assessment: Theme handed in by students at end of class period

Pre-assessment scheduled two days prior to day 2

*Abstract of language arts lesson found in Chapter 7.

Figure 9.13 Mr. Jackson's Schedule and Lesson for the Second Approach to Teaching the Skill, Identifying Tone and Mood

to predict the endings. Sample item: "Southern Democrats were disturbed with Truman's liberal views. Therefore, when it came time for the Democratic party to nominate a candidate for President . . .."

Ten of his students were not able to pass the pre-assessment, but the remainder of the students were able to complete it with ease. Therefore, Mr. Lentz decided to differentiate instruction on the skill Predicting Outcomes. Those students who passed the pre-assessment would complete an enrichment activity related to the content of the reading skill. The lesson plans for both groups are shown in Figure 9.14. Mr. Lentz did not use the pre-assessment from the original plan as he had already had the students complete a pre-assessment.

Mr. Lentz adapted these plans in the following manner for the students who did not complete the pre-assessment satisfactorily:

Day 1: All students participated in the introductory class discussion concerning the Truman era. After the discussion, students who had passed the pre-assessment were given time to read silently. Those students who had not passed the pre-assessment on predicting outcomes met with Mr. Lentz. The introductory class discussion had begun the initial teaching lesson, which continued with Mr. Lentz' showing them how to make simple predictions. For example, one of the tasks he asked them to do was to read the following sentence. "The public opinion polls, many newspapers, and numerous citizens assumed Dewey would win. But, Truman . . .."

At that point, the students were told to close their books and make guesses about Truman's chances for re-election. Mr. Lentz asked questions such as, "What do you think is going to happen to Truman?" "What words give you clues that he might win?"

After several sentences were read in a similar manner, Mr. Lentz gave the students a guided reading sheet that paralleled the activities done during the initial teaching lesson. The students were then instructed to read their textbook assignment by themselves and to complete the tasks required by their guided reading sheet. This guided reading sheet served as their first reinforcement activity for the skill Predicting Outcomes.

Day 2: All students were able to participate in the oral reading and discussion. Those students who had passed the pre-assessment had read the chapter with the discussion questions in mind. The students who had not passed the pre-assessment had been given a guided reading sheet the previous day that helped them focus on these same questions. Furthermore, the oral reading and discussion served as a second reinforcement activity. Following the oral reading and discussion, all students began projects that predicted how Truman would be perceived in 1985. These projects served as a third reinforcement activity for those students who did not pass the pre-assessment.

Day 3: While the other class members worked on their projects, Mr. Lentz met with the group of ten students for their fourth reinforcement activity—that of specifically reviewing the tasks they had been asked to complete on their guided reading sheets. After this fourth reinforcement lesson, all students showed their projects to the remainder of the class. The final activity on the third day, a class discussion of how other Presidents might be perceived forty years after their terms, was participated in by all students and served as a fifth reinforcement activity for the students who had not passed the pre-

222

Schedule for Teaching the Skill, Predicting Outcomes

	Monday	Tuesday	Wednesday	Thursday	Friday
Week 1				14.1 (Pre)	
Week 2		14.1 (In) 14.1 (1st)	14.1 (2nd) 14.1 (3rd)	14.1 (4th) 14.1 (5th)	
Week 3				14.1 (Post)	

Note: 14.1 is the skill of Predicting Outcomes, a subskill of skill 14, Making Generalizations and Conclusions.

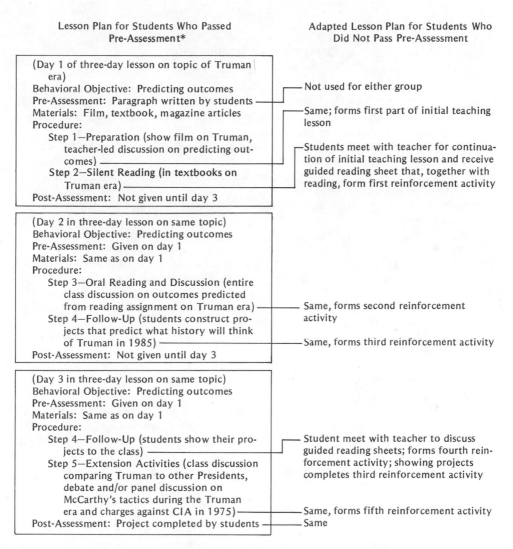

Lesson Plan for Students Who Passed
Pre-Assessment*

(Day 1 of three-day lesson on topic of Truman era)
Behavioral Objective: Predicting outcomes
Pre-Assessment: Paragraph written by students
Materials: Film, textbook, magazine articles
Procedure:
    Step 1—Preparation (show film on Truman, teacher-led discussion on predicting outcomes)
    Step 2—Silent Reading (in textbooks on Truman era)
Post-Assessment: Not given until day 3

(Day 2 in three-day lesson on same topic)
Behavioral Objective: Predicting outcomes
Pre-Assessment: Given on day 1
Materials: Same as on day 1
Procedure:
    Step 3—Oral Reading and Discussion (entire class discussion on outcomes predicted from reading assignment on Truman era)
    Step 4—Follow-Up (students construct projects that predict what history will think of Truman in 1985)
Post-Assessment: Not given until day 3

(Day 3 in three-day lesson on same topic)
Behavioral Objective: Predicting outcomes
Pre-Assessment: Given on day 1
Materials: Same as on day 1
Procedure:
    Step 4—Follow-Up (students show their projects to the class)
    Step 5—Extension Activities (class discussion comparing Truman to other Presidents, debate and/or panel discussion on McCarthy's tactics during the Truman era and charges against CIA in 1975)
Post-Assessment: Project completed by students

Adapted Lesson Plan for Students Who
Did Not Pass Pre-Assessment

— Not used for either group

— Same; forms first part of initial teaching lesson

— Students meet with teacher for continuation of initial teaching lesson and receive guided reading sheet that, together with reading, form first reinforcement activity

— Same, forms second reinforcement activity

— Same, forms third reinforcement activity

— Student meet with teacher to discuss guided reading sheets; forms fourth reinforcement activity; showing projects completes third reinforcement activity

— Same, forms fifth reinforcement activity
— Same

*Abstract of social studies lesson found in Chapter 7.

Figure 9.14   Mr. Lentz' Schedule and Lesson on Predicting Outcomes in a Diagnostic-Prescriptive Program

223

assessment on predicting outcomes. Mr. Lentz post-assessed all the students' progress by their projects, which were completed on the third day of instruction.

One week later: After one week, Mr. Lentz gave a small-group post-assessment to those ten students who had not passed the pre-assessment. Those who passed the post-assessment were considered to have mastered the skill. Those who did not, would be given more lessons during the following weeks.

Mr. Lentz' schedule for teaching the skill Predicting Outcomes to those students who had not mastered it is illustrated in Figure 9.14.

References and Bibliography

Askov, E., and Otto W. *Teacher's Planning Guide—Study Skills.* Wisconsin Design for Reading Skill Development. Minneapolis, Minn.: National Computer Systems, 1972.

Bergman, F. L. *The English Teacher's Activities Handbook: An Idea Book for Middle and Secondary Schools.* Boston: Allyn & Bacon, 1976.

Bond, G. L., and Wagner, E. B. *Teaching the Child to Read.* 4th ed. New York: Macmillan, 1966.

Burmeister, L. E. *Reading Strategies for Secondary School Teachers.* Reading, Mass.: Addison-Wesley, 1974.

Dallmann, M., et al. *The Teaching of Reading.* 4th ed. New York: Holt, Rinehart & Winston, 1974.

Ekwall, E. E. *Locating and Correcting Reading Difficulties.* Columbus, Ohio: Merrill, 1970.

Fry, E. *Reading Instruction for Classroom and Clinic.* New York: McGraw-Hill, 1972.

Guszak, F. J. *Diagnostic Reading Instruction in the Elementary School.* Harper & Row, 1972.

Harris, L. A., and Smith, C. B. *Reading Instruction Through Diagnostic Teaching.* New York: Holt, Rinehart & Winston, 1972.

Heilman, A. W. *Principles and Practices of Teaching Reading.* 3rd ed. Columbus, Ohio: Merrill, 1972.

Herr, S. *Learning Activities for Reading.* 2nd ed. Dubuque, Iowa: Brown, 1970.

Houghton Mifflin Readers. Boston: Houghton Mifflin, 1972.

Niles, O., et al. *Tactics in Reading.* Glenview, Ill.: Scott, Foresman, 1972.

Otto, W., and Askov, E. *The Wisconsin Design for Reading Skill Development: Rationale and Guidelines.* Minneapolis, Minn.: National Computer Systems, 1972.

Otto, W., and Smith, R. J. *Administering the School Reading Program.* Boston: Houghton Mifflin, 1970.

Reader's Digest New Advanced Reading Skill Builders. N. Y.: Reader's Digest Services, Educational Division, 1973.

Sanches, R. A., et al. *The Fountain Valley Teacher Support System in Reading.* Huntington Beach, Calif.: Zweig and Associates, 1975.

Spache, G. D., and Spache, E. B. *Reading in the Elementary School.* 2nd ed. Boston: Allyn & Bacon, 1973.

Thomas, E. L., and Robinson, H. A. *Improving Reading in Every Class.* Boston: Allyn & Bacon, 1972.

Zintz, M. V. *The Reading Process: The Teacher and the Learner.* Dubuque, Iowa: Brown, 1970.

Chapter 10

Teaching Vocabulary, Comprehension, and Study Skills

Prerequisite 10.1

Before beginning this chapter, participants should have successfully completed the objectives for Chapters 2 through 9 or should have a broad knowledge of the reading skills, diagnosis, reading problems in instructional materials, lesson planning, instructional strategies, and diagnostic-prescriptive teaching.

Rationale 10.2

Secondary reading instruction should be looked upon as a growth process, wherein new skills are mastered and formerly learned skills are refined and applied to more difficult material. One of the most efficient ways for secondary teachers to overview the reading skills and to select those to be mastered and refined is to look at all the reading skills and how to teach them. This chapter acquaints the participant with the reading skills and an objective, assessment procedure, and teaching techniques for each.

Objectives 10.3

On successful completion of this chapter, the participant will be able to:

1. List the skills from the scope and sequence chart in which proficiency would be most valuable to students in his subject area and give reasons for his choices.

2. Design a lesson for one skill that includes (1) an objective, (2) materials, (3) a pre-assessment, (4) an introductory lesson, (5) reinforcement lessons, and (6) a post-assessment.
3. Describe his management system of reading skills, records, and teaching strategies.
4. (On the lines below, add other objectives according to your instructor's directions.)_____

5. _____
_____

6. _____
_____

7. _____
_____

*   *   *   *   *   *   *   *   *   *   *   *   *   *

Chapter 13, Experience 10 extends Chapter 10 with this performance/consequence objective.

8. During this experience, the participant teaches at least one skill to middle or secondary school students and will include in the teaching procedure a pre-assessment, an introductory lesson, two reinforcement lessons, and a post-assessment.

*   *   *   *   *   *   *   *   *   *   *   *   *   *

Self Pre-Assessment 10.4

Can you complete all the activities listed in **Objectives 10.3**? Answer "yes," "no," or "not certain."

If you answered "yes" to the question, complete the enabling activities required by your instructor and take the Post-Assessment on the date assigned by him.

If you answered "no," refer to **Enabling Activities 10.5**. If you decide to do any activities that are not required, select those that best suit you as a learner. You need not complete all the optional activities or all parts of a particular optional activity. As soon as you have the information you need to complete the objectives, answer "yes" to the **Self Pre-Assessment 10.4** question and stop the activity.

If you answered "not certain" to the question, refer to **Enabling Activities 10.5**. Select the enabling activity that best suits your style of learning and peruse it. Then make a firm "yes" or "no" answer and proceed accordingly.

Enabling Activities 10.5

Complete only as many of the activities listed below as are required and which you need in order to meet the objectives.

1. *Enabling activity one* is a *reading* alternative. This is **Information Given 10.6.** It is a brief overview of a diagnostic-prescriptive approach to teaching reading skills to students in middle and secondary schools.

2. *Enabling activity two* is another *reading* option. In this case, the material to be read is one of the textbooks used to expand the theoretical background for this course. See chart on inside front cover for keying in textbooks that may be used.

3. *Enabling activity three* is a *class session* option. Attend the class session(s) on the date(s), at the time(s), and at the place(s) announced.

_____	_____	_____
(Date)	(Time)	(Place)
_____	_____	_____
(Date)	(Time)	(Place)
_____	_____	_____
(Date)	(Time)	(Place)

4. *Enabling activity four* (These lines are left blank so that you may add other enabling activities as suggested by your instructor.) _____

_____

_____

5. *Enabling activity five* _____

_____

6. *Enabling activity six* _____

_____

Now that you have completed the appropriate number of required and/or optional learning alternatives, look back at **Self Pre-Assessment 10.4.** If you feel you can answer "yes" to all of the questions, you are ready to proceed to the Post-Assessment. This may be given to you immediately or after completion of a series of chapters.

After completion of a workshop on techniques for teaching reading skills in the middle and secondary school, both Miss Hyde, a reading teacher, and Mr. Hudson, a social studies teacher, decided to rearrange their teaching methods to include all the tasks involved in a diagnostic-prescriptive technique. In order to develop this type of program in their classes, they asked the consultant several questions.

1. Where can we locate an overview of all the reading skills that middle and secondary school students should know?
2. What types of objectives, assessments, and procedures should be used in developing teaching strategies concerning each of these reading skills?
3. What is an efficient format for keeping records of reading skills assessed and taught?
4. How can a teacher coordinate the reading skills, records, and teaching strategies?

The remainder of Chapter 10 answers the questions asked by Miss Hyde and Mr. Hudson.

SCOPE AND SEQUENCE OF READING SKILLS

Chapters 2, 3, and 4 of this text describe a wide variety of vocabulary, comprehension, and study skills that should be known by middle and secondary school students. An overview of all the skills presented in those three chapters are listed in the scope and sequence of skills shown in Figure 10.1.

ANNOTATED SCOPE AND SEQUENCE OF SKILLS

An annotated scope and sequence of skills, which presents objectives, assessments, and procedures for developing teaching strategies for all reading skills discussed in this text, makes up the core of Chapter 10.

Components of the Annotated Scope and Sequence of Skills

Each skill listed in the scope and sequence of skills shown in Figure 10.1 is

1. Using Illustration Clues	18. Identifying Fact, Fiction, and Opinion
2. Using Context Clues	19. Identifying Propaganda
3. Using Phonic Analysis	20. Identifying Author's Purpose
4. Using Structural Analysis	21. Scheduling Time
5. Using Dictionary Skills	22. Setting Purposes
6. Expanding Background in Vocabulary	23. Using a Study Technique
7. Using a Combination of Vocabulary Skills	24. Using Locational Aids in the Library
8. Identifying Details	25. Recording References
9. Identifying Main Ideas	26. Using the Library Call System
10. Identifying Sequence	27. Using Locational Aids Within Books
11. Following Directions	28. Using Footnotes
12. Identifying Cause-Effect Relationships	29. Using Glossaries
13. Making Inferences	30. Using Maps, Graphs, and Tables
14. Making Generalizations and Conclusions	31. Matching Materials with Purposes
15. Identifying Tone and Mood	32. Understanding the Organization of Paragraphs
16. Identifying Theme	33. Organizing Information
17. Identifying Characterization	34. Adjusting Rate to Purpose

Figure 10.1 Scope and Sequence of Skills

described in more depth in the annotated scope and sequence of skills, which forms the last section of this chapter. For each skill presented, there is an annotation that contains the following components:

1. *A descriptor*, which matches the name on the scope and sequence of skills and which summarizes the objective.
2. *A skill number*, which matches the skill number on the scope and sequence of skills and which helps in locating a skill.
3. An *objective*, which states in behavioral terms what students must be able to do to prove that they are competent in the skill.
4. The term *criterion level* followed by a blank space. Because the number of correct responses as well as the percentage of correct responses required for competence will vary from situation to situation and teacher to teacher, a blank space has been left so that the teacher may indicate criterion level. For example, one teacher may ask three questions and require that two of the three (66 per cent) be answered correctly for proof of competence; another teacher may ask four questions and require that three of the four (75 per cent) be answered correctly for proof of competence.
5. A *pre-assessment* suggestion, which indicates how the objective might be pre-assessed.
6. A *sample generic teaching strategy*, including suggestions for an *initial teaching procedure* and two *reinforcement procedures*.
7. A *post-assessment* suggestion, which indicates how the objective might be post-assessed.
8. *Correlated materials*, which include a listing of *professional texts written for teacher use* and a recommendation that a list of *instructional material written for student use* be added.

229

Professional Texts Written for Teacher Use. For each skill annotated, teaching suggestions located in other secondary reading methods textbooks have been identified and referenced under the heading Professional Texts Written for Teacher Use. These texts include the following:

Aukerman, R. C. *Reading in the Secondary School Classroom.* New York: McGraw-Hill, 1972.

Burmeister, L. E. *Reading Strategies for Secondary School Teachers.* Reading, Mass.: Addison-Wesley, 1974.

Herber, H. L. *Teaching Reading in Content Areas.* Englewood Cliffs, N. J.: Prentice-Hall, 1970.

Karlin, R. *Teaching Reading in High School.* 2nd ed. Indianapolis, Ind.: Bobbs-Merrill, 1972.

Olson, A. V., and Ames, W. S. *Teaching Reading Skills in Secondary Schools.* Scranton, Pa.: Intext Educational Publishers, 1972.

Robinson, H. A. *Teaching Reading and Study Strategies: The Content Areas.* Boston: Allyn & Bacon, 1975.

Thomas, E. L., and Robinson, H. A. abridged edition *Improving Reading in Every Class.* Boston: Allyn & Bacon, 1972. (The pages referenced in Chapter 10 refer to the abridged edition of this text rather than to the unabridged edition referenced on the inside front cover.)

Instructional Materials Written for Student Use. Teachers may wish to correlate instructional materials written for student use with teaching suggestions found in the annotated scope and sequence of skills. Hence a section entitled Instructional Materials Written for Student Use has been included with each skill presented.

Record-Keeping Format

There are many forms for record keeping and teachers should select one that best suits their individual needs. One form for record keeping has already been illustrated in Chapter 9 in Figures 9.4, 9.5, 9.10, and 9.12. This format is shown again in Chapter 10 in Figures 10.2, 10.3, and 10.4.

MANAGEMENT OF READING SKILLS, RECORDS, AND TEACHING STRATEGIES

There are many ways by which teachers may coordinate materials found in this textbook with materials found elsewhere. The pages of *Personalizing Reading Instruction in Middle, Junior, and Senior High Schools* have been perforated to facilitate the following procedure. It is suggested that the teacher remove the following sections of Chapter 10 along the perforated edges: (1) the scope and sequence of skills shown in Figure 10.1, (2) the checklists shown in Figures 10.2, 10.3, and 10.4, and (3) the annotated scope and sequence of skills, which forms the last part of this chapter. By doing so, teachers may place materials in a three-ring binder and then mark

Skill Descriptor	Skill Number	Students' Names												
Using Illustration Clues	1													
Using Context Clues	2													
Using Phonic Analysis	3													
Using Structural Analysis	4													
Using Dictionary Skills	5													
Expanding Background in Vocabulary	6													
Using a Combination of Vocabulary Skills	7													

Suggested Key: Blank Space — Not Assessed

√ — Passed Pre-Assessment

◯ — Did Not Pass Pre-Assessment; Needs Instruction

⊘ — Did Not Pass Pre-Assessment; Has Received Instruction and Passed Post-Assessment

Figure 10.2   Teacher's Checklist of Skills—Vocabulary

231

	Students' Names												
Skill Descriptor **Skill Number**													
Identifying Details 8													
Identifying Main Ideas 9													
Identifying Sequence 10													
Following Directions 11													
Identifying Cause-Effect Relationships 12													
Making Inferences 13													
Making Generalizations and Conclusions 14													
Identifying Tone and Mood 15													
Identifying Theme 16													
Identifying Characterization 17													
Identifying Fact, Fiction, and Opinion 18													
Identifying Propaganda 19													
Identifying Author's Purpose 20													

Suggested Key: Blank Space — Not Assessed

                          √ — Passed Pre-Assessment

                          ◯ — Did Not Pass Pre-Assessment; Needs Instruction

                          ⊘ — Did Not Pass Pre-Assessment; Has Received Instruction and Passed Post-Assessment

Figure 10.3   Teacher's Checklist of Skills—Comprehension

| | | Students' Names | | | | | | | | | | | |
Skill Descriptor	Skill Number												
Scheduling Time	21												
Setting Purposes	22												
Using a Study Technique	23												
Using Locational Aids in the Library	24												
Recording References	25												
Using the Library Call System	26												
Using Locational Aids Within Books	27												
Using Footnotes	28												
Using Glossaries	29												
Using Maps, Graphs, and Tables	30												
Matching Materials with Purposes	31												
Understanding the Organ- ization of Paragraphs	32												
Organizing Information	33												
Adjusting Rate to Purpose	34												

Suggested Key: Blank Space — Not Assessed

√ — Passed Pre-Assessment

◯ — Did Not Pass Pre-Assessment; Needs Instruction

⊘ — Did Not Pass Pre-Assessment; Has Received Instruction
and Passed Post-Assessment

Figure 10.4 Teacher's Checklist of Skills—Study Skills

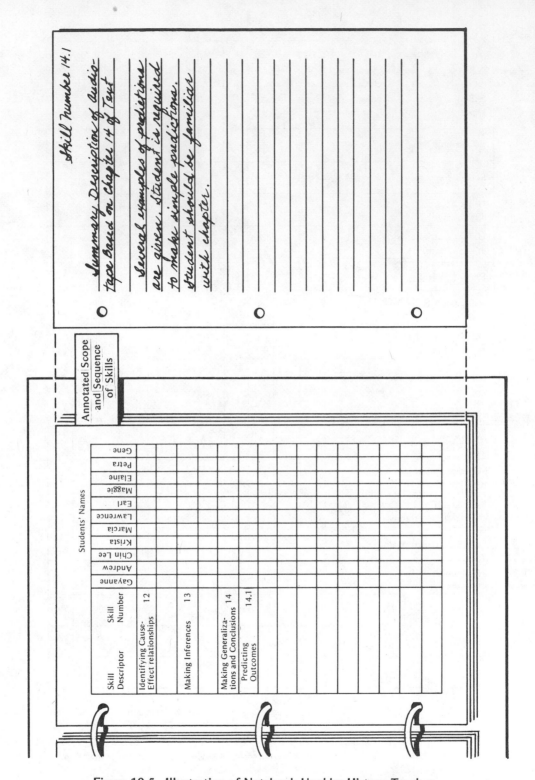

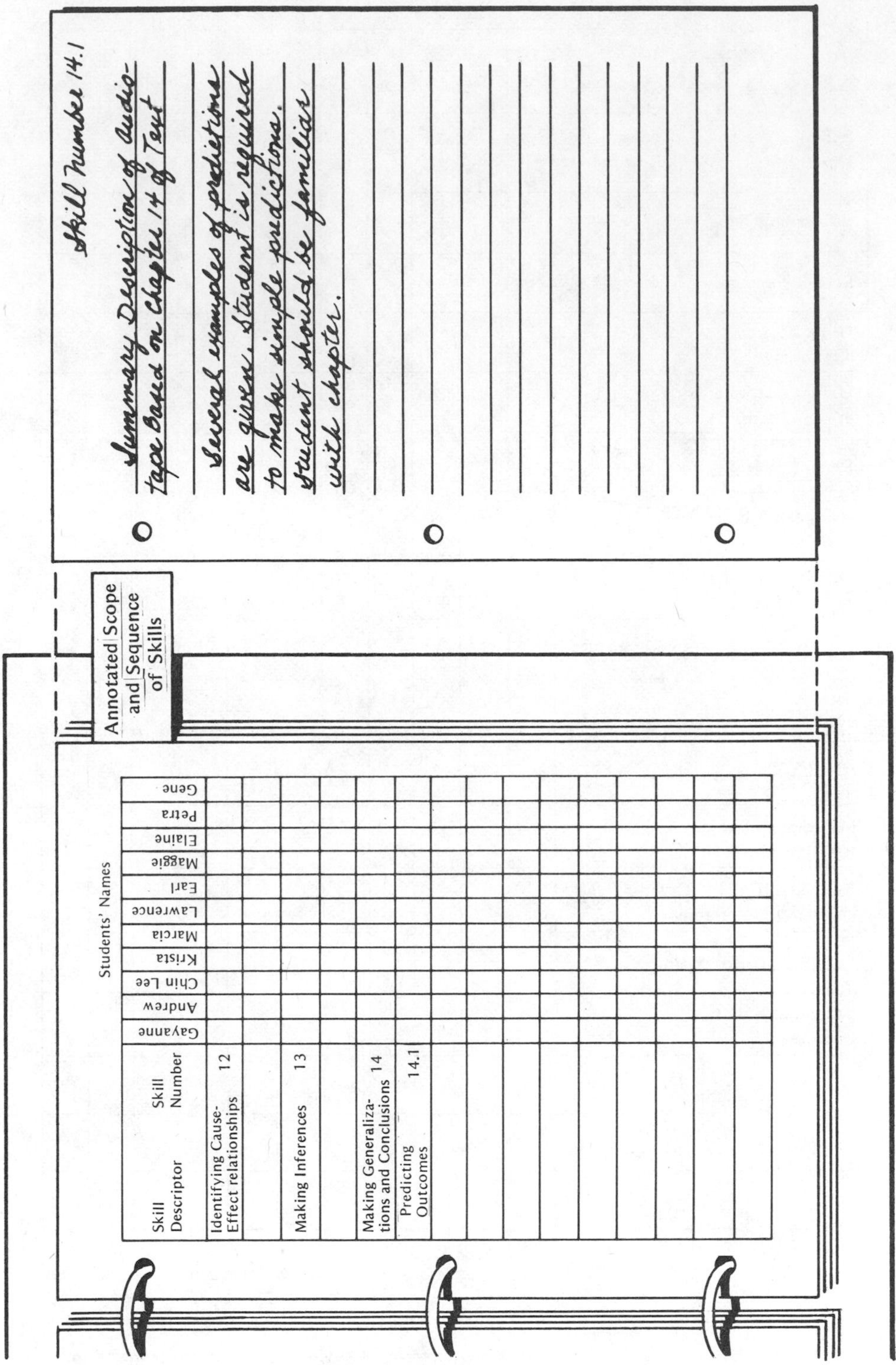
Skill Number 14.1
Summary Description of Audio-tape Based on Chapter 14 of Text
Several examples of predictions are given. Student is required to make simple predictions. Student should be familiar with chapter.
Annotated Scope and Sequence of Skills
Students' Names
Skill Descriptor
Skill Number
Gayanne
Andrew
Chin Lee
Krista
Marcia
Lawrence
Earl
Maggie
Elaine
Petra
Gene
Identifying Cause-Effect relationships
12
Making Inferences
13
Making Generalizations and Conclusions
14
Predicting Outcomes
14.1

Figure 10.5 Illustration of Notebook Used by History Teacher

each section with a tab. This provides them with a systematic means for keeping together all teaching suggestions that they consider useful. In addition, such a notebook allows teachers to easily add materials as they locate them or to delete procedures that they have found to be ineffective.

For example, if a history teacher had made an audiotaped lesson coordinated with the Truman era to reinforce the skill Predicting Outcomes, his notebook might look like the one illustrated in Figure 10.5

Close inspection of Figure 10.5 shows the following: first, the teacher has added the subskill Predicting Outcomes to the checklist that includes the other comprehension skills. Second, he has designated it as skill number 14.1, a subskill to skill number 14, Making Generalizations and Conclusions. Third, on notebook paper he has written a summary description of his audiotape on predicting outcomes. He then filed the description under the heading Materials for Student Use in the section describing the skill Making Generalizations and Conclusions.

Teachers who chose to use other scope and sequence charts or only some of the skills listed on the scope and sequence chart in this text would have to adapt their notebook accordingly. For example, if a teacher chose only five skills listed in this chapter, he might renumber them 1 through 5 rather than use the numbers assigned to them in this textbook. Likewise, he would probably pull out only the section of the annotated scope and sequence of skills that correlated with the skills he had chosen.

The remainder of this chapter will consist of the "Annotated Scope and Sequence of Skills." Each skill is presented in the order in which it was listed in Figure 10.1. The teacher may wish to use Figure 10.1 as a table of contents for the teaching techniques that follow.

Descriptor: Using Illustration Clues

Subject Areas: This skill is needed in any subject area in which students' reading materials contain illustrations that aid in explaining words or terms in the text.

Objective: Given a sentence containing a term that the student does not immediately recognize and an illustration depicting the term, the student will be able to use the illustration to define the unknown term.

Criterion Level: (Note: The teacher should fill in the number and percentage of correct responses that he feels students should complete to

receive credit for the objective.)_____.

Pre-Assessment: Locate a term with which the students are not familiar and which can best be understood by using an accompanying illustration. Ask the students to answer a question that requires their understanding of the term and observe which students make use of the illustration.

Sample Generic Teaching Strategy

Initial Teaching Procedure

Since most students know how to use illustrations to help recognize words, but often forget to do so, this lesson will be directed toward reminding the students to use illustration clues. Locate several illustrated terms which can be most quickly understood by their illustrations. Divide the class into groups of five and then give all teams three terms and the page numbers on which they occur. Then ask the students to define the terms. The team that can correctly define the terms first, wins. When asking the winning team for their definitions, ask them how they found the answers, eliciting the response that they used the illustrations. Student teams should then be asked to locate in their text five words that can be defined through the use of illustrations. The first team finding five terms that are explained by illustrations, wins.

Students working individually should then be given two terms and the page numbers on which they occur. They should be asked to define the terms and should use illustration clues to ascertain the definitions.

Reinforcement Procedures

1. Ask students to draw a picture that depicts the meaning of a word.
2. Ask students to meet in small groups. Give each small group an illustration from their content area textbook and ask them to summarize the illustration. Those students whose summary most closely matches the original description in the text selects the next illustration to be summarized.

Post-Assessment: Same as pre-assessment.

Correlated Materials

Professional Texts Written for Teacher Use

   Karlin (1972) pp. 213–216.

Instructional Material Written for Student Use

   (Attach notebook paper with brief description of instructional material designed for student use here. Examples of a few possible resources that might be used by a mathematics teacher are shown below. The mathematics teacher has also annotated his materials to help remind himself of the content of the materials.)

   1. *The Reading Line: Mathematics* by Irene Reiter, p. 32. (On this page students are shown how drawings of geometric figures may be interpreted.)
   2. Concentration game developed by Miss Smith. (The game shows drawings of various geometric figures. Students match figures with correct geometric terms in game played like "Concentration".)

Descriptor: Using Context Clues

Subject Areas: This skill is needed in all subject areas in which students are required to read.

Objectives: Given one or more sentences containing unknown words or blanks, the student should be able to use context clues to fill in the blanks with words that make sense in the sentence or to provide meanings for the unknown words.

Criterion Level:_____

Pre-Assessment: Select a short paragraph from the student's text. When re-typing the passage, replace 10 per cent of the words with blanks. Give credit for each blank filled in with an appropriate word. A sample from history follows:

> Traditionally, there_____been tolerance for ethnic and religious minor-
> ities in_____ Middle East. Each group has been_____to
> live peacefully within its own section of the city or part of the_____ .
> Today, there are still many such minorities; they exist in_____ all the
> countries of the region. (Tachau, 1970, p. 28)

Sample Generic Teaching Strategy

Initial Teaching Procedure

Most students are aware of context clues, but many neglect to use them. The purpose of this lesson is to remind students to use context clues when they encounter words they do not know. Introduce the lesson with a dis-cussion of the statement, "Often when we don't know the meaning of a word, we ask, 'How is it used?' What does the answer to this question tell us about a word we don't know?" Ask leading questions to elicit a brief discussion regarding context.

Ask students the meanings of five course-related words that they are not likely to know. Then show them five sentences from their text that can help them discover the meanings. Each sentence should contain a context clue. If possible, several types of context clues (e.g., definition, implica-tion, example, contrast) should be used. Students should then be given a brief practice session in the use of context clues. The teacher might in-troduce a topic that the class has recently studied or is about to study. Students could then list words that they might expect to find in their reading.

Students could then be shown one or more paragraphs that contain words unknown to them. The teacher might ask leading questions to help students use context to unlock the meanings of the words. Next, students could be assigned to locate, in their class materials, five words whose mean-ings can be found through context clues. Students could then list five words

239

that they might expect to find in the portion of the book that they are about to read. After reading, they could indicate whether each word was or was not included.

Reinforcement Procedures

1. Give students a list of words and the numbers of the pages on which they can be found. Ask them to use context to arrive at a rough definition of the words.
2. Substitute blanks for a few words in a story. Have class use context to fill in the blanks with appropriate words.

Post-Assessment: Same as pre-assessment.

Correlated Materials

Professional Texts Written for Teacher Use

Burmeister (1974) pp. 112–114
Herber (1970) pp. 163–164
Karlin (1972) pp. 121–123, 152–155
Olson and Ames (1972) pp. 80–82
Thomas and Robinson (1972) pp. 19–29

Instructional Material Written for Student Use

(Attach notebook paper with brief description of instructional materials designed for student use here.)

Descriptor: Using Phonic Analysis

Subject Areas: This skill is needed by subject areas in which students are required to read.

Objective: Given an unknown multisyllabic word, the student will be able to use phonic analysis to decode it.

Criterion Level:_____

Pre-Assessment: Show students nonsense words such as those in the sample below or words from their text with which they are not familiar. Then ask them to (1) divide each word into syllables, (2) indicate which syllable is accented, and (3) write another word in which the syllables would sound the same. (Note: This assessment does not include a test of blending syllables. If teachers wish to assess this skill, they must ask each student to pronounce the words after completing steps one, two, and three.)

> *Sample:* Instructions to the student: Follow steps 1, 2, and 3 below for each of the following words: (a) cepia (b) arbuous (c) pluvions (d) dakary
>
>   1. Divide it into syllables.
>   2. Place the primary accent.
>   3. Write another word in which each syllable is pronounced the same way.

The first word has been done for you.

    word   : cepia
    1. syllables   : ce/pi/a
    2. accent   : ce′
    3. other words for each syllable: ce—*see*
                                        pi—*opi*um
                                        a—Nevad*a*

Sample Generic Teaching Strategy

Initial Teaching Procedure

Most students have mastered syllabication and the pronouncing and blending of syllables by the time they reach middle or secondary school. However, many students do not use the important skill of phonic analysis to unlock many multisyllabic words that they meet in their textbooks. Therefore this lesson will be directed toward reinforcing the student's ability to use phonic analysis skills when meeting unknown words in the content areas.

Present students with a few multisyllabic words that they might possibly encounter in their reading in your content area. For example, the algebra teacher might include words such as tangent, symmetrical, postulate, and vertex. Explain to students that they should try phonic analysis when they come to a word that they do not recognize immediately and that they are unable to decode using illustration and/or context clues. Then discuss the four steps in phonic analysis:

1. Dividing the word into syllables.
2. Identifying the accented syllables.
3. Pronouncing the syllables.
4. Blending the syllables to make a word.

Students can then practice this procedure with sample words.

Next, students should be introduced to the fact that English words do not always follow the rules the students have been taught for structural analysis and phonics. When they are unable to pronounce and/or gain meaning from a word by following the rules, students should try one or two other possible ways of pronouncing it before giving up on the procedure. The class should be presented a few words that follow the rules and a few that do not. Then they could try to figure out whether the words followed the rules. If the words did not, the students could try some alternate ways of decoding them.

> *Sample:* ordinate, polygon, notation
>
>> Polygon does not follow the rules for phonic analysis. If it did, it would be pronounced po/ly/gon. The first *o* would rhyme with *go*. Ordinate and notation do follow the rules.

Ask leading questions to elicit the information that the goal of phonic analysis is to be able to pronounce the word closely enough to its actual pronunciation that its meaning can be determined. Accurate pronunciation or accurate application of all rules is not the goal.

The class can be divided into teams of two or three members. Each team locates five terms which it believes will be unknown to another team. Teams exchange lists and use phonic analysis to discern the meanings of the words. The group with the highest number of correct responses wins.

Reinforcement Procedures

1. *Checkers.* Make a checkerboard on the inside of a manila folder. In the place where the checkers are to be placed, print a word right side up and upside down so that both players can read it. The students play checkers in the usual manner, but they must be able to correctly divide the word into syllables, mark its accent, pronounce the word, and define it before they can move into that space.

Example from geography:

242

plateau		tamarack		bituminous		asbestos	
	irrigable		pampa		butte		juxtaposition
exploitation		muskeg		fjeld		intracoastal	
	humid		sorghum		sequoia		nutria
reservoir		forestry		boreal		atoll	
	taiga		pedologic		lespedeza		acreage
ethnology		detritus		piedmont		caribou	
	tundra		bauxite		kayak		strait

2. *Dart Game.* A target is purchased or made on the inside of an opened manila folder and multisyllabic course-related words that are new to the student and are from the course of study are tacked in the spaces. The youngsters take turns throwing rubber darts at various words. When they hit a word, they must correctly indicate its syllables, its accented syllable, its pronunciation, and its meaning.

Example from literature:

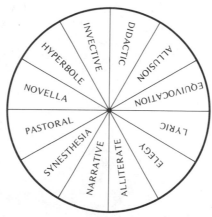

Post-Assessment: Same as pre-assessment.

Correlated Materials

Professional Texts Written for Teacher Use

Burmeister (1974) pp. 116–122, 136–141
Herber (1970) p. 168
Karlin (1972) pp. 136–142, 155–161
Olson and Ames (1972) pp. 82–84
Thomas and Robinson (1972) pp. 28–32

Instructional Material Written for Student Use

(Attach sheet.)

Descriptor: Using Structural Analysis

Subject Areas: This skill is needed in those subject areas in which students are required to read.

Objective: Given unknown terms, the student will be able to give an appropriate meaning of each through the use of structural analysis.

Criterion Level:_____

Pre-Assessment: Select course-related terms that the student is not likely to know and that contain common affixes or Greek or Latin roots. Give credit for responses that indicate a knowledge of the affix or the Greek or Latin root. Sample words from science are *calorie, equatorial, herbivorous, adrenalin, commutator, decomposition, galvanometer, pasteurization.*

Sample Generic Teaching Strategy

Initial Teaching Procedure

The ability to recognize, pronounce, and know the meanings of affixes and Greek and Latin roots aids students in the steps of structural analysis. It helps in (1) recognizing morphemes and (2) determining the word meaning.

Begin the discussion by stating to the class that "one can make twenty." Ask leading questions concerning affixes and Greek and Latin roots to make the students see that one of these elements (one) can help them to understand many (twenty) words. Then give students one prefix, one suffix, or one Greek or Latin root. (For a list of common prefixes, suffixes, and Greek and Latin roots, see Chapter 2 of this text.) Ask the students to write as many words as they can think of that contain that element. After a one-minute period, all the words the students thought of can be written on the chalkboard so that students can see how "one can make twenty." The class can then be divided into groups of about six students. Half the groups could be assigned to complete the following form with as many words as they can. One sample entry is given in the chart.

Word	Number of page on which word occurs in text	Greek or Latin root	Meaning of Greek or Latin root
reflex	p. 52	flexus (Latin)	bend, curve

The remaining groups could be assigned to complete the following form with as many words as they can.

245

Word	Number of page on which it occurs	Affix (Each affix may be used only once.)	Meaning of affix
return	p. 85	re	again
export	p. 92	ex	out

All groups may use dictionaries as aids. The winning group is the one with the most Greek or Latin roots or affixes correctly identified and defined.

Reinforcement Procedures

1. *Structural Analysis Dominoes.* Draw a line down the middle of a 3 by 5 index card and print two inflected words, each with a different Greek or Latin root, on each side of the line. Each student draws six cards and proceeds as in dominoes by attempting to match words that have the same roots. In order to play, the student must be able to define the Greek or Latin root, to give its meaning and the meanings of the inflectional endings, and to make up a new word using the root. (Dictionaries may be used as references in this game.)

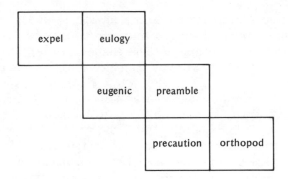

2. *Prefix and Suffix of the Day.* Have students make up words that contain the prefix or suffix of the day. This activity can be varied to include Greek or Latin roots. (Kaufman, Vol. 63, No. 5, p. 71)

Post-Assessment: Same as pre-assessment.

Correlated Materials

Professional Texts Written for Teacher Use

Thomas and Robinson (1972) p. 209

Instructional Material Written for Student Use

(Attach sheet.)

Descriptor: Using Dictionary Skills

Subject Areas: This skill is required by all subject areas in which students may need to use the dictionary in order to understand their reading material.

Objective: Given an unknown word in a sentence, the student will be able to (1) locate the word in the dictionary, (2) pronounce the word using the diacritical markings, and (3) discern the meaning of the word appropriate to the sentence.

Criterion Level:_____

Pre-Assessment: Give students identical dictionaries. First, write a main entry word on the chalkboard and ask the students to locate the word in their dictionaries. While the students are completing this task, note whether they turn to the appropriate part of the dictionary (first, middle, last), whether they use guide words, and whether they find main entry words and words that are not main entry words. Give credit for completing each of these activities appropriately. Second, write on the chalkboard a word which the students would not be able to pronounce. Tell them the page number of the dictionary where the word can be found and ask the students to pronounce the word. Give credit for correct pronunciation. Third, give the students a word whose meaning is unknown in a given sentence, such as, "The *runner* fell off the sled." The given word must have more than one meaning listed in the student's dictionary. Tell the students the number of the page in the dictionary on which the word may be found. Give credit for locating the correct meaning for the sentence.

Sample Generic Teaching Strategy

Initial Teaching Procedure

Begin the lesson by writing on the board the two guide words from a page in the dictionary. Then have students think of as many words as they can that might appear on that page. Ask leading questions to help students realize that by using guide words, they will be able to locate words in the dictionary more quickly.

Write several words that are main entries and several that are subentries on the chalkboard. Ask students which words would be main entries and which would be subentries in the dictionary and why. Have students locate the words in the dictionary to verify their responses. Ask students to formulate ideas they might use to find words that are not listed as main entries.

Ask students where the pronunciation key is located in their dictionaries. Ask them to find the key. Then discuss facets of the pronunciation key such as the following: How many sounds are shown? How many are foreign sounds? How many are consonant sounds? How many are vowel sounds? How many sounds are shown for the a, e, i, o, and u? How is the

247

schwa sound shown? What letters can it stand for? How is primary accent shown? How is secondary accent shown? Show students several words written according to the pronunciation key and ask them to pronounce each word; for example, branch, kŏn vā′.

Present words in sentences to students. Each word must have more than one meaning in the students' dictionaries. For example, "Eventually John saw the breach of a great white whale." The students would decide which dictionary meaning of breach is used in the sentence.

Reinforcement Procedures

1. *Dictionary Bingo.* Mark off 25 two-inch squares on the inside of an opened manila folder. In each except the center square, write a synonym for a vocabulary word from class materials. Prepare such a folder for each youngster, but write synonyms in different orders. As the teacher, or leader, writes a word on the chalkboard, each youngster covers the word that means the same. (Students should be given time to locate words in the dictionary.) The first student to correctly cover a row of words calls "bingo" and wins the game. Example: Teacher says "artistic" and student covers "aesthetic."

Example from art:

aesthetic	icon	frieze	tint	realism
splay	surrealistic	tier	synthetic	detailed
modillion	veneer	FREE	genre	tactile
pictorial	symbolist	volute	gilt	sculpture
truncate	abutment	stain	ostentatious	abstract

gilt	abutment	veneer	ostentatious	modillion
genre	realism	frieze	abstract	pictorial
surrealistic	volute	FREE	truncate	synthetic
tactile	stain	aesthetic	icon	splay
detailed	tint	sculpture	symbolist	tier

2. *Dictionary Old Maid.* Write out sentences containing underlined vocabulary words on separate index cards. Make one card that reads, "Old Maid." All cards are dealt and the game proceeds exactly like "Old Maid" except that when a student wants to put down a matching set, he must pronounce the underlined word and define it correctly. If he fails to do so, he must relinquish the pair in exchange for the "Old Maid." If he already holds the "Old Maid," he must award the pair to the player on his right. Dictionaries may be used.

Example:

Victims of meningitis produce *soporific* symptoms.	The queen's loyal guards performed *assiduous* tasks.	

Victims of meningitis produce *soporific* symptoms.	The queen's loyal guards performed *assiduous* tasks.	OLD MAID

Post-Assessment: Same as pre-assessment.

Correlated Materials

Professional Texts Written for Teacher Use

Karlin (1972) pp. 142–146
Olson and Ames (1972) pp. 85–87

Instructional Material Written for Student Use

(Attach sheet.)

Descriptor: Expanding Background in Vocabulary

Subject Areas: This skill is useful in all content areas in which reading is required.

Objective: Given one or more sentences that contain unknown words that may be learned through (1) an expanded conceptual background or (2) sight word skills, the student will be able to provide meanings for the unknown words.

Criterion Level:_____

Pre-Assessment: (1) Select several short passages from content-related materials that contain words that may be learned through an expanded conceptual background, and ask students to identify the words. Give credit for each word defined correctly. (2) Select several short passages from content-related materials which contain words which must be learned through sight skills, and ask students to identify the words. Give credit for each word defined correctly.

Sample Generic Teaching Strategy

Initial Teaching Procedure (Expanding conceptual background)

Explain to the students that the English language is dynamic and always changing, but that the changes follow certain patterns that are characteristic of American speakers of English. For example, discuss the tendency that Americans have for blending words (e.g., chortle—chuckle and snort; grumble—growl and rumble); and borrowing words (e.g., Bengali—bungalow, Persian—bazaar, Slavic—vampire, Malaysian—gong, Australian—boomerang, Polynesian—taboo).

Group the students into trios and give them time to locate several examples of blending and borrowing in their content area textbook. Then give the students from each group time to share the words they have located with the other class members.

Reinforcement Procedures (Expanding conceptual background)

1. Use the content area textbook as the basic resource and locate words that have been borrowed from several different languages. After presenting several such words to the students, ask them to locate as many examples as they can within a five-minute time period. At the end of the time period see how many different words have been located and determine from what language they were borrowed.

2. Ask students to make up words that could be used in the content area which are blends or acronyms. See if other students understand the words.

3. When technical words occur that have a history, relate it to the students. For example, *mesmerize* comes from Dr. Anton Mesmer, a man

who cured many people's illnesses through hypnosis. Other examples include, *pasteurize* from Louis Pasteur, *cardigan* from the Earl of Cardigan, and *gerrymander* from a signer of the Declaration of Independence named Elbridge Gerry and the word *salamander*.

Initial Teaching Procedure (Sight word skills)

Explain to students that some words and symbols can best be learned through memory techniques. Show them how symbols such as ↑, ≅, °, ∖, and ¶ cannot be decoded by any of the word attack skills and must be memorized. Place a set of content area symbols on a transparency and display it on an overhead. Let the students look at the symbols and their meanings for a short period of time. Then cover up the definitions of the symbols and ask students to define as many of the symbols as they can. As soon as the first student has finished, compare his answers with the ones on the transparency. Ask him how he was able to remember all the meanings of the symbols. Explain to the class that the flashcard technique, with the symbol on one side of the card and the definition on the other, is a good way to learn the symbols.

Some examples from several content areas are given below:

Mathematics: ∺ (geometrical proportion)
| | (absolute value)
≐ (approaches)
∪ (logical sum)
≡ (identical with)

Music: ♯ (sharp)
♭ (flat)
♮ (natural)

English: ¶ (paragraph)
i.e. (that is)
e.g. (for example)
viz. (namely)
N.B. (mark well)
f.v. (on the back of the page)

Science: ↔ (reaction goes both right and left)
↑ (gas)
♂ (male)
♀ (female)
μ (micron)

Reinforcement Procedures (Sight word skills)

1. Since memorizing may become a tedious task, encourage students to use techniques for learning symbols in an enjoyable manner. For example, a bingo game containing symbols for a content area could be developed. One student could call out the meaning and the other students could cover up the symbols on their bingo boards. The winner could be the director of the next game.

2. Encourage students to use their spare time to learn these symbols. If they place them on index cards, they may carry the cards with them and use spare time to learn them; for example, while waiting in line at the grocery store or while riding the bus to school, the students could look at the symbol, recite to themselves what they thought the answer was, and then turn the cards over to verify their answers.

Post-Assessment: Same as pre-assessment.

Correlated Materials

Professional Texts Written for Teacher Use

Burmeister (1974) pp. 134–135
Karlin (1972) pp. 146–147
Thomas and Robinson (1972) pp. 56–61

Instructional Materials Written for Student Use

(Attach sheet.)

Descriptor: Using a Combination of Vocabulary Skills

Subject Areas: This skill is needed by all subject areas in which students are required to read.

Objective: Given several sentences containing unknown words, the student will be able to give the meaning of each of the words.

Criterion Level: _____

Pre-Assessment: Select five words from reading material that the student might use in class. Present these words in sentences and ask the students to state their meanings. They may use the dictionary to locate the meanings of no more than one word. An example from a consumer awareness course follows. "Boating enthusiasts who want a closer look at buoys have created a market for *binoculars.*" Through the use of such techniques as structural analysis, phonic analysis, and context clues, the students should be able to assess the meaning of *binoculars.*

Sample Generic Teaching Strategy

Initial Teaching Procedure

Explain to the students that there are many ways to approach a word that they do not recognize immediately. Ask them to list these ways and elicit the answers: illustration clues, context clues, phonic analysis, structural analysis, and dictionary skills. Then write on the board one or more sentences that contain unknown words; for example, the term "cognitive dissonance" might be introduced in the sentence, "When a person is faced with a lack of agreement between his thoughts and his actions, *cognitive dissonance* is present." The context can then be used as a springboard to a discussion of the term.

Once its meaning is explicated, the term can be examined through structural and phonic analysis; for example the term *cognitive dissonance* can be broken into syllables, the accents placed, and the syllables pronounced. Ask students which skills they are using and whether these can be used in conjunction with context.

Other words can be approached in the same manner. In addition, words for which there are illustration clues and those that cannot be approached by context, structural analysis, or phonic analysis and that must be looked up in the dictionary can be used. Ask leading questions as to the necessity for looking up in the dictionary every unknown word; for example, "Under what circumstances should a word be looked up?"

Students can also be reminded to use other ways of identifying words. For example, the meaning of the word *quisling* in the sentence, "His countrymen considered him a quisling," cannot be determined by any means except looking up *quisling* in the dictionary or remembering the historical meaning of the word. Students can recall the meaning *collaborator* quickly

255

if they have heard the story of Quisling's role in Norway during the Second World War.

Reinforcement Procedures

1. *Scavenger Hunt.* Each student or pair of students is given a list of words to define. The first student to find the meaning of each word on the list is the winner. Suggestions from science might include the following:

    a. Give the meaning of *autoclave.* Page 27 of your text will help you. (Page 27 contains a picture clue—an illustration of an autoclave.)
    b. Give the meaning of *endoplasmic reticulum.* Page 36 of your text will help you. (Page 36 contains adequate context clues to help the student unlock the term.)
    c. Divide the word *pronghorn* into syllables. Place the accent. Write a word that rhymes with each syllable. Define *pronghorn.*
    d. Locate the word *estuaries* in your dictionary. Write its pronunciation. Write a word that rhymes with each syllable. Draw an illustration of an estuary.

2. Have students keep individual lists of words not instantly recognized. They can write the words on 3 by 5 cards. One side of the card can have only the word, and the other side can show the dictionary pronunciation and the word used in a sentence.

Post-Assessment: Same as pre-assessment.

Correlated Materials

Professional Texts Written for Teacher Use

    Burmeister (1974) pp. 135–141

Instructional Material Written for Student Use

    (Attach sheet.)

Descriptor: Identifying Details

Subject Areas: This skill is required by all subject areas in which students are required to read for information.

Objective: Given questions that require detailed reading and that are based on course-related material written on an appropriate instructional level, students will be able to locate the required details.

Criterion Level: _____

Pre-Assessment: Tell students the main idea of the content of a few pages of some of the material that they will be expected to read as part of class instruction. Then ask them to read these pages to find details that support the main idea. Give credit for accurate identification of details. *Example* (from biology): "List three details from pages 10 and 11 of your textbook that support the statement that species are capable of changing."

Sample Generic Teaching Strategy

Initial Teaching Procedure

Explain to students that the author of a textbook often gives readers hints about details. Ask students to locate words or phrases that authors might use to give clues to details. (Students might locate phrases such as "a more familiar example" and "for example.") Students might also be asked to locate the place in paragraphs where details often occur. (Details tend to occur more often in the sentences in the middle of paragraphs.) Leading questions should be asked to elicit answers of the above nature.

Give students practice in locating details as a group. Write a main idea on the chalkboard. Then ask students to find some details to support it. For example, a science teacher might ask students to read page 204 to find two details that support the theory that there is no life on Mercury.

Give students practice in locating pertinent details in small student-led groups. Give each group leader a main idea and a list of page numbers on which supporting details might be found. Then have them lead their groups in attempting to find the details that support their main idea. For example, one group might be asked to find details that support the idea that there is no life on Jupiter, another that there is no life on Saturn, and another that there is no life on Mars. After completing the activity, each group may give feedback in its particular area of expertise.

Reinforcement Procedures

1. Give students main ideas and ask them to find the supporting details. Ask them to record the details in standard or novel form.

Standard Form

Main Idea: The Rush-Bagot Agreement (1817) was a momentous achievement.

Detail 1: The treaty was the first step in disarming the United States–Canada border.

Detail 2: The entire border was eventually disarmed.

Detail 3: Neither Great Britain nor the United States trusted each other.

Novel Forms

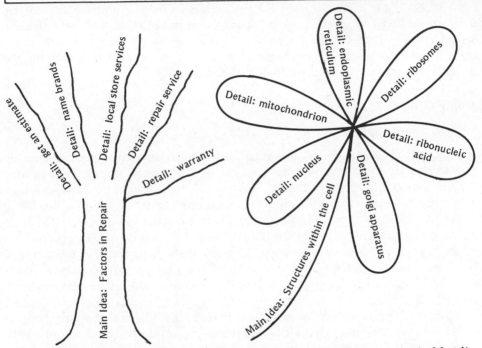

2. Give students a paragraph and an idea that may be supported by it. Have them mark each sentence in the paragraph as significant or not significant to the support of that idea.

Post-Assessment: Same as pre-assessment.

Correlated Materials

Professional Texts Written for Teacher Use

Olson and Ames (1972) pp. 42–43, 49–56

Instructional Material Written for Student Use

(Attach sheet.)

Descriptor: Identifying Main Ideas

Subject Areas: This skill is required by all subject areas in which students are required to locate main ideas.

Objective: Given course-related sentences; paragraphs with the main idea in the initial, medial, and final positions; paragraphs with the main idea not directly stated; and chapter subsections and chapters written on an appropriate instructional level, the student will be able to identify the main ideas.

Criterion Level:_____

Pre-Assessment: Tell students to state the main ideas of sentences; paragraphs with the main idea in initial, medial, and final positions; a paragraph in which the main idea is not directly stated; and one chapter subsection and one chapter.

Sample Generic Teaching Strategy

Initial Teaching Procedure

Main ideas of sentences: Students having trouble with this skill need practice in locating subjects, verbs, objects, and important modifiers in sentences. The teacher should introduce the concept of main idea by having students work through several sample sentences to find the subjects, verbs, objects, and important modifiers. If students encounter particular difficulty at this stage, then extensive group and individual practice should be given in identifying only one of each of these sentence parts in particular sentences before attempting to name all the parts of one sentence.

Once the class has completed a teacher-directed activity in finding subjects, verbs, objects, and important modifiers, the students are paired. Each pair is given a guide sheet containing sentences. One student reads the first sentence aloud to the other. The second student has thirty seconds to write down the core of the sentence. After the first student has read ten sentences, the roles reverse and the second student uses the guide sheet to locate and read sentences to the other student. A key is given on the guide sheet to help students assess their accuracy.

Practice in both the teacher-led and the student-led activities should begin with simple sentences and proceed through compound, complex, and compound-complex sentences. Final practice should be given from course-related material on the students' instructional levels.

Main ideas of paragraphs: The teacher can introduce the concept of main ideas of paragraphs by listing a common factor and the objects that share it. Students can then identify the common factor, or main idea, from the given list. *Example:* The teacher gives the students the following list: paper, pencil, school supplies, book, eraser. *Answer:* The main idea is indicated by the term *school supplies.* A teacher-led discussion can then focus on

259

finding the main idea of a paragraph. Leading questions should elicit the information that main ideas can occur at the beginning, middle, or end of a paragraph or may not be directly stated at all. The teacher can then show paragraphs whose main ideas occur as indicated above and students can underline the main idea of each in one color and the details in another.

The class can then be divided into four groups. The members of one group read a few pages of class material to identify those paragraphs in which the main idea occurs in the initial sentence; another group identifies those paragraphs in which the main idea is stated in the medial position; another finds the paragraphs in which the main idea is placed at the end; and a fourth group locates those paragraphs in which the author does not directly state the main idea. After twenty minutes, each group shares its findings in terms of the number of times that the particular pattern was found in the material used.

The class can then be divided into small groups of two or three. Each group should locate the main idea of a chapter and of a chapter subsection. A class discussion could follow.

Reinforcement Procedures

Main ideas of sentences:

1. *It's Your Money.* Students are given a list of sentences in which they are to find the core. Then they are to send messages stating the main ideas of each. The instructions read that the message must be sent at a cost of $10.00 per word. The object of the activity is to send the messages for the least possible expense. *Example:* "Since the hospital is just across the street, Belinda leaves the car in its stall and walks to work." The least expensive message would cost $40.00—"Belinda walks to work."

2. *Stump Your Partner.* Students are grouped into pairs and are given fifteen minutes to write ten sentences and to locate their main ideas. The students then exchange lists and try to find the main ideas of each of their partner's sentences. The partner with the highest number of accurate answers wins.

Main ideas of paragraphs

1. *Decision.* Three students work together. In each group of three, two students participate while the third acts as moderator. The moderator reads from index cards that direct the students to a given paragraph in their class material. After the two participants have read the appropriate passage, the moderator reads the three possible main ideas written on the index cards. The other two students decide individually which is the true main idea and each writes down his choice. When the moderator gives the signal, each participant reads his choice and the moderator tells which is correct as shown on the index card. If the participants are both correct, they each gain a point. If they disagree, they discuss why one answer was better than another. The participant with the most points at the end of the session becomes the moderator during the next exercise.

2. *Challenge.* The class is divided into two teams. Using specified pages

of their class material, each team constructs questions designed to stump the opposition. However, the questions must be designed so that a knowledge of only the main idea of a paragraph is needed to answer them correctly. After formulating questions for twenty minutes, each team takes turns asking members of the opposing team to answer their questions. If the team member responds correctly, his team gains one point. If an opponent does not believe that the question asked of him represents a main idea, he may challenge the question. If his charge is correct, his team receives three points; but if the question does represent a main idea, the team loses one point. The teacher may act as referee.

Main ideas of chapter subsections and chapters

1. Students are given a choice of three main ideas for a chapter or chapter subsection. They are instructed to choose the appropriate idea. Explanation of why one choice is correct is provided by an answer key.

2. Give students a copy of a chapter or chapter subsection from which the headings and subheadings have been removed. Students supply the new headings. Then students can verify their responses against the original headings.

Post-Assessment: Same as pre-assessment.

Correlated Materials

Professional Texts Written for Teacher Use

> Burmeister (1974) pp. 158–163, 187–190
> Karlin (1972) pp. 190–198
> Olson and Ames (1972) pp. 39–40
> Thomas and Robinson (1972) pp. 118–123

Instructional Material Written for Student Use

(Attach sheet.)

Descriptor: Identifying Sequence

Subject Areas: This skill is required by all subject areas in which students are required to sequence information according to time or space.

Objective: Given course-related reading material on an appropriate instructional level, the student will be able to identify sequences of time or space.

Criterion Level: _____

Pre-Assessment: Given a selection in which a sequence of time may be discerned and a selection in which a sequence of space may be discerned, students will identify and correctly sequence the items in each selection.

Sample Generic Teaching Strategy

Initial Teaching Procedure

The teacher introduces the topic by verbally giving some sequences that students are to complete.

> *Example of time sequence:*
> 4 P.M., 5 P.M., 7 P.M., 8 P.M.,_____,_____. *Answer:* 10 P.M., 11 P.M.
>
> *Example of spatial sequence:*
> Nome, Winnipeg, Seattle,_____,_____. *Answer:* Any cities south of Seattle.

The teacher focuses the discussion on the reasons why it is necessary for students to be able to locate sequence. The students locate in their content area textbooks examples of sequences of time or space. These examples are then listed on the chalkboard under the heading "Sequence of Time" or "Sequence of Space." Examples are read aloud and students are encouraged to listen for key words that indicate relationships in time or space. (Sample key words for time: after, following, consequently, later, sequentially, subsequently, successively. Sample key words for space: clockwise, horizontal, leeward, parallel, reverse, windward, northerly, easterly, starboard, sinistral, straight, perpendicular, plumb, upright.) Students also listen to decide whether the sequence is directly stated or merely implied. Other examples are then read.

Reinforcement Procedures

1. Give students a paragraph that contains a sequence and have them underline the clue words.
2. Have students list the sequence found in a given selection. Then have them scramble the items in the sequence so that they may be sequenced by another student.
3. Draw a map of a fully described situation and write directions for getting from place to place. Other members of the class can check the map and the directions for accuracy.

4. Draw a map, diagram, or floor plan for a situation that is fully described.

5. Give students an unfinished sequence and ask them to hypothesize the next item.

6. Ask students to guess what incident might have taken place between two listed ones.

7. Have students discuss how the content of a piece of expository material might have differed if the sequence of events had been changed.

Post-Assessment: Same as pre-assessment.

Correlated Materials

Professional Texts Written for Teacher Use

Karlin (1972) pp. 169–170
Robinson (1975) pp. 119–124, 146–150

Instructional Material Written for Student Use

(Attach sheet.)

Descriptor: Following Directions

Subject Areas: This skill is required by all subject areas in which following directions is important.

Objective: Given a set of printed directions on an appropriate instructional level, the student will be able to follow them accurately.

Criterion Level:_____

Pre-Assessment: Locate commonly used directions in your subject area and list them. Give credit to students who can accurately respond.

> *Example:*
>
> 1. Write out the formulas found on page 6.
>
> 2. Use only one side of your notebook paper.
>
> 3. Write with pencil only.
>
> 4. Fold your paper vertically.
>
> 5. Turn to Appendix B in your text.
>
> 6. Remove the seal from your test booklet.

Sample Generic Teaching Strategy

Initial Teaching Procedure

Begin the lesson with the following activity. Hand the students a sheet similar to the one below and tell them to follow the directions in Steps 1 and 2.

Step 1: Read the directions below and then proceed to Step 2.

    a. Turn to page 56 of your text and count the number of times that the word *the* appears.
    b. Stand up and turn around three times.

Step 2: Turn over this sheet and look at your teacher.

This activity will demonstrate to those students who performed the activities in Step 1 that they do not know how to follow directions well.

Discuss and perform examples of instructions that occur frequently in your subject area. For example, discuss terms such as *list, name, classify, compare, contrast,* and *compare and contrast.* Then give examples from your course.

The speed at which directions should be read should also be discussed and practiced. Students should be questioned to elicit the information that directions should be read first to obtain the overall view and then read and reread slowly one or more times until the student knows exactly what to do.

Reinforcement Procedures

1. Students who are encountering difficulty are given one simple direction at a time. When they have become proficient at following one simple direction, they may be given two simple directions at one time. The number of directions given can be slowly increased until the students can handle the number that the instructor would normally assign. (Karlin 1972, p. 213)

2. Those students who have mastered reading and accurately following simple directions might be given the assignment of writing directions that might be used in your course. This activity increases their knowledge of the difficulty of writing clear directions and alerts them to the fact that all written directions may not be absolutely descriptive. These directions can be used for students working on reinforcement procedure 1 above. (Burmeister 1974, p. 154)

Post-Assessment: Same as pre-assessment.

Correlated Materials

Professional Texts Written for Teacher Use

Burmeister (1974) pp. 150–156
Herber (1970) pp. 169–170, 185–191
Karlin (1972) pp. 212–213

Instructional Material Written for Student Use

(Attach sheet.)

Descriptor: Identifying Cause-Effect Relationships

Subject Areas: This skill is required by those subject areas in which cause-effect relationships are important, such as history, literature, and science.

Objective: Given a course-related selection on an appropriate instructional level, the student will be able to identify the cause-effect relationships contained in the selection.

Criterion Level:_____

Pre-Assessment: Give the student a course-related selection that contains one or more cause-effect relationships. Ask the student to read the selection and to identify the cause(s) and the effect(s) therein. Give credit for accurate identification of cause(s) and effect(s).

Sample Generic Teaching Strategy

Initial Teaching Procedure

The teacher opens the discussion by asking leading questions as to the reasons why being able to locate cause-effect relationships is important. (His leading questions might elicit the answer that identifying cause and effect helps the student organize and recall details.) Using the chalkboard, an overhead projector, or handouts, make sentences containing stated cause-effect relationships available to the entire class. Have the students note the cause and the effect in each sentence. Then discuss with the class how they determined the causes and the effects. Repeat this procedure with paragraphs and units longer than paragraphs in which the cause(s) and the effect(s) are openly stated. Using these selections, have students identify the author's key words (*since, because, therefore*) which may indicate the cause-effect relationship. Additional examples of stated cause-effect relationships that use these key words could also be located in class materials.

Students could then be presented with some cause-effect relationships in which key words are not used and shown how clue words could be added to make the relationships more clear. Some content area examples follow. Clue words have been italicized.

> *Example from agricultural education:*
> The unfertilized corn did not yield large ears.
> *Since* the corn was unfertilized (cause), it did not yield large ears (effect).

> *Example from science:*
> The solvent was not added within one minute and the element did not dissolve.
> *If* the solvent is not added within one minute (cause), the element will not dissolve (effect).

267

Example from mathematics:
> In the example, the formula was applied correctly and the right answer was obtained.
>
> In the example, the formula was applied correctly (cause). *Therefore*, the right answer was obtained (effect).

Using content materials, the students could practice adding key words to samples of cause-effect statements in which clue words were not used. The class could then be divided into groups of two or three and each group could attempt to locate as many directly and nondirectly stated cause-effect relationships as possible in a given length of time.

Reinforcement Procedures

1. Students could be given a guided reading sheet that includes all the causes but only some of their effects as contained in a given selection. The students could then read and supply the omitted effects.

2. Students could be given a sequential list of causes based on material that they are to read along with a jumbled list of the effects. They could then read to find out which effect goes with each cause.

3. Students who are skilled in locating cause-effect relationships might be given questions which would require them to hypothesize why an event occurred or what the effect of a given cause might be. For example, the students might hypothesize why the author of a piece of literature chose to include certain words.

Post-Assessment: Same as pre-assessment.

Correlated Materials

Professional Texts Written for Teacher Use

Burmeister (1974) pp. 185–187, 211–212
Herber (1970) pp. 107–113, 128–130
Karlin (1972) pp. 171–172
Robinson (1975) pp. 151–153

Instructional Material Written for Student Use

(Attach sheet.)

Descriptor: Making Inferences

Subject Areas: This skill is needed in those subject areas such as literature, history, and science in which inferences play an important part.

Objective: Given a selection that is written on an appropriate instructional level and that contains an inference, the student will be able to identify the inference.

Criterion Level:_____

Pre-Assessment: Give students course-related selections that contain inferences and ask them to identify the inferences.

Sample Generic Teaching Strategy

Initial Teaching Procedure

Introduce the concept of inference by showing students a picture that is accompanied by a list of statements. Some of the statements should be based directly on the picture and some should be inferred. For example, a picture of the characters of *The Merchant of Venice* could be used. Statements such as the following could be presented:

1. Portia is dressed in a gown of blue. (factual)
2. Shylock looks shrewd. (inferred)

The teacher could lead a discussion on distinguishing inferential statements.

Samples of course-related reading material that contain inferences should be shown to the students along with a list of accompanying statements. The students should be instructed to first overview each selection to gain some understanding of its content. As a group, they should decide which statements are factual and which are inferred. They should discuss whether there is a need to verify the inference or whether their backgrounds are sufficient to assume that the inference is correct. The class could then be divided into groups of two or three and the students could proceed to answer questions such as the following about a selection from course material.

1. Are most of the ideas in the statements in the first paragraph directly stated or must they be inferred?
2. Which idea in the second paragraph must undeniably be inferred?

Reinforcement Procedures

1. Give the students a passage from class materials in which the statement containing an inference has been underlined. A guide sheet with questions concerning the underlined statement could be provided.

Example: A guide sheet in literature might read:

A. The time of this story is probably

    (a) 25 B.C.   (b) A.D. 1200   (c) A.D. 1900

(Underlined passages concern dress and customs of people.)

B. This story takes place

    (a) in a mountainous region   (b) in a plains region   (c) near an ocean

(Underlined passages describe a violent storm.)

2. Give the students partial information on a topic and have them try to accurately infer the missing information.

Post-Assessment: Same as pre-assessment.

Correlated Materials

Professional Texts Written for Teacher Use

Burmeister (1974) pp. 191–193
Olson and Ames (1972) p. 70

Instructional Material Written for Student Use

(Attach sheet.)

Descriptor: Making Generalizations and Conclusions

Subject Areas: This skill is needed in those subject areas such as mathematics and history in which generalizations and conclusions play an important part.

Objective: Given two course-related selections on an appropriate instructional level, one of which contains a generalization and one of which contains a conclusion, the student will identify each.

Criterion Level:_____

Pre-Assessment: Locate one or more course-related selections on the student's instructional level. Each selection should contain at least one generalization and at least one conclusion. Give credit for accurate identification of a generalization and a conclusion.

Sample Generic Teaching Strategy

Initial Teaching Procedure

Show students two examples of conclusions and two of generalizations. Whenever possible, examples should be drawn from course material.

> *Example of generalization:* All matter is made of atoms.

> *Example of conclusion:* Since snakes are cold-blooded chordates, they may be classified as reptiles.

Then discuss with students how some generalizations and conclusions may be inaccurate due to incomplete evidence or fallible reasoning. Examples of an inaccurate generalization and of an inaccurate conclusion are given below.

> *Example of inaccurate generalization:* Since a snake doesn't have paired appendages, it is not similar to the sunfish.

> *Example of inaccurate conclusion:* Since robins have two wings, sharks have two fins, and frogs have two legs, the basis for their biological classification is paired appendages.

The teacher should then discuss with students the methods by which tentative initial generalizations and conclusions can be verified. Points to be brought out in the discussion should include verifying by past experience, by discussion, and by other reading. After the discussion, the class could be divided into groups of two or three students. Each group could be given examples of generalizations and conclusions from course-related material and the students could be asked to decide whether each has sufficient evidence to support it or whether there is evidence of inaccurate reasoning. Following this activity, a whole-group discussion should center on these points.

271

Reinforcement Procedures

1. Students can be asked to describe poor generalizations or conclusions and then to create examples of each which illustrate inadequate evidence or inaccurate reasoning.

2. Students can attempt to locate cases of poor generalizing or concluding in course-related materials.

3. Students can be shown specific examples of conclusions (such as the transitive property shown here) and can be asked to provide other examples of their own.

$$a = b$$ Warren has hayfever.
$$b = c$$ or Hayfever sufferers sneeze frequently.
$$\therefore a = c$$ $\therefore$ Warren sneezes frequently.

Post-Assessment: Same as pre-assessment.

Correlated Materials

Professional Texts Written for Teacher Use

Burmeister (1974) pp. 212–220
Robinson (1975) pp. 108–114, 142–146

Instructional Material Written for Student Use

(Attach sheet.)

Descriptor: Identifying Tone and Mood

Subject Areas: This skill is required by those subject areas such as literature and history in which identification of tone and mood is an important consideration.

Objective: Given a selection on an appropriate instructional level and from which tone and mood can be ascertained, the student will be able to identify the tone and mood.

Criterion Level:_____

Pre-Assessment: Locate a selection that students might be asked to read as part of their course work and from which tone and mood may be ascertained. Ask students to describe the tone and mood. Give credit for appropriate responses.

Sample Generic Teaching Strategy

Initial Teaching Procedure

Define tone and mood for the students. (These terms may be confusing to the students since their meanings vary among authors.) Have students read one or more short selections and then, as a group, decide on the tone and mood of each. Have them list several adjectives that describe tone (*serious, unsympathetic, factual*) and mood (*happy, threatening, bleak*).

Discuss with students guidelines for ascertaining tone and mood. Such guidelines might include the following:

1. Understand the content of the work thoroughly before trying to ascertain tone or mood.
2. Look for clue words, such as *stern, love, hate,* or *fascination,* that might indicate tone or mood.
3. Read descriptive passages as well as any dialogue that might indicate tone or mood.

Break the class into small groups of two or three and provide each group with one or more short selections. Ask the students to decide the tone and mood of the selection(s) and to support their answers with references from the passage(s).

Students should be given additional instruction before they try to identify the tone and mood of longer selections. The teacher should demonstrate to the students how to select representative passages as a means of identifying tone and mood and how to support their choices. Then he should reteach how to identify tone and mood and how to support choices as with shorter selections.

Reinforcement Procedures

1. Provide students with a short selection accompanied by multiple

273

choice questions for assessing its tone and mood. Students decide which answers are correct and then explain their reasons for accepting or rejecting each choice. This activity can be completed independently or in groups.

2. Assign students the following exercise: Assume that you have just been employed as a salesman for the XYZ Product Company. You wish to write ads to help sell a product of your choice to two different groups of people; namely, middle-aged blue-collar workers and young high school students. Describe what the tone and mood of each ad should be.

Post-Assessment: Same as pre-assessment.

Correlated Materials

Professional Texts Written for Teacher Use

Robinson (1975) pp. 202–203

Instructional Material Written for Student Use

(Attach sheet.)

Descriptor: Identifying Theme

Subject Areas: This skill is needed in those subject areas such as literature in which identification of theme is important.

Objective: The student will be able to identify the theme of a selection which is written on his instructional level.

Criterion Level: _____

Pre-Assessment: Locate a selection that students might be asked to read as part of their course work and from which the theme can be ascertained. Ask students to state the theme and the reasons for their choices. Give credit for accurate responses.

Sample Generic Teaching Strategy

Initial Teaching Procedure

This procedure assumes that the students have mastered the subskills necessary for identifying theme. An alternate procedure can be carried out with short works (no more than a few paragraphs long) from which themes can be more easily deduced.

The general nature of *theme* can be discussed. Students should then be asked to identify the themes of short selections composed of no more than a few paragraphs. This exercise can be simplified by giving students two or more possible themes from which to choose their answers. Students can then discuss their choices.

Once students have mastered the concept of theme through the use of short works, they should read a well-written article concerning the theme of a longer work that they have already read. One excellent source of such articles is exemplary papers written by students during previous semesters. Discussions can center on the way in which students supported their theses. This analysis could include a study of tone, mood, characterization, and the author's purpose.

Working with the teacher, the class can then attempt to identify the theme of a short work that has been previously studied in class. Earlier analyses of tone, mood, characterization, and author's purpose could be brought to bear upon the choice of theme. Students could then work individually or in small groups to identify the themes of works read.

Reinforcement Procedures

1. Students write a short paper based on a poem that has a theme similar to the prose material being read in class. (Kaufman, Vol. 64, No. 7, p. 66)

2. Give students several pictures that reflect the same theme and that contain the same cast of characters. Working singly or in groups, have students invent stories that portray the theme of the pictures as they perceive it. (Kaufman, Vol. 62, No. 9, p. 1,283)

Post-Assessment: Same as pre-assessment.

Correlated Materials

Professional Texts Written for Teacher Use

Robinson (1975) p. 203

Instructional Material Written for Student Use

(Attach sheet.)

Descriptor: Identifying Characterization

Subject Areas: This skill is important in those subject areas, such as literature and history, in which an understanding of personages is important.

Objective: Given a selection on an appropriate instructional level and from which a description of a character could be made, the student will be able to describe the character.

Criterion Level:_____

Pre-Assessment: Locate a selection that students might be asked to read as part of their course work and from which a characterization could be ascertained. Ask students to describe the character. Give credit for an accurate description.

Sample Generic Teaching Strategy

Initial Teaching Procedure

Explain to students that to identify characterization, they will need to proceed through three steps. First, they will have to collect all evidence on the character, including his thoughts, speech, appearance, and actions; other people's thoughts and speech about him and actions toward him; and the author's description of him. Second, they need to decide which of these thoughts, words, and actions are in character and which are not. And third, they need to ascertain the personage's dominant characteristics and which of his actions support his contentions.

Students could then be given the page numbers on which to find information concerning a character in a book that had been read in class. Each piece of information could be evaluated in terms of its consistency with the other information presented about the character.

Another activity would involve giving students the page numbers on which information regarding the character could be found, along with some sample characteristics (*loving, simple, warm*). Students could then decide which words or actions support each characteristic.

The class could then be divided into groups of five students. Inform each group that they have ten minutes to find the five main characteristics of a character they have been studying. They will need to support their character descriptions. At the end of the assigned time period, each group gives their description and supporting reasons. Differences in descriptions between the groups can act as a source of discussion.

Ask students to write character sketches of personages in short selections. Allow them to work individually or in small groups. When they become proficient with short selections, have them use longer works. Eventually, each student should write a character sketch of a personage in a short selection and a long selection.

Reinforcement Procedures

1. Ask students to select an object that they carry with them throughout the school day and to have that object tell its "thoughts" for one day. This exercise is designed to give students an insight into the interior monologue often used in novels to reveal the personage's character. (Kaufman, Vol. 64, No. 5, p. 79)

2. Design an activity based on the "Today Show." Ask one student to be the "host" and others to be the "guests" to be interviewed. Each guest will assume the identity of a character or a historical figure that the class has been studying. A group of students then decide on the topics they want to discuss and design questions based on those topics. After students acting as guests study their characters, all the students participating in the activity should be given one period to rehearse before presenting their show to the class. The major emphasis during the activity should be the portrayal of the characters. A discussion following could center on whether the guests acted as the other members of the class would have perceived the characters as acting. (Kaufman, Vol. 62, No. 7, p. 1,023)

3. Each student in a group is given a different personality characteristic (*friendly*, *mean*, *generous*) and asked to create a character having that trait and to write his description. However, the trait itself may not be mentioned anywhere in the description. Students then read their papers and the remainder of the class tries to guess what characteristic is being described. (Kaufman, Vol. 64, No. 5, p. 76)

Post-Assessment: Same as pre-assessment.

Correlated Materials

Professional Texts Written for Teacher Use

Robinson (1975) pp. 202–203

Instructional Material Written for Student Use

(Attach sheet.)

Descriptor: Identifying Fact, Fiction, and Opinion

Subject Areas: This skill is required by those subject areas in which the ability to identify fact, fiction, and opinion is necessary.

Objective: Given a selection on an appropriate instructional level, the student will be able to identify it as fact, fiction, or opinion.

Criterion Level:_____

Pre-Assessment: Locate three course-related selections—one fact, one fiction, and one opinion. Ask students to decide which is fact, fiction, and opinion and to give reasons for their choices. Give credit for accurate responses adequately supported.

Sample Generic Teaching Strategy

Initial Teaching Procedure

Begin class by having students read an editorial and a newspaper report on the same topic and then discuss whether each is fact, fiction, or opinion. This discussion should lead to the ways of determining whether a piece of writing is fact, fiction, or opinion. Clues given by librarians, editors, and writers can be discussed and listed by the students.

Three additional selections could be analyzed. These pieces should include factual, opinionative, and fictional writing on the same topic. For example, a history teacher might present three selections: a factual account of an incident, an opinionative account of the same incident, and a fictionalized account of the incident. Students can decide how to categorize each piece of writing and can add to their list of editorial and writer clues. Students should then work individually or in groups to classify the materials.

Reinforcement Procedures

1. Give students a list of book titles with editorial notes and ask them to classify each using the labels *fact, fiction, opinion,* or *insufficient information to decide.* For example, the following teacher-made descriptions of nonexistent books would both be classified as fact:

> *Birds of the Southwest:* "The authors have described with utmost precision all the important species, living habits, life histories, and ecological relationships. Ninety-seven photographs show living birds in their natural habitats."

> *Growing Plants Indoors:* "This book suggests ways to choose appropriate plants for your home."

2. Students read a novel concerning their class work; for example, in history, a historical novel could be read; in science, a science fiction book or a piece of fiction dealing with ecology or another scientific issue could

279

be read. Students react to the novel indicating how the fictional account added to their feelings about the period or situation. Then they decide which makes the stronger statement—fact or fiction. (Kaufman, Vol. 64, No. 6, p. 58)

Post-Assessment: Same as pre-assessment.

Correlated Materials

Professional Texts Written for Teacher Use

Burmeister (1974) pp. 206–207
Olson and Ames (1972) pp. 68–69

Instructional Material Written for Student Use

(Attach sheet.)

Descriptor: Identifying Propaganda

Subject Areas: This skill is required by any subject area—for example, history, literature, and science—in which the ability to recognize propaganda is needed.

Objective: Given a selection on an appropriate instructional level and which contains propaganda, the student will be able to identify the propaganda statements.

Criterion Level:_____

Pre-Assessment: Locate material that contains propaganda and that students might be required to read as part of their course work. Ask students to identify the propaganda in the selection. Give credit for accurate identification.

Sample Generic Teaching Strategy

Initial Teaching Procedure

To introduce this concept, use copies of newspaper advertisements to demonstrate to students examples of those propaganda techniques that might occur in your field of study. (See Identifying Propaganda in Chapter 3 for a list of the types of propaganda.) Next, give examples of propaganda statements from course-related materials (texts, articles, supplementary readings). Divide the class into groups of two or three and have the students find examples of propaganda in advertisements and course-related materials. List the following five questions that students should ask themselves when attempting to detect propaganda.

1. What is the writer's purpose?
2. How competent is the writer on this topic?
3. How familiar am I with the topic?
4. Do any propaganda techniques appear to be used?
5. Should I accept, reject, or delay my opinion of this source?

Reinforcement Procedures

1. Have students locate two pieces of writing (e.g., books, articles, speeches, editorials) on the same course-related subject and then answer the five questions listed above in relation to them.
2. Have students locate one piece of course-related material and accept or reject it on the basis of the five questions above.

Post-Assessment: Same as pre-assessment.

Correlated Materials

Professional Texts Written for Teacher Use

Burmeister (1974) pp. 207–211

Instructional Material Written for Student Use

(Attach sheet.)

Descriptor: Identifying Author's Purpose

Subject Areas: This skill is needed in those subject areas in which a study of the author's purpose for writing is required.

Objective: Given a selection on an appropriate instructional level, the student will be able to ascertain its author's purpose for writing it.

Criterion Level:_____

Pre-Assessment: Locate a selection that students might be required to read as part of class material and in which the author's purpose might be identified. Ask students to assess the author's purpose and to give reasons for their choices. Give credit for responses that are adequately supported.

Sample Generic Teaching Strategy

Initial Teaching Procedure

Present students with a simple piece of writing, such as a two- or three-paragraph description of a product that relates to your subject area. Tell them that the piece was written by the president of the company promoting the product, and ask them to judge the authenticity of the paragraphs. Then inform the students that you made an error and that the ad was actually written by an objective consumer agency. What changes do they now make in their evaluation of the ad?

Explain to students that our view of written material changes drastically when it is based on the author's purpose for writing. This fact has just been demonstrated in the foregoing activity. Explain further that all responsible writing has a purpose and ask leading questions to elicit some of the purposes—for example, to entertain, inform, sell, change attitudes, or change behavior.

With the students, analyze the purposes of a few short selections. Then ask them to work in small groups to ascertain the purposes of some other selections. For example, students in a biology class could analyze their textbook author's purpose (to inform); the purpose of the writer of an article concerning the dwindling numbers of grizzly bears in Alaska (to have pressure brought upon lawmakers to set up a sanctuary for grizzly bears); or an article on pollution (to refrain from further infractions on environmental safety).

Reinforcement Procedures

1. An easy reinforcement activity is having students identify the author's purpose in short selections. This activity could be made even easier by providing multiple answers from which to choose.

2. A more difficult reinforcement activity is having superior students analyze the author's purpose in longer selections. Before they could arrive at a valid decision, the students would need to study all aspects of the work as well as background information.

Post-Assessment: Same as pre-assessment.

Correlated Materials

Professional Texts Written for Teacher Use

Thomas and Robinson (1972) pp. 115–116

Instructional Material Written for Student Use

(Attach sheet.)

Descriptor: Scheduling Time

Subject Areas: This skill is needed in those subject areas in which students are required to schedule their study time either in or out of school.

Objective: The student will be able to schedule study time appropriately.

Criterion Level:_____

Pre-Assessment: Ask students to write a time schedule that indicates their plan for scheduling study time for the course they are taking. Give credit for any response that appears feasible.

Sample Generic Teaching Strategy

Initial Teaching Procedure

The teacher introduces the topic by discussing with students what the teacher will do to help the students and what they are expected to do on their own. For example, the teacher of German might explain to students that he will assign a given number of words to be learned and a given number of passages to be translated each day. In addition, it is the students' responsibility to keep current the words they have learned during the preceding month. The teacher then requires each student to keep a *study card* such as that found below. The cards may be turned in to the teacher at the end of each week for about a month, so that the teacher may assess the students' progress in time scheduling.

A sample study card follows:

	Planned Time			Actual Time	
Mon.	Sept. 19	7:00–7:45 P.M.	Mon.	Sept. 19	7:00–7:50 P.M.
	homework	7:00–7:30		homework	7:00–7:50
	review	7:30–7:45			
Wed.	Sept. 21	7:00–7:45 P.M.	Wed.	Sept. 21	7:00–7:30 P.M.
	homework	7:00–7:30		homework	7:00–7:15
	review	7:30–7:45		review	7:15–7:30
Sat.	Sept. 24	10:00–10:45 A.M.	Sat.	Sept. 24	10:00–10:45 A.M.
	homework	10:00–10:30		homework	10:00–10:15
	review	10:30–10:45		review	10:15–10:45

Reinforcement Procedures

1. Remove the names of students from exemplary study cards and put the cards in a file box. Allow all students to use these cards as a reference source for study ideas.

285

2. Have students plot a graph showing number of hours studied on one axis and grade received on tests on the other axis. Let students generalize about the results.

Post-Assessment: Same as pre-assessment.

Correlated Materials

Professional Texts Written for Teacher Use

(Attach own list here.)

Instructional Material Written for Student Use

(Attach sheet.)

Descriptor: Setting Purposes

Subject Areas: This skill is required by any subject area in which students are required to read.

Objective: Before starting to read a selection, the student will be able to state the purpose for reading.

Criterion Level: _____

Pre-Assessment: Ask student to state the purpose for reading a given selection. Give credit for responses that are sufficiently specific (e.g., "to find the main idea" rather than, "to pass the test").

Sample Generic Teaching Strategy

Initial Teaching Procedure

The teacher introduces the topic by asking the class to brainstorm on some purposes for reading. Take several minutes to gain a variety of ideas and write them on the chalkboard. Then ask students what value they see in knowing their purpose for reading. Elicit such answers as (1) affects reading rate and (2) affects amount remembered. Take several of the reasons for reading listed on the chalkboard and decide how the purpose would affect the rate and the amount remembered. For example, reading directions to make a model airplane would require slow, careful reading and detailed recall, whereas reading a novel for pleasure would not require such slow, careful reading or detailed recall of the contents. Impress on students the need to know their purpose for reading and ask them if they are able to note the cue to teacher purpose when he asks questions prior to giving a reading assignment. Pursue, with the students, methods of their making up their own questions when teachers do not give them a purpose for reading. Show them how to change titles and subtitles into questions. The teacher can give a guided practice session for students in making up questions based on the headings in their textbook. A practice session of this nature will provide a background for skill 23, Using a Study Technique.

Reinforcement Procedures

1. Prepare a list of purposes for which students should read. Students should respond to each item with the speed at which they should read and the amount that they should remember.

2. Ask students to write down their purposes for reading everything that they read for one week. Have them also state the speed at which they read it and the amount they hoped to remember.

Post-Assessment: Same as pre-assessment.

287

Correlated Materials

Professional Texts Written for Teacher Use

Karlin (1972) pp. 293–295
Thomas and Robinson (1972) pp. 53–62

Instructional Material Written for Student Use

(Attach sheet.)

Descriptor: Using a Study Technique

Subject Areas: This skill is needed in all subject areas in which studying is necessary.

Objective: Given a selection that is written on an appropriate instructional level and that requires studying, the student will be able to apply an efficient study technique.

Criterion Level:_____

Pre-Assessment: Give students course-related selections that require studying and ask them to read the selections using their most efficient study technique. (If they fail to skim the selection for headings and typographical aids, or in other ways illustrate lack of a systematic approach to studying, they need instruction on this skill.)

Sample Generic Teaching Strategy

Initial Teaching Procedure

Inform the students that previewing a lesson familiarizes them with the content and makes them better able to cope with the ideas presented. Then preview the lesson with the students by doing the following together.

1. Carefully examine the title of the selection, its opening paragraph, headings, and concluding paragraph. Observe the format of the selection. Look at the pictures and their captions and talk about them. Notice the charts, graphs, maps, and other diagrams. How informative are they? Anticipate the vocabulary to be met. Examine the new words. Consider carefully the italicized and/or bold-faced words and phrases. Notice any formulas, abbreviations, and summaries. What are the formulas for? What do the abbreviations stand for? What is the purpose of the summaries?

2. As all go through the selection, list on the board questions that will probably be solved and issues that will probably be discussed. Encourage the students to relate their past experiences to the material.

3. Allow the students time to read the selection.

4. After most of the students have completed the selection, go back to the questions listed on the board and recite the answers.

5. Review ideas presented in the selection. Summarize major points and emphasize important details.

Reinforcement Procedures

1. Construct a checklist that contains the five letters *S, Q, R, R, R.* Each time students are given an assignment, the teacher reminds them to check off the steps as they proceed through the material. Give the class time to complete the two steps in class.

2. Tell the students that they will have only ten minutes to study a new chapter. At the end of ten minutes, give them a quiz on the chapter, based

on information that they could have gotten merely through previewing correctly.

3. Construct a guided reading sheet on a specific chapter that asks the student to provide the following information: (1) title of selection (2) reason why selection is titled as it is, (3) clues to important information (e.g., italics, boldface, illustrations), (4) any background information they may already possess on the topic, and (5) predictions that they can make about contents and/or outcomes of the selection.

Post-Assessment: Same as pre-assessment.

Correlated Materials

Professional Texts Written for Teacher Use

Aukerman (1972) pp. 59–62
Thomas and Robinson (1972) pp. 69–104

Instructional Material Written for Student Use

(Attach sheet.)

Descriptor: Using Locational Aids in the Library

Subject Areas: This skill is required by any subject area in which students must locate information in the library.

Objective: The student will use the card catalog, indexes, and an encyclopedia to locate references and information on a topic.

    Criterion Level:_____

Pre-Assessment: Locate a topic that students might be required to study as part of your course. Ask them to locate a list of references in the library and to note how they found the references. Give credit to students who made use of the card catalog, indexes, and encyclopedia.

Sample Generic Teaching Strategy

Initial Teaching Procedure

The first lesson on this topic may be carried out in the classroom. Using the overhead projector, show students facsimiles of title, subject, and author cards. Briefly note that the call number occurs on each, as well as the author, title, publisher, place of publication, and date of publication. Describe sample situations in which various types of references should be used. For example, ask, "If you wish to locate a book entitled *Artists of the Midwest*, what type of card should you use?"

Using the overhead projector, show students a page of the *Readers' Guide to Periodical Literature.* Study the format with the students carefully. Project the key that interprets the symbols used. Discuss with the students the information that is contained in the *Readers' Guide* but not in the card catalog. A brief discussion of other indexes—such as *Who's Who*, dictionaries, and *Roget's International Thesaurus*—and their purposes might follow.

Ask students what information they might gain from an encyclopedia. Elicit answers such as a brief summary of the topic and bibliographic references. Ask students how they might find information in an encyclopedia. Be sure students realize that there are both subject headings and an index. Discuss the arrangement of entries in the encyclopedia.

Give students a subject that they might need to research in the library and ask them to decide which topics they might look under to find information. For example, students might be asked what topics they might look under to find information on the role of Serbia in the First World War.

The last step in this lesson would be to take students to the library and have the librarian show them the location of the card catalog, the indexes, and the encyclopedias. A natural follow-up activity would be to have students find several references on a topic using the card catalog, indexes, and encyclopedias.

Reinforcement Procedures

1. Write topics on slips of paper, place them in a hat, and ask each student to draw one. The student is to make up two cards: (1) a title card in which he makes up the name of a book that fits the topic; and (2) an author card in which he is the author. All the title cards are then gathered and shuffled. The class is divided into small groups and the title cards are divided among the groups. Students are instructed to make subject cards from the title cards. As soon as the groups finish making the new subject cards, they locate the original author to check their answers.

2. Give the students a list of questions that require them to look in the card catalog, indexes, and encyclopedias to find the answers. (Bergman 1976, #754*)

Post-Assessment: Same as pre-assessment.

Correlated Materials

Professional Texts Written for Teacher Use

Karlin (1972) pp. 210–212
Thomas and Robinson (1972) pp. 176–188

Instructional Material Written for Student Use

(Attach sheet.)

*Refers to activity number 754 in F. L. Bergman, *The English Teacher's Activities Handbook*, Boston: Allyn and Bacon, 1976.

Descriptor: Recording References

Subject Areas: This skill is required by any subject area in which students need to locate references in the library.

Objective: The student will record references on note cards.

Criterion Level:_____

Pre-Assessment: Show students (1) two cards from the card catalog, (2) an index such as the *Readers' Guide to Periodical Literature*, and (3) the bibliography following a topic in an encyclopedia. Ask students to make a note card for one reference from each source. Give credit for each card containing adequate information to locate the material (e.g., call number) and a format that can easily be transferred to a list of references.

Sample Generic Teaching Strategy

Initial Teaching Procedure

Ask students what information they need to write a list of references. Student should mention author, title, place of publication, publisher, and date of publication. Have students write on the chalkboard sample bibliographic entries such as the one below.

> Graham, Hope. *The Everbearing Strawberry Plant.* Newark, N. J.: Crepe Press, 1975.

Then, using the overhead, project a facsimile of another card, such as the following one, from the card catalog:

BF 121 1963	**Kindem, Charles Steven, 1930–**
K 135	Basic psychology (by) Charles S. Kindem.
	New York, Appleton–Century–Crofts (1963)
	xii, 723 p. illus. 27 cm.
	Includes bibliographies
1. Psychology. BF 121.K 135	63–55215
Library of Congress	

Ask students to identify information on the card. Be sure they identify call number, author, title, place of publication, publisher, and date. Students should understand that the call number aids them in locating the book in the library.

Ask students what information they need from the card to locate a book in the library and to record the reference. Students should answer, "call number, author, title, place of publication, publisher, and date of publication." Next, develop a form with the students for writing the call number and the reference that would be helpful in (1) locating the book and (2) writing the bibliography. A sample form, which shows the call number in an easily identifiable form and the information regarding the book in the same form in which it will appear in the bibliography, follows:

BF121   Kindem, Charles. *Basic Psychology.*
1963   New York: Appleton-Century-Crofts,
K 135   1963.

Give each student five 3 by 5 cards. On the first card, have the student copy the reference card above. Then, using the overhead projector, show students a title card and a subject card. Have them write a reference card for each.

Using the overhead projector, show students a list of bibliographic references. Discuss with students the information that should be recorded and the form in which it should be recorded in order that they may transfer it directly to their bibliographies. Write one reference on the chalkboard. Have students write a different reference on a 3 by 5 card.

Using the overhead projector, show students typical entries from the *Readers' Guide* or other indexes. Then, proceed with discussion, demonstration, and card completion as above.

Reinforcement Procedures

1. Prepare an exercise that contains typical card catalog, encyclopedia,

294

and index references. Have students write reference cards.

    2. Divide the class into groups of three and ask them to share ideas on writing reference cards. Have one member of each group tell the entire class his group's best idea.

    3. Have students use the card catalog, indexes, and bibliographies in the library as a basis for writing references.

Post-Assessment: Same as pre-assessment.

Correlated Materials

Professional Texts Written for Teacher Use

    Thomas and Robinson (1972) pp. 180, 185

Instructional Material Written for Student Use

    (Attach sheet.)

Descriptor: Using the Library Call System

Subject Areas: This skill is required by any subject area in which students must use the library to locate information.

Objective: The student will be able to locate material in the library using the Dewey decimal classification or the Library of Congress system for information retrieval.

Criterion Level:_____

Pre-Assessment: Give students three complete note cards that contain information that might have been taken from (1) the card catalog, (2) the *Readers' Guide to Periodical Literature*, or (3) an encyclopedia. Give credit to students who can locate the written materials within a reasonable time period.

Sample Generic Teaching Strategy

Initial Teaching Procedure

A lesson on the library call system should be conducted in the library. The teacher or librarian should explain that books in the library are shelved according to the organizational system used in that library, whether it be the Dewey decimal classification or the Library of Congress system. The general classes of the systems should be explained. The students should be shown how to locate books using the call numbers found on the cards in the card catalog. Students should be given the call numbers and titles from five books and asked to locate them. Discussion of any difficulties should follow.

The teacher should show students reference cards for magazine articles made from the *Readers' Guide to Periodical Literature* and should instruct students in the location of periodicals. Similarly, students should be shown reference cards for books based on materials taken from bibliographies in an encyclopedia. Students should be questioned as to how they would locate the books. The teacher should elicit the answer that students should look up the title or author card for each book in the card catalog.

Reinforcement Procedures

1. Divide the class into teams. Give each team a list of books and journal articles. The teams must use the library reference tools to decide whether the materials are in the library and, if so, to locate them. The first team to correctly finish wins. (Bergman 1976, #37)

2. Provide a box with book catalog cards. Divide the class into teams of five. The first member of each team chooses a card from the box and goes to find the book. When he finds it, the next member of the team repeats the procedure. This system is followed until all the members of one team have found a book. (Bergman 1976, #728)

Post-Assessment: Same as pre-assessment.

Correlated Materials

Professional Texts Written for Teacher Use

Thomas and Robinson (1972) pp. 176–188

Instructional Material Written for Student Use

(Attach sheet.)

Descriptor: Using Locational Aids Within Books

Subject Areas: This skill is required by any subject area in which the students need to use the table of contents, chapter headings, subheadings, or index in a book to locate information.

Objective: Given a topic that can be located using the table of contents, chapter headings, and subheadings, and another that can be located from the index, the student will be able to locate the appropriate pages.

Criterion Level:_____

Pre-Assessment: Give students a topic that can be located using the table of contents, chapter headings, and subheadings in a book that they might read as a part of course work. Assign credit to those students who locate the topic through use of the table of contents, chapter headings, and subheadings. Give students a topic listed in the index of a book that they might be required to read in class. Ask students to locate the discussion of the topic in the text. Give credit for appropriate use of the index.

Sample Generic Teaching Strategy

Initial Teaching Procedure

Use the table of contents from a textbook available to all the students and the tables of contents from several other course-related materials. Design questions in which students must use the tables of contents in order to answer the questions; for example, "In which source would you find information about the principle of chromatography?"

After the students have had time to answer the questions, discuss the correct answers with them. Show them that the purpose of a table of contents is merely to be a guide to the kind of material contained in the book.

After the students understand the use of the table of contents, show them how headings and subheadings may be used to locate information. Explain to them that by using the table of contents to locate a general topic, they may skim through the portion of the chapter looking at headings and subheadings in order to determine whether the information contained therein is related to the topic in which they are interested. For example, if they were looking for information on the camel, they could look in the table of contents to determine where the topic was discussed. The chapter heading "Biological Classification of Animals" might indicate to the students to turn to that chapter. Instead of reading the entire chapter, they could then look through headings and subheadings until they found the heading "Mammals." Then they could look through the subheadings until they found the topic, "Family Camelidae."

Tell the students to turn to a given page in the index and ask them to locate the answers to the questions that they cannot answer from the table of contents alone (for example, "What is the name of the man who developed the principle of chromatography?" After they locate the answer, explain that (1) all topics in an index are in alphabetical order, (2) pages on which the information related to the topic may be found are given in the index, (3) topics are arranged in the index according to key words (i.e., the key words for the *principle of chromatography* would be *chromatography, principle of*), and (4) commas often separate topics and page numbers. Demonstrate the four rules by showing students several examples in their own textbooks.

Explain to the class that the primary technique in using an index is in determining the key words to locate a topic. Present a list of topics from the content area and ask the students to identify the key words that they would use in order to find the topic in the index. An example from biology follows:

1. distribution of the camel family
2. structure of the cell
3. reproduction in plants
4. rise in liquids in plant stems
5. characteristics of classification systems

After the students locate the correct key words, discuss some of the problems with locating key words. For example, if the topic cannot be located, try to find a (1) synonym for the key word—for example, the Arabian camel may be listed as *dromedary*; (2) more general term for the key word—for example, *camel* may be listed under *mammal*; (3) more specific term for the key word—for example, *camel* may be listed under *llama*; (4) related term—for example, *camel* may be listed as *domesticated beast.*

Reinforcement Procedures

1. Construct a list of questions that may be answered from the textbook. Ask the students to locate the answers and then state whether they used the table of contents, the headings and subheadings, the index, or all three. Later discuss the most efficient source that should have been used. Point out the questions that obviously could be located only through the use of the index, and explain to students why they should not use all three aids if they do not have to. Likewise, explain that some of the questions would be best answered by reference to the table of contents because the index would be too narrow to give the general response required. Questions of this type include the following: "What is the author's order of presentation of topics in this text? Why do you think he presents them in this order?"

2. Give students a list of topics and see how many key words they can make up that relate to the topics. They are to use their knowledge of synonyms, specific terms, general terms, and related terms to make their lists of key words as expansive as possible. Have them indicate which terms they think would be the ones actually used in the index.

3. Make up a "Concentration" game. One card contains a key word; its match contains a broader term, narrower term, related term, or synonym. Let students play the game in pairs. Encourage them to make up more

cards so that the game may be played with different topics.

4. Time the students on the speed with which they can locate a list of topics in the text. Let the student who finished first explain why he was able to locate the correct information so quickly.

Post-Assessment: Same as pre-assessment.

Correlated Materials

Professional Texts Written for Teacher Use

Karlin (1972) pp. 207–210
Thomas and Robinson (1972) pp. 188–189

Instructional Material Written for Student Use

(Attach sheet.)

Descriptor: Using Footnotes

Subject Areas: This skill is required by any subject area in which the students need to use footnotes to gain information.

Objective: Given a book containing footnotes, the number of a page on which a footnote may be found, and a term that is explained in the footnote, the student will be able to use the footnote for clarification or further reference.

Criterion Level: _____

Pre-Assessment: Give students a page from a book that they might use as part of their class materials and ask them a question that may be answered in the footnote found on that page. Give credit to those students who use the footnote to answer the question.

Sample Generic Teaching Strategy

Initial Teaching Procedure

Ask students why they think authors include footnotes. Elicit answers that footnotes include explanatory notes and references to material in another source. Have students turn to several footnotes of the first type in their text. Make certain that students can understand how the number in the text refers to the footnote number, the type of information included (i.e., author, title, place of publication, publisher, and date of publication), and any abbreviations used. Discuss with students the reasons why authors include footnotes (in order that the reader may pursue the subject).

Next have students turn to footnotes which contain explanatory notes. Have them analyze the type of information included. Complete the lesson by having students read material in their texts using a guided reading sheet that requires them to use information contained in the footnotes.

Reinforcement Procedures

1. Design a treasure hunt by developing questions that students must answer by referring to footnotes. Divide the class into teams of four or five. The team finding the correct answers to all the questions first, wins.

2. Ask students to locate a footnote that contains a reference to a topic in which they are particularly interested. Then have students locate the book or periodical in the library.

Post-Assessment: Same as pre-assessment.

Correlated Materials

Professional Texts Written for Teacher Use
(Attach own list here.)

Instructional Material Written for Student Use
(Attach sheet.)

Descriptor: Using Glossaries

Subject Areas: This skill is required by any subject area in which students need to use glossaries.

Objectives: Given a book containing a glossary and words to be defined, which are included in the glossary, the student will be able to locate the words in the glossary.

Criterion Level: _____

Pre-Assessment: Give the students a course-related textbook that contains a glossary. Have them find the meanings of words listed in the glossary. Give credit to those students who turn immediately to the glossary to locate the meanings.

Sample Generic Teaching Strategy

Initial Teaching Procedure

This lesson is designed to remind students to use the glossary, since most students mastered the skills necessary for using a glossary in elementary school. Discuss with the students the purpose and location of the glossary. Ask them to locate a few words. Have them compare the glossary with the dictionary in terms of scope and function. Assign students a lesson to read with one or more terms that they may need to look up in the glossary. Discuss the use of the glossary following the reading of the selection.

Reinforcement Procedures

1. Divide the class into teams of four. Give each team six words whose meanings are to be found by using the glossary. Each team has fifteen minutes to locate the meanings of the words and to practice a method of presenting the meanings in some novel form. Students then present their word meanings. (Adapted from Bergman 1976, #312)

2. Have students make a glossary of words that they encounter in their text and whose meanings they do not know. This exercise is particularly profitable when the text the student is using does not include a glossary. (Adapted from Bergman 1976, #364)

Post-Assessment: Same as pre-assessment.

Correlated Materials

Professional Texts Written for Teacher Use

(Attach own list here.)

Instructional Material Written for Student Use

(Attach sheet.)

Descriptor: Using Maps, Graphs, and Tables

Subject Areas: This skill is required by any subject area in which the student must take information from maps, graphs, or tables.

Objective: Given a map, graph, or table, the student will be able to answer questions pertaining to it.

Criterion Level:_____

Pre-Assessment: Provide students with maps, graphs, or tables that they might be required to read as part of your course. Ask them to answer course-related questions whose answers may be obtained using the maps, graphs, or tables. Give credit to those students who can accurately answer the questions using the appropriate diagram.

Sample Generic Teaching Strategy

Initial Teaching Procedure

Locate a map, graph, or table in content-related materials and ask the student to listen as you read the information contained (e.g., science: the path blood takes from the heart to the thumb; history: growth of the population in the United States from 1860 to 1900; mathematics: the point-slope equation of the line; auto shop: steps to take in rebuilding a carburetor).

Then give students a quiz over the materials you read aloud to them. Explain to them that words alone are often inadequate to clearly communicate some concepts. Show them the map, graph, or table that you read to them and discuss its worth in helping the reader understand the message intended by the author.

Explain to the class that diagrams usually contain information to help the reader understand an object, a process, or an operation. Give the students a diagram they have not seen before and ask them to answer specific questions about it. Discuss the correct answers to the questions and the procedure that should have been followed to locate the correct answers.

Finally, explain how to use the following graphic aids that are relevant to your content area: maps, graphs, tables, or other diagrams.

Maps: Show the student maps that all have *legends*. Demonstrate the meanings of the symbols on various legends. Give them a map they have not seen before and ask them to locate answers to several questions that require them to use its legend correctly. Discuss the correct answers to the questions and the procedure that should have been followed to locate the correct answers.

Graphs: Tell the student that several different kinds of graphs exist. Explain that *pictorial graphs, bar graphs. line graphs*, and *circle graphs* all contain similar elements. The students should always (1) read the title to get an idea of what the graph is about; (2) look for the scale of measure or legend (e.g., a picture of an oil can may represent the oil industry or a figure of a man may represent 2,000 people); (3) note what types of relationships are being presented (e.g., relationships of objects, places, or ideas); (4) identify the relationships shown by the graph (e.g., comparison of change in rate of population growth from 1860 to 1900, comparison of functional relationships between number of calories consumed and gain in weight). Give the students a graph they have not seen before and ask them to answer specific questions about it. Discuss the correct answers to the questions and the procedure that should have been followed to locate the correct answers.

Tables: Explain to the class that a table is usually a listing of facts and information. It is helpful in showing comparisons between facts as well as in helping the reader locate specific facts. The approach to reading a table is similar to that of reading a graph. Students should follow the succeeding steps: (1) Read the title to determine the contents of the table. (2) Look at the headings for the various columns. Note any subheadings. (3) Read the details along the vertical and horizontal columns of the chart. (4) Begin to draw some conclusions about the information contained. Give students a table they have not seen before and ask them to follow the four steps given above in order to answer specific questions. Discuss the correct answers to the questions and the procedures that should have been followed to locate the correct answers.

Reinforcement Procedures

1. Ask students to construct a map, graph, or table of something in their content area textbook that is not already in such a format. Then ask the students to share their illustrations with the remainder of the class. Discuss whether the map, graph, or table makes the original idea of the author any clearer.

2. Place students in pairs. Ask them to sit back to back. One student is to read from a map the directions for getting from one place to another. The second student is to draw a map of the oral directions and then compare the actual map with the one he drew. Then the students switch roles and repeat the process. Examples from several content areas follow: science—one student describes the distribution of two forms of hamsters in southern Russia while the other fills in a map; English—one student describes the route of Huckleberry Finn and Jim down the Mississippi while the second fills in a map; history—one student describes the status of slavery in each state after the Missouri Compromise, while the second student fills in a map.

3. Group students into threes and give them a set of questions concerning maps, graphs, and tables. The group that finishes first should compare answers with the other groups and then discuss the procedures the winning three used to locate the information so quickly.

Post-Assessment: Same as pre-assessment.

Correlated Materials

Professional Texts Written for Teacher Use

Karlin (1972) pp. 213–216
Olson and Ames (1972) pp. 56–58

Instructional Material Written for Student Use

(Attach sheet.)

Descriptor: Matching Materials With Purposes

Subject Areas: This skill is required by any subject area in which students must assess the worth of a selection for a given purpose.

Objective: Given three selections on the same topic and written on an appropriate instructional level, the student will state which selection is most relevant for a given purpose.

Criterion Level:_____

Pre-Assessment: Show students three selections on a given topic. Be sure to include qualifications of the author and date of writing. Ask students to indicate which selection they would choose to use as a reference for a term paper and to give reasons for their choices. Give credit for an appropriate choice adequately supported.

Sample Generic Teaching Strategy

Initial Teaching Procedure

Introduce the topic by explaining that reference materials must match the purpose for reading in two ways. First, the selection must fit the need. Second, the person who wrote the materials should be an "authority."

Ask the class how they would find out if a book or article that they had located in the library contained information that was appropriate to their needs. Answers might include looking at the index, table of contents, headings, and subheadings, as well as skimming the book in general. The class could then be asked to locate information on various topics. The students could use an unread chapter from their text as a resource. Note which parts of the text the students use. Give practice in locating appropriate portions of the text or give further explanation of the portion of the text that they do not use.

Give to the class descriptions of three different authors who all wrote on the same topic. In each case, give the writer's background, in so far as it concerns the topic, and the date the book was published. Ask students to decide which author they feel is best qualified to write about the topic. Ask students where they could find information pertaining to the author's expertise on the topic and the date the book was copyrighted. For example, information about the author may be found in material in the book itself, on the book jacket, or in the preface, as well as in references such as *Who's Who.* The copyright date should always be located in the book's introductory material.

Take the class to the library and ask them to find three books or articles on the topic and then assess each of the materials located for suitability to their purposes. Discuss students' answers and any difficulties that may have arisen.

Reinforcement Procedures

1. Prepare a question sheet that includes a description of a topic to be researched and the copyright dates and qualifications of the authors of articles or books on the topic. Ask students to decide which references would probably be most useful for the topic being researched. Several sets of questions and descriptions could be included in one worksheet.

2. Place several books on a general topic on one shelf in the classroom library. Give the class a specific topic to research. Ask students to evaluate the books in terms of the given topic, for suitability of content and authorship.

Post-Assessment: Same as pre-assessment.

Correlated Materials

Professional Texts Written for Teacher Use

Burmeister (1974) pp. 203–206
Olson and Ames (1972) p. 70
Thomas and Robinson (1972) pp. 192–194

Instructional Material Written for Student Use

(Attach sheet.)

Descriptor: Understanding the Organization of Paragraphs

Subject Areas: This skill is required by all subject areas in which students need to perceive the author's organization.

Objective: The student will be able to recognize the following paragraph organizations: cause-effect, comparison-contrast, enumerative, and chronological sequence.

Criterion Level: _____

Pre-Assessment: Show students four paragraphs, each of which exemplifies one of the following types of organization: cause-effect, comparison-contrast, enumerative, and chronological. Ask them to identify each type. Give credit for correct identification.

Sample Generic Teaching Strategy

Initial Teaching Procedure

Explain to students that ideas are often arranged in patterns and that if they learn to recognize the pattern and use it when they study, they will have an easier time remembering what they read or hear. Place on the overhead a transparency of content-related paragraphs that provide examples of the following four types of paragraph organization: (1) cause-effect, (2) comparison-contrast, (3) enumerative, and (4) chronological.

Go through the paragraphs one at a time and underline the key words that the reader may use as clues to help him understand the pattern used. An example of the chronological pattern is given below:

> Garbage *once* meant the wastes from butchering animals for meat. *Later* it included solid organic wastes, such as discarded foods from kitchens. *Now* it often refers to solid household wastes of all kinds . . .. (Haynes 1973, p. 685)

In this paragraph, the teacher would point out to the students that the words *once*, *later*, and *now* should help them identify the pattern as chronological.

Once the students understand how to identify the various patterns, tell them they should always ask themselves the following questions about the patterns they have identified: (1) What *caused* the effect to occur? (2) What is being compared or contrasted? (3) What types of things are listed? (4) What is the time order?

Reinforcement Procedures

1. Select several paragraphs from the content area textbook or from other content-related materials and ask students to identify the paragraph pattern.

2. Group students into threes and give each group a different type of

313

paragraph pattern to look for in their textbooks. After ten minutes, ask members of each group to identify the paragraphs they have located. Compare the number of each type of paragraph found in the text and discuss why the author would tend to use one type of paragraph more than another. For example, in history, the chronological pattern would probably prevail; and in mathematics, the enumerative.

3. Group the students into pairs and give the groups the task of locating one specific type of paragraph pattern. After ten minutes find out which pair has located the most. If the paragraphs located by the pair are the correct pattern, ask them to tell the remainder of the class what clue words they used to locate the paragraphs so quickly. Then discuss how these same clue words should give the students aids to interpreting the meanings of the paragraphs.

Post-Assessment: Same as pre-assessment.

Correlated Materials

Professional Texts Written for Teacher Use

Burmeister (1974) pp. 190–191
Herber (1970) pp. 171–172
Karlin (1972) pp. 170, 172, 173–174
Robinson (1975) pp. 102–108, 114–119, 135–142, 150–151, 153–156, 174–181

Instructional Material Written for Student Use

(Attach sheet.)

Descriptor: Organizing Information

Subject Areas: This skill is needed in any subject area in which the student is required to outline, take notes, summarize, compare and contrast, or classify information.

Objective: The student will be able to organize information in a variety of ways; namely, outlining, taking notes, summarizing, comparing and contrasting, and classifying.

Criterion Level:_____

Pre-Assessment: Provide students with reading material that they might read as part of their course work. Ask them to take notes on one paragraph, outline a second section, summarize a third section, compare and contrast two additional sections, and classify information in a final section. Give credit for demonstration of the appropriate skill.

Sample Generic Teaching Strategy

Initial Teaching Procedure

Discuss with students the role of outlining. Stress that this technique should be used when students need to note main ideas and details in relation to a specific purpose. Show students a completed outline. Discuss the placement of headings and details. Then give students a partial outline as shown in the following example and have students complete it. (Karlin 1972, pp. 200–207)

"Markets also vary widely in geographical scope. The markets for such basic foodstuffs and raw materials as wheat, cotton, rubber, coffee, sugar, copper, and oil are international in scope with buyers and sellers all over the world. Other markets are regional or local. The market for black-eyed peas tends to be limited to the South. The market area covered by a small barber shop is likely to be the neighborhood. For many familiar products, such as automobiles, lumber, and clothing, the market is national." (Calderwood and Fersh 1974, p. 77)

I. Markets vary widely geographically

  A. International

    1. basic foodstuffs

    2._____

  B._____

    1. black-eyed peas

  C. Neighborhood

    1._____

  D._____

    1. automobiles

    2. lumber

    3. clothing

315

As the students become more skilled, the teacher can present outlines with more blanks, as shown in the following example:

"In the Middle East, a large number of distinct groups have been able to live together while maintaining separate group identities. They have done so by living in clearly defined parts of cities and towns, by following certain occupations and professions, and by maintaining their own community organizations and customs—particularly religious beliefs and modes of dress. In addition, each group often spoke its own language and belonged to a separate religious denomination." (Tachau 1970, p. 19)

I. Middle Easterners maintain separate group identities

   A. Living in defined areas

   B. _____

   C. _____

      1. _____

      2. _____

   D. _____

   E. Separate religious denominations

Note-taking skills can be introduced as a technique to be used when the more structured outline is not needed. The teacher can show students various types of notes including single-word notes, incomplete sentence (phrase) notes, and complete sentence notes. Then the teacher might ask students to take notes on a paragraph and follow this activity with a discussion.

For example, the history teacher instructs her students to read the following paragraph in order to be able to name some of the articles of clothing worn by the Kiowas.

Clothing, too, came from the buffalo. In the old days, men dressed literally from head to foot in buffalo skins. Their moccasin soles were cut out of rawhide; the uppers were made from soft-tanned buffalo-calf skin, which wore better than buckskin. Leggings, to protect the legs from mesquite thorns and low-growing brush, were also made from buffalo-calf skins, as were the breechcloths and the belts tied around the men's waists to secure leggings and breechcloth. (Marriott 1968, p. 147)

One student's notes might be

Kiowa clothes: moccasins, leggings, breechcloths, belts

Following this activity, a student's notes could be evaluated by discussing the following:

1. Is information appropriate to purpose?
2. Are author's points restated in student's words?
3. Are all important points recorded?
4. Were any shorthand techniques used to increase speed of note-taking?
5. Would notes be readable at a later date?

Classifying can be taught in the following manner. Students can be assigned questions to which the answers can best be found by classifying. For instance, the students might be asked to answer the question, "Which of Shakespeare's plays are comedies and which are tragedies?" After reading a selection which answers this question and then listing which plays belong in each category, formats for classifying could be discussed. Formats that may be used follow:

Tragedies	Comedies

Tragedies: _____ , _____ ,

_____ , _____ ,

_____ _____

Comedies: _____ , _____ ,

_____ , _____ ,

_____

Tragedies

1. _____
2. _____
3. _____
4. _____
5. _____

Comedies

1. _____
2. _____
3. _____
4. _____
5. _____

Summarizing can be taught as an outgrowth of instruction in note-taking, outlining, and classifying. The teacher might ask a specific question and have students read material concerning its answer. They could take notes or outline the material and summarize the information they recorded. The summaries could then be evaluated by discussing the following criteria:

1. Are all the necessary points included?
2. Are all extraneous points excluded?
3. Is the material in the student's own words?
4. Is the material written in complete sentences?
5. Does the summary consist of a complete and organized paragraph?

Comparing and contrasting can be taught as a method of taking notes when the purpose is to note similarities and differences. The teacher can show formats for comparing and contrasting. Students can be given a paragraph that lends itself to this skill and asked to compare and contrast the items described. The students' comparisons and contrasts can then be discussed.

Reinforcement Procedures

1. Give students several paragraphs or longer selections and ask them a question on each selection. Students decide whether outlining, note-taking, classifying, summarizing, or comparing and contrasting would be the most appropriate way of organizing information. They then would organize the information in the way they chose.

2. Divide the class into teams of five students. Ask students to compare two objects not usually compared. For example, the teacher might say, "A book is like a pencil." The teams are given five minutes to compare the objects. Each team reads its comparisons aloud. The entire class then votes for the best comparisons. (Class members cannot vote for their own team's contribution.) (Adapted from Bergman 1976, #49)

3. The class can visit a place of interest in or near their school. During the visit each member organizes the information he obtains. The teacher can instruct students to (1) take notes, (2) classify information under the headings, *What I Saw*, *What I Heard*, and *What I Smelled*, or (3) compare and contrast. When the students return to the classroom, the teacher may request that they write a summary paragraph based on their written notes. (Adapted from Bergman 1976, #50.)

Post-Assessment: Same as pre-assessment.

Correlated Materials

Professional Texts Written for Teacher Use

Burmeister (1974) pp. 158–159
Herber (1970) pp. 171–172
Karlin (1972) pp. 200–203
Olson and Ames (1972) pp. 43–44
Thomas and Robinson (1972) pp. 195–203

Instructional Material Written for Student Use

(Attach sheet.)

Descriptor: Adjusting Rate to Purpose

Subject Areas: This skill is required in all subject areas in which students must independently gain information from texts.

Objective: Given several selections written on an appropriate instructional level, but for different purposes, the student will be able to read them at a rate that is suitable to the purpose.

Criterion Level:_____

Pre-Assessment: Give students course-related selections that are written for different purposes and ask them to read them within a certain time limit. (Those who read all at the same rate need instruction on this skill.)

Sample Generic Teaching Strategy

Initial Teaching Procedure (In general)

Place transparencies of three different textbook passages on the overhead. Ask the students to read the first one in order to locate a specific detail, the second one for the main idea, and the third one to apply the information to a homework assignment to be given at the end of the period. As soon as the first student finishes the task, turn off the overhead and ask him to tell the class his answers. If he is correct, ask him to explain how he was able to finish so quickly. Explain to the class that the first passage could be scanned, the second passage could be skimmed, and the third passage had to be read carefully. Then explain the relationships among the three techniques.

Show the students how to locate the answers to the questions by searching for key words that relate to a specific question. Demonstrate the procedure using several textbook passages that have been placed on transparencies.

Select several pages from the content area textbook that require slow, careful reading, as well as some passages that may be read at a faster rate (e.g., mathematics—an introductory paragraph about the nature of *probability*, followed by a word problem requiring the application of mathematical concepts concerning probability). Tell the students that they will be expected to know all the relevant details in the assigned reading and that they will be given a time limit for completing their reading. At the end of the time limit, give the students a quiz in which they are to close their textbooks and list the relevant details they found in the assignment. Then place a transparency of the textbook pages on the overhead and demonstrate to the students clue words that should have helped them determine the pace at which they were to read the materials. Point out that words in italics or boldface are usually considered important, and the reader should slow down and carefully read such portions of the text. Also explain that some material does not have to be read so slowly and should be read at a faster pace. Show them that words in very tiny type

319

are usually minor details about some subtopic and can be skimmed unless the student's purpose for reading is one that requires that they learn those details.

Reinforcement Procedures (In general)

Tell the students that they are to read several pages in their textbook in order to locate most of the relevant details. Before they read, give them a few minutes to look over the pages and place an *S* by those portions that they think should be read at a slow, careful rate, an *M* by those portions that they think should be read at a moderate rate, and an *F* by those portions that they think could be read at a fast rate.

At the end of the time limit, assemble the students in small groups and ask them to compare their markings to those of their peers. After several minutes, ask a member of each of the small groups to report any differences of opinion. Discuss with the whole class how the purpose relates to the rate and what the rates for each of the portions of the textbook should have been.

Give the students a new purpose for reading the pages (e.g., identify main ideas) and repeat the above procedures.

Initial Teaching Procedure (Skimming)

Explain to students that the purpose of skimming is to quickly pass over an entire selection to get a general impression of it. Skimming means that students do not have to read every word in a line or paragraph. The method might include reading the first few words of a sentence, reading phrases within sentences, reading a word here and there, or all three. Show the students how to develop their own method of skimming. They should try to find words or ideas in a paragraph or page that will give them a clue to the information they are to look for.

Use the content area textbook and ask specific questions that students may answer by skimming. For example, in history, "What was Truman's speech about?"; in mathematics, "What does the author say is the purpose for the chapter on congruence?"; or in science, "State several ways in which a midlatitude deciduous forest is different from a tropical rain forest."

Reinforcement Procedures (Skimming)

1. Group students into pairs. One student is to read a portion of the text as rapidly as he can. The reading time is recorded and then the student relates the main idea to his partner. The roles are exchanged and the partner then reads the same passage as rapidly as possible. The reading time is recorded, and then the student verifies or refutes the main ideas given previously by his partner. Continue this procedure for several passages in the text.

2. Group students into pairs. All students are to have their own textbook. Give the students time to look through an assigned portion of the textbook and note which paragraphs contain information too important to skip if the purpose of the assignment is to understand the main idea of

the total chapter. The partners should compare their answers and then check their answers with a key made by the teacher. If further practice is needed, develop guided reading sheets on this topic or place the student with a partner who has successfully completed this assignment.

Initial Teaching Procedure (Scanning)

1. Explain to students that this is a technique to locate specific information. The scanning should be done so rapidly that no other information is retained. Using transparencies of paragraphs related to course content, show students how to scan for target words. Ask specific questions and demonstrate what words or phrases they should look for in order to find answers to the questions.

2. Then use the content area textbook and ask specific questions that students may answer by scanning. For example, in science, "What are fossils?"; in history, "When was Truman elected President?"; in mathematics, "Using the table of square roots, tell me the square root of 15."

Reinforcement Procedures (Scanning)

1. Make a guided reading sheet that contains questions and page numbers on which the answers may be located. Ask students to locate the answers and then state the key word or words that helped them locate the answer.

2. Make a list of specific questions from the textbook that may be answered by scanning. Tell students that they will gain a point each time they are first to answer the question. Continue in a like manner until many questions have been asked. The student with the most questions correctly answered at the end of ten minutes is next to design questions, which he will ask the class the next day.

Post-Assessment: Same as pre-assessment.

Correlated Materials

Professional Texts Written for Teacher Use

> Burmeister (1974) pp. 235–249
> Karlin (1972) pp. 236–250
> Olson and Ames (1972) pp. 92–98
> Robinson (1975) pp. 190–192
> Thomas and Robinson (1972) pp. 65–104, 136–165, 190–192

Instructional Material Written for Student Use

(Attach sheet.)

References and Bibliography

Aukerman, R. C. *Reading in the Secondary School Classroom.* New York: McGraw-Hill, 1972.

Beach, R. "Conceiving of Characters." *Journal of Reading,* 17:7 (April 1974), pp. 546-551.

Bergman, F. L. *The English Teacher's Activities Handbook: An Idea Book for Middle and Secondary Schools.* Boston: Allyn & Bacon, 1976.

Burmeister, L. E. *Reading Strategies for Secondary School Teachers.* Reading, Mass.: Addison-Wesley, 1974.

Calderwood, J. D., and Fersh, G. L. *Economics for Decision-Making.* New York: Macmillan, 1974.

Cramer, L. "Setting Purposes and Making Predictions: Essential to Critical Reading." *Journal of Reading,* 13:4 (January 1970), pp. 259-262, 300.

Finder, M. "Teaching to Comprehend Literary Texts—Drama and Fiction." *Journal of Reading,* 17:4 (January 1974), pp. 272-278.

Giroux, J. A., and Williston, G. R. *Recognizing Tone.* Providence, R. I.: Jamestown, 1974.

Giroux, J. A., and Williston, G. R. *Understanding Characters.* Providence, R. I.: Jamestown, 1974.

Hart, C., et al. *Free to Be . . . You and Me.* New York: McGraw-Hill, 1974.

Haynes, N. L. *Biological Science: An Ecological Approach.* 3rd ed. Chicago: Rand McNally, 1973.

Herber, H. L. *Teaching Reading in Content Areas.* Englewood Cliffs, N. J.: Prentice-Hall, 1970.

Karlin, R. *Teaching Reading in High School.* 2nd ed. Indianapolis, Ind.: Bobbs-Merrill, 1972.

Kaufman, B. B., ed. "EJ Workshop." *English Journal,* **62-66** (October 1973–October 1975).

Marriott, A. *Kiowa Years: A Study in Culture Impact.* New York: Macmillan, 1968.

Olson, A. V., and Ames, W. S. *Teaching Reading Skills in Secondary Schools.* Scranton, Pa.: Intext Educational Publishers, 1972.

Pauk, W. *Getting the Author's Tone.* Providence, R. I.: Jamestown, 1975.

Pauk, W. *Perceiving the Author's Intent.* Providence, R. I.: Jamestown, 1975.

Paul, W. *Recognizing Traits of Character.* Providence, R. I.: Jamestown, 1975.

Reiter, I. *The Reading Line: Mathematics.* Philadelphia: Polaski Company, 1973.

Roberts, E. V. *Writing Themes About Literature.* Englewood Cliffs, N. J.: Prentice-Hall, 1965.

Robinson, H. A. *Teaching Reading and Study Strategies: The Content Areas.* Boston: Allyn & Bacon, 1975.

Schneider, H., and Schneider, N. *Science and Your Future.* Boston: Heath, 1961.

Skillin, M. E. *Words Into Type.* Englewood Cliffs, N. J.: Prentice-Hall, 1974.

Smallwood, W. L., and Green, E. R. *Biology.* Morristown, N. J.: General Learning Corp., 1968.

Spencer, H. C., and Dygdon, J. T. *Basic Technical Drawing.* New York: Macmillan, 1974.

Steinman, M., and Willen, G. *Literature for Writing.* 2nd ed. Belmont, Calif.: Wadsworth, 1967.

Tachau, F. *The Middle East.* New York: Macmillan, 1970.

Thomas, E. L., and Robinson, H. A. *Improving Reading in Every Class.* abridged edition Boston: Allyn & Bacon, 1972.

Part Four

Developing an Effective Reading Program

Chapter 11

Utilizing Materials Designed for Teaching Reading

Prerequisite 11.1

Participants should have successfully completed the objectives for Part One of this text, or should have some knowledge of the skills involved in reading before beginning this chapter.

Rationale 11.2

In order to match reading materials to adolescent needs, teachers should have some idea of the types of instructional and nontext materials that are available commercially, a means for constructing their own materials, and the characteristics of adolescents that alter the effectiveness of these materials. This chapter gives a brief overview of these aspects.

Objectives 11.3

On successful completion of this chapter, the participant will be able to:

1. Describe and differentiate between the following terms: instructional materials, comprehensive instructional materials, specific skill-building instructional materials, and nontext materials.
2. Briefly describe and give an example of the following comprehensive instructional materials: basal reader, unit, anthology, collections of reading passages, workbooks, periodicals, kits, and programmed materials.

3. Briefly describe and give an example of the following specific skill-building instructional materials: (1) written format, including workbooks, kits, programmed materials; (2) multimedia format, including mechanical devices, films, filmstrips, and reading pacers; (3) games, tapes, and records.

4. Describe and distinguish between games, tapes, and records designed to motivate and those designed for instructional purposes.

5. Briefly summarize the reading interests of early adolescence, middle adolescence, and late adolescence.

6. Describe at least three ways in which classroom teachers might use their knowledge of the adolescent's stage of "developmental tasks," according to Havighurst, and of cognitive growth, according to Piaget, in order to provide students with a meaningful understanding of what they read.

7. Identify and discuss at least one means by which the interests of a specific adolescent may be diagnosed.

8. Describe, give examples of, differentiate between, and discuss the utility in the various content areas of the following: nonfiction, biography, popular adult literature, significant modern literature, classics, poetry, the adolescent novel, subliterature, and other types of nontext materials.

9. Define the term *special learner* and give at least three examples of instructional materials and of nontext materials geared to the needs of this population.

10. Briefly describe how the following three aspects may provide teachers with a means of helping their students improve their reading without the aid of commercially produced reading materials: (1) changing content area lessons into reading lessons, (2) developing teacher-made games and reinforcement activities, (3) developing teacher-made nontext materials.

11. Describe a checklist that might be used to help locate appropriate instructional materials.

12. Describe at least one source teachers might use to help them locate instructional materials and at least one source they might use to locate nontext materials.

13. (On the lines below, add other objectives according to your instructor's directions.)_____

_____

14. _____

_____

15. _____

_____

16. _____

_____

*   *   *   *   *   *   *   *   *   *   *   *   *   *

Chapter 13, Experience 11 extends Chapter 11 with these performance/consequence objectives:

17. Construct and utilize an instrument to diagnose the reading interests of adolescents;

and/or

18. Utilize a checklist to help locate appropriate reading materials;

and/or

19. Develop and use a game or activity designed to reinforce a reading skill within a content area.

*   *   *   *   *   *   *   *   *   *   *   *   *   *

Self Pre-Assessment 11.4

Can you complete all the activities listed in **Objectives 11.3**? Answer "yes," "no," or "not certain."

If you answered "yes" to the question, complete enabling activities required by your instructor and take the Post-Assessment on the date assigned by him.

If you answered "no," refer to **Enabling Activities 11.5**. If you decide to do any activities that are not required, select those that best suit you as a learner. You need not complete all the optional activities or all parts of a particular optional activity. As soon as you have the information you need to complete the objectives, answer "yes" to the **Self Pre-Assessment 11.4** question and stop the activity.

If you answered "not certain" to the question, turn to **Enabling Activities 11.5**. Select the enabling activity that best suits your style of learning and peruse it. Then make a firm "yes" or "no" answer and proceed accordingly.

Enabling Activities 11.5

Complete only as many of the activities listed below as are required and which you need in order to meet the objectives.

1. *Enabling activity one* is a *reading* alternative. This is **Information Given 11.6**. It is a brief overview of commercially available instructional and nontext materials, ways to construct teacher-made materials, and the characteristics of adolescents that alter the effectiveness of these materials.

2. *Enabling activity two* is another *reading* option. In this case, the material to be read is one of the textbooks used to expand the theoretical background for this course. See chart on inside front cover for keying in textbooks that may be used.
3. *Enabling activity three* is a *class session* option. Attend the class session(s) on the date(s), at the time(s), and at the place(s) announced.

(Date)	(Time)	(Place)
(Date)	(Time)	(Place)
(Date)	(Time)	(Place)

4. *Enabling activity four* (These lines are left blank so that you may add other enabling activities as suggested by your instructor.)＿＿＿

＿＿＿＿＿＿＿＿＿＿＿＿＿＿＿＿＿＿＿＿＿＿＿＿＿

5. *Enabling activity five*＿＿＿＿＿＿＿＿＿＿＿＿＿＿＿＿

＿＿＿＿＿＿＿＿＿＿＿＿＿＿＿＿＿＿＿＿＿＿＿＿＿

6. *Enabling activity six*＿＿＿＿＿＿＿＿＿＿＿＿＿＿＿＿

＿＿＿＿＿＿＿＿＿＿＿＿＿＿＿＿＿＿＿＿＿＿＿＿＿

Now that you have completed the appropriate number of required and/or optional learning alternatives, look back at **Self Pre-Assessment 11.4.** If you feel you can answer "yes" to all of the questions, you are ready to proceed to the Post-Assessment. This may be given to you immediately or after completion of a series of chapters.

Information Given 11.6
Utilizing Materials Designed
for Teaching Reading

A group of teachers from neighboring middle and secondary schools were visiting LaSalle High School's resource center, where all content area teachers could find resources and materials to aid them in teaching the reading skills needed by their students. The visiting teachers were greatly impressed by the types and quantity of materials in the center. There were mechanical devices such as projectors, recorders, pacers and tachistoscopes, as well as games, tapes, films, and records and a wide assortment of commercially published and teacher-made materials. Some of these materials were designed to be used in teacher-directed activities, while others could be used independently by students. Some were specific to certain content areas, while others were geared toward teaching reading as a subject.

At the end of their visit to LaSalle's resource center, the teachers had many questions:

1. What types of instructional materials are available from publishers?
2. What are the purposes of the various types of commercially published instructional materials?
3. What are the purposes of the various types of nontext instructional materials?
4. Why should various types of instructional materials be used with adolescents?
5. How can teachers make their own instructional materials?
6. How does one identify the interests of specific adolescents?
7. How does one locate and select needed materials?

OVERVIEW

In an effort to answer these questions, this chapter will discuss ways in which commercially published materials may be obtained and methods for producing teacher-made materials. Throughout this text, *instructional materials* refers to those designed specifically to teach reading skills (for example, basal readers) and *nontext materials* refers to those used to provide personally relevant ways to practice reading skills (for example, cookbooks).

Commercially Published Instructional Materials

There are a great many commercially published instructional materials that can prove helpful to the teacher in setting up a reading improvement program. Materials such as these, which may be used by content area or reading teachers in teacher- or student-directed situations, are described in the following paragraphs.

Comprehensive Instructional Materials

Comprehensive instructional materials attempt to present reading skills in an inclusive manner. These materials are available in a variety of forms, including basal readers, anthologies, units, collections of reading passages, workbooks, periodicals, kits, and programmed materials. Each of these formats may be used either as a total program or as an adjunct to a program. For example, one teacher might decide to use the basal reader on a daily basis as his only instructional material. A second teacher might decide to use the basal reader once a week in addition to periodicals and units. In the first case, the basal reader would be used as a total program. In the second, it would be used as an adjunct to a program.

Basal Readers

Basal reader texts usually consist of a series of books that contain reading materials on increasingly difficult levels and that teach all the reading skills in an orderly fashion. A variety of content areas are represented, but most of the reading selections are of a literary type. The three basic components are (1) a student's book that contains the material to be read by the middle and secondary school student, (2) a student's workbook that contains exercises in reading to be completed by the student, and (3) a teacher's manual that gives suggestions to the teachers for teaching each lesson. Most series also include correlated testing and teaching materials designed to extend the three basic components.

Testing Materials. Assessment instruments in basal reader materials include (1) placement tests, which the teacher may use to determine the level basal in which to place the student, (2) achievement tests, so that the teacher may be kept aware of each student's progress, and (3) diagnostic tests, which measure specific skills that might be needed by a student.

Teaching Materials. Teaching materials include aids such as duplicating masters for activities designed to reinforce concepts and skills presented in the student's books. Many of the series include filmstrips, games, and programmed materials to supplement core materials. Often a series will key in and make available a variety of books written on different reading levels and on topics that expand ideas presented in the basic text.

In general, these series are very similar to the basals used in the elementary school, and in some cases they are an extension of an elementary series. Other series are made specifically for the secondary school and extend only from grades seven through nine, or seven through twelve.

Usually the catalog description for basal reader materials would be on the order of the following one:*

> *Houghton Mifflin Readers Levels 13 and 14.* Boston: Houghton Mifflin, 1972. Designed for grades seven and eight. Zeroes in on a variety of skills, such as skimming, evaluating writing styles, interpreting figurative language, understanding implied messages—in all over one hundred seventy specific skills. Literary skills are emphasized, comprehension and reference skills and study skills are developed in depth, decoding skills are assessed and reinforced. The anthologies are entitled *Serendipity* and *Diversity* and include short stories, excerpts from "masterworks," informational articles, drama, poetry, biographies, personal narratives on such diverse topics as Indian culture, feminist leaders, and ski touring. Fully correlated teaching and learning materials at each level. Includes hardcover anthology; a comprehensive, spiral bound teacher's guide; a workbook; basic reading tests; plus extra skill lessons and independent practice on duplicating masters.

*Note: Since there are so many fine products on the market and space is not available to list them all, this text presents the readers with a "typical" catalog description to help them differentiate among the types of materials that exist and to help them choose their own materials based on some knowledge of what to look for in catalog descriptions when ordering materials.

Units

The unit-type reading textbook approach is similar to the basal reader approach in that the teacher has available (1) a student's book (in most cases, an anthology), (2) a student's workbook, and (3) a teacher's manual. Students are usually asked to read a short selection in the anthology and then respond to exercises in the workbook. However they may also be asked to make a second selection from a given list of books that accompany the unit and that are written on various reading levels. This second book usually extends a theme around which the unit is built. Often the students' workbook asks them to respond to both the anthology and the self-selected book. For example, while completing a thematic unit on *humor*, a student might be asked first to participate in a class discussion on the effect of figurative language upon humor and then to read a short story in the anthology. In addition, since he has a self-selected collection of short stories by James Thurber, he reads a selection from the Thurber book. He is then asked to complete several pages in his workbook. The workbook asks him specific questions about figurative language as found in his anthology and asks him to write a short passage in which he identifies several instances of figurative language as found in one of the short stories by Thurber that he has selected to read.

Units are found primarily in the disciplines of literature, social studies, and vocational arts, though a few are available in the other content areas. One such unit designed for adolescents who read well below grade level is described here:

> *Scholastic Action Unit.* Englewood Cliffs, N. J.: Scholastic Book Service. Incorporates basic word attack and reading comprehension skills into 18 intensive weeks of reading, role-playing, discussions, writing. Contains materials for twenty students, including one LP record, twenty copies of the three-unit books, twenty copies of short stories, twenty copies of short plays, six posters, and a teacher's guide. Reading levels are between 2.0 and 4.0. *An Action Word Attack Skills Supplement*, which includes forty ditto masters to provide additional skills work for students, is available as well as an *Action Library*. This is a supplement to the Action Kit and consists of twenty books on the second grade level and fifty ditto masters.

Anthologies

A reading textbook of the anthology type is similar to the basal reader or unit type. However the basal reader and the unit are written for the sole purpose of teaching reading skills. Most anthologies that are accompanied by material that directly teaches the reading skills have been designed primarily to present the subject matter, not the reading skills. For example, the major purpose of an American literature anthology with accompanying reading skill development material is to make the reader more aware of American literature. The reading skill-building material is provided in order that the reader may read the content more efficiently. Teachers who choose the anthology approach to teaching reading skills do so because they not only need to teach their content areas but also to assure themselves that they are giving their students instruction in the reading skills, which they need to be able to read their assignments.

Anthology texts are usually found in such content areas as literature and social studies, but they should not be confused with the literary anthologies used in these content areas. Anthologies that may be considered reading textbooks are those in which the publisher has provided vehicles for teaching reading skills by including accompanying workbooks and/or reading tests and/or a teacher's manual. The following is a description of a literature anthology that may be used as a reading textbook:

> *Adventures in Literature Series: Classic Edition.* New York: Harcourt Brace Jovanovich. Each of the anthologies for grades nine, ten, eleven, or twelve presents soundly organized collections of literature, study aids, and a fine arts program that enriches the literature. The scope and in-depth background materials permit a wide variety of teaching approaches: major authors, humanities, history, aesthetics. Each book contains over forty full-page, full-color reproductions of art masterpieces, with commentaries on the artists, their school, and their periods.
>
> Paperbound Reading/Writing Workshops extend the reading and composition programs in the anthologies, and Lessons in Critical Reading and Writing contain complete texts of major works and critical commentaries on them. A teacher's manual is available for each anthology. In addition a teacher's manual with a key to tests and teaching instructions for the reading/writing workshop is available.

Collections of Reading Passages

Collections of reading passages is another common format for secondary school reading textbooks. These collections often consist of assorted short essays preceded by a brief overview describing a reading skill to be presented. Students read the overview and then may or may not be asked to apply the skill when reading the subsequent passage. After they read the passage, they respond to comprehension questions and often to vocabulary skill-building questions related to the reading selection. They are usually asked to time themselves to determine the rate of reading the passage, to correct their own comprehension and vocabulary responses, and to keep a record of their reading progress. They are expected to improve in rate of comprehension and size of vocabulary by proceeding through the textbook in the prescribed manner. The following is an example of the collections-of-reading passages format:

> Schumacher, Melba, et al. *Design for Good Reading.* New York: Harcourt Brace Jovanovich, 1969. A developmental reading program designed to improve reading rate and comprehension. The books are divided into three sections: (1) essays for timed reading (more than half the book) and short selections to help the students sharpen their appreciation and critical perception; (2) vocabulary development; (3) lessons on how to distinguish among various kinds of readings and various purposes for reading. Paperbound for grades nine through twelve. A teacher's manual is available to accompany each of the four levels on which the books have been written.

Workbooks

The workbook format treats reading skills in a comprehensive manner, but students are usually given a very short passage and then asked to respond to the content of the selection in space provided immediately following it. Often reading skills that may or may not be related to the selections are discussed and the student is given space in the book to practice these skills.

The workbook format differs from the collection-of-reading-passages format in the percentage of time spent reading as opposed to working skill-building exercises. In other words, the collection-of-reading-passages text may touch on all the reading skills, but the exercises following each passage make up less than half the textbook. In the workbook approach, all the reading skills are also presented, but the exercises make up a much larger percentage, sometimes as much as 70 per cent.

Many workbooks are available that emphasize skills needed in the various content areas. Though students are usually shown how to complete the skill they are asked to practice, they may or may not be given direct explanation on how the skill is to be used in the content area they are being asked to read. An example of a workbook designed to help students better read content area materials follows:

> Herber, Harold. *Go.* Englewood Cliffs, N. J.: Scholastic Book Services. A reading in the content area approach which utilizes high-interest reading selections from literature, social studies, mathematics, and science to develop on-grade vocabulary, basic concepts, comprehension, and reasoning. Coordinated pre- and post-reading exercises simultaneously strengthen word attack skills, reading comprehension, and conceptual reasoning. Includes a skills text on four different reading levels, each level containing correlated ditto masters and a teaching guide. The ditto master lessons present the same skills, processes, and concepts taught in the skills text, but in a different format. Their variety and gamelike presentation make them especially useful with students who "block" textbook materials. With their own teaching notes, the ditto masters are complete enough to be used independently of the skills text as a series of 50 reading and reasoning lessons.

Periodicals

Another major way in which reading skills are taught in a comprehensive manner is through the use of periodicals.

There are several varieties of magazines available for students of all reading levels in which the primary focus is that of teaching the reading skills. These periodicals may come weekly or monthly, but the format is basically the same. The student reads a story and then is asked to respond to vocabulary and/or comprehension and/or study skill questions over the content of the story. Periodicals specifically geared to the content areas, in particular language arts and social studies, are readily available as teaching tools. Furthermore, a teacher's edition and test questions are usually available. Most periodicals are purchased as classroom sets and can be used in the same manner as other instructional materials, except that the teacher does not have access to the contents of all the issues of the magazine for use in planning the course for the year.

Some magazines, such as *Reader's Digest* and *Atlantic Monthly* have special editions labeled *educational*, which consist of the magazine as available to the regular adult reader, but containing inserts that include comprehension, vocabulary, and study skill questions about the stories found in the issue. As with the other types of periodicals, a teacher's edition is usually available to give teaching suggestions and answers to test questions. Although a magazine like *Atlantic Monthly* might be especially helpful in literature, one like *Reader's Digest* contains selections from a variety of disciplines. Thus, a science teacher who filed articles related to his content area, could accumulate a sizable collection of materials that could expand concepts and reading skills of students in his classes. Following are two examples of periodicals that teach the reading skills. The first is of a periodical written specifically to teach reading skills.

> *Scholastic Scope.* Englewood Cliffs, N. J.: Scholastic Book Services. A weekly periodical designed for grades eight through twelve to motivate students on a fourth to sixth grade reading level with high-interest articles, plays, skill-building activities, and games.

The second is of a periodical adapted to teach reading skills.

> *The Atlantic Monthly Educational Edition.* Boston: Atlantic Monthly Company. The educational edition consists of the regular monthly issue of *The Atlantic* with eight extra pages bound in the study guide. The guide is prepared by the editors of *The Atlantic* in conjunction with a panel of experienced teachers and educational consultants, and contains exercises on reading, writing, and vocabulary techniques, based on the articles, features, and poems from the issue in which it appears. It is available only on a monthly basis, ten months out of the year, and is available only to teachers.

Kits and Programmed Materials

Some publishers have chosen to publish comprehensive instructional materials in kit format rather than in book format. Usually these kits contain multilevel passages so that the students may practice their reading skills on a level consistent with their reading abilities. The kits are usually accompanied by a placement test, a progress test, and a teacher's manual. The reading selections are often color-coded by reading level. Once a student's reading level has been identified, he is assigned to read passages of a particular color. He then selects his own reading exercises by choosing any story he wishes, as long as it is of the designated color. He responds to questions about the passages read. If he is able to successfully complete criteria for a certain number of passages, he is allowed to move to the next reading level and is assigned a new color from which to choose reading materials.

A description of a kit follows:

> *Reading Laboratory Kits 3b, 4a.* Chicago: Science Research Associates. Each kit contains multilevel, skill-building materials from a variety of books and periodicals. Diversified and current content reflects young people's increasing involvement with the world they live in. This allows each student to begin at his own level, where he is assured success, and to progress as fast as his learning rate permits. Students work with reading selections and exercises, record responses in

334

the Student Record Book, and correct their own work with only occasional teacher guidance and spot checks. Immediate feedback helps reinforce skills and point out weaknesses. Students record their performance on progress charts in the Student Record Book, so that they are aware of their improvement.

Other publishers have chosen to develop programmed textbooks. In this approach students proceed through the textbook at a pace consistent with their accuracy of response to each item in the text. Usually when they give a correct response, they are rerouted by being told to skip ahead so many questions; when they give an incorrect response, they are instructed to continue to answer questions without skipping any. This continues until they complete the programmed textbook.

A description of a programmed textbook follows:

> Buchanan, Cynthia D. *Programmed Reading for Adults.* New York: Webster Division/McGraw-Hill, 1966. This text helps to bring older students and adults quickly to sixth grade reading level. The program employs the linguistic approach and is practically self-teaching. After Book 8, the student will be able to read material for meaning, at fifth grade level, will have mastered fifteen hundred words, and will be able to generalize to thousands of other words.

Specific Skill-Building Instructional Materials

Sometimes teachers want to emphasize particular skills and would rather have ten exercises on one specific skill than ten exercises on a variety of reading skills. In such a case, rather than using comprehensive materials, the teacher should use materials that may be termed *specific skill-building instructional materials*. These materials are published in a variety of formats and media. It should be emphasized that some of the specific skill-building materials are primarily designed to introduce and teach a skill, and others are intended only as reinforcement materials. (See discussion on this topic in Chapter 9.) The various formats and media follow.

Written Format

Some specific skill-building materials are written in a format identical to the comprehensive materials format discussed previously. For example, a workbook in this category might contain a series of short passages in which students are asked to locate main idea. They are not asked to respond to vocabulary questions, study skill questions, or even other types of comprehension questions. The workbook might give explanations of why particular answers are correct and then present successively harder passages to which the student is asked to respond. Not all workbooks that focus on specific skill building are this narrow. Some are almost as broad as the comprehensive variety, but would be considered basically as skill-building because they do not teach reading skills in an inclusive manner. A description of a workbook focusing on comprehension skill building is given below.

335

Pauk, Walter. *Six-Way Paragraphs.* Providence, R. I.: Jamestown Publishers, 1974. Contains a hundred one-page reading selections graded from easy to difficult, spanning levels six through college. Questions that follow each passage always include one of each of the following types which the author considers to represent the six essential categories of comprehension: subject matter, main idea, supporting details, conclusions, clarifying devices, and vocabulary in context.

Though many of the skill-building materials seem to build exercises around literary-type selections, more and more that focus on content representing the other disciplines are being published. One recent publication that presents reading skills needed for a variety of content areas is the following:

Reiter, Irene M. *The Reading Line.* Philadelphia: Polaski Company, 1971. This is a multidisciplinary reading and study skills program that contains six student books including the topics of English language and literature, science, mathematics, social studies, business and vocational and technical. There is also a teacher's guide. A unique feature of the program is the availability to the teacher of an in-service program called "Why Can't They Read?" which trains all content area teachers to direct their students' reading and studying habits. Each book develops the following skills: reading for purpose, drawing inferences, thinking critically, taking notes and tests in all content areas.

Kits that teach specific skills seem to be popular with teachers and may be used by the student with very little teacher direction. One such kit, which focuses on critical reading skills, follows:

Thurstone, Thelma G. *Reading for Understanding.* Chicago: Science Research Associates, 1958. Provides four thousand paragraphs at one-hundred difficulty levels (roughly from 3.0 to 13.0) for practice in careful reading and critical thinking about what is read. Inferences and logical implications are emphasized; word-meaning skills are essential and developed through the exercises.

Another kit designed to help students with study skills needed in the various content areas is

EDL Study Skills Library. Huntington, N. Y.: Educational Development Laboratories, 1962. A series of kits containing graded exercises for reading levels three through nine, in science, social studies, and reference skills. Each box contains ten lessons and seven hundred work sheets (i.e., seventy for each lesson) and keys.

Many programmed materials, particularly ones which focus on developing vocabulary exist. One is described below.

Markle, Susan. *Words.* Chicago: Science Research Associates, 1963. Each student test booklet contains a diagnostic test. From the result, the teacher determines which of two "tracks" the student is ready for. The slow track takes the student through each frame in sequence; the fast track is color coded to indicate which frames may be skipped by more advanced students. Although basically a linear program, some branching is incorporated. Includes a dictionary of roots and prefixes, and periodic review tests, with the answer key in the teacher's manual.

The manual shows how to operate the program. The text contains approximately twenty-two hundred frames in fourteen sequential chapters.

Multimedia Materials

The existing market is being heavily inundated with multimedia materials of all sorts. Basically, multimedia materials may be considered under two main headings: (1) mechanical devices and (2) games, records, and tapes.

Mechanical Devices. Usually these materials are designed to help improve rate of reading. Though they are useful teaching devices most reading authorities believe that their primary usefulness comes from the motivation they provide the student. Spache states

> There is no available evidence, to our knowledge, that any audiovisual aid or training device has ever taught an individual to read more critically or discriminatingly. . . . Audiovisual instruments cannot supply the stimulation of group discussion or the individualization essential in remedial reading . . . In a word, no satisfactory mechanical substitute for a competent teacher has been devised. (Spache 1961, pp. 222–225)

However, some of the mechanical devices can be useful in a reading program if used cautiously, properly, and primarily as reinforcement vehicles. Mechanical devices fall into three basic categories: (1) films or filmstrip machines, (2) pacers, and (3) tachistoscopes.

1. *Films and Filmstrips:* Films and filmstrips used to control rate are designed to expose short passages for a certain period of time, during which readers are expected to comprehend the exposed passages. One film has a shutter that exposes one third of a line at a time; other films present one phrase at a time. The filmstrip technique involves a slot that moves across the page uncovering words and then covering them again to prevent the reader from regressing. Some of the devices have more flexibility in terms of speed control, and some of them have more extensive libraries of materials. An example of a films program is

> *Iowa High School Films.* Iowa City, Iowa: State University of Iowa. This series consists of fourteen films ranging from 270 to 447 words per minute. Each phrase is dimmed after exposure; the background print is visible but not readable. The materials require three fixations per line.

An example of a filmstrips program is

> *Controlled Reader.* Huntington, N. Y.: Educational Development Laboratories, 1963. The controlled reader is a 35-mm filmstrip projector equipped with a speed control (0 to 1,000 words per minute) and a left-to-right scanning mechanism. The instrument is equipped with a means of starting and stopping the exposure slot. The left-to-right slot should be used to bring trainees up to speeds of approximately five hundred words per minute and then the free-reading slot should be used. The free-reading slot is designed for acceleration only and should not be used until the reading attack is sufficiently developed. The General content of filmstrips is persons, animals, or objects. Questions following

337

concern locale or setting, type of plot, motivating agent, and degree of realism. Each set of filmstrips (from K to adult) is accompanied by a workbook for the reader which correlates with the filmstrip.

2. *Reading Pacers:* Reading pacers are designed to control reading rate without imposing a set pattern of phrasing. A shutter gradually covers a page from top to bottom at a speed that can be regulated by the individual. Sometimes the shutter is metal or plastic; in other cases a beam of light is used to cover successive lines at a rate set by the reader.

A specialized type of pacer includes those machines that are designed to teach skimming and scanning. These are intended to help the already competent reader proceed from all-inclusive reading, in which every line of print is read, to selective reading, in which the reader looks for more significant facts and then stops to read them. These devices do not exercise the same control nor direct the reader as precisely as the regular type of pacer. One device employs a single beam of light that moves at a constant speed down the center of the text. The reader is directed to locate specific details before the beam of light reaches the bottom of the page. A description of a reading pacer follows:

> *SRA Reading Accelerator.* Chicago: Science Research Associates. The reading accelerator is a reading pacer device that is portable, lightweight, and entirely mechanical. The accelerator has a shutter, a dial control for speed setting (30 to 3,000 words per minute) and a wide range of speed settings. The shutter moves at a consistent pace down the page, forcing the individual to keep ahead, and at the same time it covers the preceding line so that the reader cannot make the regressions that he makes in normal reading.

3. *The Tachistoscope:* The tachistoscope is a device that presents timed exposure of pictures, numbers, and letters. Students learn to pay careful attention to detail, to read in a left-to-right fashion, and to remember more of what they see. Exposure time can range from .01 of a second to as long as 1.5 seconds. Valid objectives for middle and secondary school students should be to increase eye span and decrease fixation time, thereby increasing rate of comprehension. These devices range in complexity from a very simple hand-held tachistoscope, to elaborate projectors. A description of a tachistoscope of the projector variety is

> *Tach-X Tachistoscope.* Huntington, N. Y.: Educational Development Laboratories. The Tach-X is a 35 mm filmstrip projector equipped with a timing mechanism that provides exposure speeds of .01 second to 1.5 seconds. The Tach-X flashes pictures, numbers, letters, words, or phrases on the screen for a brief time. The students say or write what they saw; then material is focused for another look and the students check their work.

Games, Tapes, and Records. Games range in sophistication from simple crossword puzzles to simulation games in which small groups of students are asked to put themselves into the roles of major fictional or historical characters

338

about whom they have read. The two games described illustrate the wide range of purposes and content areas for which games may be adapted. The following game teaches vocabulary directly and is primarily intended for the teacher of English:

> *Vocabulary Beano Game.* Superior, Wis.: English Laboratory. Designed to develop interest in the study of vocabulary. It differs from conventional bingo in that instead of numbers, questions are called. The students look for the answers on their cards. The set contains thirty-six cards. Games such as Vocabulary Beano make for a refreshing departure from conventional vocabulary drills.

The following game teaches thinking skills needed to read and understand cause-effect relationships in American history:

> *American History Games.* Chicago: Science Research Associates. Each of the six history games deals with a major issue of U.S. history and requires that the student become involved in making decisions that could have affected the outcome of history. Six games with boards, tokens, chips, chance cards, thirty-five student game books, teacher's guide, spirit master book, and acetate sheets to protect game boards are contained.

Tapes and records may be designed to be motivational or instructional. Several publishers have recorded the beginnings of exciting stories onto tape and after listening to the tape, the student must read the remainder of the story in order to find out what happens. Other motivational recordings that may be used by the teacher are ones that present information about a topic in such a manner that the student actively seeks more information on the subject. Those intended to be used more directly as instructional devices may supplement a workbook activity or may be the core of the learning activity. For example, a supplementary audiotape would be one in which the student could choose to listen to a tape about context clues after reading this information in a correlated textbook. When the audiotape is used as the learning core, the student must listen to the tape to complete the exercise. For example, one company publishes a set of correlated workbooks and audiotapes designed to teach critical reading skills. Students are given oral instructions and directions and then told to complete certain reading exercises. After they complete each step, they are given feedback on what the correct answers should have been and why. Other instructional tapes simply help the student interpret meaning less directly. A recording of Dylan Thomas reading his poetry would represent a less direct instructional device. An example of each type of tape or record discussed is provided. An example of those that are designed to motivate is

> Radlauer, Ed, and Radlauer, Ruth. *Reading Incentive Language Program Audiovisual Kits.* Glendale, Calif.: Bowmar. Consists of sound filmstrips, records, or cassettes designed to correlate with high interest–low vocabulary books. The student's attention is captured with the use of action-oriented, full-color, sound filmstrips. Listeners become quickly involved through introductory music, straightforward narration, and authentic, on-location sound effects. The books

may be read without use of the audiovisual materials; they concern topics of interest to adolescents, such as motorcycles, horses, dune buggies, drag racing, and bicycles.

An example of tapes that are designed to inform but that may be used to stimulate interest is

> *Career Development Laboratory.* Tulsa, Okla.: Educational Progress Corporation. Three trays of taped interviews with people who are professionals (60 per cent) and nonprofessionals (40 per cent). Provides information about a field and an opportunity to experiment with the occupational role. This is an individualized program. No reading involved.

An example of tapes that are designed to supplement the basic instructional tool is

> *New Advanced Reading Skill Builders, Audio Lessons.* Pleasantville, N. Y.: Reader's Digest Services, Educational Division, 1973. Selections adapted from regular editions of *Reader's Digest*, written on seventh through eighth grade reading levels and accompanied by comprehension and vocabulary-building exercises, make up the content of the *New Advanced Reading Skill Builder* books. The audiotapes are designed to add another dimension to the *New Advanced Reading Skill Builder* program. These lessons are extensions of the stories and exercises presented in the skill builders, and it is not necessary to listen to the tape in order to complete the material in the skill builder books. Each audio lesson correlates with an advanced skill builder selection; and for each level there are twelve audio lessons. Each audio lesson emphasizes one particular skill, such as skimming, inferring, or detecting sequence. After students have read the selection, the audio instructor guides them through exercises based on material read in the text designed to measure their reading and reading-related skills. The tape provides help with the directions to the exercises and gives answers with explanations of why they are the best choices.

An example of tapes designed as the core of the learning activity is

> Anderson, Norena, and Dechant, Emerald. *EDL Listen and Read Program.* Huntington, N. Y.: Educational Development Laboratories, 1963. Thirty tapes and workbooks covering the understanding of words, sentences, paragraphs, stories, and articles. Other tapes give information and practice in study skills, critical reading and listening, and literature.

Many games, tapes, and records that teach the reading skills as well as the content areas are available in the content areas of English and social studies. However, in other content areas, such as mathematics or science, most media presentations are available to teach only the concepts not the reading skills necessary to cope with them. A teacher who is aware of this distinction can help students learn reading skills by developing guided reading sheets to accompany the audiotapes and workbooks so students may focus upon reading skills they need to complete exercises in the workbook while listening to the concept being explained.

Factors Related to Nontext Reading Needs

Exclusive exposure to instructional materials alone does not constitute all the needed aspects of a reading program. Though instructional materials may be useful in systematically developing needed reading skills, they do not always help in the development of reading habits and attitudes that motivate students to read outside of school, nor do they satisfy a certain "developmental needs" characteristic of adolescents. A total reading program is one that integrates both these aspects by providing activities above and beyond the skill development program. In addition, such a program gives students a chance to practice, in a personal and meaningful way, the skills they have learned in the instructional component.

Characteristics of Adolescent Growth

Adolescents have certain growth characteristics that affect their reading preferences. Havighurst (1948) believes that human individuals are influenced by three forces: (1) their own physical development; (2) their social environment, which places certain demands and expectancies on them; and (3) their own personality, and in particular their own values and aspirations. These three forces establish a series of developmental tasks that must be mastered if the individual is to become emotionally and psychologically mature. There are tasks at every stage of development. Havighurst delineates several tasks of adolescence.

Developmental Tasks of Adolescence

1. Accepting one's physique and accepting a masculine or feminine role.
2. Achieving new relationships with age-mates of both sexes.
3. Achieving emotional independence from parents and other adults.
4. Achieving assurance of economic independence.
5. Selecting and preparing for an occupation.
6. Developing intellectual skills and concepts necessary for civic competence.
7. Desiring and achieving socially responsible behavior.
8. Preparing for marriage and family life.
9. Building conscious values (aesthetic, religious, ethical) in harmony with an adequate scientific world-picture.

Though the middle and secondary school teacher cannot force youngsters to be interested in reading, by providing materials that are personally relevant to the youngsters' needs and interests, the motivation to read outside of school may be fostered. Hence books can serve as tools to further the growth toward maturity, and books that reflect the needs of youth can be extremely useful both in providing motivation to read as well as in aiding young people in their progress toward adulthood.

341

Directly related to Havighurst's tasks is the age of the adolescent when passing through each stage. Younger adolescents are much more interested in accepting their physiques than in building conscious values. Many research studies have been done that identify the characteristics of reading patterns of middle and secondary school students. The majority of the studies reveal that chronological age is more important than intelligence in determining what youngsters like to read. In addition, the sex and the cultural background of readers affect what types of books they choose to read. In other words, a fifteen-year-old boy of average intelligence and a fifteen-year-old boy of superior intelligence would be more likely to select the same type of reading material than would a bright fifteen-year-old girl and a bright fifteen-year-old boy.

Furthermore, Carlsen (1971) points out that adolescents generally choose reading material based on the contents of the book, rather than the reading level. Therefore, even if a book is quite difficult to read, if the subject matter is interesting, the youngster will try to read it; and the youngster will reject the easy-to-read book if the content does not interest him.

Stages of Reading Interest

Carlsen (1971) suggests certain periods into which middle and secondary school students may be classified when identifying stages of reading interest. The three stages are (1) early adolescence, ages eleven through fourteen; (2) middle adolescence, ages fifteen through sixteen; and (3) late adolescence, ages seventeen through adulthood. The reading interests of these age groups vary considerably. The discussion that follows attempts to summarize the interests listed by Carlsen. Obviously some students will not fit into these generalizations; the teacher should not rely upon them solely but use them as guidelines for matching reading materials to each adolescent.

Early Adolescence. Between the ages of eleven and fourteen, adolescents are greatly involved in hero worship and enjoyment of daring feats. They like their stories to be straightforward and obvious, but they also enjoy the fantastic. Their favorite fiction emphasizes such aspects as wish fulfillment, success, or physical prowess.

While boys are particularly fond of *adventure stories*, they also enjoy reading *science fiction*, stories about *mechanical devices*, and *how-to* books. Characteristically, boys prefer fact to fiction.

Girls enjoy reading almost anything, but their favorite themes concern *love* and *romance*. In particular, they enjoy *historical fiction*, stories of *home and family life*, and *career* stories. The reading material of older girls tends to contain a high percentage of sentimental fiction.

Stories concerning *animals and nature; adventure* stories of the sea, the Old West, war; *mysteries* and tales of the *supernatural; sports* stories; and *slapstick humor* are enjoyed by both boys and girls. Stories that seem to be most enjoyed by both sexes focus on adolescent main characters who learn to understand themselves better through dealings with a car, an animal, the sea, or a loving family.

342

history, travel—and very technical books relating to their hobbies and mechanical experimentation. Though they still enjoy action tales, there seems to be a waning interest in adventure simply for adventure's sake. Boys of this age want the stories they read to be about people who have experienced exciting events and revelations of character. The most popular literature with middle-adolescence girls is the romantic novel, though they also enjoy historical fiction. In general, the type of reading done by this age group reflects a maturation toward more realistic literature, such as *true-life adventures, biographies and autobiographies* of famous or unusual people, *historical fiction*, and stories centering on *adolescent life*.

Late Adolescence. From the age of seventeen through adulthood, adolescents' reading interests become even more mature and individualized. Generalizations about the interests of students in this age group are difficult to make and the teacher must know the individuals and their tastes in order to help them select a book. However, most older adolescents enjoy stories that focus upon individuals who are struggling to find their own value systems. Older adolescents are interested in global geography, social problems, scientific advancement, and problems pertaining to personality, vocations, and philosophies of life.

Adolescent Interests Related to Havighurst's Characteristics

A ready comparison can be made between Havighurst's developmental tasks of adolescence and the growth of reading interests as presented by Carlsen. Most recent texts in introductory psychology support the notion that *ego identity* is a major crisis during adolescence (Peck and Richeck 1969). The physical changes that take place and that require teenagers to learn to accept their newly changing bodies are one obvious cause of this ego identity crisis. In addition, certain hormonal and biological changes within their bodies cause them to experience entirely new emotions and feelings. Early adolescence is characterized by "an increase in the strength of the instinctual forces. The child suddenly experiences strong erotic and aggressive impulses that seem to come from nowhere and clamor for expression." (Group for the Advancement of Psychiatry 1968, p. 59) In other words, the reaction to maturational changes are most volatile during early adolescence, when the bodily changes first begin to occur. Many adolescents search for their identities by testing themselves in very aggressive ways.

But young adolescents are often not physically mature enough to experience directly the situations that help them to establish a masculine or feminine role. Therefore the boy enjoys sports stories that reinforce the stereotyped role of the male as a strong, virile man; while the girl enjoys romance stories in which the heroine's femininity is reaffirmed through the attention of a member of the opposite sex.

Books dealing with adventure help them to relate in a vicarious manner to situations involving aggression. Burton (1960) suggests that such vicarious attacks upon their personal problems through identification with fictional or real-life characters give individuals a chance to approach their problems from the objective role of observer. This helps readers gain a greater insight into their own problems because of the author's power to order experience, identify vital components, and clear away ambiguities.

Younger adolescents are more aware of and concerned with their own personal problems—problems that are more or less unique to the adolescent period—and this personal concern is greatly reflected by their reading interests. However, as adolescents mature physically, their interests in reading change. They have had some time to try out their masculine or feminine roles, to achieve new relationships with the age-mates of both sexes, and in other ways to assure themselves that they are normal, physically, mentally, emotionally, and socially. Furthermore, their hormonal and biological processes begin to stabilize and they have had an opportunity to become accustomed to the physical and emotional changes within their bodies. Their interests begin to shift to books dealing with social and personal values. Therefore, Havighurst's ninth task makes sense in terms of the normal maturation process.

Adolescent Interests Related to Cognitive Development

The varying interests of adolescents as reflected by the different types of books they prefer as they mature may be thought of in terms of cognitive development as well as in terms of Havighurst's developmental tasks. Piaget (1970) spent years conceptualizing a theory of cognitive growth. The stages he formulated may be related to books chosen by adolescents of varying ages. The young adolescent is just leaving the *concrete operations* stage (seven through eleven years) and entering the *formal operations* stage (eleven through sixteen years). The rate of maturation for each individual is different, and while the majority of secondary school students are in the formal operations stage, many middle and junior high students are still in the concrete operations stage. A characteristic of the concrete operations stage is that the level of thinking is quite literal and the mental maturity required to grasp very abstract concepts is not present. Instead those in this stage tend to translate any abstractions into concrete and highly specific terms. Therefore children at this stage prefer to read books that they can relate to their specific everyday experiences. For example, the character who climbs a mountain and captures some bandits reflects the type of masculine role they desire in their dreams. Though they themselves may never have climbed a mountain, they have no trouble relating to that type of aggressive expression of behavior. They do not relate as well to a main character who sits on a mountain and questions the meaning of life because that behavior does not reflect the active behavior of the young adolescent. At the concrete operations stage, youngsters are quite literal-minded and see stories in simplistic black and white terms (therefore they prefer stories in which good guys always win and bad guys always lose).

The preference for slapstick comedy by early adolescents can also be explained in terms of Piaget's cognitive stages. Literal-minded children delight in using explicitness and literalness as a basis for their jokes. Jokes such as

344

"What country is used by a cook?"; answer—"Chile" leaves the literal-minded child roaring with laughter. Younger adolescents enjoy playing around with literal-mindedness and often tantalize parents with their actions. For example, a mother might ask a child to, "Keep away from the television" because he has watched it all day. Several hours later when asked to turn the television on so mother can watch the news, the child will reply, "You told me to keep away from the television." (Sprinthall and Sprinthall 1974, p. 112)

However, during the formal operations stage, adolescents expand their cognitive powers. They mature enough to use logical, rational abstractions, and their choices of reading materials will reflect this maturity. Their minds begin to utilize the increased capacity for high-level abstract thinking due to biological maturation. The teenager begins to argue and reason about such philosophical issues as the meaning of life and why social inequities exist. The instinctual forces dealt with through aggressiveness in early adolescence are dealt with through thinking processes during late adolescence. The older youngsters begin to use their faculties of self-observation and self-evaluation as well as their intellectual abilities in seeking to understand themselves (Group for the Advancement of Psychiatry 1968). Hence their choices of books, which concern aesthetic, religious, and ethical values, help them as they search for answers that will help them find out "who they are." Their increased cognitive powers help them understand symbolic meanings and stories with a moral that must be generalized.

Choice of reading materials and teacher guidance is very important in both stages. Children in the concrete operations stage who read *Animal Farm* by George Orwell would understand it only as a story about animals. If students who are just entering the formal operations stage were to read *Animal Farm* and were then asked questions about it that pointed out the general principles of communism, they could be taught some generalizations about communistic theories. Thus maturity of comprehension is a two-pronged process: students must be intellectually able, and the teacher must help guide them toward increased understanding of their reading material through effective questioning and other teaching techniques. (Sprinthall and Sprinthall 1974)

Furthermore, students' cognitive growth is directly affected by the activeness of the means used to stimulate abstract thinking. In other words, passively reading a definition of metaphors is not as effective as actually locating some metaphors in the reading. (Sprinthall and Sprinthall 1974) Active guidance to stimulate the growth of abstract thinking can be done in a number of ways. One means is to develop the type of guided-reading sheet that encourages active readers (see Chapter 8). Another means is to help students react to books in as active a manner as possible (i.e., creative book reports as discussed in Chapter 12). Still another means is to encourage youngsters to read materials that stimulate active reading.

Hence the choice of books is meaningful in terms of normal growth toward maturity during adolescence, and the teacher should encourage students to read books that help them mature. In other words, the seventeen-year-old girl who continues to want to read stories of romance should be carefully guided into more mature materials that beneficially stimulate her mind and help her to develop personal values as well as reading skill.

Identifying Interests of Specific Adolescents

Though all of the above information about developmental tasks, cognitive growth, and the various stages of reading interest can be useful, it only generalizes about what members of a particular age and sex like to read. In order to develop a reading program geared to the needs of students, teachers should try to ascertain the specific reading interests of each of their students.

As teachers determine their students' hobbies, favorite television shows, interests, and personal problems, they can suggest books geared to particular interests or problems that students might have. A systematic study of each youngster's reading interests should be an important part of the instructional program in reading.

Interest Inventories

Interests may be ascertained in many ways, including observation, student reviews of books they have read, charts of their reading interests kept by students, choice of books for recreational reading, or administration of an interest inventory. The interest inventory may be a checklist on which students are asked to rank categories of interests or titles of fictitious books; it may be a questionnaire on which students are required to respond creatively to questions such as "If you were a . . . what would you read?"; or it may be a set of questions that reveals the type of reading materials in which they are most interested. The inventory shown in Figure 11.1 could be used to aid a teacher in identifying the reading interests of specific students.

Literature for Adolescents

Need for Appropriate Materials

Research indicates two very important facts about youngsters in early adolescence: (1) reading interest peaks at this age, and it is not uncommon for a thirteen-year-old girl to read between fifty and one hundred and fifty books a year; (2) unless the habit of reading for leisure is developed at this age, it will probably never become an integral part of the individual's leisure-time activities. Obviously there is a need to keep young adolescents interested in reading. There are several explanations for the decline in reading interest, including the increased demand by the academic and social world of the adolescent upon time spent formerly in reading for pleasure. Another extremely important explanation is that youngsters of this age simply run out of books to read (Pilgrim and McAllister 1968).

Pilgrim and McAllister (1968) support the notion that reading maturity depends upon the levels of concepts presented in the materials read, the levels of intellectual and emotional experience the reader possesses, and the kind of guidance given readers to enable them to read with understanding. They also speak of books as being *multilevel* or *unilevel* in nature. For example, *Animal Farm* could be considered multilevel because several levels of concepts within it make it appealing to people of different ages and reading maturities. On

346

Name_____ Age_____

School_____ Date_____

Grade_____

Directions: Below is a list of topics that some students find interesting. Some of these are things that you can actually do. Others could be watched on television or read about in books, magazines, or newspapers. Use the following marking system: 5 = dislike intensely; 4 = dislike somewhat; 3 = indifferent; 2 = like somewhat; 1 = like very much. In addition, these items have been described as "fiction," "nonfiction," "modern," and "past." If you enjoy reading or watching television shows about modern-day, fictional mysteries but are only mildly interested in mysteries that are documentary and that take place over one hundred years ago, you would mark the first item as follows:

	fiction	nonfiction	modern	past
1. mystery	1	2	1	2

Name of Area	Fiction	Nonfiction	Modern	Past
1. mystery				
2. supernatural				
3. adventure				
4. violence				
5. romance				
6. family life				
7. sex				
8. comedy				
9. westerns				
10. domestic animals				
11. wild animals				
12. sports				
13. travel				
14. social problems				
15. philosophy				
16. religion				
17. biography and autobiography				
18. history				
19. foreign countries				
20. world affairs				
21. local affairs				
22. music				
23. art				
24. mathematics				
25. applied science and technology				
26. physical science				
27. biological science				
28. vocations				
29. avocations				
30. adolescent life				
31. personal problems				
32. fairy tales and mythology		*		

*Not applicable.

Note: The teacher may adapt this inventory by administering it over several days, or he may wish to give explicit examples of books or television shows from each category. For examples, under the category wild animals, the teacher might add the phrase "novels such as Rawlings', *The Yearling*," or television shows, such as one of Walt Disney's wild animal adventures.

Figure 11.1 Reading Interest Inventory

the other hand, a play like *King Lear* is unilevel in concepts and requires a high level of cognitive development, reading ability, and experience on the part of the reader if it is to be understood. Books written expressly for children or adolescents are often unilevel and relatively simple in concept and style. As such, they have real appeal only for the age levels for which they are written.

Adolescent literature may be defined as that body of writing that has special appeal and meaning to most adolescents. Basically this type of literature is available from three main sources—the most mature of the materials written for children, the least complex of the materials written for adults, and materials written especially for adolescents. As youngsters progress through adolescence, they outgrow or have already read the most mature children's books and are not quite ready for the adult books. Though the books written especially for adolescents could provide them with the type of materials they need, until recently there was not enough quality adolescent literature available to them. Furthermore, the most mature adolescent literature is sometimes too advanced for young adolescents; they need careful guidance in order to read and enjoy it.

Regardless of the age level for which the material was originally intended, much material does exist that may be used successfully with adolescents. Some of this material could be used in almost all content areas, while some is specific to a particular content area. One of the finest books currently available on the adolescent reader is *Books and the Teen-Age Reader* by Robert Carlsen (1971). His comprehensive presentation of the types of materials that may hold appeal for young people is overviewed below.

Adolescent Literature Appropriate for All Content Areas

Nonfiction. There are many factual books available that are written especially for teenagers. These include expository accounts of the work of people in science, social studies, the arts, technology, business, hobbies, leisure activities, and personal and social problems. Much nonfiction presents with clarity and precision the extremely complicated and difficult developments in human knowledge. The broad outlines presented are accurate, so that readers may later refine and add to their knowledge through subsequent study. (Carlsen, 1971)

Biography. In addition to describing the lives of special people, biographies usually give other pertinent information, such as the social climate of a particular era, the details of a specific scientific experiment, or the development of a technological process. Adolescents usually like biographies because most are written about exciting, unusual people. As such, they help the adolescent to bridge the gap between "adventure" fiction, particularly appealing to younger adolescents, and nonfiction, appealing to more mature readers. (Carlsen, 1971)

Adolescent Literature Appropriate for Specific Content Areas

Nonfiction and biographical materials focus upon a variety of topics and can easily be used to supplement concepts presented in all content areas.

348

Sometimes books thought of as specifically geared to English or history can be used by teachers in other content areas. For example, some science fiction is written by practicing scientists, and the background of the stories they write are often based on actual scientific principles. Science teachers who carefully select science fiction written by scientists such as Isaac Asimov could use these materials to supplement, in a pleasurable way, many of the concepts touched upon in class. Other types of literature, appropriate for specific content areas, are discussed briefly. (Carlsen, 1971)

Popular Adult Literature. The majority of the essays, novels, dramas, and short stories classified as *popular adult literature* are concerned with topics that become outdated quickly. Such materials often do not have much lasting power, and many represent pure sensationalism. Often, adolescents want to read literature of this kind simply because adults are reading it, or because it presents explicit details concerning taboo topics. Unfortunately much of the material presents these topics with descriptions that are often scientifically untrue and/or have little literary merit. When students express interest in reading books about taboo topics, the teacher may help the student select appropriate and relevant reading materials which do have both scientific and literary value. For, although some popular adult literature is not particularly worthwhile, some can contribute greatly to the knowledge and development of the adolescent. (Carlsen, 1971)

Significant Modern Literature. Some popular adult literature endures longer than others because it is written more skillfully and lends itself to several levels of interpretation. Its characters are developed in greater depth, the plot patterns are more intricate in design, and the author is articulate in his word choice and use of language. (Carlsen 1971, p. 105) The writers most popular with each generation of adolescents are those who challenge the values of the period, glorify the individual as he struggles against contemporary society, and shock the older generation through unconventional use of ideas, situations, or language. Most books in this category, such as James Baldwin's *Go Tell It on the Mountain*, lend themselves well to the study of concepts usually presented in literature or social studies. Others, such as John Hershey's *Hiroshima*, can be used in science to extend concepts such as the effects of radiation upon human life. (Carlsen, 1971)

Classics. Classical literature continues to be read and to survive actively because of certain enduring qualities. It confronts the reader with an eternal human dilemma and is based on a theme that presents a profound, mature, and significant appraisal. The writing is enriched by magnificence of structure, choice of words, ordering of details, and use of symbols, all of which are exactly appropriate to the theme the author is developing. In effect, the classics represent human beings' finest use of language and are the pinnacle of our literary achievement. However, great literature is written by mature artists about mature concerns, and seldom does it center on the topics about which adolescents feel most strongly—their personal problems. For this reason, the teacher may need to actively stimulate the adolescent to read a classical selection.

Most of the classics contain concepts that reflect literary conventions or social themes usually studied in the language arts, and though it is possible that classics such as H. G. Wells' *War of the Worlds* could be easily understood by adolescents, most teenagers do not have the experiential background required to enable them to interpret great classical literature. (Carlsen, 1971, p. 128) In some cases, teachers may want their students to read a particular classic even though they know that they will not be able to understand it easily. In such a case, teachers may select rewritten material, such as the *Globe Adapted Classics.* These graded adaptations of famous stories range from fourth to tenth grade reading levels. Though the language and style of writing can not compare with the originals, adapted classics of this sort can become a means of acquainting students with a classic that they might otherwise never read. It should be remembered, however, that when students begin to read the actual classics their reading development must be mature and they must be given careful guidance. (Carlsen, 1971)

Poetry. Many contemporary songwriters have written lyrics rich in poetic imagery, containing intricate rhythms and presenting ideas of deep significance to youthful audiences. The teenager's fondness for contemporary folk and rock music lends itself well to stimulating him toward a more receptive reading of traditional poetry. Enjoyment of the rhythmic beauty of poetic words is a universal age-old aspect of human communication; and the virtue of poetry is that the exact words have been used to capture the essence of an idea. The words of poets, like the words of songwriters, can increase the youngsters' awareness and understanding of themselves and the moment.

Whether through the use of songs or other stimuli, the teacher who is able to relate poetry to adolescent needs and interests should be successful in encouraging teenagers to read poetry. But when youngsters are given standard poetry, it should be in accordance with their maturity. Early adolescents just leaving the concrete development stage especially enjoy light verse, nonsense rhymes, puns, and limericks. Adolescents of all ages like narrative poems, which tell a story. Collections particularly suited to the interests of "special populations" are especially useful in stimulating an interest in poetry. Examples of such collections are Langston Hughes' (ed.) *New Negro Poets: U. S. A.* and Nancy Larrick's (ed.) *On City Streets: An Anthology of Poetry.*

Most poetry is studied in language arts in terms of its reflection of the social protests of an era or its particular literary devices. However there is some poetry that could be used as supplementary reading in other content areas. For example, Helen Plotz has edited a book entitled *Imaginations' Other Places*, which includes poems about the sciences and mathematics. (Carlsen, 1971)

The Adolescent Novel. Sometimes called the junior novel or transitional literature, this type of material is written especially for the teenaged reader. Its writers focus upon the feelings and emotions normally experienced by the adolescent. In the past, this material has been criticized as subliterature because many of the settings, characters, and plots were stereotyped and shallow. Stories were almost always told from an omniscient point of view; and the plots usually built to a climax near the end of the story, when the hero almost always won. Subtleties in the narrative such as flashback, change from first to second person, or stream of consciousness were uncommon; and the stories

350

usually concentrated on one or two major characters. In addition, many topics considered taboo, such as sex and drugs were either avoided or dealt with in a superficial manner. There was a failure to plunge below the surface into the deeper and most complex human emotions and motivations (Burton, 1960).

However in recent years, the quality of the adolescent novel has improved and currently there are many well written and worthwhile nonformula adolescent novels on the market. Themes now include protagonists in real-life situations who do not always solve their problems by the end of the book. Many formerly taboo subjects are dealt with in depth, and characters from all walks of life are represented.

These novels can be quite useful in extending concepts presented in certain content areas. For example, the novel *Johnny Osage* by Janice Holt Giles tells the story of the Osage Indians in a historically accurate manner. Thus this book could provide meaningful supplementary reading for students studying the 1820s in American history. Likewise, for example, the biology teacher might use Isaac Asimov's *Fantastic Voyage* to extend concepts dealing with the circulatory system. This novel tells of a nuclear submarine, a team of experts, and a crew who are miniaturized so that they may travel through the blood stream of a famous scientist in an attempt to remove a blood clot from his brain. The author, Dr. Asimov, is a practicing biochemist and the scientific data presented as background is based on factual aspects of the human circulatory system. (Carlsen, 1971)

Subliterature

All of the categories of adolescent literature just described have included materials that contain great literary value. However, most people, including adolescents, sometimes enjoy reading subliterature, materials with little or no literary value. These materials include comic books, juvenile series books, and some of the sensational adult novels. They are usually characterized by formula writing in which the author could practically write the story by simply filling in the blanks on a prewritten outline. The characters, settings, and themes are stereotypes, but do present in exaggerated form some of the basic conventions of good literature. As such, they may prove useful to the literature teacher who wants to introduce students to some elementary literary concepts. Subliterature is also of some use in that students often get so involved in easy reading of this type that they learn to practice reading skills in a pleasurable way. However, subliterature is of limited value if the teacher wishes to develop mature readers. While adapted versions of classics presented in comic book form may be used successfully with the reluctant reader, the teacher must be careful to see that students learn to transfer their reading skills to materials of greater depth. If they do not, they will never learn to enjoy reading because as they mature, the content of subliterature will begin to bore them and will fail to hold their attention. Many newspapers have cartoon sections that stress mathematical or scientific concepts in a simple, straightforward manner. These cartoons represent a good way to reinforce or even teach a basic concept. However, materials such as these should be used only as transitional materials that help youngsters understand and learn to enjoy the content area. The student must eventually be led into reading material that deals with these concepts in depth and in a skillful, accurate, and mature manner. (Carlsen, 1971)

Other Types of Nontext Materials

Much of the literature read by adults has not been neatly labeled as nonfiction, modern fiction, or poetry, and readers must decide for themselves the purpose of the material, their purpose for selecting it, and the best approach to reading it. Just as adolescents need guidance in reading and selecting books, essays, and short stories, they also need guidance in selecting and interpreting magazines, newspapers, and warranties.

Just as books do, nontext materials span the range of quality, maturity, and interests. For example, instructions on how to build a model airplane would be more appealing to the young adolescent boy than an article on how to apply for a job, which would appeal to the older adolescent boy. The articles in a magazine such as *Mad* could have particular appeal to the young adolescent who enjoys slapstick humor, while some of the short stories of high literary quality, such as those which might appear in *Atlantic Monthly*, might appeal to the more mature reading interests of an older boy. The magazine *Young Miss*, geared to girls ages seven through fourteen, would probably not appeal to the older girl, who would prefer a magazine such as *Seventeen.* The teacher who has a variety of magazines in his classroom will enhance his chances of having something geared to the individual interests of the adolescents in his class. Examples of the variety that exists include such titles as *Sports Illustrated, Mechanix Illustrated, Ebony, Time, Psychology Today, Popular Science, Mother Earth News, Outdoor Life, Motor Trend, Reader's Digest, House and Garden, Black Sports,* and *Glamour.*

Newspapers geared to the interests of young people are also available. For example, American Education Publications produces several newspapers for different content areas and grade levels. One of their publications is the *Science and Math Weekly* written for grade levels nine through twelve. The local daily or weekly paper contains many features that can be used with students of a variety of reading maturities and in almost any content area. For example, most of the comic strips are less sophisticated and simpler to interpret than the editorials. However, both usually contain content that reflects current thinking and could be used in social studies as supplementary reading on a topic such as environmental pollution. The sports section usually appeals to boys, and the fashion section to girls. The math teacher could make available articles that extend concepts discussed in class. A lesson in algebraic functions could become more relevant to boys who read a supplementary article concerning the experience of quarterbacks and points scored in a football game; or to girls who did free reading on the type of fabric used to make a garment and the price of the garment. However the teacher should encourage the adolescent to read more than one type of nontext material. He should steer youngsters into more mature reading materials and help them understand the multilevels of the more complex writings. Many of these materials are also

352

excellent sources for the teacher to use when developing exercises to teach reading skills needed in his content area.

Commercially Produced Materials for Special Populations

A good reading program should contain instructional and nontext materials for a variety of reading levels and interests. Sometimes students will not read because they do not possess the reading skills necessary to understand the grade level materials; other students are reluctant to read because they are bored by the skills or content. In either case, a teacher needs access to materials that are geared to the needs of this special group of learners.

Instructional Materials Focused on the Special Learner

A teacher frequently needs to locate materials for the adolescent who reads below grade level. In the past, teachers were forced to use elementary school materials with these youngsters, which were often uninteresting and/or embarrassing for them to read. Lately there has been much material designed specifically for adolescent interests but written at an elementary reading level. However it is still hard to find much material of this nature written below fourth grade reading level. Therefore the teacher who has some youngsters who are severely retarded in their reading development should not ignore the use of material intended for the elementary school population. If elementary school materials are used judiciously and presented to the adolescent in a straightforward, helpful manner, they can prove effective. Whenever possible, however, the high-interest, low-vocabulary materials especially geared to adolescents should be used. An example of one of these follows. It is interesting to note that it contains various components that would be particularly useful in health, social studies, and literature.

> *Contact Units.* Englewood Cliffs, N. J.: Scholastic Book Services. A multimedia program of thematic reading units for hard-to-reach students reading at a fourth to sixth grade level. Each unit includes thirty-six illustrated paperback anthologies of short stories, plays, open-ended material, letters from students, and poetry organized for sequential development of the unit theme; thirty-six student logbooks; and an LP of real-life interviews with teenagers and adults who amplify the theme through actual life experiences, eight theme-related posters, and a comprehensive teaching guide. The units deal with drugs, environments, the future, imagination, maturity, law, personal problems, loyalties, and prejudice.

Another group of learners who could be considered as part of a special group are those youngsters who are reading well above grade level and need sophisticated extension of their reading skills. An example of materials geared to this group follows. This material lends itself to the content areas of science, music, and social studies.

353

College Reading Skills. Englewood Cliffs, N. J.: Prentice-Hall Educational Division. A text that provides extensive aids to students who are preparing to deal effectively with reading tasks in college. Practice materials include such topics as electronics, music, and politics, and tasks such as note-taking, studying, and term-paper development.

Still another group of learners for whom specialized materials are available is the youngster who is a member of a minority group. Materials for this population are usually of two kinds: (1) those that provide motivation because they deal with geographic setting and/or populations to which the minority-group member can relate and (2) those that provide skill development particularly geared to the reading needs of a member of a specific type of minority group. An example of each type will be given. Components of each lend themselves to the content area of literature or social studies. An example of material geared to the interests of "special populations" is

Women's Liberation. Jacksonville, Ill.: Perma-Bound. A series of fourteen books that deal with the new feminism. Titles include *Black Women, Born Female, Second Sex, Sisterhood Is Powerful* plus ten others.

An example of material geared to skill building for "special populations" is

Spanish Edition Reading Incentive Language Program. Glendale, Calif.: Bowmar. Spanish edition classroom kits contain Spanish audiotapes correlated with high-interest, low-vocabulary books written in Spanish that appeal to adolescent interests. Topics include *Carros Chistosos de Carreras de Arrastre* (Drag Racing Funny Cars), *Los VW "Bugs," Mini-Motos,* and the like. Since the same books and correlated audiotape are available in English, the teacher may use any combination of English and Spanish audiotapes and stories to reinforce the skills needed in reading by the Spanish-speaking youngster. For example, the teacher could ask the Spanish-speaking youngster to read a story first in Spanish then in English, while following along with the English tape.

It should also be noted that most of the instructional materials discussed throughout this chapter contain components particularly suited to the special learner. Most of the basal reader series include correlated extension reading books that are written at various grade levels and focus on different minority or ethnic groups. Likewise, most of the anthologies and units are available in versions particularly suited to members of special populations. Some of the topics of anthologies that are currently on the market include "Afro-American literature," "women in literature," and "multiethnic literature." An example of a periodical that publishes a version geared to the below grade level reader follows. Components could be used in science, social studies, or health.

Adult Education Leaflets. Pleasantville, N. Y.: Reader's Digest Services. Sixty high-interest articles on health, safety, community action, education, and government. Each article was selected from a recent issue of *Reader's Digest* and rewritten to readability levels ranging from grades three to five based on the Spache and Flesch formulas.

Students of different reading levels and ethnic backgrounds should have access to instructional materials that are motivating and readable, as well as to supplementary reading materials that fit their needs. Just as there should be high-interest, low-vocabulary books available for the below grade level reader of all minority and/or ethnic groups, there should also be comparable books available for the above grade level reader. As Carlsen (1971) points out, above average, college-bound readers need to have access to books that challenge their intellects without overwhelming them and also to reading materials that expand their backgrounds thereby facilitating their success in college. Most college curricula expect students to be familiar with a central body of literature before entering the institution. In essence, while students do not need to read everything they will be assigned to read in college, they do need to read materials on philosophical and humanistic issues that will challenge them and prepare them for the type of reading that they will be asked to do in college.

Likewise, since most youngsters like to read about people like themselves, with whom they can identify, it is desirable to have materials available that concern a variety of ethnic and/or minority backgrounds. Carlsen (1971) suggests that books dealing with the ethnic and/or minority experience can be grouped in an almost infinite number of ways. Some of the literature focusing on the minority and/or ethnic experience is written by individuals who are themselves members of that minority and/or ethnic group; some center primarily on the problems faced because one is a member of an ethnic and/or minority group; others focus on a theme concerning a general human problem and the characters are only incidentally members of an ethnic and/or minority group.

Carlsen (1971) also believes that both the book that centers on the ethnic/minority experience and the one in which the minority/ethnic experience is incidental are useful for all students to read. The one provides insight into the particular problems of a specific group of people at a certain point and place in history. The second kind of book deals with the individual as part of the ongoing human experience. The study of the first should make students aware that generalizations about the entire ethnic experience of the minority group in question can only be made for that specific moment in history and not for all time; the second should stress to students that what happened to the central character happened because he was a human being and not because his experience was typical of all people in his minority group.

TEACHER–MADE MATERIALS

Instructional Materials

Both the classroom teacher and the reading specialist often make their own teaching-of-reading materials because their budgets will not allow them to purchase commercial materials, or they prefer to tie in the curriculum of the school more closely by integrating the teaching of reading with materials actually used in course work. These teacher-made materials fit into two broad categories: (1) changing content area lessons into reading lessons and (2) developing games and reinforcement activities.

Changing Content Area Lessons into Reading Lessons

In some cases content area teachers determine that their students need to learn a specific reading skill before they can complete their assignments and thus change their content area lesson into a reading lesson. For example, the math teacher might look at his algebra lesson and determine that much of the vocabulary will be new to his students. Therefore he might make a guided reading sheet, which helps the student learn the new vocabulary while completing the required assignment.

In other cases, the content area teacher might be the teacher assigned by the school to teach reading skills. If commercial materials are unavailable or undesirable, he may transform the content lesson into a reading lesson in a much more direct fashion than that used by the math teacher described in the preceding paragraph; that is, the teacher may determine that the students in his class need to learn the skill Using Context Clues. Instead of locating commercially available materials on this skill, the classroom teacher designs his own lesson that teaches this skill around the content area.

In both situations, reading skills are being taught in the content area lesson, but the stress is different. The first lesson emphasized needed reading skills to understand a content area lesson; the second lesson emphasized a reading skill and then located a lesson that would reinforce the teaching of that skill.

For example, Mrs. Inez was teaching reading to her class of tenth graders. She had no funds available to purchase commercial reading materials and had to use what was available to her. Therefore she used the tenth grade literature books to teach her students all the reading skills. The first book she adapted for this purpose was *Lord of the Flies* by William Golding. Her procedure for adapting this book was consistent with the diagnostic-prescriptive teaching procedures discussed in Chapter 9 of this text; that is, she (1) used an IRI to assess the reading levels of the students in her class, (2) used a scope and sequence chart to determine what reading skills they should know, (3) assessed their achievement on the reading skills selected for them. Then she used the generic teaching strategies discussed in Chapter 10 to help her design lessons to teach the designated reading skills. Her lesson for tenth graders reading on grade level on the vocabulary skill of Using Context Clues follows:

> *Objective:* At the completion of this lesson, the student will be able to identify the meaning of at least eight British idioms found in *Lord of the Flies* from their use in context.
>
> *Pre-Assessment:* Ask students to look through a list of ten sentences containing British idioms used in context and to identify the meaning of at least

356

eight of the idioms. Those can who do so, have met the objective and should go on to another lesson.

Materials: Lord of the Flies, paper and pencil, handouts.

Procedure: (Initial Teaching Lesson) Define idioms and ask students to think of American idioms, listing them on the board. Discuss word usages that are characteristic to different cultural groups in the United States and make more lists on the board. Explain that the British have their own idioms and ask if students know any. Show students that the way words are used in sentences can give clues to meaning. Explain the different types of context clues; for example, synonyms and antonyms.* Divide the class into small groups to examine Chapter 1 of *Lord of the Flies* for British idioms. One student in each group acts as a recorder, making a list of the idioms. Then the groups exchange lists.

Post-Assessment: This is to be administered after the completion of a reinforcement lesson given to the students the following day.

In a like manner, Mrs. Inez could have used *Lord of the Flies* to teach structural analysis (e.g., Locate ten words that are based on Greek roots and define them according to the meanings of their Greek roots and the meanings of their affixes); identifying propaganda (e.g., What is Golding's purpose in writing this book? What is his background? Does the fact that the author was in World War II make you suspect that his story is attempting to persuade readers that humans have much potential for brutality to fellow humans?); or scanning (e.g., Locate as many British idioms as you can in a two-minute period of time).

Even though Mrs. Inez used *Lord of the Flies* to teach reading skills, she could have just as easily used another literary work, assorted magazines, or the daily newspaper. In other words, since reading is a skill and not a content, reading skills may be taught through any content area and through any material designed to be read.

Reinforcement Activities

Often teachers make up games and other activities that are designed to reinforce a particular reading skill. It should be pointed out that games are primarily useful as reinforcement activities but often are not suitable for teaching a reading skill. Most games can be used with any age group; however some would be more suitable to a middle or junior high class than to a senior high class, and vice versa. The teacher should diagnose the maturity of his own students to determine their receptivity and ability to benefit from the games he would like to use as a means for reinforcing a specific reading skill.

Ideas for teacher-made activities may be gleaned from a variety of sources. Many activities are described in Chapter 10 of this text in the reinforcement

*See skill number 2 in Chapter 10 for more information on teaching this skill.

section of the generic teaching strategies. Other ideas for games may be adapted from commercially made reading activities or from suggestions made by inservice classroom teachers. In addition many professional journals for teachers contain detailed descriptions for teacher-made activities that have been used successfully with secondary school students. The activity shown in Figure 11.2 and used by Mrs. Inez to reinforce the use of context clues, was adapted from a suggestion given by a teacher in the "EJ Workshop" section of the *English Journal.* *

It is also interesting to note that whenever possible Mrs. Inez made her game boards on manila folders and stored all parts of the games inside the folders. This enabled her to close the folder and store it in a file cabinet for easy accessibility. In addition, she usually "laminated" the game boards, or placed clear plastic paper with a sticky back on them, to make them last as long as possible.

Though teacher-made activities have the advantage of helping students transfer needed reading skills to the content material that the students are required to read, their construction can be a time-consuming task for the teacher. Sometimes the task may be made easier by locating materials that are easily adaptable to the skill being taught; at other times, the task may be made easier by eliciting student help. For example, the teacher could use both of these facilitating aspects by (1) asking a student to cut out examples of propaganda from newspaper advertisements and (2) subsequently using pictures gathered by the students as the basis for an activity developed by the teacher. Likewise the Magic Numbers box shown in Figure 11.2 could be adapted by students to any other novel as part of their reinforcement activities for using context clues to identify meanings of British idioms. Once students located eighteen more sentences containing British idioms and their synonyms, it would be relatively easy for the students to adapt the Magic Numbers exercises to them as long as they were told the correct combinations; namely, A and 2, L and 3, and so forth. Again, the resulting exercises could be used by Mrs. Inez as the basis of an exercise to be given to other students. While these strategies would not eliminate all the teacher's work, they would cut down the amount of time spent on developing teacher-made activities.

It should be noted here that some English teachers feel that certain works of literature should not be dissected but that they should be studied in their entireties. While this has some validity, particularly in great literature whose beauty of style might be subordinated by overattention to "structural analysis," the skillful reading teacher can make reading skills relevant to the content at hand. For example, Mrs. Inez taught context clues because they were needed by the class and because they helped students understand needed vocabulary within the book. Had she had them use *Lord of the Flies* as an instructional tool to teach Greek roots, she would have been wise to tie the study of Greek roots into the effect of these types of words upon an author's style of writing. In other words, students might look at Golding's use of words with Greek roots in terms of his precise use of language, a characteristic that made him the author of a modern classic.

Taken to its extremes, this concept could be used to teach even nonreaders.

*M. Cotton, "EJ Workshop," *English Journal,* 64:7 (October 1975), p. 66–67.

Objective: (reinforcement lesson) Same as initial teaching lesson.
Pre-Assessment: Already given on previous day with initial teaching lesson.
Materials: List of idioms, synonyms in context, and Magic Numbers exercise.
Procedure for Reinforcement Lesson: Give students the following Magic Numbers exercise.

Directions to student: Choose the numbered statement from Column I that answers the lettered statement in Column II. The letter in each box corresponds with the lettered statement in Column II. Place the number from Column I in the correct box. Each row should add up to the magic number 39, both vertically and horizontally. Work in pairs to complete this task.

Column I	Column II
1. "It wasn't half dangerous with all them tree trunks falling."	A. my breath
2. "Can't catch me breath."	B. words understood only by a particular group
3. "I ought to be chief, . . . because I'm chapter chorister and head boy. I can sing C sharp."	C. taking a short break for relaxation
4. "I was the only boy in our school what had asthma."	D. British obscenity
5. "My dad's dead," he said quickly, "and my mum . . ."	E. fainting
6. "I used to get ever so many candies."	F. mother
7. "This last piece of shop brought sniggers from the choir."	G. gone
8. "He's always throwing a faint."	H. empty your bladder
9. "If this isn't an island we might be rescued straight away."	I. doesn't look very good
10. "When they had done laughing, . . ."	J. come to get us
11. "Now you've been and set the whole island on fire."	K. very many
12. "They let the bloody fire go out."	L. the boy in charge
13. "It don't look much."	M. constantly present
14. "There isn't more than a ha'porth of meat in a crab."	N. finished
15. " . . . if you're taken short . . . "	O. who had
16. "Simon's always about."	P. soon
17. ". . . until they fetch us."	
18. "I bet it's gone tea-time. . ."	

Student's Copy

A	B	C	D
E	F	G	H
I	J	K	L
M	N	O	P

Answer Key

A–2	B–7	C–18	D–12
E–8	F–5	G–11	H–15
I–13	J–17	K–6	L–3
M–16	N–10	O–4	P–9

Post-Assessment: Ask the students to look through the remainder of the *Lord of the Flies* for more British idioms used in context. Those who can identify the meanings of at least eight out ten from their use in the context of a sentence have met the objective and may go on to another skill.

Figure 11.2 Context Clues Lesson

For example, the tenth grade nonreading boy could be asked to identify initial consonants in words with the letters *b* and *r*. The teacher could stress that Golding liked to use alliteration and could ask the youngster to look for alliterative words such as *birds* and *bee-sounds*, *returning* and *roost*. This would not only help him to learn the alphabet, but also would contribute something meaningful to his knowledge of literary style, both for his own benefit and to discuss with the remainder of the class.

Teacher-Made Nontext Materials

Teachers usually do not have time to author books or articles geared to the needs and interests of their students; but they can search through current magazines, newspapers, or informational pamphlets and build a resource file geared to the interests of their classes. For example, the mathematics teacher who cuts out articles in newspapers or nontechnical magazines dealing with the projected conversion to the metric system, would be developing nontext materials geared to his content area. Often teachers assign students to collect articles on particular topics. Such student-located articles, which have special appeal, may be subsequently filed in folders and placed in an area for free reading.

LOCATING MATERIALS

Locating Instructional Reading Materials

There are so many commercial materials currently available on the market that it is almost overwhelming to the average teacher. Perhaps the easiest way for teachers to select materials for a reading program is to use a checklist in conjunction with the purpose for teaching reading. The checklist appearing in Figure 11.3 might be helpful in this task.

In order to use this checklist with efficiency, teachers should examine their specific type of reading program and then select materials that suit their purpose. Obviously, the teacher who is a reading specialist and teaches a class in reading would want to select different materials than the content area teacher who merely wants materials to supplement needed reading skills in his content area of biology. Ideally, the reading specialist would like at least one copy of the materials in each of the vertical categories suitable to the reading levels, needs, and interests of all adolescents. However, most reading teachers do not have the budget to permit them to purchase this massive amount of materials. Therefore, the simplest means of reaching all students would probably be to build up a fund of materials that represents at least one comprehensive reading program for adolescents, ranging in reading levels from K through twelve. Then the reading specialist could add to the comprehensive programs by purchasing skill-building materials focusing on the skills most needed by the students in his particular school. A teacher would be well advised to build up a

Instructional Materials	a. Commercially Produced	b. Teacher Made	c. Comprehensive	d. Skill Building (Write Out Skill Number)	e. Intended as Total Program	f. Intended as Adjunct to Program	g. Primarily Teacher Directed	h. Primarily Non-Teacher Directed	i. Intended as Teaching Activity	j. Intended as Reinforcement Activity	k. Content Concerns Developmental Tasks for Early Adolescence	l. Content Concerns Developmental Tasks for Middle Adolescence	m. Content Concerns Developmental Tasks for Late Adolescence	n. Content Concerns Reading Interest for Early Adolescent Boy	o. Content Concerns Reading Interest for Early Adolescent Girl	p. Content Concerns Reading Interest for Middle Adolescent Boy	q. Content Concerns Reading Interest for Middle Adolescent Girl	r. Content Concerns Reading Interest for Late Adolescent Boy	s. Content Concerns Reading Interest for Late Adolescent Girl	t. Content Geared to Cognitive Development of "Concrete Stage"	u. Content Geared to Cognitive Development of "Formal Operations Stage"	v. Intended Reading Level (Write Out Grade Level)
1. Basal Reader Type																						
2. Unit Type																						
3. Anthology Type																						
4. Collections-of-Reading Type																						
5. Workbook Type																						
Periodicals																						
6. Reading Focus																						
7. Adapted, Regular																						
8. Kits																						
9. Programmed Materials																						
10. Multimedia Materials																						
Mechanical Devices																						
11. Films or Filmstrip Machines																						
12. Pacers																						
13. Tachistoscopes																						
14. Games, Records, Tapes																						
Nontext Materials																						
15. Nonfiction																						
16. Biography																						
17. Popular Adult Literature																						
18. Significant Modern Fiction																						
19. Classics																						
20. Poetry																						
21. Adolescent Novel																						
22. Subliterature																						
23. Other Types of Materials (e.g., newspapers, magazines)																						

Directions for Use: Place a check mark by materials which you already have that fit into the delineated categories. For more preciseness, put the skill number instead of a check mark in the fourth column from the left. For more descriptive recording, attach a sheet of paper to this checklist and describe components by number; e.g., number 14 might include a description of 14b, d—a teacher-made game that teaches the skill Using Context Clues.

Figure 11.3 Context Clues Lesson

plethora of noninstructional materials geared to the needs, interests, and reading levels of all adolescents, instead of overlooking them for the purchase of a massive amount of skill-building materials.

In cases of limited budgets, it is recommended that the teacher purchase books rather than mechanical devices. The book format is much less expensive and does the same thing as the machine. In fact, many authorities believe the main value in mechanical devices is the motivational value. If money were not limited, mechanical devices could be purchased to support the program and a variety of comprehensive programs and alternative materials for teaching the same specific skills could be obtained.

Currently, there are many excellent materials available, which will not be described in this text because of space limitations. In addition, more good material is being produced daily, and the classroom teacher should ask for catalogs from publishing company representatives at professional meetings in order to keep as current as possible on these new developments.

Locating Nontext Reading Materials

Because the term *nontext* is used in this chapter to identify materials not directly designed to teach reading skills, the amount of materials in this category is massive. Basically, the best thing a classroom teacher can do is to be quite familiar with the library and the resource tools that may be used to locate materials geared to the needs of his students. Though teachers should check with their own librarians to see what references exist in their school libraries, the following descriptions give teachers some idea of the types of references that would be most useful to them.

Reference Guides to Periodical Literature

Reference guides to periodical literature include indexes to general and nontechnical magazines, specialized indexes, indexes to newspapers, and selection aids for periodical literature. All types of periodicals are indexed, and one particularly useful aid is the *World Dictionary of Youth Periodicals* by Lavina Dobler and Muriel Fuller.

Reference Guides for Book Selection

Reference guides to help select books according to students' interests and content areas include bibliographies classified by student interest, bibliographies for book selection classified by content areas, and books and readings about the adolescent reader. An example of each type is the New York Public Library's *Books for the Teen Age*, The National Council of Teachers of Mathematics' *The High School Mathematics Library*, and Robert Carlsen's *Books and the Teen-Age Reader*.

362

Many free and inexpensive materials are available which teachers of all content areas may use to build up their nontext resources. One example of this type of reference guide is *Free and Inexpensive Learning Materials*, published biennially by George Peabody College for Teachers.

References and Bibliography

Adelstein, M., and Pivel, J. eds. *Women's Liberation.* Jacksonville, Ill.: Perma-Bound, Division of Hertzberg—New Method, Inc., 1972.

Adult Education Leaflets. Pleasantville, N. Y.: Reader's Digest Services, 1971.

American Education Publications, Columbus, Ohio. *Weekly Reader*, reading level 1–5; *Senior Weekly Reader*, reading level 6; *Current Events*, reading level 7–8; *Every Week*, reading level 9–10; *Our Times*, reading level 11–12; *Science and Math Weekly*, reading level 9–12; *How to Study Workshop*, reading level 7–9; *Reading Treasure Chest*, reading level 7–9; Low-priced periodicals and supplementary materials that cover a wide range of topics to interest adolescents and youths.

American History Games. Chicago: Science Research Associates, 1970.

Anderson, N., and Dechant, E. *EDL Listen and Read Program.* Huntington, N. Y.: Educational Development Laboratories, 1963.

Anderson, Q., et al. *Adventures in Literature Series: Classic Edition.* New York: Harcourt Brace Jovanovich, 1973.

Asimov, I. *Fantastic Voyage.* New York: Bantam, 1966.

The Atlantic Monthly Education Edition. Boston: Atlantic Monthly.

Aukerman, R. C. *Reading in the Secondary Classroom.* New York: McGraw-Hill, 1972.

Baldwin, J. *Go Tell It on the Mountain.* New York: Dell, 1963.

Blake, K. A. *College Reading Skills.* Englewood Cliffs, N. J.: Prentice-Hall Educational Division, 1973.

Buchanan, C. D. *Programmed Reading for Adults.* New York: Webster Division/McGraw-Hill, 1966.

Burton, D. *Literature Study in the High Schools.* New York: Holt, Rinehart & Winston, 1960.

Career Development Laboratories. Tulsa, Okla.: Educational Progress Corporation, 1970.

Carlsen, R. G. *Books and the Teen-Age Reader.* Harper & Row, 1971.

Classics Illustrated. New York: Gilberton, 1965–1966.

Contact Units. Englewood Cliffs, N. J.: Scholastic Book Services.

Controlled Reader. Huntington, N. Y.: Educational Development Laboratories, 1963.

Cotton, M. "EJ Workshop." *English Journal* 64:7 (October 1975), p. 66–67.

Dobler, L., and Fuller, M. *World Dictionary of Youth Periodicals.* New York: Citation Press, 1970.

EDL Study Skills Library. Huntington, N. Y.: Educational Development Laboratories, 1962.

Free and Inexpensive Learning Materials. Nashville, Tenn.: George Peabody College for Teachers (bienially).

Giles, J. H. *Johnny Osage.* Boston: Houghton Mifflin, 1960.

Globe Adapted Classics. New York: Globe, 1945–1955.

Golding, W. *Lord of the Flies.* New York: Putnam, 1959.

Group for the Advancement of Psychiatry. *Normal Adolescence: Its Dynamics and Impact.* New York: Scribner, 1968.

Havighurst, R. J. *Developmental Tasks and Education.* New York: McKay, 1948.

Herber, H. *Go.* Englewood Cliffs, N. J.: Scholastic Book Services, 1974.

Hershey, J. *Hiroshima.* New York: Bantam, 1946.

Houghton Mifflin Readers Levels 13 and 14. Boston: Houghton Mifflin, 1972.

Hughes, L., ed. *New Negro Poets: U.S.A.* Fort Wayne, Inc.: Indiana University Press, 1964.

Iowa High School Films. Iowa City, Iowa: State University of Iowa, 1959.

Larrick, N., ed. *On City Streets: An Anthology of Poetry.* New York: Bantam, 1968.

Markle, S. *Words.* Chicago: Science Research Associates, 1963.

Matterson, D. R. *Adolescence Today: Sex Roles and the Search for Identity.* Homewood, Ill.: Dorsey, 1975.

National Council of Teachers of Mathematics. *The High School Mathematics Library,* 3rd ed. Washington, D. C.: National Council of Teachers of Mathematics, 1967.

New Advanced Reading Skill Builders. Audio Lessons. Pleasantville, N. Y.: Reader's Digest Services, Educational Division, 1973.

New York Public Library. *Books for the Teen Age.* The New York Public Library, annually.

Orwell, G. *Animal Farm.* New York: Harcourt Brace Jovanovich, 1954.

Parker, D. H. *Reading Laboratory Kits 3b, 4a.* Science Research Associates, 1963 and 1959.

Pauk, W. *Six-Way Paragraphs.* Providence, R. I.: Jamestown, 1974.

Peck, R. F., and Richeck, H. "Adolescence." *Encyclopedia of Educational Research.* 4th ed. Robert Ebel, ed. New York: Macmillan, 1969, p. 44

Piaget, J. *Science of Education and the Psychology of the Child.* New York: Viking, 1970.

Pilgrim, G. H., and McAllister, M. K. *Books, Young People, and Reading Guidance.* 2nd ed. New York: Harper & Row, 1968.

Plotz, H., ed. *Imagination's Other Places.* New York: Crowell, 1958.

Radlauer, E., and Radlauer, R. *Reading Incentive Language Program Audiovisual Kits.* Glendale, Calif.: Bowmar, 1968-1971.

Radlauer, E., (translated from Covarrybies, A.) *Reading Incentive Language Program Spanish Language Edition.* Glendale, Calif.: Bowmar, 1973.

Reiter, I. M. *The Reading Line.* Philadelphia: Polaski Company, 1971.

Scholastic Action Unit. Englewood Cliffs, N. J.: Scholastic Book Services.

Schumacher, M., Spache, G., and Schmidt, B. *Design for Good Reading: New Edition.* New York: Harcourt Brace Jovanovich, 1969.

Spache, G. "Auditory and Visual Materials." *Development in and Through Reading.* 60th Yearbook, University of Chicago, NSSE, 1961, pp. 222-225.

Sprinthall, R. C., and Sprinthall, N. A. *Educational Psychology: A Development Approach.* Reading, Mass.: Addison-Wesley, 1974.

SRA Reading Accelerator. Chicago: Science Research Associates.

Tach-X Tachistoscope. Huntington, N. Y.: Educational Development Laboratories.

Thomas, D. *An Evening with Dylan Thomas Reading His Own and Other Poems.* (Produced by Caedmon Recording Company for National Council of Teachers of English.) Urbana, Ill.: National Council of Teachers of English, 1971.

Thurstone, T. G. *Reading for Understanding.* Chicago: Science Research Associates, 1958.

Vocabulary Beano Game. Superior, Wis.: English Laboratory.

Chapter 12

Using a Variety of Organizational Approaches for Teaching Reading

Prerequisite 12.1

Participants should have successfully completed the objectives for Chapters 1, 2, 3, 4, and 11 or should have some knowledge of the reading skills and materials available to teach reading before beginning this chapter.

Rationale 12.2

To teach reading efficiently, the reading skills should be presented in a manner that facilitates learning. This chapter discusses several ways in which the teaching of reading may be organized, and also presents ways in which all middle and secondary school teachers may become involved in reading instruction.

Objectives 12.3

On successful completion of this chapter, the participant will be able to:

1. Describe characteristics of and distinguish between the following types of organizational approaches for teaching reading within the school: (1) developmental reading as a required course, (2) advanced developmental reading as an elective course, (3) corrective reading as a required course, (4) reading as part of an English course, (5) content area teachers as teachers of reading, and

365

(6) the reading laboratory.

2. Describe characteristics of and distinguish between the following types of organizational approaches for teaching reading within the classroom: (1) comprehensive reading textbook approach, (2) individualized reading approach, (3) independent study approach, (4) language experience approach, (5) eclectic approach, and (6) diagnostic-prescriptive technique.

3. Describe the role of supplementary reading materials in the reading program.

4. Describe and give at least one example of how the classroom teacher might do the following concerning supplementary reading materials: (1) motivate students to read nontext materials, (2) provide for a creative means of book sharing, (3) use criteria for evaluating the success of the supplementary reading program.

5. Describe and give at least one example of each of the following components of a management system for teaching reading: (1) grouping for reading achievement, needs, and interests, (2) keeping records, and (3) arranging the physical aspects of the classroom.

6. Given a description of a secondary school teacher who teaches reading, the participant will be able to (1) identify and describe the materials used; for example, basal reader, unit; (2) identify the approach being used; for example, individualized, reading textbook, (3) describe the management system being used; for example, grouping procedures, record keeping, physical arrangement of the classroom.

7. Describe and give at least one example of how the organization of a reading program may vary because of the age of the students, materials available, content area being taught.

8. Describe and give an example of each of the following as teachers of reading: (1) English teacher, (2) teacher of another content area, (3) reading specialist.

9. Describe and distinguish between the following roles that may be played by reading specialists in the middle and secondary school: (1) reading lab instructor, (2) inservice consultant to other reading teachers, (3) inservice consultant to all content area teachers.

10. Describe at least one way in which a school-wide reading program may be developed for all content area teachers.

11. Given a description of a group of students functioning above grade level, on grade level, or below grade level, state how to design a developmental reading program. The answer should include approaches, materials, and management.

12. (On the lines below, add other objectives according to your instructor's directions.) _____

_____

_____

_____

13. _____

_____

14. _____

_____

15. _____

_____

*   *   *   *   *   *   *   *   *   *   *   *   *   *

Chapter 13, Experience 12 extends Chapter 12 with these performance/consequence objectives:

16. Design a reading lesson during which three different approaches to developmental reading are used with three different groups of students; e.g., one group by the textbook approach, one group by the individualized approach, and one group by the independent study approach;

and/or

17. Design and teach a lesson based on an eclectic approach; e.g., the lessons for one group might include aspects of the language experience, the independent study, and the individualized approaches.

*   *   *   *   *   *   *   *   *   *   *   *   *   *

Self Pre-Assessment 12.4

Can you complete all the activities listed in **Objectives 12.3**? Answer "yes," "no," or "not certain."

If you answered "yes" to the question, complete the enabling activities required by your instructor and take the Post-Assessment on the date assigned by him.

If you answered "no," refer to **Enabling Activities 12.5**. If you decide to do any activities that are not required, select those that best suit you as a learner. You need not complete all the optional activities or all parts of a particular optional activity. As soon as you have the information you need to complete the objectives, answer "yes" to the **Self Pre-Assessment 12.4** question and stop the activity.

If you answered "not certain" to the question, refer to **Enabling Activities 12.4**. Select the enabling activity that best suits your style of learning and peruse it. Then make a firm "yes" or "no" answer and proceed accordingly.

Enabling Activities 12.5

Complete only as many of the activities listed below as are required and which you need in order to meet the objectives.

1. *Enabling activity one* is a *reading* alternative. This is **Information Given 12.6.** It is a brief overview of several ways in which the teaching of reading may be organized and by which all middle and secondary school teachers may become involved in reading instruction.

2. *Enabling activity two* is another *reading* option. In this case, the material to be read is one of the textbooks used to expand the theoretical background for this course. See chart on inside front cover for keying in textbooks that may be used.

3. *Enabling activity three* is a *class session* option. Attend the class session(s) on the date(s), at the time(s), and at the place(s) announced.

| _____ | _____ | _____ |
| (Date) | (Time) | (Place) |

| _____ | _____ | _____ |
| (Date) | (Time) | (Place) |

| _____ | _____ | _____ |
| (Date) | (Time) | (Place) |

4. *Enabling activity four* (These lines are left blank so that you may add other enabling activities as suggested by your instructor.)_____

_____

_____

5. *Enabling activity five*_____

_____

6. *Enabling activity six*_____

_____

Now that you have completed the appropriate number of required and/or optional learning alternatives, look back at **Self Pre-Assessment 12.4.** If you feel you can answer "yes" to all of the questions, you are ready to proceed to the Post-Assessment. This may be given to you immediately or after completion of a series of chapters.

Students at LaSalle Junior-Senior High School were provided several formats for improving their reading skills.

1. All seventh, eighth, and ninth graders spent some time in required "developmental" reading courses.
2. An elective English course called Advanced Developmental Reading was available to students who wished to improve their reading skills.
3. An English course entitled Corrective Reading was required for students who were having trouble reading classroom materials.
4. Each English teacher in school divided his individual course of study into the three areas of literature, grammar, and communication. At least one three-week unit under the category of literature focused on reading skills.
5. All content area teachers spent a few minutes each day teaching and reinforcing reading skills needed for their content areas.
6. A reading lab was available for all students.

ORGANIZATIONAL APPROACHES WITHIN THE SCHOOL

The organizational formats used at LaSalle are typical of those used in secondary schools, though other schools may offer fewer formats. Each of the approaches presented above is discussed on the following pages.

Developmental Reading As a Required Course

Students past the eighth grade are not always taught reading as a content area subject. However, developmental reading as a required year-long course is relatively common in the middle school and junior high school, and teachers often use a basal reader series that extends from grades K through 8 as the core material for this course. In the senior high school, developmental reading is frequently found at the ninth or tenth grade level; and often instruction utilizes the unit or the comprehensive workbook as the core of the instructional materials. (See Chapter 11 for more discussion of these materials.) In the senior high school, this organization may be found in combination with a block of other required courses and, as such, may be offered for a specific time block rather than for an entire school year.

For example, LaSalle's junior high curriculum required all seventh and eighth graders to take reading as a subject. The classes met daily for the entire school year, and students used a basal reader series as the major instructional tool. However, the senior high curriculum required all ninth graders to take one semester of developmental reading from one of two teachers, whose course structures varied. Both teachers administered a standardized reading test, asked students to respond to a reading interest inventory, and then helped students set self-improvement goals in terms of their vocabulary, comprehension, rate of comprehension, and study skills. One teacher usually spent part of the time discussing such topics as ways to take efficient notes, means for skimming textbooks, and the meanings of Latin and Greek roots. The remainder of the time was spent in individual work in the comprehensive workbook, used as the main instructional tool, as well as in various programmed materials, in kits, and with machinery designed to increase proficiency with specific reading skills. The second teacher based instruction around work in nontext materials that had been self-selected by the students.

Advanced Developmental Reading As an Elective Course

In the elective course approach, reading is offered as a subject and the focus may range from a basic skills course to one geared specifically to study skills or speed-reading. When offered primarily as a basic skills improvement course, stress is placed on improving vocabulary and comprehension skills. When offered as a study skills course, the student is presented with techniques for improving note-taking, skimming, scanning, and library usage skills. Because seniors often enroll in courses of this type in order to prepare for college, time may be spent on general techniques for improving test-taking skills, as well as on reviewing the reading skills required for the American College Testing Program Examination and the Scholastic Aptitude Test.

When this course is offered as a speed-reading course, students may be shown techniques for increasing rate of comprehension and may then be given materials designed to push them to read faster so that they may practice the techniques. For example, in LaSalle's senior high division, the developmental reading course was basically a speed-reading course. Most of the students who enrolled were good readers who felt they were spending too much time on reading assignments in their textbooks. They wanted to learn skills that would help them read classroom materials in a more efficient and rapid manner. The students usually spent the first part of each period participating in a lecture/discussion in which techniques for improving rate of reading were presented by the teacher. During the remainder of the period, most of the students worked on their own, reading a selected passage from a collection of readings as rapidly as possible and then responding to accompanying questions about the content. Students would calculate rate and degree of comprehension and then place the calculations on a graph, which helped students visualize their reading progress. Afterwards most were asked to select a book on their own, which they were to read with the help of a reading pacer, a mechanical device that forces one to read faster. This device contains a shutter that gradually covers a page from top to bottom at a speed set by the individual.

370

Corrective Reading Required for Some Students

A corrective reading course is geared toward students who are below grade level in some aspect of their reading skills. Sometimes the course involves group discussion; but often it is centered around independent study. Students are provided materials to use in improving their reading skills in order to keep up with their content area studies.

In LaSalle's senior high division, students were scheduled to substitute the course for other English electives on the recommendation of their counselors. If their reading did not improve as much as needed, they could be scheduled to take the corrective reading course again. The teacher usually gave them a group standardized test and then further assessed their reading skills, using a variety of diagnostic tests based on the response of each student on the group test. After each student's reading strengths and weaknesses were identified, an independent program of study was set up for him; and a variety of skill-building materials, geared to the specific skills needed by each, were individually assigned. The teacher spent most of the time acting as a resource person who checked on students' daily work and kept continuous track of their progress on materials that had been individually assigned.

Reading As Part of an English Course

Reading as part of an English course is more frequently part of the curricula in middle and junior high than in senior high. Often the teacher is given a reading textbook and is asked to incorporate instruction from the text into the regular course work. Teachers may spend as many as six weeks on the reading unit. Though the unit could be presented in one six-week block, many teachers divide the time so that a certain number of minutes a day or a week is devoted to teaching reading skills.

At LaSalle, all senior high English teachers spent at least three weeks teaching reading skills. They did not use a reading textbook but rather relied upon a teaching packet that had been prepared for them by their reading consultant. Since reading was taught by all the English teachers, the reading consultant had sequenced the material in the instructional packets so that the students would not receive instruction on the same reading skills each year. (This packet is explained later on in the chapter.)

Content Area Teachers As Teachers of Reading

When content area teachers function as teachers of reading they spend a few minutes each day teaching and reviewing reading skills particularly needed to complete the daily reading assignments. Some schools purchase workbook type skill-building textbooks that emphasize skills needed for a particular content area. Most often the teacher teaches the skills in the order they are presented in the workbook and helps the students to make the correlation between their workbook assignments and their textbook reading assignments.

For example, a science teacher might spend half an hour a week instructing students from the science component of the *Reading Line*, which stresses reading skills needed in science. The same teacher might then help the students make the transfer from materials discussed in the *Reading Line* to the current assignment being read by the student.

In LaSalle's senior high curriculum, no textbook was used; instead the reading consultant went from classroom to classroom, helping content area teachers identify needed reading skills in their specific daily assignments. Then she showed the teachers how to construct differentiated guided reading sheets to teach the skills and help the students read the assignment. (See guided reading sheets in Chapter 8.)

Reading Laboratory Approach

Another frequently used approach is to set up an area in the school that is open on a very flexible basis to all students, either for developmental or corrective reading. Frequently, this lab will be a classroom provided with many resource materials and individual carrels. Students are individually tested and then assigned materials for independent study to meet their individual reading needs.

In LaSalle's senior high division, a reading specialist manned the reading lab. Students were not scheduled into the lab the same way they were scheduled into the other reading programs; the time in the reading lab was dependent upon the student's time schedule and reading needs. For example, one very poor reader in the eleventh grade came every day for the entire school year. One superior reader wanted to improve his note-taking skill in order to improve his grade point average. When he had improved his note-taking skill, he stopped coming to the lab because his goal had been accomplished.

ORGANIZATIONAL APPROACHES
WITHIN THE CLASSROOM

Regardless of the format set up by the school, teachers responsible for teaching reading must design instruction according to the needs of their students and within the context of an approach with which they feel comfortable. Because the reading courses just discussed were developed for differing purposes, the instructional approaches used by the classroom teachers varied considerably.

Approaches to Teaching Reading

Of the courses listed above, five were taught in a format in which reading was a separate subject and in which the instructor was a reading teacher. One course was presented in a format in which only the specific reading skills needed to understand the content area were taught. In this format, the instructor was the content area teacher.

Basically, there are six commonly used means by which teachers may organize their classrooms in order to teach reading skills. While these intraclassroom structures are indigenous to the teaching of reading as a subject, they exist to a lesser extent in content area courses. These six structures are (1) comprehensive reading textbook approach, (2) individualized reading approach, (3) independent study approach, (4) language experience approach, (5) eclectic approach, (6) diagnostic-prescriptive technique. The following sections will define each structure and give examples of the ways in which both reading teachers and content area teachers may use them.

Comprehensive Reading Textbook Approach
Definition of Terms

Chapter 11 discusses, in depth, materials that deal with the reading skills in an inclusive manner and hence can be considered *comprehensive*. In this approach, the teacher selects materials that may be used as a total program and then centers the reading program around these materials.

Components

Most of these comprehensive programs include (1) a teacher's manual, which contains detailed teaching suggestions and carefully delineates day-by-day instruction; (2) a student's text, in which the vocabulary is carefully selected, most of the stories are primarily narrative, and most of the stories are based upon concepts believed to be interesting to the adolescent; (3) a student's workbook, in which all the reading skills are presented and practiced in an orderly fashion; and (4) usually a large amount of correlated supplementary material designed to extend skills, concepts, and stories.

Individualized Reading Approach
Definition of Terms

Individualized reading is a term that has been used for more than thirty years to denote a system of teaching reading in which skill development is based on books that have been selected by the student rather than the teacher. The plan provides for individual instruction in reading by (1) carefully guiding students in their choice of books, (2) developing independent study activities for each youngster, and (3) developing reading skills through frequent individual conferences with each youngster. The sequence of skills developed is determined by the youngster's reading needs, which are reflected in his individual conference.

Components

Motivation and Self-Selection of Materials. The focus of motivation is to stimulate adolescents to select books that they would like to read. There are many ways to stimulate interest in book selection. Teachers using an individualized approach usually decorate their rooms with book covers, magazines, and a wide variety of attractive paperback books designed to interest adolescents. Though the teacher is helpful in suggesting specific books for each student based on his or her interests, reading level, and needs, the final choice of reading matter is left to the student.

Self-Pacing in Instruction and Individual Conferences. Although the student reads his own book at his own rate, his skill instruction is based upon the results of frequent individual conferences during which the teacher carefully questions him on the content of his self-selected book. If the instructor determines that the student needs to know the skill of, for example, Identifying Main Idea, he assigns the student lessons to develop this skill. The rate at which the student is expected to complete his specific skill exercises is based on his individual manner of working and the number of skills he has been assigned.

Peer Interaction. One of the most important components of the individualized approach is peer interaction. During adolescence, youngsters are particularly aware of peer opinion. Therefore one of the best ways to encourage teenagers to read a book is to have other teenagers recommend it to them. Two very important dimensions make up the peer interaction component of individualized reading: (1) book sharing and (2) grouping for various purposes.

1. *Book Sharing.* Teachers who use this approach usually set aside some time each week so that adolescents may meet in large or small groups to tell others about the book they read. The teacher often encourages creative book reporting similar to the suggestions given in a later section of this chapter.

2. *Grouping for Various Purposes:* In order to make the most efficient use of his time, the teacher often schedules group instruction for students who need help on the same skill. Students are given assignments to work together on a task—with or without the teacher present—in order to practice or reinforce reading skills needed by each. As in book sharing, peers can learn from each other by occasionally working together on tasks. Sometimes these tasks are gamelike activities that provide students a chance to work in groups. The natural inclination of this age level to form peer groups makes the task more enjoyable and hence, reinforces needed reading skills in a pleasurable way.

It should be stressed that "individualized reading" does not mean always working alone, but rather developing reading skills based on individual needs. Many of the strengths of "individualized" reading are lost if youngsters don't interact in sharing activities. For example, if a youngster learns best in a small group, his learning has not been individualized if all his lessons are designed so that he must work alone.

Independent Study Approach

Definition of Terms

Many teachers currently use organizational formats in which students are given individual work in materials based on their test scores in reading. Often the youngsters self-select materials and work on them in a self-paced manner. Sometimes materials used in these programs are primarily kits or programmed books, in which youngsters are assigned material through the use of a color code and told to progress at their own rate. Other times, these materials span a wide range of instructional vehicles and include free reading, teacher-made materials, and a fairly rigid time line for completion of specific tasks.

Sometimes teachers erroneously label this type of program as *individualized* because each student is working on his own materials and at his own pace. If the program revolves around a book (not a self-selected reading exercise), if it involves a teacher conference during which skills are diagnosed through a self-selected book (not a diagnosis based on percentage correct on a self-selected reading passage or teacher-assigned reading textbook), and if the teacher has some peer interaction (students do not just work alone or with the teacher on their reading materials), the program is probably an *individualized reading program* and not the type of *independent study* described in this chapter.

Components

In addition to including many materials that may be used independently, teachers using the independent study approach usually schedule frequent individual conferences with the students in order to assess student progress as well as to assign new materials. Because much work is done independently, the ways in which instructions are given and records are kept are an important part of this approach. Often students are given individual assignment sheets that are placed in folders along with worksheets they use to complete reading exercises. The students read their assignments and progress accordingly. They check in with the teacher whenever they run out of assignments or need help.

Language Experience Approach

Definition of Terms

The language experience approach to teaching reading is applied most beneficially to middle and secondary school students whose reading development is severely retarded. Many teachers have found success in using this approach with middle, junior, and senior high school students who have not learned to read by other methods. In this approach, the experiential background of the students is used as the basis for the content of their reading materials. Their experiences and viewpoints are first written in their own words, and then they build their reading skills through reading practice on content that is already familiar to them.

Components

In order to use this approach effectively, the teacher must identify the language facility, interests, and background of each youngster and then plan instruction around these existing elements.

Spache and Spache (1973) suggest that the development of the language experience approach follow these five steps: (1) encourage learners to share their ideas and experiences; (2) help students clarify and summarize their ideas and experiences; (3) transcribe the learners' stories exactly as they dictate them, but with correct spelling; (4) encourage the youngsters to share

375

their written ideas with the whole class; and (5) design skill development and extension activities.

Sharing Experiences. Sharing ideas may be done in large-group discussions in which the teacher transcribes a story written by the entire class. Youngsters who have little to say may benefit from listening to the experiences of their peers. Students may be asked to meet in small groups and discuss specific issues. If the teacher does not meet with the group and the members of the group do not know how to write, the teacher may ask them to tape their discussion for later transcription. Often youngsters discuss topics more freely when the teacher is not present. A teacher may also meet with an individual student and transcribe portions of the subsequent discussion for use as reading materials for the student.

The teacher can usually stimulate adolescents to react to topics such as movies, television, job opportunities, drugs, values, dating, war, racial issues, pollution, and the energy crisis.

Clarifying Ideas and Transcribing Thoughts. The teacher can help the students clarify their thoughts by recording key words and making an outline of the topic. This helps youngsters to identify main ideas and important details and to organize their thinking when learning to write. They begin to realize that reading material is more than talk written down and that writing is easier to understand when authors summarize their thoughts and use only the ideas necessary to deliver the message.

Teacher-Transcribed Stories: The teacher can help youngsters transfer their experiences into reading skills by the way in which he transcribes their stories. For example, if he first jots down key words, he is helping the students see how main ideas are formed. If he makes an outline before he writes, he is helping them see the relationships between ideas. The awareness of main ideas, the relationships between ideas, and the effect upon the content of the order in which they occur are needed by the youngster in order to apply such comprehension skills as identifying cause-effect relationships and drawing conclusions.

Though the teacher uses correct spelling, he does not attempt to control vocabulary, sentence length, or dialectal or syntactical patterns.

Student-Transcribed Narrations: Youngsters also need to learn to write their own narrations. The means by which this is done varies according to the reading and writing abilities of the youngsters. A student who is unable to write at all may dictate a narration into a tape recorder. A small group of youngsters who are unable to write may tape record their narrations or have a peer who is a good reader transcribe their narrations for them.

Sharing Ideas with the Class. Since youngsters build their own experiences by communicating with one another, they should share both the materials they have written and their ideas for further writing. The sharing of written ideas adds to the relevancy of writing down one's ideas. If the material the student writes is to be read by a peer, it becomes more meaningful to him because he must communicate his thoughts. It must be written so that it may be understood. (E.g., The writer must use standard spelling and must eliminate extraneous ideas that may interfere with the reader's comprehension.)

376

Ideas can be effectively shared through silent reading by distributing copies of student's stories, and through oral reading by having the "author" read his story to a small or large group of peers.

Designing Skill Development and Extension Activities. Essential to the success of a language experience program is a record-keeping system by which students keep track of the words they know. This enables the teacher to develop activities to extend the students' reading skills by using these known words. Students usually keep a notebook in which both the stories they have transcribed for themselves and the stories the teacher has transcribed are kept. In addition, students usually keep a vocabulary list of all the words they know. The words may be placed on index cards and kept in a file box so that the students may rearrange them in any order they wish. For example, if using them to practice structural analysis, the student might pull out only words with the prefixes, *re*, *dis*, and *un*. It is important to note that *only* teacher-transcribed words are on this list. Because this list and the teacher-transcribed stories are the student's personal resource file for functional spelling, the words that are included must be spelled correctly.

Materials. It is important to note at this point that sources of reading materials other than the students' own stories are an integral part of this approach. In order to expand their core of words and their experiences, books and materials on topics of interest to adolescents should be made available. If students are unable to read them independently, they may listen as the teacher, a tape recorder, or a peer orally conveys the contents of material to them.

Eclectic Approach

Definition of Terms

Though it is possible to use any of the previously described approaches in isolation, teachers commonly use a combination of methods in order to meet the reading needs of all students. Such an approach is called eclectic.

Components

A program that is eclectic might use language experience components with the poorest readers, an independent study program with readers who are on grade level, and an individualized approach with readers who are above grade level. Further, portions of a comprehensive textbook might be presented in a large-group discussion in order to introduce a certain skill needed by all the students.

Diagnostic-Prescriptive Technique

Definition

For an extensive discussion of this technique, see Chapter 9 of this text.

In essence, the diagnostic-prescriptive approach is merely a management system to assure the teacher that students are being taught all the reading skills they need. It centers around a scope and sequence of reading skills and requires that the teacher proceed through the following sequence of steps for each student:

1. Ascertain each student's instructional level.
2. Delineate skills in which the student should be competent.
3. Pre-assess to determine the skills in which the student is not yet competent.
4. Give instruction in the skills in which the student is not yet proficient.
5. Post-assess after instruction to determine whether the student has mastered the skills he has been taught.
6. Administer additional instruction until the student does become competent in the needed skills.

Relationship Between Diagnostic-Prescriptive Technique and Other Approaches to Teaching Reading. The reading textbook approach, the individualized approach, the language experience approach, the independent study approach, and the eclectic approach are all structures that may be presented in a diagnostic-prescriptive manner. That is, the teacher who wants a means to correlate the diverse needs of students reflected in an individualized or language experience approach could use a diagnostic-prescriptive technique to approach the skills in a systematic manner. Furthermore, though the reading textbook approach frequently contains all the components needed for it to be a diagnostic-prescriptive technique, unless it is used by the teacher according to the six-step sequence described previously, it would not be considered a diagnostic-prescriptive technique. In other words, regardless of the instructional approach chosen, to teach in a diagnostic-prescriptive manner, the reading teacher should always (1) determine youngsters' reading levels and specific skill requirements so that they are working with materials appropriate to their needs, (2) give them reading materials and skill-building exercises geared to those reading needs, and (3) continuously assess their progress so that when new skills are needed or previously presented skills are mastered, instruction can be varied accordingly.

The Role of Supplementary Reading Materials

Regardless of the school organization or the classroom organization used by the teacher, unless students are motivated they will not read. Perhaps one of the best ways to help students practice their reading skills and learn content area subject matter at the same time is to provide them with supplementary, nontext materials that they may read for enjoyment.

Some teachers encourage supplementary reading through extrinsic means, such as giving students points toward higher grades for each book they read. However, much can be done by all content area teachers to motivate students in an intrinsic manner to read supplementary, nontext materials concerned with their content areas.

Teachers of all content areas may take advantage of adolescent growth patterns, existing nontext materials (see Chapter 11), and current events in order to make reading in their content areas more enjoyable for their students. For example, the biology teacher might cut out and place on the bulletin board an article on implanting an artificial kidney in the human body. She might then encourage discussion on how the artificial kidney would have to be constructed if it were to function like a natural human kidney. A list of books available on an appropriate reading level for school students could be provided so that students could pursue the discussion topic if they so desired.

The math teacher might pose questions about the use of hand calculators and their effect upon the ability of future generations to work mathematical problems by hand. He could make available to the students books such as *Computers* by Richard B. Rush, which explains how computers were developed, how they work, and how they affect humans now and potentially in the future.

The social studies teacher could keep track of the currently popular movies. If a movie like *Becket* were popular, discussion on the movie in class could stimulate youngsters to read more about English history in order to find out what really happened to Becket while he was archbishop of Canterbury. The availability of novels in historically accurate settings as well as nonfiction on the topic could quench their momentary curiosity and also extend it into a more in-depth pursuit of the topic.

In a like fashion, all content area teachers could encourage students to read supplementary materials about their content areas.

Provide for a Creative Means of Book Sharing

Another procedure for stimulating interest in supplementary reading is to establish a means by which the students can share books or react creatively to what they read. Assigning traditional book reports on supplementary reading can destroy some of the interest the teacher has encouraged in the students to read books related to the content area. Instead, the teacher should try to allow each student the opportunity to respond to a book in an individualized manner and should avoid assigning standardized book reports. The teacher can encourage creative and interpretative reporting through a variety of means. For example, if a student reads the book *Becket* as well as sees the movie *Becket*, he might be asked to tell the class how the movie distorted or supported the information presented in the book.

Other creative sharing could be accomplished by having students select one of the following activities:

379

1. Construct a mobile or collage about the book.
2. Make a map of the location and illustrate key points about the topic read.
3. Report to the teacher in an individual conference.
4. Conduct a panel discussion.
5. Draw a picture of an important object or character.
6. Construct a book jacket.
7. Tape-record a dramatization of the book as a radio or television show.
8. Dress up as a character and tell about one event.
9. Pretend to be a radio or television interviewer and interview one of the main characters.
10. Retell the story in poetry or song.
11. Assume the identity of the main character but pretend to be ten years older and tell about your life.
12. Design a television or radio commercial in which you tell the high points of the book in an effort to sell it.

Many more such activities could be used to extend means by which books are usually reported upon by students. Some of these activities lend themselves better to language arts and social studies than to the other content areas, and some of them are more appropriate for one age group than for another. However, most of the activities can be used by any content area teacher with any age group. For example, a student good in biology might read *The Double Helix* by James D. Watson, which delineates steps in the isolation of DNA. His report on the book might consist of a mobile that represents the components of DNA. A geometry student might read *String, Straightedge and Shadow* by Julia E. Diggins, which concerns the development of geometry. To report on this book, the student might dress up as Euclid and give the class an overview of the important events in the history of geometry.

Criteria for Evaluating the Success of the Supplementary Reading Program

The following factors should be considered in evaluating the success of a supplementary reading program: (1) the number of supplementary books students choose to read, (2) the growth the students demonstrate in the quality of supplementary literature they select to read, (3) the enjoyment youngsters experience when reading, (4) the effect that the supplementary reading has upon the student's attitude toward reading in general and toward content area reading in particular, (5) the information students accumulate, (6) the growth in the length of time students spend reading at one sitting, and (7) the effect the reading has on the student's achievement in the content area.

Management Techniques for Teaching All Youngsters

Perhaps one of the most difficult tasks for the teacher is to organize instruction within the classroom so that the needs of all students are met. This organizational task might be termed *management* and includes (1) grouping for reading and achievement levels, specific skill needs, or interests, (2) keeping records and (3) arranging the physical aspects of the classroom.

Grouping for Reading Achievement, Needs, and Interests

Students may learn by themselves, in a group with one other person, in a small group of three or more, or in a large group. Grouping is one way that a teacher may make more efficient use of his time and materials. Grouping also allows for peer interaction, which is particularly important to the developmental needs of the adolescent (see Chapter 11). Groups vary in purpose and may be designated as reading achievement level groups, needs groups, or interest groups. Each of these is discussed below in the context of approaches used by specific teachers.

Achievement Level Groups. Youngsters who read on or nearly on the same level may be grouped together for instructional purposes. The way in which they are grouped depends on the approach used by the classroom teacher. For example, Mr. Lentz discovered that he had a range of reading levels from grade five to grade twelve in his American history class. Therefore, he selected three different history texts that contained basically the same information. One was written on the fifth grade level, one on the seventh grade level, and one on the eleventh grade level. He made lesson plans so that he taught the material in each book in the form of a "directed reading lesson" (see Chapter 7). He developed differentiated guided reading sheets to help his students read the materials (see Chapter 8). Then he arranged students in his history class into three groups, one for each of the basic texts.

Interachievement-Level Group Sharing. Interachievement-level grouping is desirable. First, youngsters can learn a tremendous amount from each other. Second, interachievement-level grouping helps alleviate the stigma that often accompanies ability-type grouping. By changing group membership frequently, students do not get labeled as readily as they would if they were always in the "top" group or always in the "bottom" group.

Needs Groups. Needs groups are formed when more than one youngster needs help on the same reading skill. For example, Mrs. Fitzpen discovered that neither Ruth, who read on the fifth grade level, nor Paul, who read on the eighth grade level, nor Rick, who read on the twelfth grade level, could interpret the graphs found in their ninth grade algebra book. Therefore Mrs. Fitzpen designed a lesson for these three students in which they were taught to use graphs.

Interest Groups. Often teachers find that students are interested in reading about the same topics even though they are reading different materials on different achievement levels. For example, one of Mr. Morphew's biology students, Doug, read at fourth grade level and another, Carol, at college level. However, both youngsters were extremely interested in the human heart. Therefore, Mr. Morphew grouped Carol and Doug in a project in which they investigated the cause of heart failure. Carol did most of the library research, while Doug used a tape recorder to interview several local heart specialists.

In addition, Doug used a laboratory model of the human heart to illustrate to the class what went wrong when people had heart attacks.

Keeping Records

Record keeping is one of the teacher's most difficult tasks. The record-keeping charts discussed in Chapter 9 of this text lend themselves well to keeping track of reading skills needed by students in any reading program. However, the classroom teacher also needs to keep records of student interests, past academic achievements, and emotional and psychological needs. The teacher who is aware of these needs can locate books that not only will interest the youngsters but that can help them in their adjustment to maturity. Another valuable record is that of learning style. Some youngsters learn best by listening, some by seeing, and others by writing; some learn best alone and others learn best with assorted numbers of other people. Hence, assignments that take these factors into consideration can facilitate a youngster's learning.

Another type of record keeping is that done by the students themselves. If done correctly, this record-keeping system allows students to visually assess their own progress and to keep track of the materials they should complete. One of the most common types of student records is based on the contract system. In this system, students are given several choices of materials and told to self-pace themselves through the materials. The following procedure is often practiced by the teacher who uses contracts: (1) Students are given individualized folders in which all their lessons and assignments are kept. (2) The teacher and student meet to discuss the choices of assignments and what kinds of things the student must do to make the grade contracted for. An "A" contract may require that more exercises or more sophisticated exercises be completed than a "B" contract, and so forth. (3) Each student is given a separate contract based on his reading skills and reading needs. For example, the youngster reading on fourth grade level would be given a different choice of activities than the youngster reading on ninth grade level. (4) The teacher periodically goes through each student's folder to see if the student has completed the contracted number of assignments; and when alternative assignments were given on the same skill the teacher checks to see which alternatives the student selected. If exercises are done in a sloppy manner or incorrectly, the teacher may write a note and place it in the student's folder asking the student to redo the exercise. Likewise, if the student has done a particularly good job, the teacher may compliment the student and tell him to stop working on a particular skill and to begin work on another skill area.

Arranging the Physical Aspects of the Classroom

Some activities may be completed equally as well in groups or independently. In either case, the physical structure of the classroom can facilitate aspects of lessons.

Learning Center. Reinforcement activities can frequently be set up in *learning centers* around the room. In such a situation, the teacher allows students a certain number of minutes each day to participate in activities located in a center. Activities include free reading; playing reinforcement games independently or with peers; working independently in programmed materials, kits, or work sheets; working with a task group researching a particular topic; working in a needs group practicing particular reading skills; or working in an interest group sharing books that have been read. In his text, *Explorations in the Teaching of Secondary English*, Stephen Judy (1974), discusses many practical ways in which the classroom may be arranged in order to provide a stimulating environment for learning. Figure 12.1 shows several classroom floor plans that Dr. Judy has found to be effective with secondary school students.

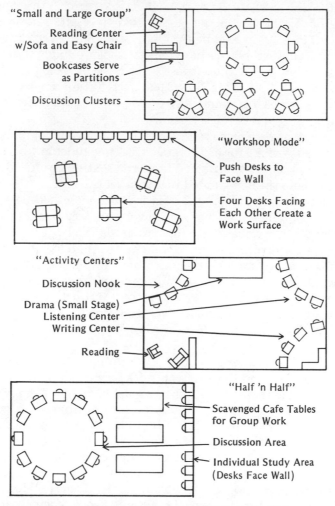

Fig. 1 "Classroom Floor Plans" Illustrated by David Kirkpatrick (p. 172) in *Explorations in The Teaching of Secondary English* by Stephen N. Judy (Harper & Row, 1974). Used with permission.

Figure 12.1   Classroom Floor Plans

383

Developing a Reading Program in a Variety of Ways

In order to clarify the relationships among materials, classroom organization, and school organization, various approaches to teaching reading will be illustrated.

Mr. Evans's Reading Textbook Approach to a Required Reading Course

Mr. Evans taught an eighth grade required reading course in which students in his class spent an hour a day throughout the entire school year in reading instruction. When he tested his students in September, he found that he had among his students a nonreader and a college level reader. Since the range in reading levels spanned thirteen years, he decided to group the youngsters into three basic groups: those who read above grade level, those who read on grade level, and those who read below grade level. Mr. Evans knew that three was not a magic number, but his experiential background and his own individual needs made him decide to use these three basic groups.

Mr. Evans's Materials. Since Mr. Evans had such a wide range of reading levels, he decided to use three different types of comprehensive instructional materials (see Chapter 11 for more description).

1. The group that read close to grade level or above would be assigned a basal reader series written for eighth graders. The students who read on the seventh grade level would be assigned the same text but watched carefully and given extra help through guided reading sheets.

2. The group that read on grade levels five and six would be assigned an anthology that contained high-interest, low-vocabulary selections written for adolescents who read on the fifth and sixth grade levels. The anthology would be accompanied by a correlated, comprehensive skill development program.

3. The group that contained the nonreader as well as those who read through grade four would be assigned materials from a unit that contained materials written for adolescents who read on the second through fourth grade levels. Those who read below second grade level would be given audiotapes of the materials written on second grade level so they could follow along in that material.

It should also be noted, at this point, that though Mr. Evans used the basal reader, the anthology, and the unit as his primary teaching tools, they were not his only teaching tools. He also had available many of the materials discussed in Chapter 11 of this text. Therefore, in addition to assigning students materials produced by the basal, the anthology, or the unit, he assigned students materials on their reading levels from assorted kits, games, workbooks, and programmed materials. He also had a large classroom library to provide students with the opportunity to do much nontext type reading.

Mr. Evans's Achievement Level Groups. Though Mr. Evans divided his class by achievement level into three groups, he did not expect each student to remain in the same group for the entire year. Some of those reading just below grade level would move to the on-grade level group as their reading skills improved or as review of skills they needed improved their over-all reading achievement.

Since Mr. Evans wanted to use different materials with each of the three groups, he developed an organizational system that would help him do so. However, when he began to plan instruction, he knew that he wanted to spend some time each day with each group. Furthermore, he wanted to make certain that each group had the opportunity to "read" each day. Mr. Evans did not consider doing work sheets or group discussions as "reading." He knew that in order to improve reading skills as well as to enjoy reading, his pupils had to actually confront the pages of print in a meaningful, relevant context. To Mr. Evans, "reading" meant allowing the youngsters to react to the stories in the reader, the supplementary books, or other nontext reading materials.

When Mr. Evans closely examined the five-step directed reading lesson format (see Chapter 7), he realized that some of the steps did not require his presence. While he felt it important that he be with a group in order to present new words and motivate them to read the story, he didn't feel his presence was necessary when they began to read silently. Because he knew oral reading and group discussion revealed a lot about each youngster's word recognition and comprehension skills, he felt he would have to be with a group when they were working on step 36. Depending on the skill or activity being planned, he might or might not need to be with the youngsters when they were completing step 4, follow-up, and step 5, extension. He knew that if he were well organized he could set up a schedule for their lessons that would allow him to be with a group when they were working on a step during which he was needed. Figure 12.2 shows the organizational format he designed in order to reach each group each day as well as a list of suggestions he wrote out for himself to make certain that he was teaching the reading lessons in the best possible manner.

Mr. Evans knew that he had only one hour a day to work with the achievement level groups. In order to work with each group each day, this hour was divided into fifteen-minute segments. At the end of each fifteen-minute period, each group worked with a new skill and Mr. Evans went to work with another group. The symbol T by the step in Figure 12.2 indicates that the teacher is almost always present at that step; the symbol T/N means that the teacher does not necessarily have to be there to assure successful completion of the step.

Mr. Evans's weekly schedule is shown in Figure 12.3.

By looking at Figure 12.3 it can be seen that Mr. Evans worked with the three achievement level groups four days a week. Though he asked all the students in each group to read some stories in common, their follow-up and extension activities varied with the individual. For example, the students who read well above grade level in the basal group were not required to complete all the workbook exercises but were assigned materials in a text that focused upon increasing critical reading and study skills. Specifically, on Wednesday during the third, fifteen-minute time segment, while the remainder of the basal group was working with Mr. Evans on learning and practicing the new skill of identifying propaganda (4a and b), the students who read well above grade level and already knew the skill were working in a workbook that stressed the skills of skimming and scanning. Likewise, some of the poorest readers in the unit group were assigned audiotaped skill-building activities rather than being assigned activities that were originally designed to accompany the unit.

ORGANIZATIONAL FORMAT

1. Preparation
   - T   a. Motivation
   - T   b. New words
   - T   c. Concept development

2. T/N   Silent reading

3. Oral reading and discussion
   - T/N   a. Interpretation and sharing
   - T   b. Discussion

4. Follow-up
   - T   a. Learn a new skill
   - T/N   b. Practice a new skill—the skill just learned in step 4a
   - T/N   c. Practice an old skill—a skill formerly learned

5. Extension
   - T/N   a. Supplementary reading
   - T/N   b. Dramatization
   - T/N   c. Rereading for a different purpose
   - T/N   d. Creative activities

Key: T = Teacher present, T/N = Teacher may or may not be present.

Teaching Suggestions for Planning for Each Group

a. Steps 1 and 2 should be completed the same day.
b. Step 3a can be completed by reading to another student or onto a tape.
c. Steps 1, 2, and 3 should be included in the same week.
d. Step 4a should be completed before step 4b is introduced.
e. Steps 4a and 4b should be completed the same day.
f. Step 4 may sometimes be completed out of sequence.
g. Steps 5a–5d may be completed between steps 1 through 5. (Students do not have to go through all the steps to get to 5a–5d.)
h. Some free reading (may or may not be 5a) should be included each week.
i. Steps 5b, 5c, and 5d do not have to be included with each directed reading lesson.
j. Step 3b (discussion) should be completed before step 5c (rereading for a different purpose) is introduced.
k. Each group should do some reading each day. (Steps 2, 5a, 5b, 5c, and sometimes 5d include activities classified as reading.)
l. The teacher should work with each group each day.

Figure 12.2   Organizational Format and Teaching Suggestions

		Basal Group	Anthology Group	Unit Group
MON	15 min. 15 min. 15 min. 15 min.	T1 (a, b, c) 2 3 (a) Intergroup activities	5 (c) T1 (a, b, c) 2 Intergroup activities	5 (a) 5 (d) T3 (b) Intergroup activities
TUES	15 min. 15 min. 15 min. 15 min.	5 (d) T3 (b) 5 (c) Intergroup activities	3 (a) 5 (d, b) T3 (b) Intergroup activities	T1 (a, b, c) 2 5 (b) Intergroup activities
WED	15 min. 15 min. 15 min. 15 min.	5 (a) 3 (a) T4 (a, b) Intergroup activities	T4 (a) 4 (b) 5 (a) Intergroup activities	3 (a) T3 (b) 5 (a) Intergroup activities
THUR	15 min. 15 min. 15 min. 15 min.	T1 (a, b, c) 2 4 (c) Intergroup activities	5 (a) T1 (a, b, c) 2 Intergroup activities	5 (c) 5 (d) T4 (a, b) Intergroup activities
FRI	15 min. 15 min. 15 min. 15 min.	Free reading Free reading Free reading Intergroup activities	Free reading Free reading Free reading Intergroup activities	Free reading Free reading Free reading Intergroup activities

Key:

1. Preparation
   a. Motivation
   b. New words
   c. Concept development
2. Silent reading
3. Oral reading and discussion
   a. Interpretation and sharing
   b. Discussion

4. Follow-up
   a. Learn a new skill
   b. Practice a new skill
   c. Practice an old skill
5. Extension
   a. Supplementary reading
   b. Dramatization
   c. Rereading for a different purpose
   d. Creative activities

T = Teacher present

Figure 12.3   Mr. Evans's Weekly Schedule

Mr. Evans's Needs Groups. By looking at Figure 12.3 one can tell that Mr. Evans also included needs groups in his program. Though step 4c, *practice an old skill*, could be interpreted in terms of a specific skill that the students' core material (i.e., basal, unit, anthology) had introduced previously and was reinforcing, it also could apply to any skill the youngsters had not adequately learned. For example, when teaching his class, Mr. Evans discovered that one member from the basal group, three members from the anthology group, and two members from the unit group did not know the skill of discriminating fact from opinion. Therefore, Mr. Evans developed a lesson that used the cartoon section of the paper, an editorial, and a series of newspaper advertisements to teach the skill. On Tuesday, during the time allotted for intergroup sharing and free reading, he gathered together the six youngsters and presented the lesson on discriminating fact from opinion. Then he allowed each student some time during that same time period to practice that skill in materials appropriate to their reading levels.

Mr. Evans's Interest Groups. Mr. Evans allowed his students at least an hour a week for free reading. He felt that his students needed time to practice reading in a pleasurable, personally relevant manner. Many of the students read books on similar topics. Mr. Evans kept careful track of the free reading books selected by each youngster and often assigned projects to meet the interests of a specific group of students. For example, one group of youngsters seemed particularly interested in learning more about drugs. Mr. Evans located a literature unit on drugs. This unit was designed to reinforce reading skills through providing high-interest materials written on the fourth through sixth grade levels. In addition to the materials that accompanied the unit, Mr. Evans gathered together pamphlets from local drug prevention agencies to expand the contents of the unit. Some of the materials were written for adults who were functionally illiterate and, therefore, could be read by students who read on the second and third grade levels. Other materials on drugs which he located were quite sophisticated and were to be used by the most able readers in the group. Since the unit contained a teacher's manual with explicit teaching directions, Mr. Evans, with the aid of the suggestions for teaching and expanding ideas within the unit, was able to develop guided reading sheets on several different reading levels. The "drug" group was then given time to meet on Mondays, Wednesdays, and Thursdays during the time allotted for intergroup sharing.

Teacher Substitutes to Facilitate Groups. Though Mr. Evans knew that it was best for him to be with all groups during the steps that he had marked with a *T*, he learned over the years that there were teacher substitutes that he could utilize in order to help him be in "two places at the same time." Some of his substitutes were supplementary materials, tape recorders, and student group leaders. To illustrate, one of the three textbook series he used had developed coordinated filmstrips and records to introduce many of their stories. Mr. Evans was able to motivate the youngsters and introduce them to new words and concepts with the aid of the audiovisual material provided, thereby reducing his actual time with the group because he did not have to be present during the filmstrip presentation. Nevertheless, he was quite careful to make certain that he motivated the students to watch the filmstrip and that he conducted follow-up activities after the presentation before asking the students to proceed to the silent reading step.

Another useful substitute was the tape recorder. He discovered that if he taped instructions, the youngsters became self-directed. They would listen to the tape and follow the oral instructions without even being told to do so. He found the tape recorder to be particularly useful with the steps during which his presence was not essential. He especially liked to ask his students

388

to practice old skills through tape-recorded directions. The step, *practicing old skills* lent itself well to that approach because the youngsters were already somewhat familiar with the skills and enjoyed the motivating introduction to the skill-building lesson, which Mr. Evans always utilized.

The youngsters themselves were probably the most useful substitutes he had. He tried to give each youngster a chance to be group leader and found the leaders to be more strict than he was in terms of demanding that the exact directions and procedures be followed on the exercises. (See Chapter 8 for more information on the use of students as teacher substitutes.)

Mr. Cilak's Individualized Reading Program in a Required Reading Course

Mr. Cilak taught a class in developmental reading required of all ninth graders, in which the reading levels ranged from nonreader to college level. To accommodate the wide range of reading levels, Mr. Cilak decided to use an individualized approach to teaching reading. Since his class met for an hour a day, five days a week, he arranged his instruction so that he could have a ten-minute conference with each student at least once every two weeks.

Figure 12.4 shows how he scheduled sixteen students in individual conferences during a one-week time period. He divided his class period into ten-minute segments. On Monday, Tuesday, Wednesday, and Thursday, the first twenty minutes were spent by Mr. Cilak in activities related to groups of students. The last forty minutes were spent in individual conferences with four different students.

Looking at Figure 12.4, it can be seen that on Monday Mr. Cilak spent the first ten minutes reading a story aloud to his students. The book, *Tuned Out* by Maia Wojciechowska, was selected because he felt that it would interest the students and that they would be motivated to finish it if he began it for them. After ten minutes of oral reading, he checked individual folders while students who wanted to continue reading *Tuned Out* picked up one of the multiple copies he had made available and read it on their own. Those who did not wish to read *Tuned Out* at that time continued to read their own previously self-selected books.

Mr. Cilak's Individual Conferences. Mr. Cilak's individual conferences were the heart of his skill development program. Each time a youngster sat with him, Mr. Cilak (1) assessed what skills he needed, (2) helped him select a book, (3) gave him instruction on a needed skill, (4) gave him further assignments for skill instruction, (5) post-assessed him on a needed skill to see if he had learned the skill, (6) assessed his interests, or (7) helped him decide how he wanted to share his book with others.

Before Mr. Cilak held his individual conference with any of his students, he determined to pre-assess each member of the class on the comprehension skill of making inferences, the study skill of scanning, and the vocabulary skill of interpreting affixes. Mr. Cilak made up questions to assess each of these skills and then varied the questions to suit the specific book chosen by the student. Mark had chosen the book, *The Pigman* by Paul Zindel, a tale

389

	Mr. Cilak	Students
M O N	10 min. Motivate by reading story 10 min. Check individual folders 10 min. Individual conference—Mark 10 min. Individual conference—Susan 10 min. Individual conference—Phil 10 min. Individual conference—Nancy	Listen to Mr. Cilak Read stories Skill groups, individual skill work, free reading Skill groups, individual skill work, free reading Skill groups, individual skill work, free reading Skill groups, individual skill work, free reading
T U E S	10 min. Large group instruction on skimming 10 min. Rotate from group to individuals to assess work 10 min. Individual conference—Fred 10 min. Individual conference—Georgia 10 min. Individual conference—Bob 10 min. Individual conference—Christy	Listen to Mr. Cilak Individual and group activities on skimming Interest groups, free reading Interest groups, free reading Needs groups, free reading Needs groups, free reading
W E D	10 min. Small group instruction on inferences (5 students) 10 min. Small group instruction on morphemes (5 students) 10 min. Individual conference—Paul 10 min. Individual conference—David 10 min. Individual conference—Betty 10 min. Individual conference—Emmy	Read, skill exercises, free reading Read, skill exercises, free reading Needs groups, free reading Needs groups, free reading Needs groups, free reading Interest groups, free reading
T H U R	10 min. Small group instruction on skimming (5 students) 10 min. Rotate from group to group 10 min. Individual conference—Greta 10 min. Individual conference—Gene 10 min. Individual conference—Cindy 10 min. Individual conference—Gary	Skill groups, individual skill work, free reading Skill groups, individual skill work, free reading Interest groups Interest groups Interest groups Interest groups
F R I	10 min. Large-group book sharing 10 min. Large-group book sharing 10 min. Move from group to group 10 min. Move from group to group 10 min. Move from group to group 10 min. Move from group to group	Listen and share Listen and share Small-group book sharing Small-group book sharing Small-group book sharing Regroup for interest groups

Figure 12.4 Mr. Cilak's Grouping Chart

of a teenage girl and a teenage boy who take turns telling about their relationship with lonely old Mr. Pignatti as they seek to determine if they were responsible for his death. Mr. Cilak used the following questions to pre-assess Mark's reading skills.

Pre-Assessment Questions for Making Inferences

1. Look at the sentence on page 112 in which John refers to a "transylvanian-looking nurse" and tell me how you think John felt about the hospital? (Answer: Reference to Dracula theme would reflect his feeling as negative. Mark answered incorrectly.)

390

2. How can you tell that John dislikes Norton? (Answer: John says only negative things about Norton. Mark didn't know the answer.)
3. On page 140 of your book Mr. Pignatti is crying. Why do you suppose this is so? (Answer: Probably because he believes Lorraine and John were just using him and had no real fondness of him. Mark answered incorrectly.)

Since Mark answered the three pre-assessment questions incorrectly, he obviously needed practice in this skill.

Pre-Assessment Questions for Scanning
1. Can you find the part in the book in which Lorraine says, "We murdered him"? (Answer: The student should begin toward the back of the book and then turn pages rapidly to find the answer. Mark did this correctly.)
2. Can you locate at least three statements made by Lorraine that tell us something about her? (Answer: The student should run eyes rapidly down the pages, stopping only when he locates statements made by Lorraine. Mark did this correctly.)
3. Can you locate at least three words that contain the Latin prefix *re*? (Answer: Student should run his eyes down the page, stopping only when he locates words with the *re* prefix. Mark located *repress*, page 13; *replace*, page 31; *realist*, page 96; and *refreshments*, page 99. Because three of the four contain the Latin prefix *re* the teacher determined he knew the skill of scanning for the prefix *re*.)

Because Mark was able to scan to find a given sentence, quotations, and the prefix *re*, Mr. Cilak decided that Mark knew the skill of scanning.

Pre-Assessment Questions for Interpreting Affixes
1. Can you tell me the meanings of the prefix *re* and also the meaning of the three words with the prefix *re* that you located? (Answer: Student should respond that *re* means *back* or *again*, *replace* means *put back*, *repress* means *hold back*, and *refreshments* means *that which makes fresh again*. Mark knew the answers.)
2. Can you tell me the meanings of the prefixes *com* or *con* and the words, *commemorative*, page 9; *compassion*, page 16; and *congealing*, page 118? (Answer: Student should reply that *com* and *con* are Latin prefixes meaning *with* or *together*, that *commemorative* means *with the memory of*, *compassion* means *with passion*, and *congealing* means *gelling together*. Mark answered correctly.)
3. Can you tell me the meaning of the prefix *dis* and the words *disinfectant*, page 23; *discomfort*, page 31; and *dismember*, page 40? (Answer: Student should reply that *dis* is a Latin prefix meaning *apart* or *away*, *disinfectant* means *away from infection*, *discomfort* means *away from comfort*, and *dismember* means *apart from members* or *to remove the limbs of the body*. Mark knew the answers.)

Because Mark answered the pre-assessment questions on *re, com, con,* and *dis* accurately, he obviously needed no practice in this skill.

During the next forty minutes, Mr. Cilak had individual conferences with four different students. While he was in the individual conferences, the remainder of the students followed instructions that had been given to them in individual folders. Individual student assignments included a variety of activities such as (1) individual skill work with a kit, work sheets, programmed material, or guided reading sheets geared to their self-selected book; (2) group skill work through playing a game with peers, work sheets completed in pairs, pairs of students working together researching a topic of mutual interest, small groups of students working together on a task related to a topic that each had read about in his self-selected book, and book sharing among students who had read books of about the same reading level; and (3) free reading in self-selected materials.

Mr. Cilak's Materials. Mr. Cilak based his instruction around a plethora of materials selected because they appealed to a wide range of adolescent interests. He used components from basal reader series, units, and anthologies if they contained materials that he thought his students would read.

He also had a massive amount of skill-building materials in his classroom. After individual conferences with youngsters, he would assign a series of skill-building materials that focused on the skills needed by the specific youngster. Whenever possible, he made up guided reading sheets that stressed the needed skill in the books being read by the youngster. For example, Mark was reading *The Pigman* by Paul Zindel and needed practice with the skill of making inferences. Therefore Mr. Cilak placed an assignment sheet inside Mark's individual folder that instructed him to read *The Pigman* according to directions on the enclosed guided reading sheet. The guided reading sheet contained a short definition of inferences and then pointed out inferences, made from action, conversation, and description, that Mark was to pay particular attention to as he read the book. In addition to reading *The Pigman* with the help of the guided reading sheet, Mark was given the following assignment sheet and told to complete his guided reading sheet as well as four out of six of the assignments in category I, and one out of three assignments in category II before his next individual conference.

Category I contained (1) an audiotape and work sheet exercise on inferences found in the *Listen and Read* series published by EDL; (2) a basal reader work sheet exercise on the eighth grade level dealing with inferences; (3) an exercise from a kit titled *Tactics II*, published by Scott, Foresman, which focused on inferences; (4) an audiotape and work sheet correlated with a selection from the *New Advanced Reading Skill Builders*, which focused on making inferences; (5) a group activity in which the student was to select one other peer who also needed the skill of inferences and who had read *The Pigman*. They were to sit together with a list of statements made by the major characters and then construct inferences that could be made about the characters from their own statements; (6) a group activity in which the student was to participate in a contest called Who Can Make the Most Inferences. The contest was to be completed by selecting a group of peers to work with who also needed the skill of making inferences. A current photograph from the daily paper was to be selected, and students would be given two minutes to make as many inferences as possible about the picture. The student who made the most correct inferences was allowed to choose the next picture from the newspaper. The contest was to continue until the class ran out of time.

Category II was to be started only after the student had completed the four activities chosen from category I. Then the student was to select one of the following three activities: (1) construct a crossword puzzle based on inferences made in *The Pigman*, (2) write a paragraph in which the student interprets at least three inferences located in *The Pigman*, (3) construct a collage made out of objects inferred but not directly stated in *The Pigman* (e.g., clothing worn by the main characters, furnishings of Mr. Pignatti's house not directly mentioned in the novel).

Mr. Cilak's Achievement Levels Groups. Usually Mr. Cilak only grouped his students by achievement level during book sharing sessions in which he wanted to assure himself that students would share books that were on the same reading level. The purpose for such a grouping was to interest students in books that were written at levels they could read. For example, *Dr. Zhivago* would not be readable to the student reading on third grade level. However, Mr. Cilak did have some interachievement-level book sharing on occasion because students could sometimes find books on a similar topic written at a level they could read. For example, after hearing about *Huckleberry Finn* from another student, one very weak reader found a third grade version he could read.

Mr. Cilak's Needs Groups. Whenever two or more students worked together on a specific skill, Mr. Cilak was using a needs group to make his teaching time more efficient. For example, when Mark chose a peer or group of peers to work with him on the skill of making inferences, he was in effect a member of a needs group.

Mr. Cilak's Interest Groups. Mr. Cilak utilized interest groups a great deal in his individualized approach. Whenever he noticed several students reading materials that had something in common, he tried to group the students together so they could share their books with each other in a meaningful manner. Reference to Figure 12.4 shows that interest groups met on Thursday, while Mr. Cilak was involved in individual conferences. For example, Mark was a member of the interest group that was made up of students who were all reading books that concerned the theme of "death." The members of the group spanned a wide range of reading levels and included the following students: Mark, at the ninth grade level, who was reading *The Pigman* by Paul Zindel; Susan, on the eighth grade level, reading *Death Be Not Proud* by John Gunther; Phil, on the sixth grade level, reading the *Three-Legged Race* by Charles P. Crawford; and Nancy, on the twelfth grade level, reading *Death Is a Noun* by John Langone. They shared their books with each other and also used guided reading sheets constructed by Mr. Cilak to look for various aspects of death in their own individual books. Each was asked different questions about why and how death was faced by the characters they read about, and what insight into human behavior the student gained from reading that particular selection.

For example, the guided reading sheet used by Mark with his book *The Pigman* not only stressed that he look for ways in which the various characters reacted to death but also helped him reinforce the needed reading skill

Making Inferences. Some of the questions were

1. John goes to a cemetery to drink. What sort of inferences can you make about the foreshadowing of a death that is to come? (page 15)
2. What is one of John's chief reasons for going to the cemetery? (page 65)
3. What sort of inferences can you make about his visit there? (page 65)

Mr. Cilak's Independent Study Approach to an Elective Reading Course

Mr. Cilak also taught an elective course in developmental reading, which consisted of students who had no particular problem with their reading but wanted to improve their reading efficiency. With this class he decided to use an independent study approach. As such, his students rarely worked in skills or needs groups but rather were assigned individual tasks according to the results of Mr. Cilak's testing. However he did begin the class each day with a large-group discussion on techniques for increasing reading efficiency and then allowed the students to practice their techniques in materials he individually helped them select. Most of the students used mechanical pacers to push themselves to read faster, as well as timed reading passages, which they read without the help of any mechanical device. The students were given most of their directions through an assignment sheet placed in their individual folders, which they completed at their own pace. Though Mr. Cilak scheduled frequent individual conferences with each student, he discussed their progress on their skill-building materials and then assigned them new tasks. Some of the activities completed were as follows.

Carol was a student who read well but seemed to have difficulty adjusting rate to purpose and wanted to read everything at a slow, careful pace. Mr. Cilak assigned her materials of varying purposes, all of which she was to read with the help of the mechanical pacer. In addition, she was assigned some exercises that correlated with a second machine designed to help her learn the technique of scanning.

Bob was a student who read well but seemed to have difficulty determining what details were important and what details were not important when studying textbook materials. Mr. Cilak asked Bob to divide his time between reading textbooks with the help of a pacer and outlining the books according to a prepared format that Mr. Cilak had worked out for him. Mr. Cilak showed Bob how headings in textbooks could be used to interpret content area aspects that the author thought to be important. Bob was to use a timer and to practice surveying the textbook chapter for specific information about a topic according to the SQ3R technique (see Chapter 4 on study techniques for more information).

Susan was a student who read on grade level but had no idea how to take notes. Mr. Cilak recommended that Susan complete the work sheets that taught techniques for efficient note-taking and that were contained in a commercially prepared kit.

Mr. Cilak's Language Experience Approach in a Corrective Reading Course

Mr. Cilak also taught a course in corrective reading, which was required of all students enrolled in the senior high division of LaSalle who were reading two or more years below grade level. These youngsters, who were referred to Mr. Cilak on the basis of counselor recommendation, varied in reading levels from grades one to ten and in ages from fourteen to nineteen years. When they entered his class in September, Mr. Cilak gave each student an individual test and then assigned instruction accordingly.

All of the students reading on the first and second grade levels were grouped together for instruction in the language experience approach. Mr. Cilak usually encouraged writing about events that were currently occurring in the school. For example, when one of the students was suspended because he violated the dress code, the group wrote out their feelings about the code. The students also wrote narratives on their own. If they could not write well enough to express themselves in print, Mr. Cilak let them dictate into a tape recorder.

Mr. Cilak's Eclectic Approach in a Corrective Reading Course

Mr. Cilak's corrective reading class described previously, ranged ten years in reading level, therefore the language experience approach was not Mr. Cilak's only teaching method. He used a variety of approaches, which included the comprehensive textbook, individualized and independent study, as well as the language experience approach.

Since the remainder of the students in Mr. Cilak's class were above the grade two reading level, he used approaches other than the language experience approach with them. All the students reading on the third and fourth grade levels were grouped together for work in an anthology that contained an extensive skill-building program. The anthology, written on third and fourth grade reading levels, was geared to the interests of senior high students.

Most of those who read on the fifth grade level and above were placed in an individualized reading program and given much guidance by Mr. Cilak in locating books on their interest and reading levels. Several students were enrolled in the class because they were learning English as a second language and were therefore encountering difficulties in reading. Though Mr. Cilak could have used the individualized approach, he located some tapes that were geared specifically to teaching reading to the speaker of English as a second language; and he set up an independent study program in which the students spent most of their time with material developed to be used in a bilingual reading program.

Mrs. Sperry's Diagnostic-Prescriptive Technique in the Reading Component of the English Course

Mrs. Sperry was an English teacher who had prepared reading units that she included as a regular part of her English curriculum. However, she decided that these reading units were not enough reading practice for her students, and therefore she made a point to teach a reading lesson daily. While teaching the novel *Huckleberry Finn*, she referred to the scope and sequence of skills to determine the skills listed there that would be helpful to her students in reading *Huckleberry Finn*. She decided that the skills of phonic analysis (needed to pronounce Huck's speech as Clemens had intended), of identifying characterization (needed to determine what a given person was like), and of outlining were needed. She pre-assessed her class and found out which students needed help in the three skills. Because she already knew she had a range of reading levels from grade four to college, she divided her class into three groups.

Mrs. Sperry's Achievement Level Groups

1. *Groups of Students Reading Above Grade Level:* The students reading above grade level read *Huckleberry Finn* and were given guided reading sheets that asked them to locate specific examples of dialect that reflected the following themes running throughout the novel: (1) the conflict between society and the individual (e.g., Widow Douglas wanted to "sivilize" Huck); (2) quest for freedom; (3) Huck's birth and rebirth; (4) loneliness and isolation (e.g., "I felt so lonesome I most wish I was dead.").

2. *Groups of Students Reading on Grade Level:* The students reading on grade level read *Huckleberry Finn* and were given guided reading sheets that asked them to locate specific examples of dialect spoken by Huck, Jim, the Duke, the King, and the Grangerfords that they felt reflected the theme of conflict between society and the individual.

3. *Groups of Students Reading Below Grade Level:* The students reading below grade level were given a guided reading sheet and asked to locate speeches made by characters on specific pages in *Huckleberry Finn*. They were then to match each quotation with the theme of (1) conflict between society and the individual, (2) birth and rebirth, (3) quest for freedom, and (4) loneliness and isolation.

Her organizational chart for teaching each group for three days is shown in Figure 12.5.

It can be seen from Figure 12.5 that Mrs. Sperry spent the first fifteen minutes on Monday discussing with the entire class the dominant themes found in *Huckleberry Finn*. She related these themes to events in her students' lives and asked questions such as, "Have you ever felt that today's values conflict with your personal beliefs?" (conflict between individual and society); "Do you ever wish you could just get away for a while and find out who you are?" (quest for freedom); "Have you ever felt that no one really understands you and that the only person who can work out who you are is you yourself?" (loneliness and isolation); "Have you ever had anything traumatic happen in your life that really changed it? Something so significant that you in fact emerged a different person?" (birth and rebirth).

After making certain that the students understood the themes, she gave the group reading above grade level and the group reading on grade level their

		Above Grade Level Group	On Grade Level Group	Below Grade Level Group
M O N	15 min.	T1 (a, b, c)	T1 (a, b, c)	T1 (a, b, c)
	15 min.	2	2	T1 (c)
	15 min.	T3	2, 5 (a)	2
	15 min.	Intergroup activities — Interest groups		
T U E S	15 min.	T3 (a, b)	T3 (a, b)	T3 (a, b)
	15 min.	5 (a)	5 (c)	T4 (a)
	15 min.	5 (a)	T3 (a, b)	4 (b)
	15 min.	T3 (a, b)	4 (c)	5 (a)
W E D	15 min.	T1 (a, b, c)	T1 (a, b, c)	T1 (a, b, c)
	15 min.	2	2	2
	15 min.	Intergroup activities — 2 — free reading — T needs groups		
	15 min.	Intergroup activities — 2 — free reading — T needs groups		

Key:

1. Preparation
   a. Motivation
   b. New words
   c. Concept development
2. Silent reading
3. Oral reading and discussion
   a. Interpretation and sharing
   b. Discussion

4. Follow-up
   a. Learn new skill
   b. Practice a new skill
   c. Practice an old skill
5. Extension
   a. Supplementary reading
   b. Dramatization
   c. Rereading for a different purpose
   d. Creative activities

T = Teacher present

Figure 12.5 Mrs. Sperry's Diagnostic-Prescriptive Approach

guided reading sheets and asked them to read silently. While these groups read silently, Mrs. Sperry worked with the group reading below grade level to make certain they understood their assignment. After fifteen minutes of discussion, Mrs. Sperry let the below grade level group complete their silent reading with their guided reading sheet, while she worked with the above grade level group to see if they were identifying the themes and the dialects that they had been asked to locate. She also discussed issues with them, such as "How accurate is Clemens's use of dialect?" "Why did the author use the type of dialect he did for Huck? Jim?"

Mrs. Sperry's Interest Groups

The last fifteen minutes of Monday were spent in interest groups on four different research topics. Mrs. Sperry had given the class members their choice of the following themes. (1) The theme of loneliness—Students in this group were reading books on a variety of reading levels. Some titles were *Dinky Hooker Shoots Smack* by M. E. Kerr, *A Separate Peace* by John Knowles, and *Siddhartha* by Hermann Hesse. The students were sharing their own ideas about loneliness as well as discussing the loneliness reflected by the main character in their specific supplementary reading book. In addition, these youngsters were going to present a panel discussion to the class on the theme of loneliness. (2) The theme of the quest for freedom—Students in this group were reading books that included the following titles: *The Call of the Wild* by Jack London, *Inherit the Wind* by Jerome Lawrence and Robert E. Lee, and *By the Highway Home* by Mary Stolz. They were making a model of the raft used by Huck during his trip down the river to illustrate Huck's quest for freedom. In addition, their presentation to the class would relate the quest for freedom by Huck to the quest for freedom by each of the main characters in their self-selected supplementary reading. (3) The theme of conflict between society and the individual—Books read by students in this group included: *The Effect of Gamma Rays on Man-in-the-Moon Marigolds* by Paul Zindel, *I Never Promised You a Rose Garden* by Hannah Green, and *Sounder* by William H. Armstrong. These students were going to present their topic to the class in the form of a drama in which they would dress as a main character from their individually read novels and express a conflict. Then a student dressed as Huck would share ideas with each on why they disagreed with society and what means they would use to resolve their conflicts. (4) The theme of birth and rebirth—Students in this group were reading *Profiles in Courage* by John F. Kennedy, *Bridges at Toko-Ri* by James Michener, *The Soul Brothers and Sister Lou* by Kristin Hunter, and *A Man Called Horse* by Dorothy M. Johnson. Members of this group elected to make a group collage that was going to show the theme of birth and rebirth in *Huckleberry Finn*. In addition, each member of the group was going to make a collage reflecting this theme in his individual reading matter. On the day of their presentation they intended to ask each member of the group to present their individual collages to the rest of the class and explain how the theme of birth and rebirth fit into each. Then they would show the group collage to the entire class and see if the class members not in their group could identify the aspects of birth and rebirth in the collage from the novel *Huckleberry Finn*.

Mrs. Sperry's Needs Groups

On Wednesday, Mrs. Sperry spent the first fifteen minutes motivating the students, presenting new words, and developing new concepts so that all the students would be prepared to read another chapter of *Huckleberry Finn*, which they began to read silently during the next fifteen minutes with the aid of their guided reading sheets. During the last half hour, most of the class continued reading *Huckleberry Finn* silently or read their supplementary reading books just for enjoyment. Additionally, during the last half hour, Mrs. Sperry met simultaneously with those members of each of the achievement level groups who were having trouble pronouncing the dialect in *Huckleberry Finn*. After fifteen minutes when she finished teaching this new skill to the members of this needs group, she let these students practice it on their own reading levels. During the last fifteen minutes, she met with a second needs group. This group was having difficulty with the skill, Identifying Characterization, so Mrs. Sperry introduced and gave them practice in this skill.

Mrs. Sperry was an English teacher who was using *Huckleberry Finn* to teach reading in a diagnostic-prescriptive manner. Like most content area teachers, her major concern was with her content area rather than with directly teaching reading skills. Her textbook, like the textbook in most other content areas, stressed the content and not the reading skills needed to understand it. As such, it did not include a scope and sequence of reading skills, suggestions for teaching those skills, and a means of record keeping. The diagnostic-prescriptive approach is one technique that can provide this structure for the content area teacher.

The teachers who taught reading as an entire course also used components of the diagnostic-prescriptive technique and, hence, could also be considered diagnostic-prescriptive teachers. All the approaches discussed in the previous section were diagnostic-prescriptive because of the following aspects:

1. Mr. Evans used the scope and sequence in his basal, unit, and anthology series to provide the systematic presentation of skills, and he did not present a lesson without pre-assessing to see if the students needed the skills. Furthermore, after he introduced the student to the skill, he made certain that he provided reinforcement activities to practice the skill. If reinforcement activities were not provided with the basic teaching materials, he supplemented the basic materials with the needed materials to provide reinforcement activities. Though the basal, unit, or anthology series did not suggest that he post-assess after each skill, he did so in order to use the materials in a manner that he considered diagnostic-prescriptive.

2. Mr. Cilak used the diagnostic-prescriptive technique in his individualized approach in order to provide a sequence of skill development for his students. He did not haphazardly pre-assess Mark on the skills of inference, structural analysis, or scanning. He chose these skills because they were on the scope and sequence chart he was using to make certain that he would pre-assess all the skills during the course of his instruction. He began with those particular skills because there seemed to be a more urgent need for them than for other skills listed on the chart. However, in the course of the school year, he would continue to assess other skills on the chart until he had covered as many as he could, depending on his student program, by the end of the school year.

3. Mr. Cilak found the diagnostic-prescriptive technique invaluable to him when setting up his independent study approach. Though many of the materials contained their own pre-assessments, introductory lessons, reinforcement lessons, and post-assessments, he needed some means to coordinate the wide assortment of skill-building materials. Therefore, he keyed each piece of material and/or equipment in his classroom to the scope and sequence chart and generic teaching strategies. In this manner he was able to keep track of the materials he had that he could use to teach the skills in a systematic manner. For example, one of his teaching tools was a programmed book that taught vocabulary words through the use of context clues. This book was available on grade levels seven through twelve. Therefore, he turned to the scope and sequence chart and noted that the vocabulary skill of identifying context clues was described as a specific skill. He then turned to the generic teaching strategy on the skill and wrote down the name of the programmed text

as an additional teaching option. Since the programmed text was accompanied by a diagnostic test to determine the grade level of the book in which the student should begin, Mr. Cilak also indicated that pre-assessment questions on context clues could be gathered from this source.

4. Just as he had done in the individualized and independent study approach, Mr. Cilak also depended upon the diagnostic-prescriptive technique to coordinate materials and instruction when teaching his corrective reading class in an eclectic manner. He found it particularly useful in providing him with a systematic approach to teaching the reading skills for those students involved in the language experience approach.

Varying Organization to Meet Any Situation

The approaches illustrated in the previous section were placed in the context of specific classrooms for purposes of clarity. However any of the approaches could have easily been varied. For example, the individualized program was illustrated in the context of a required ninth grade developmental reading class. This same organization could be used quite successfully in an elective course for advanced students. Books would be written for more mature readers and skills emphasized would probably be higher level comprehension skills as well as study skills. Likewise, the independent study approach was shown in the context of a developmental reading class but could just as easily be used in a corrective reading class.

Age Level and Material Variation

Some of the approaches described at the senior high school level are also used at the middle and junior high levels, and vice versa. It is usually more common for reading to be taught daily for an entire school year in the middle and junior high than in the senior high. In addition, basal readers, and other such comprehensive textbooks are more often used in a year-long program than in a six-week program. Obviously a basal series containing enough materials for an entire school year could not be covered completely in a six-week unit on reading. However some teachers use comprehensive instructional reading programs intended for a year of study by simply emphasizing certain skills and omitting others. For example, Mr. Cilak could have used a basal reader with his ninth graders enrolled for one semester in developmental reading if he decided to select only those instructional components that emphasized certain skills, such as the higher level comprehension skills. Students might be asked to read a story in the basal reader and then complete only the correlated exercises that dealt with the critical reading skills. In a like manner, all instructional approaches could be adapted to almost any situation.

Most of the approaches discussed previously were in the context of a reading course; however, components of all the approaches could be adapted to the content area class.

Textbook Approach. Though a content area teacher would probably not use a comprehensive textbook such as a basal reader, it is feasible that the content area teacher could utilize a textbook emphasizing specific skills needed in his content area and then use the skill-building text on a regular basis. For example, the mathematics teacher might elect to use the *The Reading Line/ Mathematics* by Irene M. Reiter prior to and concurrent with regular teaching from textbooks in the field. The following materials, which are part of *The Reading Line/Mathematics* program, are intended to be used with the content area mathematics book issued by the school: (1) a student's workbook titled *The Reading Line/Mathematics*, which contains passages correlated with the content area of mathematics and written at varying reading levels, (2) a pre- and post-test to evaluate student progress, (3) a teacher's manual that contains lesson plans and a complete study skills guide, and (4) references to supplementary materials to extend basic concepts.

Individualized Reading Approach. All content area teachers may use nontext materials, which have been self-selected by students, to teach and reinforce concepts and skills needed to understand content area materials. For example, Mr. Morphew, a biology teacher, might determine that the biology text used by his students was too difficult for five of his students and too easy for three. Hence he could try to locate materials written on other reading levels which concerned his topic. He could use the scope and sequence chart to determine what reading skills would be most needed by those reading the core text. If he determined that Identifying Cause-Effect Relationships, Making Inferences, and Identifying Main Ideas were important skills and that identifying components of the human heart" was his subject area objective, he could set aside fifteen minutes at the end of the period each day for individual conferences. While the other students were given time to read lessons silently, work on homework assignments, or complete dissections, Mr. Morphew could spend five minutes or so with each youngster who had been given a book on his own reading level. Mr. Morphew could ask him questions that required a variety of reading skills and that related to the content area; for example, "What is this paragraph about?" (Identifying Main Idea); "Why does the blood from the arteries spurt and the blood from the veins flow?" (Identifying Cause-Effect Relationships); "If blood was "spurting out" of a man's arm would he have cut a vein or an artery?" (Making Conclusions).

Likewise, those who read well above grade level could be given time for conference on books that treated the topic in more depth; for example, "What is this section about?" (Identifying Main Idea); "Why do they discuss the issue that one of the arteries is only 3 mm in diameter if the idea concerns the rate at which the heart pumps blood?" (Identifying Cause-Effect Relationships); "If a person taking medication which affected the size of the arteries suddenly fainted, what could you infer would have made him faint?" (Making Inferences).

401

Language Experience Approach. Components of this approach lend themselves well to teachers of any content area who have students reading at the beginning levels. For example, Mr. Edwards was a driver's education instructor who had Roger, a nonreader, in one of his classes. Mr. Edwards read the driver's license manual into the tape recorder and thus produced an audio version of the manual for Roger. Roger was instructed to listen to the tape and follow along in the pamphlet, underlining those terms he thought he knew. Before he began to read and listen to the manual, he was given an oral and written version of a guided reading sheet, which told him what he needed to know in order to understand the chapter. After he listened to the audiotape, he would record his answers on another tape and then make index cards for the words that he had underlined as ones he knew. Mr. Edwards would listen to the oral answers Roger had recorded and transcribe them into a notebook for Roger. These answers became Roger's resource material, which he could read better than the manual because it was written in his own words. Furthermore, Mr. Edwards often had Roger reread and relisten to the tape for new purposes, particularly when he felt Roger was not learning what he needed to know in order to pass the driver's license test.

Independent Study Approach. Many materials designed to be used in independent study are available for most content areas. For example, if the teacher of a general mathematics class had a student who read on the third grade level, he could assign him material in a kit produced by SRA entitled *Arithmetic Fact Kit*, which consists of fact cards that develop accuracy and mastery of addition, subtraction, multiplication, and division. In addition, the teacher could audiotape the regular mathematics book or design guided reading sheets (See Chapter 8) so that the student could be given an independent means for learning the basic skills required in his mathematics class.

Eclectic Approach. Most content area teachers would probably not use any of the above approaches in an isolated manner but rather components of each to help their students understand their subject areas. Hence the mathematics teacher cited in the previous paragraph might give his students independent study from the mathematics kit, choose a mathematics book on third grade level, schedule an individualized conference to build reading skills in mathematics or request that the students describe an experiment they had completed in which they had had to use mathematical principles.

PERSONNEL FOR THE VARIOUS ORGANIZATIONAL APPROACHES

Most secondary schools provide personnel to teach reading in the form of (1) content area teachers who function part-time as reading teachers, (2) reading specialists whose primary tasks are to act as reading teachers.

English Teachers As Reading Teachers

The ways in which content area teachers might be assigned to teach reading are varied. In some cases a secondary school has a reading department, but in many cases reading is included in the English department, as is the case of La Salle Junior-Senior High School discussed previously. Secondary schools are probably organized in this fashion because the English teacher is the content area teacher most often given the task of teaching the students how to read.

This responsibility has fallen on the English teacher for many reasons. One primary cause is that English teachers usually spend over half their instructional time teaching literature. Though any content area that uses a textbook requires reading for information, the type of material included as literature to be used in English classes often requires interpretative reading, which is not needed to understand other content areas. In other words, English teachers, more than other content area teachers, are aware that they are teaching their students how to interpret what they read. Though in English classes literature is read and carefully interpreted, other subject areas use the text as a means of imparting information, and the focus is usually on information rather than on interpretation.

Often an English teacher will teach both reading classes and English classes. In the case of LaSalle Junior-Senior High School, Mr. Cilak, an English teacher, taught three classes of reading and two classes of English.

Content Area Teachers Other Than English Teachers As Reading Teachers

Though the English teacher is usually the content area teacher who teaches reading, occasionally other content area teachers are given the task of teaching the reading courses. However, in most situations they do not teach courses in reading per se but rather emphasize reading skills particularly needed in their content area. Chapter 8 in this text explains in great detail how content area teachers may be most helpful to students in showing them how to read their assignments.

Reading Specialists As Reading Teachers

Role As Reading Lab Instructor

In some schools, the courses taught by Mr. Cilak would be taught by a teacher who did nothing else but teach reading. However, LaSalle Junior-Senior High School had a reading specialist, Mrs. Lawson, who performed an entirely different role in the reading program. Mrs. Lawson spent part of her time in the reading lab. Students of all reading abilities would come to Mrs. Lawson for help in improving their reading skills. She tested each individually and then set up an independent study program for them to follow.

For example, Pete was highly involved in school activities and only had time to attend lab during his lunch hour. He was a senior and wanted to go to a prestigious college. He knew competition for admission would be high, and he wanted to improve his vocabulary and test-taking skills so that he could do well on the entrance exams and get into the college of his choice. Mrs. Lawson assigned Pete material that focused on increasing his vocabulary and test-taking skills. Sue also wanted to go to college, but she was an average student and felt she might have trouble keeping up. Mrs. Lawson helped her learn and practice more efficient study skills. Roger was a tenth grade student who had never learned to read. Mrs. Lawson was working with him on basic readiness skills.

Role As an Inservice Consultant

In addition to her role as reading teacher in the reading lab, Mrs. Lawson acted as a reading consultant for the entire faculty at LaSalle Junior-Senior High School.

Role As Inservice Consultant to Other Reading Teachers. Though Mr. Cilak taught reading as a subject three hours a day, he was a member of the English department, and most of his training had been in that discipline before he was hired as a faculty member. However, since he had expressed a willingness to teach reading and had had one undergraduate course in teaching reading methods, he had been hired to teach some reading courses at LaSalle. Mrs. Lawson worked closely with Mr. Cilak when he planned his instruction for the reading courses he would be teaching.

In addition, each of the English teachers in the school was teaching reading as a subject as part of the yearly curriculum. In order to avoid unnecessary overlap in skills taught and to provide instruction to teachers who had had little background in teaching reading methods, Mrs. Lawson had developed instructional packets.

The packets were made at a workshop during which Mrs. Lawson and the English teachers had determined what skills should be taught to the junior and senior high school students. This was accomplished by first presenting the teachers with an overview of the skills that exist in reading, along with some description of each skill. Specifically, Mrs. Lawson presented the teachers with a scope and sequence of reading skills and then discussed with them the meaning of each skill. (See the scope and sequence of skills presented in Chapter 10 of this text.) The teachers in each content area at each grade level then met to decide on those reading skills that they would stress.

For example, the freshman English teachers decided to spend more time on vocabulary building and basic comprehension skills, while the senior English teachers decided to focus their reading unit on developing sophisticated library skills as well as efficient study techniques.

The teachers divided into groups according to the skill they were interested in teaching, and they studied the generic teaching techniques found in Chapter 10 of this text. After the teachers understood techniques for teaching

404

the skills they had selected, Mrs. Lawson helped them adapt lessons to the content area of English to reinforce the reading skills. At the conclusion of the inservice workshop, all the English teachers had a teaching-of-reading packet geared to the particular content of the course and to the reading levels of their students.

Role As Inservice Consultant to All Content Area Teachers. Since the faculty at LaSalle Junior-Senior High School was particularly concerned about the reading skills of their students, the administration had required all content area teachers to spend some time each day making their students aware of the reading skills needed for their particular content area lessons. To help them identify the needed reading skills, the school administrators provided a summer workshop headed by the reading specialist and required the reading specialist to visit all content area teachers periodically in order to help them design lessons to teach reading skills needed within their content areas.

The summer workshop was one in which teachers were made aware of the reading skills that were particularly needed in their content areas, and were instructed in such techniques as making guided reading sheets to adapt lessons to students of varying reading abilities. Another purpose of the summer workshop was to make the reading specialist known to all the content area teachers so that she could work with them throughout the school year.

During the regular school year, Mrs. Lawson had a teacher's aide come in and watch the reading lab so that she could visit classes and help various content area teachers with instructional problems relating to reading.

The results of the emphasis upon the fact that "all teachers are teachers of reading" and the cooperation between the reading specialist and the content area teachers are reflected in the teaching strategies used by the teachers. (1) Mr. Morphew was able to locate materials on the human heart on Doug's instructional level and to design a guided reading sheet so that Doug could research the causes of human heart disease. (2) Mr. Lentz was able to diagnose his students' wide range of reading abilities and locate American history textbook materials written on three different reading levels. In addition, he was able to make guided reading sheets for each group so that they could be helped to understand the content as they went through their reading materials. (3) Mrs. Fitzpen determined that Phil, Ruth, and Bill did not know how to read graphs. She located the generic teaching strategy in Chapter 10 of this text and adapted it to fit the specific graphs in her students' mathematics books.

The cooperative relationship between the content area teachers and the reading specialist made coordination between their programs possible. For example, when Mr. Edwards, the driver's education teacher, discovered that Roger could not read, Mrs. Lawson helped him design lessons using the language experience approach and the driver's manual in order to teach the content area as well as the skills of reading. When Roger went to the reading lab, directed by Mrs. Lawson, he brought his materials and she showed him reading skills through words in the driver's manual and his own notes. For example, he learned to identify sequence (put steps in parallel parking in the order in which they should be completed), to use phonics (put all words containing digraphs together), and to use the index (put all words together that would fit under the heading *parking*).

DEVELOPING A SCHOOL–WIDE READING PROGRAM
FOR ALL CONTENT AREA TEACHERS

The reading program at LaSalle Junior-Senior High School was the result of several years of inservice training as well as strong faculty and administrative support. Their reading program had first begun five years previously. Initially, the school administration had hired Mrs. Lawson, the reading specialist. She began the total school program by asking three English teachers to teach developmental reading skills as part of the regular work in English. The teachers had learned how to teach the needed reading skills by going with their classes to the reading laboratory for a six-week unit of instruction. The major objective of the plan was the improvement of the reading abilities of the students. In addition, the plan served as an inservice program for the teaching of reading by the English teachers. After a few semesters, the three English teachers who had been involved in the plan were able to teach reading skills in their own English classes; they no longer needed the services of the reading teachers. Furthermore, their enthusiasm for teaching reading encouraged the remaining members of the English faculty to request inservice programs in the teaching of reading. This led to the type of inservice workshop program described earlier in which all the English teachers developed packets for teaching reading skills to their students.

During the fourth year of the project, members of the social studies department expressed interest in the reading program and a desire to help their students read social studies materials more effectively. Schedules were arranged so that the freshman social studies classes and their teachers would come to the reading lab for three weeks in order to improve their skills in areas needed in social studies classes and also to give the teachers some inservice help in teaching reading.

During the fifth year, the remaining content area teachers requested that the reading specialist work with their classes and provide training for the teachers as well.

Since Mr. Morphew was one of the science teachers, he went with his students to the reading lab. By this time, his students knew the developmental reading skills from their reading course in the English class. They also knew skills particularly important in reading social studies. Hence, the reading specialist felt she had three main tasks when working with the science teachers during their three weeks in the reading lab: (1) show the students what reading skills were particularly important in science, (2) show Mr. Morphew what reading skills were particularly important in science so that he could continue to make his students aware of these skills after they left the reading lab, and (3) show Mr. Morphew how to differentiate instruction for students of varying reading abilities.

The day before his class was to go to the reading lab, the reading specialist had met with Mr. Morphew in order to obtain a copy of the lesson plans that he was going to use with his class the following week. She perused the plans and the reading materials to be assigned to the students, determined what sorts of reading skills were particularly important, and then outlined guided reading sheets for above level readers, below level readers, and on level readers. Then she checked with Mr. Morphew to see if he had any suggestions for teaching the reading skills. She continued in a like manner until she had outlined biology lessons for the week. When Mr. Morphew came to the reading lab with his class, he was given a copy of the lesson plans and asked to react to them.

The first day the class was in the lab, the reading specialist administered a content area IRI based on biology materials. She also administered an interest inventory geared to the varieties of topics that existed in biology. The second day of class, Mrs. Lawson reviewed skills which she thought were particularly important to the students in order for them to read their biology materials effectively. The third day of class, the reading specialist assigned the students their regular biology materials based on the lesson plans Mr. Morphew had shown her. However, she differentiated instruction according to reading ability and provided students with guided reading sheets, which she had constructed. Thus for the next three days, each student completed the objectives Mr. Morphew had outlined for the week, but each worked with materials appropriate to his reading level.

After their week of instruction in the reading lab, both the students and Mr. Morphew had a better idea of the reading skills needed in the content area. In addition, Mr. Morphew learned enough about the reading abilities and interests of his students as well as enough of the terminology for him to be able to go to the reading specialist for specific help with his students. After that week, Mr. Morphew felt he could ask Mrs. Lawson to observe his class and give him specific suggestions for adapting his lessons.

References and Bibliography

Anderson, N., and Dechant, E. *Listen and Read Program.* Huntington, N. Y.: Educational Development Laboratories, 1963.

Armstrong, W. H. *Sounder.* New York: Harper & Row, 1969.

Aukerman, R. C. *Reading in the Secondary School Classroom.* New York: McGraw-Hill, 1972.

Bamman, H., Dawson, M., and McGovern, J. *Fundamentals of Basic Reading Instruction.* 3rd ed. New York: McKay, 1973.

Burmeister, L. E. *Reading Strategies for Secondary School Teachers.* Reading, Mass.: Addison-Wesley, 1974.

Burron, A., and Claybaugh, A. *Using Reading to Teach Subject Matter: Fundamentals for Content Teachers.* Columbus, Ohio: Merrill, 1974.

Clemens, S. *Adventures of Huckleberry Finn.* New York: Dodd, Mead, 1953.

Crawford, P. *Three-Legged Race.* New York: Harper & Row, 1974.

Cushenbery, D. *Remedial Reading in the Secondary School.* West Nyack, N. Y.: Parker, 1972.

Diggins, J. E. *String, Straightedge and Shadow.* New York: Viking, 1965.

Green, H. *I Never Promised You a Rose Garden.* New York: Holt, Rinehart & Winston, 1964.

Gunther, J. *Death Be Not Proud.* New York: Harper & Row, 1949.

Herber, H. *Teaching Reading in Content Areas.* Englewood Cliffs, N. J.: Prentice-Hall, 1970.

Hesse, H. *Siddhartha.* Philadelphia: New Directions, 1951.

Hunter, K. *The Soul Brothers and Sister Lou.* New York: Scribner, 1968.

Johnson, D. *A Man Called Horse.* New York: Balantine Books, 1970.

Judy, S. *Explorations in the Teaching of Secondary English.* New York: Dodd, Mead, 1974.

Karlin, R. *Teaching Reading in High School.* 2nd ed. Indianapolis, Ind.: Bobbs Merrill, 1972.

Karlin, R. *Teaching Reading in High School: Selected Articles.* Indianapolis, Ind.: Bobbs-Merrill, 1972.

Kennedy, J. F. *Profiles in Courage.* New York: Harper & Row, 1964.

Kerr, M. E. *Dinky Hooker Shoots Smack.* New York: Harper & Row, 1972.

Knowles, J. *A Separate Peace.* New York: Macmillan, 1960.

Langone, J. *Death Is a Noun.* Boston: Little, Brown, 1972.

Lawrence, J., and Lee, R. E. *Inherit the Wind.* New York: Bantam, 1969.

London, J. *The Call of the Wild.* New York: Macmillan, 1963.

Michener, J. *Bridges at Toko-Ri.* New York: Random House, 1953.

New Advanced Reading Skill Builders. Pleasantville, N. Y.: Reader's Digest Services, Educational Division, 1973.

Niles, O. S., et al. *Tactics in Reading II.* Glenview, Ill.: Scott, Foresman, 1964.

Olson, A., and Ames, W. *Teaching Reading Skills in Secondary Schools.* Scranton, Pa.: Intext Educational Publishers, 1972.

Olson, A., and Ames, W. *Teaching Reading Skills in Secondary Schools: Readings.* Scranton, Pa.: Intext Educational Publishers, 1970.

Pasternak, B. *Dr. Zhivago.* New York: Pantheon, 1953.

Rapp, D. R. *Arithmetic Fact Kit.* Chicago: Science Research Associates, 1973.

Reiter, I. M. *The Reading Line.* Philadelphia: Polaski Company, 1971.

Reiter, I. M. *The Reading Line/Mathematics.* Philadelphia: Polaski Company, 1971.

Robinson, H., and Thomas, E. eds. *Fusing Reading Skills and Content.* Newark, Del.: International Reading Association, 1969.

Robinson, H. *Teaching Reading and Study Strategies: The Content Areas.* Boston: Allyn & Bacon, 1975.

Rush, R. *Computers.* New York: Simon & Schuster, 1959.

Spache, G. D., and Spache, E. B. *Reading in the Elementary School.* 3rd ed. Boston: Allyn & Bacon, 1973.

Stolz, M. *By the Highway Home.* New York: Harper & Row, 1971.

Watson, J. D. *The Double Helix.* New York: Atheneum, 1968.

Wojciechowska, M. *Tuned Out.* New York: Harper & Row, 1968.

Thomas, E., and Robinson, H. *Improving Reading in Every Class: A Source Book for Teachers.* Boston: Allyn & Bacon, 1972.

Zindel, P. *The Effect of Gamma Rays on Man-in-the-Moon Marigolds.* New York: Harper & Row, 1971.

Zindel, P. *The Pigman.* New York: Harper & Row, 1968.

Part Five

Practicing Teaching Reading

Practicing Teaching Reading at the Performance and Consequence Levels

Chapters 1 through 12 of this book have stressed knowing—knowledge level objectives. However, what prospective teachers know matters very little if they are unable to stimulate their students to learn. The thrust in Chapter 13 is to demonstrate how well they can *do* what they have learned theoretically. It stresses both what teachers *do*—performance level objectives—and the effect that they have on their students—consequence level objectives.

These objectives can be met in several ways. Ideally, each participant should have the opportunity to work with a small group of secondary school students. However, if this option does not exist, each experience can be assessed in a microteaching situation with a participant's peers playing the roles of students.

In either case, it will be found that the experiences are quite flexible and can be adapted to almost any classroom situation. For example, secondary school students may be given a questionnaire that assesses some of the factors that make a textbook difficult, regardless of the content area in which they are enrolled. Likewise, the technique for administering the questionnaire could be practiced by a college student with a peer, using a college level textbook.

HOW TO USE CHAPTER 13

Chapter 13 includes 12 experiences, one of which correlates with each of the preceding 12 chapters. Each experience contains the following sections:

Prerequisite tells which chapter the participant needs to have completed before proceeding with the experience.

Objectives informs participants of what they are expected to be able to do after they have completed the experience.

Participant's Instructions gives participants suggestions of several things they might do to complete the activity successfully. It often includes step-

411

by-step instructions for completing the activity.

Participant's Follow-Up is designed to help participants summarize their activities at the completion of the experience.

Observer's Checklist contains questions to be answered by an observer; that is, peer, cooperating teacher, or instructor, who watches the participant perform the activity. If no observer is available, participants may assess their own progress by answering the questions.

OVERVIEW

The following brief descriptions provide an overview of the experiences.

Experience 1—Chapter 1: Identifying the Role of the Secondary School Teacher in Reading Instruction
During this experience, the participant will (1) select two comprehension or senior high school teacher and one middle, junior, or senior high school student to ascertain their views on reading and reading instruction.

Experience 2—Chapter 2: Identifying the Vocabulary Skills
During this experience, the participant will analyze an adult's or a student's reading and accurately identify the vocabulary skills used.

Experience 3—Chapter 3: Identifying the Comprehension Skills
During this experience, the participant will (1) select two comprehension skills that apply to his area, (2) design questions on low, medium, and high levels of difficulty for each skill using singly or in combination the readability hierarchy, the unit hierarchy, and the usage hierarchy, and (3) present the questions to a student.

Experience 4—Chapter 4: Identifying the Study Skills
During this experience, the participant will (1) select those study skills that apply to his area, (2) design questions or tasks for each skill to ascertain the extent to which students use it, and (3) present the questions or tasks to a student.

Experience 5—Chapter 5: Determining Student's Reading Ability
During this experience, the participant will (1) evaluate a standardized reading test according to a checklist given in this experience and/or (2) administer, score, and interpret the results of an informal reading inventory.

Experience 6—Chapter 6: Identifying Reading Problems with Textbooks
During this experience, the participant will administer and interpret a questionnaire that assesses some of the factors that make a textbook difficult for a middle, junior, or senior high school student.

Experience 7—Chapter 7: Planning Reading Instruction in the Content Area Classroom
During this experience, the participant will design and teach at least one step of a directed reading lesson using a format that includes a behavioral objective, a pre-assessment, a list of materials, a description of procedures, and a post-assessment.

Experience 8—Chapter 8: Adapting Content Area Materials to Student's

412

Reading Ability

During this experience, the participant will construct, administer, score, and interpret an IRI based on a content area textbook.

Experience 9—Chapter 9: Using Diagnostic-Prescriptive Techniques

During this experience, the participant will describe a diagnostic-prescriptive reading program that he has observed.

Experience 10—Chapter 10: Teaching Vocabulary, Comprehension, and Study Skills

During this experience, the participant will teach to secondary school students at least one skill and will include a pre-assessment, an introductory lesson, two reinforcement lessons, and a post-assessment.

Experience 11—Chapter 11: Utilizing Materials Designed for Teaching Reading

During this experience, the participant will (1) construct and utilize an instrument to diagnose the reading interests of adolescents and/or (2) utilize a checklist to help locate appropriate reading materials and/or (3) develop and use a game or activity designed to reinforce a reading skill within a content area.

Experience 12—Chapter 12: Using a Variety of Organizational Approaches for Teaching Reading

During this experience, the participant will (1) design a reading lesson during which three different approaches to developmental reading are used with three different groups of students; e.g., one group by the textbook approach, one group by the individualized approach, and one group by the independent study approach and/or (2) design and teach a lesson based on an eclectic approach; e.g., the lessons for one group of students might include aspects of the language experience, the independent study, and the individualized approaches.

413

EXPERIENCE 1: CHAPTER 1

Prerequisite: Before beginning this experience, the participant should have satisfactorily completed the objectives for Chapter 1.

Objective: During this experience, the participant will interview one middle, junior, or senior high school teacher and one middle, junior, or senior high school student to ascertain their views on reading and reading instruction.

Participant's Instructions

1. Check with your instructor for any special directions.
2. Arrange a time and place to talk with (a) a teacher and a student who will be your subjects and (b) a classmate or other colleague who will be your observer.
3. Read the Participant's Checklist in this experience until you are familiar enough with your role to perform the interviews. Plan only a few minutes for each interview.
4. Give the Observer's Checklist in this experience to your observer.
5. Complete the interviews.
6. After concluding the above steps, complete the Participant's Follow-Up.

Participant's Checklist

Teacher Interview

Teacher's subject area:_____ Grade level(s):_____

Ask the teacher the following questions:

1. What is the percentage of students in your classes who do not have adequate reading ability to complete your reading assignments?

   _____

2. What are some of the problems that students have in relation to reading?_____

   _____

   _____

   _____

3. What techniques do you use to help students read content material? (e.g., providing questions to be answered)_____

_____

_____

_____

Interview with Middle, Junior, or Senior High School Student

Student's first name:_____ Grade level:_____

Ask the student the following questions:

1. What do you think reading is?_____

_____

_____

_____

2. Is learning the meanings of words part of reading?_____

_____

_____

3. Is looking for the main idea in a paragraph part of reading?_____

_____

_____

4. Is locating information in the library part of reading?_____

_____

_____

Participant's Follow-Up

Do the following:

1. List what you consider to be the two most important reading-related problems that you expect to face as a teacher._____

_____

_____

2. Compare and contrast your definition of reading with the one given by the student you interviewed._____

_____

_____

416

Observer's Checklist

This assessment was completed by: (circle one)

self   peer   cooperating teacher   course instructor   other_____

1. Participant asked teacher what percentage of students had problems completing reading assignments? (circle one)   yes   no

2. Participant asked teacher to state some problems that students had in relation to reading? (circle one)   yes   no

3. Participant asked teacher what techniques he used to help his students read? (circle one)   yes   no

4. Participant asked middle/junior/senior high school student to give his definition of reading? (circle one)   yes   no

5. Participant asked middle/junior/senior high school student if learning word meanings, looking for the main idea, and locating information in the library are part of reading? (circle one)   yes   no

6. Answer to all of the above questions is "yes"? (circle one)
   yes   no

7. General comment._____

   _____

   _____

EXPERIENCE 2: CHAPTER 2

Prerequisite: Before performing this experience, the participant should have satisfactorily completed the objectives for Chapter 2.

Objective: During this experience, the participant will analyze an adult's or a student's reading and accurately identify the vocabulary skills used.

Participant's Instructions

1. Check with your instructor for any special directions.
2. Arrange a time and place where you can work with (a) a student or an adult who will be your subject and (b) a classmate or other colleague who will be your observer.
3. Read the Participant's Checklist and Subject's Copy in this experience carefully so that you will understand your task. Remember that this activity is designed to familiarize you with the vocabulary skills. It is not intended to serve as a definitive assessment of the subject's skills in this area.
4. Locate the word *gavotte* in the dictionary that you will take with you when you complete this experience. Be sure that (1) *gavotte* is included in the dictionary, (2) the pronunciation is shown and, (3) at least two meanings are given. If *gavotte* does not meet these criteria, locate another word in your dictionary that does. Then use the word in a written sentence and substitute that sentence for the one in Box 5 of the Subject's Copy.
5. Provide your observer with the section entitled Observer's Checklist.
6. Complete the activity. Introduce the task to the subject by saying, "I am going to show you some words and I would like for you to pronounce each one. Some of them are real words, and some are nonsense words. Say each as best you can." Then, hand your subject the Subject's Copy that you have torn from this book.
7. After concluding the above steps, complete the Participant's Follow-Up.

Participant's Checklist

1. Directions for *Box 1* on Subject's Copy: Say to the subject, "What does the word in Box 1 mean?" When the subject indicates that he does not know the meaning, point to Box 1A and say, "This is an illustration of it." Did the subject arrive at a correct response after seeing the picture?

419

_____ yes

_____ no

2. Directions for *Box 2* on Subject's Copy: Say to the subject, "Read the sentence in Box 2. What word goes in the blank?" Place a check mark beside the following phrase that best describes the subject's response.

      _____ provided a noun or pronoun that made sense in the sentence

      _____ provided a word that did not make sense

      _____ did not respond

3. Directions for *Box 3* on Subject's Copy: Say to the subject, "Read the word in Box 3," and point to Box 3.

  a. Place a check mark beside the phrase that best describes the subject's response.

      _____ subject pronounced word correctly; that is, *pre* as in *premium*, *dom* as in *dominant*, *thol* as in *menthol*

      _____ subject pronounced word incorrectly

  b. If the subject pronounced the word *correctly*, proceed to instructions for Box 4. If the subject pronounced the word *incorrectly*, do the following:

    (1) Ask subject to draw a line at the end of the first syllable, at the end of the second, and at the end of the third. Place a check mark beside the phrase that most closely matches subject's response.

      _____ pre/dom/thol (correct)

      _____ other (Please specify.)

    (2) Ask subject which syllable is accented. Place a check mark beside his response.

      _____ dom (correct)

      _____ pre

      _____ thol

    (3) Ask subject, "How would you pronounce the first part?" Pause. "The second part?" Pause. "The last part?" Place check marks beside the responses that best match subject's.

      _____ pre as in *pre*mium (correct)

      _____ dom as in *dom*inant (correct)

      _____ thol as in men*thol* (correct)

      _____ other (Please specify.) _____   _____   _____

(4) Say to the subject, "Blend the sounds to make a word." Mark his response below.

_____ prē / dŏm / thŏl (correct)

_____ other (Please specify.)_____

4. Directions for *Box 4* on Subject's Copy: Say to the subject, "What is the meaning of the word in Box 4," and point to Box 4.
   a. Place a check mark beside the phrase that best describes the subject's response.

   _____ subject gave correct meaning of the word; that is, *act of killing one's father.*

   _____ subject could not give correct meaning of the word.
   b. If the subject gave the correct meaning of the word, proceed to instructions for Box 5. If the subject could not give the correct meaning of the word, do the following:
   (1) Ask subject to draw a line between the two meaningful units. Place a check mark beside the phrase that most closely matches subject's response.

   _____ patri / cide (correct)

   _____ other (Please specify.)_____
   (2) Ask subject, "What is the meaning of the first part?" Pause. "The second part?" Place a check mark beside the response that best matches the subject's response.

   _____ patri, meaning *father* and cide meaning *to kill* (correct)

   _____ other (Please specify.)_____

5. Directions for *Box 5* on Subject's Copy: Ask the subject to pronounce and give the meaning of the word *gavotte* as used in the sentence in Box 5.
   a. Mark the subject's response.

   _____ word was correctly pronounced and defined

   _____ word was not correctly pronounced and defined

   b. If subject was *unable* to pronounce and define the word, hand him the dictionary and ask him to look up the word, pronounce it, and find the correct meaning to fit the sentence. Mark results.

   _____ subject *was* able to locate word in dictionary

   _____ subject *was not* able to locate word in dictionary

   _____ subject *was* able to use diacritical markings to arrive at correct pronunciation

   _____ subject *was not* able to use diacritical markings to arrive at correct pronunciation

_____ subject *was* able to locate appropriate meaning

_____ subject *was not* able to locate appropriate meaning

6. Directions for *Box 6* on Subject's Copy: Say to the subject, "Read the word in Box 6 aloud and tell me what it means." Place a check mark beside the following phrase that best describes the subject's response.

_____ used sight word skills for meaning and pronunciation

_____ used word attack skills for meaning and pronunciation

_____ could identify neither meaning nor pronunciation

Participant's Follow-Up

1. (Box 1) Subject used the illustration clue? (circle one)   yes   no
Why or why not?_____

_____

2. (Box 2) Subject used context clues? (circle one)   yes   no
Why or why not?_____

_____

_____

3. (Box 3) Subject pronounced word *predomthol* correctly either with or without your help? (circle one)   yes   no   If any difficulties were encountered, at which step did they occur?_____

_____

_____

4. (Box 4) Subject could give meaning of *patricide*? (circle one) yes   no   If any difficulties were encountered, at which step did they occur?_____

_____

_____

5. (Box 5) Subject pronounced and defined the italicized word? (circle one)   yes   no   If no, describe any difficulties the subject encountered using the dictionary. _____

_____

_____

6. (Box 6) Subject used sight word skills to read the word *republic*?
   (circle one)   yes   no   Why or why not?_____

   _____

   _____

1.

> ognif

1A.

2.

> _____ran for president of the club.

3.

> predomthol

4.

> patricide

5.

> Mary Sue played a *gavotte* at the piano recital.

6.

> republic

Observer's Checklist

This assessment was completed by: (circle one)

    self   peer   cooperating teacher   course instructor   other

1. (Box 1) Subject used the illustration clue? (circle one)   yes no

    Why or why not?_____

    _____

    _____

2. (Box 2) Subject used context clues? (circle one)   yes   no

    Why or why not?_____

    _____

    _____

3. (Box 3) Subject used phonic analysis? (circle one) yes no

    Why or why not?_____

    _____

    _____

4. (Box 4) Subject used structural analysis? (circle one) yes   no

    Why or why not?_____

    _____

    _____

5. (Box 5) Subject used dictionary skills? (circle one)   yes   no

    Why or why not?_____

    _____

    _____

6. (Box 6) Subject used sight word skills? (circle one)   yes   no

    Why or why not?_____

    _____

    _____

7. General comments._____

    _____

    _____

    _____

EXPERIENCE 3: CHAPTER 3

Prerequisite: Before performing this experience, the participant must have satisfactorily completed the objectives for Chapter 3.

Objective: During this experience, the participant will (1) select three comprehension skills that apply to his area, (2) design questions on low, medium, and high levels of difficulty for each skill using singly or in combination the readability hierarchy, the unit hierarchy, and the usage hierarchy, and (3) present the questions to a student.

Participant's Instructions

1. Check with your instructor to see if he has any special directions.
2. Arrange a time and place where you can work with (a) a student who will be your subject and (b) a classmate or other colleague who will be your observer.
3. Select two comprehension skills to work with.
4. Write the name of each of these skills beside Name of Skill under skills number one and two on the Record Sheet.
5. Complete the Record Sheet except for the "response accurate" questions.
6. Give the Observer's Checklist to your observer.
7. Ask the student the questions and record the accuracy of his answers in the space provided on the Record Sheet.
8. After completing the above steps, complete the Participant's Follow-Up.

Participant's Checklist

Comprehension skill 1:

Name of skill: (e.g., Making Inferences)_____

1. Least difficult question: (e.g., Did Huck like Widow Douglas?)

_____

Reading material: (e.g., *Huckleberry Finn*, p. 2)_____

Response accurate? (circle one)   yes   no

2. More difficult question:_____

_____

Reading Material:_____

429

Why did the question increase in difficulty?_____

_____

Response accurate? (circle one)   yes   no

3. Most difficult question: _____

_____

Reading material:_____

Why did the question increase in difficulty?_____

_____

Response accurate? (circle one)   yes   no

Comprehension skill 2:

Name of skill:

4. Least difficult question:_____

_____

Reading material:_____

Response accurate? (circle one)   yes   no

5. More difficult question: _____

_____

Reading material:_____

Why did question increase in difficulty? _____

_____

Response accurate? (circle one)   yes   no

6. Most difficult question: _____

_____

Reading material: _____

Why did question increase in difficulty? _____

_____

Response accurate? (circle one)   yes   no

Participant's Follow-Up

Answer the following questions:

1. Did your student find question two more difficult than question

430

one? (circle one)   yes   no   Why or why not?_____

_____

_____

2. Did your student find question three more difficult than question two? (circle one)   yes   no   Why or why not?_____

_____

_____

3. Did your student find question five more difficult than question four? (circle one)   yes   no   Why or why not?_____

_____

_____

4. Did your student find question six more difficult than question five? (circle one)   yes   no   Why or why not?_____

_____

_____

Observer's Checklist

This assessment was completed by: (circle one)

self   peer   cooperating teacher   course instructor   other_____

1. Did the participant put the student at ease?

   (circle one)   yes   no   If yes, how?_____

   _____

2. Did the participant give clear instructions?

   (circle one)   yes   no   If yes, how?_____

   _____

3. Did the participant have the necessary books ready?

   (circle one)   yes   no

4. Was the participant otherwise prepared?

   (circle one)   yes   no   Why or why not?_____

   _____

5. Was the first question appropriate for the first skill?

   (circle one)   yes   no   Why or why not?_____

   _____

6. Did the second question match the first skill listed?

   (circle one)   yes   no   Why or why not?_____

   _____

7. Was the second question more difficult than the first question?

   (circle one)   yes   no   Why or why not?_____

   _____

8. Did the third question match the first skill listed?

   (circle one)   yes   no   Why or why not?_____

   _____

9. Was the third question more difficult than the second question?

   (circle one)   yes   no   Why or why not?_____

   _____

10. Was the fourth question appropriate for the second skill?

    (circle one)   yes   no   Why or why not?_____

    _____

11. Did the fifth question match the second skill listed?

(circle one)   yes   no   Why or why not?_____

_____

12. Was the fifth question more difficult than the fourth question?

(circle one)   yes   no   Why or why not?_____

_____

13. Did the sixth question match the second skill listed?

(circle one)   yes   no   Why or why not?_____

_____

14. Was the sixth question more difficult than the fifth question?

(circle one)   yes   no   Why or why not?_____

_____

EXPERIENCE 4: CHAPTER 4

Prerequisite: Before performing this experience, the participant should have satisfactorily completed the objectives for Chapter 4.

Objective: During this experience, the participant will (1) select those study skills that apply to his area, (2) design questions or tasks for each skill to ascertain the extent to which students use it, and (3) present the questions or tasks to a student.

Participant's Instructions

1. Check with your instructor for any special directions.
2. Arrange a time and place where you can work with (a) a student who will be your subject and (b) a classmate or other colleague who will be your observer.
3. Complete the first two columns in the Participant's Checklist in this experience. You should use at least three skills but you may use as many skills as you feel apply to your subject area.
4. Give the Observer's Checklist in this experience to your observer.
5. Complete the interview, recording the subject's responses in the third column of the Participant's Checklist.
6. After concluding the above steps, complete the Participant's Follow-Up.

Participant's Follow-Up

1. Describe the student's strengths and weaknesses in the study skills as you perceived them through your interview with or your tasks for the student.

435

Participant's Checklist

Skill Name	Interview Questions or Tasks	Subject's Response

e.g., Using Glossaries	e.g.,
	    Interview Question: Tell me how you would use the glossary in your textbook to locate the meaning of *neurosis*.
	    Interview Task: Locate the meaning of *neurosis* in the glossary in your textbook.	

Observer's Checklist

This assessment was completed by: (circle one)

self   peer   cooperating teacher   course instructor   other

1. Did the participant put the student at ease?

   (circle one)   yes   no   If yes, how?_____

   _____

2. Was the participant prepared? (e.g., questions and any necessary materials ready?)

   (circle one)   yes   no   Why or why not? _____

   _____

3. Were the questions asked appropriate to the skills selected?

   (circle one)   yes   no   Why or why not?_____

   _____

4. Did the participant appear to be arriving at a complete understanding of the student's study skills?

   (circle one)   yes   no   Why or why not?_____

   _____

EXPERIENCE 5: CHAPTER 5

Prerequisite: Before performing this experience, the participant should have satisfactorily completed the objectives for Chapter 5.

Objectives: During this experience, the participant will (1) evaluate a standardized reading test according to a checklist given in this experience and/or (2) administer, score, and interpret the results of an informal reading inventory.

Participant's Instructions

1. Check with your instructor for any special directions.
2. Arrange a time and a place where you can work with (a) at least one student who will be your subject (if you are completing the second objective) and (b) a classmate or other colleague who will be your observer (for either objective).
3. Use the Standardized Test Evaluation Form in this experience or another evaluation form of your choosing, if you plan to complete the first objective. Use the IRI found in Appendix A or construct one of your own, if you plan to complete the second objective.
4. If you have completed materials for the first objective, give the Observer's Checklist—Form A to your observer. If you have completed materials for the second objective, give the Observer's Checklist—Form B to your observer.
5. Complete the experience you have chosen.
6. After concluding the above steps, complete the Participant's Follow-Up—Form A if you have chosen Objective 1. Complete Participant's Follow-Up—Form B if you have chosen Objective 2.

Standardized Test Evaluation Form

1. Name of test_____

2. Publisher_____

3. Cost_____

4. Length of time to administer_____

5. Ease of administration (Comment on what has been done to simplify this task.)_____

   _____

   _____

439

6. What was the population on which the norms for this test were based? (comment)_____

_____

7. How does this population compare with your local population?_____

_____

_____

8. What type of format was used to report results (i.e., stanine, grade level, and so forth)?_____

_____

_____

9. How easy to understand was the manual? (comment)_____

_____

_____

10. Look closely at the vocabulary section and answer these questions:

a. Are the following types of vocabulary skills measured on the test? (Circle ones that were measured.)

(1) using illustration clues

(2) using context clues

(3) using phonic analysis

(4) using structural analysis

(5) using dictionary skills

(6) using a combination of vocabulary skills

(7) size of existing vocabulary

b. Write down one sample item from the vocabulary section._____

_____

_____

c. How many vocabulary items are there?_____

_____

d. What is the time limit?_____

_____

e. Do the items get progressively harder? (e.g., is item 6 easier than item 25?)_____

_____

11. Look closely at the comprehension section and answer these questions.

    a. Does the content deal with school subjects or recreational reading?

    b. Would the content appeal to both boys and girls?

    c. Which of the following types of comprehension skills were measured on the test? (Circle ones that were measured.)

        (1) identifying details

        (2) identifying main ideas

        (3) identifying sequence

        (4) following directions

        (5) identifying cause-effect relationships

        (6) making inferences

        (7) making generalizations and conclusions

        (8) identifying tone and mood

        (9) identifying theme

      (10) identifying characterization

      (11) identifying fact, fiction, and opinion

      (12) identifying propaganda

      (13) identifying author's purpose

    d. Give an example of three questions that each measure a different comprehension skill. If three of the above types are not represented, give three examples of the skills that are measured.

    _____

    _____

    _____

    e. How many comprehension items are there?_____

    _____

    f. What is the time limit?_____

    _____

    g. Do the items get progressively harder?_____

    _____

12. Look closely at the rate of comprehension section and answer the following questions:

    a. Is the rate score figured separately or as part of the comprehension

441

score? (That is, is the student asked to circle a number on the line he is reading after so many minutes or are no directions given for rate, and is the score determined simply by how long it took him to finish the test?)_____

_____

_____

_____

b. If the test gives a separate score for rate, and the student is asked to circle a number on the line he is reading at the end of so many minutes, comment on this procedure. (That is, can you think of any reason why this score might not be valid or reliable?)_____

_____

_____

_____

13. If another reading skill is measured, describe it below. (For example, the Iowa gives more than just vocabulary, comprehension, and rate. This test also gives some separate scores for study skills, such as directed reading.)_____

_____

_____

_____

14. Give your general impression of this test in terms of its worth to you as a classroom teacher._____

_____

_____

_____

Participant's Follow-Up — Form A

Answer the following:

1. Is there anything in particular that you liked about the standardized test you reviewed?

(circle one)   yes   no   Briefly explain._____

_____

2. Is there anything in particular that you disliked about the standardized test you reviewed?

(circle one)   yes   no   Briefly explain._____

_____

3. Were there any content areas for which you felt the test you reviewed would be particularly appropriate?

(circle one)   yes   no   Briefly explain._____

_____

Participant's Follow-Up — Form B

Do the following:

1. State the name, age, and grade for each student worked with:

Name	Age	Grade
_____	_____	_____
_____	_____	_____
_____	_____	_____

2. Copy the results from your score sheet in the spaces below.

Name	12		11		10		9		8		7		6		5		4		3		2		1	
	O	S	O	S	O	S	O	S	O	S	O	S	O	S	O	S	O	S	O	S	O	S	O	S

3. On the chart, circle the instructional level for each student.

4. State the level on which you would instruct each student and any special strengths or weaknesses noted during testing.

Name	Instructional Level	Strengths or Weaknesses
_____	_____	_____
_____	_____	_____
_____	_____	_____

Observer's Checklist — Form A

This assessment was completed by: (circle one)

self   peer   cooperating teacher   course instructor   other_____

1. Did the participant use the Standardized Test Evaluation Form found in Experience 5 of this textbook to help identify characteristics of a specific standardized reading test? (circle one)

   yes   no   If no, briefly describe the checklist that was used by

   the participant._____

   _____

   _____

   _____

2. Did you agree with the participant's comments about the following aspects mentioned on the checklist? (Circle the ones with which you agreed.)

   a. ease of administration

   b. norm population

   c. type of format used to report results

   d. understandability of test manual

   e. type of vocabulary skills measured

   f. type of comprehension skills measured

   g. manner in which rate of comprehension was assessed

   h. other types of reading skills measured

   i. general impression of test

3. Briefly discuss any of the items in question 2 with which you disagreed and state your reasons for disagreement._____

   _____

   _____

   _____

Observer's Checklist—Form B

This assessment was completed by: (circle one)

self   peer   cooperating teacher   course instructor   other_____

1. Did the participant use the IRI in Appendix A? (circle one)

   yes   no   If no, briefly comment on the following:

   a. Content area from which most of the passages seemed to have
   been selected._____

   _____

   b. Type of vocabulary questions asked._____

   _____ _____

   c. Type of comprehension questions asked. _____

   _____

2. Participant's administration of test:

   a. Was testing begun at appropriate levels? (circle one)   yes   no

   Why or why not?_____

   _____

   b. Were errors tallied correctly? (circle one)   yes   no

   Why or why not?_____

   _____

   c. Were students asked not to look back when answering silent reading comprehension questions? (circle one)   yes   no

   Why or why not?_____

   _____

   d. Were adequate instructions given? (circle one)   yes   no

   Why or why not?_____

   _____

3. Was participant's test scoring on the oral passages accurate?

   (circle one)   yes   no   Why or why not?_____

   _____ _____

   _____ _____

4. Was participant's scoring of the silent passages accurate?

   (circle one)   yes   no   Why or why not?_____

_____

_____

5. Was participant's interpretation of test results accurate?

   (circle one)   yes   no   Why or why not?_____

   _____

   _____

6. Were students taking the test cooperative?

   (circle one)   yes   no   Why or why not?_____

   _____

   _____

EXPERIENCE 6: CHAPTER 6

Prerequisite: Before performing this experience, the participant should have satisfactorily completed the objectives for Chapter 6.

Objective: During this experience, the participant will administer and interpret a questionnaire that assesses some of the factors that make a textbook difficult for a middle, junior, or senior high school student.

Participant's Instructions

1. Check with your instructor for any special directions.
2. Arrange a time and a place where you can work with (a) at least one student who will be your subject and (b) a classmate or other colleague who will be your observer.
3. Read the participant's copy of the Questionnaire on Textbook Difficulty in this experience and be sure you understand exactly what you are to do while you are completing the exercise.
4. Try to develop some rapport with the student(s) before administering the questionnaire.
5. If you are going to administer the questionnaire in a group situation, it might be wise to duplicate the student's copy of the Questionnaire on Textbook Difficulty for each student who will be responding to the questionnaire. In such a case, oral directions could be given to the group, but individual responses could be obtained by asking students to write their answers on their own student's copies.
6. Give the Observer's Checklist to your observer.
7. Administer the questionnaire to the student(s).
8. After completing all the above steps, complete the Participant's Follow-Up.

Participant's Follow-Up

Do the following:

1. State the age(s), grade(s), and content area(s) of the student(s) you worked with.

Age	Grade	Content Area
_____	_____	_____
_____	_____	_____
_____	_____	_____

2. Summarize the factors that you feel might make textbooks difficult

449

for the student(s)._____

_____

_____

3. Briefly describe a procedure for overcoming at least one of the difficulties you identified._____

_____

_____

4. Briefly discuss student reaction to the questionnaire. (I.e., Do you
consider answers to be honest, unbiased, colored by nervousness, and
so forth?)_____

_____

_____

Questionnaire on Textbook Difficulty

Name of major textbook(s) used in course_____

_____

Author of text(s)_____

_____

Publisher of text(s)_____ _____

_____

Readability level_____

Description of specific topic being covered (e.g., Truman in history, functions in mathematics)_____

Directions: Use this questionnaire for recording your answers to the questions that you ask the students. If you need more room, attach a sheet of notebook paper to the back. The words in regular type are the questions you are to ask the student(s). The words in italics are special directions and suggestions for you.

1. Do you like this textbook? Do you find it easy to read? Do you find it enjoyable to read? Why or why not? *(Note: If you suspect that the student is unable to read the textbook, continue with the rest of the interview but check with your instructor later to see if you may also do Experience 5 with this student in order to determine whether or not he can read the textbook.)*_____

_____

_____

2. Do you find this topic interesting? Why or why not?_____

_____

3. Have you had any past experience with this topic? In what way?____

_____

_____

4. What would you like to get out of this topic? *(e.g., high grade to get into the college of his choice, high grade to get financial reimbursement from family, not interested in grade but has special interest in the topic)*_____

_____

_____

5. Do you get anything special from the school if you finish this topic? *(e.g., extra credit, released time to work on a project student is par-*

*ticularly interested in, a grade of F if he does not finish)*_____

_____

_____

6. Do you know the meanings of these terms? Do you know more than one meaning for these terms? If so, what are the other meanings? *(Locate list of terms at the end of the chapter or words in italics or boldface. Try to find technical words as well as words that have more than one meaning.)*_____

_____

_____

7. Do you think this topic relates to today's world? *(e.g., look for concepts such as the energy conservation aspect of a function in terms of the relationship between miles per gallon and speed at which the car is driven)*_____

_____

_____

8. Do you think this topic has any relationship to your life at all? Why or why not? *(e.g., ask student how the energy crisis and the function of gas versus speed affects his life)*_____

_____

_____

Questionnaire on Textbook Difficulty

Name of text_____

Author of text_____

Publisher of text_____

1. Do you like this textbook? Do you find it easy to read? Do you find it enjoyable to read? Why or why not?_____

   _____

   _____

2. Do you find this topic interesting? Why or why not?_____

   _____

   _____

3. Have you had any past experience with this topic? In what way?____

   _____

   _____

4. What would you like to get out of this topic?_____

   _____

   _____

5. Do you get anything special from the school if you finish this topic?

   _____

   _____

6. Do you know the meanings of these terms? Do you know more than one meaning for these terms? If so, what are the other meanings?

   _____

   _____

7. Do you think this topic relates to today's world?_____

   _____

   _____

8. Do you think this topic has any relationship to your life at all? Why or why not?_____

   _____

Observer's Checklist

This assessment was completed by: (circle one)

self   peer   cooperating teacher   course instructor   other_____

1. Participant developed rapport with the student(s) before administering the questionnaire? (circle one)   yes   no
   Briefly describe how this was or was not done._____

   _____

2. Participant was well prepared and administered the questionnaire in a proficient, professional manner? (circle one)   yes   no
   Briefly explain why or why not._____

   _____

3. Participant administered the questionnaire in such a manner that the questions were clearly understood by the student(s)?
   (circle one)   yes   no   Briefly explain._____

   _____

   _____

4. Student(s) appeared comfortable and honest in responding to the questionnaire? (circle one)   yes   no
   Briefly explain._____

   _____

EXPERIENCE 7: CHAPTER 7

Prerequisite: Before performing this experience, the participant should have satisfactorily completed the objectives for Chapter 7.

Objectives: During this experience, the participant will design and teach at least one step of a directed reading lesson, using a format that includes a behavioral objective, a pre-assessment, a list of materials, a description of procedures, and a post-assessment.

Participant's Instructions

1. Check with your instructor for any special directions.
2. Arrange a time and a place where you can work with (a) student(s) who will be your subject(s) and (b) a classmate or other colleague who will be your observer.
3. Select the reading skill and the content area subject matter that you wish to teach to your subjects. You should select a reading skill that you feel is particularly appropriate to the content area lesson you will be teaching.
4. On a separate sheet, design the lesson according to the format illustrated in the section titled "sample lesson plans" in Chapter 7.
5. Give the Observer's Checklist in this experience to your observer.
6. Teach the lesson you have designed to the students.
7. After completing all the above steps, complete the Participant's Follow-Up.

Participant's Follow-Up

Answer the following questions:

1. If the content area textbook contained a teacher's manual, did it suggest any procedures for teaching reading skills that you were able to use in your lesson?

   (circle one)   yes   no   Briefly explain why or why not._____

   _____

   _____

2. Do you have any suggestions for varying the same lesson next time or for improving upon the suggestions in the teacher's manual?

   (circle one)   yes   no   If so, briefly describe at least one

   suggestion._____

   _____

Observer's Checklist

This assessment was completed by: (circle one)

self   peer   cooperating teacher   course instructor   other_____

1. Did the participant develop a lesson that involved one of the five
    steps of a directed reading lesson?

    (circle one)   yes   no   If yes, what was the step?_____

    _____

2. Did the participant use a lesson plan format that contained a be-
    haviorally stated reading skill objective?

    (circle one)   yes   no   If yes, describe the reading skill objec-

    tive._____

    _____

3. Did the participant use a lesson plan format that contained a be-
    haviorally stated content area objective?

    (circle one)   yes   no   If yes, describe the content area

    objective._____

    _____

4. Did the reading skill objective seem to be appropriate for the con-
    tent area lesson that was being taught?

    (circle one)   yes   no   Briefly explain why or why not._____

    _____

5. Did the participant use a lesson plan format that contained a pre-
    assessment, materials, procedures, and post-assessment?

    (circle one)   yes   no   Briefly explain how student did this.

    _____

    _____

6. Was the post-assessment appropriate to the objectives and the pre-
    assessment?

    (circle one)   yes   no   Briefly explain why or why not._____

    _____

    _____

7. Did the students show the behavior intended by the reading objec-
    tive?

    (circle one)   yes   no   Describe a behavior that reflected that the objective had been met._____

_____

_____

8. Did the students show the behavior intended by the content area
objective?

(circle one)   yes   no   Describe a behavior that reflected that

the objective had been met._____

_____

_____

EXPERIENCE 8: CHAPTER 8

Prerequisite: Before performing this experience, the participant should have satisfactorily completed the objectives for Chapter 8.

Objectives: During this experience, the participant will (1) construct, administer, score, and interpret an IRI based on a content area textbook and/or (2) design three guided reading sheets according to the following criteria: (a) select a specific content area lesson and identify one reading skill particularly needed to understand the lesson, (b) construct a lesson plan that uses at least one step of a directed reading lesson in a format that includes a behavioral objective, a pre-assessment, a list of materials, a description of procedure, and a post-assessment, and (c) include in the procedure section of the lesson plans three guided reading sheets—one for the below grade level reader, and one for the grade level reader, and one for the above grade level reader. Use at least one of the guided reading sheets to teach part of the above lesson.

Participant's Instructions

1. Check with your instructor for any special directions.
2. Arrange a time and place where you can work with (a) a student who will be your subject and (b) a classmate or other colleague who will be your observer.
3. If you plan to complete the first objective, give the Observer's Checklist—Form A to your observer. If you plan to complete the second objective, give the Observer's Checklist—Form B to your observer.
4. Complete the activity you have prepared.
5. After you have concluded all the above steps, complete the Participant's Follow-Up—Form A and/or the Participant's Follow-Up—Form B.

Participant's Follow-Up — Form A

Do the following:

1. State the name, age, grade, and content area for the student you worked with.

Name	Age	Grade	Content Area

2. Write the results of your testing below:

Name	Errors on Silent Reading Comprehension Questions	Errors on Oral Reading
_____	_____	_____

3. Can this student read that textbook?   (circle one)   yes   no

   Briefly explain why or why not._____

   _____

4. Briefly describe a procedure for teaching this student the material contained in the textbook you used for diagnosis._____

   _____

   _____

   _____

   _____

Participant's Follow-Up — Form B

Answer the following questions:

1. Did you notice any students whom you taught previously who seemed to learn more because of the differentiated guided reading sheet?

   (circle one)   yes   no   Briefly explain your answer._____

   _____

2. Did you gain any more ideas about how to construct another lesson on the same lesson you taught for the students who read above grade level?

   (circle one)   yes   no   Briefly describe your idea(s)._____

   _____

3. Did you gain any more ideas about how to construct another lesson on the same lesson you taught for the students who read on grade level?

   (circle one)   yes   no   Briefly describe your idea(s)._____

   _____

4. Did you gain any more ideas about how to construct another lesson on the lesson you taught for the students who read below grade level?

   (circle one)   yes   no   Briefly describe your idea(s)._____

   _____

Observer's Checklist—Form A

This assessment was completed by: (circle one)

self   peer   cooperating teacher   course instructor   other_____

1. Did the participant ask the student to read silently a passage of about one hundred words?

   (circle one)   yes   no   Briefly describe the content of the pas-

   sage._____

   _____

2. Did the participant construct ten comprehension questions that were appropriate to the passage?

   (circle one)   yes   no   Why or why not?_____

   _____

3. Did the participant give the student adequate instructions concerning the passage?

   (circle one)   yes   no   Why or why not?_____

   _____

4. Did the participant ask the student not to look back when answering silent reading questions?

   (circle one)   yes   no   Why or why not?_____

   _____

5. Did the participant ask the student to read aloud another passage of about a hundred words?

   (circle one)   yes   no   Why or why not?_____

   _____

6. Did the participant tally correctly errors made by the student when answering the comprehension questions and when reading aloud?

   (circle one)   yes   no   Why or why not?_____

   _____

   _____

7. Was the test subject cooperative?   (circle one)   yes   no

   Briefly describe the subject who took the test._____

   _____

Observer's Checklist—Form B

This assessment was completed by: (circle one)

self   peer   cooperating teacher   course instructor   other_____

1. Did the participant identify a specific reading skill particularly
    needed in the content area lesson?

    (circle one)   yes   no   Briefly describe the reading skill and the

    content area lesson._____

    _____

2. Did the participant's lesson plan include at least one step of a di-
    rected reading lesson?

    (circle one)   yes   no   Briefly describe why or why not._____

    _____

    _____

3. Did the participant's lesson plan contain a behavioral objective, a pre-
    assessment, a list of materials, a description of procedure, and a post-
    assessment?

    (circle one)   yes   no   Briefly describe why or why not._____

    _____

    _____

4. Did the participant construct a differentiated reading guide designed
    for a student who was reading below grade level?

    (circle one)   yes   no   Briefly describe the lesson._____

    _____

5. Did the participant construct a differentiated reading guide designed
    for a student who was reading on grade level?

    (circle one)   yes   no   Briefly describe the lesson._____

    _____

6. Did the participant construct a differentiated reading guide designed
    for a student who was reading above grade level?

    (circle one)   yes   no   Briefly describe the lesson._____

    _____

    _____

7. Did the participant teach the content area lesson?

   (circle one)   yes   no   Briefly describe the lesson._____

   _____

   _____

8. Did the student learn the intended skill?

   (circle one)   yes   no   Briefly describe why or why not._____

   _____

   _____

9. Did the student react favorably to the lesson?

   (circle one)   yes   no   Briefly explain the student's reaction.

   _____

   _____

EXPERIENCE 9: CHAPTER 9

Prerequisite: Before performing this experience, the participant should have satisfactorily completed the objectives for Chapter 9.

Objective: During this experience, the participant will describe a diagnostic-prescriptive reading program that he has observed.

Participant's Instructions

1. Check with your instructor for any special directions.
2. Arrange a time and place to observe diagnostic-prescriptive instruction. This experience does not require you to have an observer.
3. Read the Participant's Checklist in this experience until you are familiar enough with your role to complete the observation.
4. Complete the observation.
5. After concluding the above steps, complete the Participant's Follow-Up.

Participant's Checklist

1. Is a scope and sequence of skills used?   yes   no

   If so, where did the teacher obtain it?_____

2. Has an instructional level been found for each student?   yes   no

   If so, how?_____

3. Does the teacher pre-assess before instruction?   yes   no

   If so, from what source does he obtain his items?_____

   Describe or include a sample of an assessment for one skill._____

   _____

   _____

   _____

   _____

4. Do the instructional strategies include an initial teaching lesson and a reinforcement lesson?

   yes   no   If so, describe each. If not, describe the strategies

   used._____

   _____

_____

_____

_____

_____

5. Does the teacher post-assess following instruction?   yes   no

   If so, from what source does he obtain his items?_____

   _____

   Describe or include a sample of an assessment for one skill._____

   _____

   _____

   _____

   _____

   _____

6. Describe or include a sample of the lesson plan used._____

   _____

   _____

   _____

   _____ ____

   _____

7. Describe or include a sample of the teacher's schedule for diagnostic-
   prescriptive instruction._____

   _____

   _____

   _____

   _____

8. Other observations:_____

   _____

   _____

   _____

   _____

   _____

Answer the following question:

1. Did this observation give you any ideas for establishing a diagnostic-prescriptive program of your own?   (circle one)   yes   no

    If so, briefly describe at least one of those ideas. Use additional sheets as needed.

EXPERIENCE 10: CHAPTER 10

Prerequisite: Before performing this experience, the student should have satisfactorily completed the objectives for Chapter 10.

Objective: The participant will

1. Pre-assess subjects on reading skills until a skill that one or more subjects have not mastered is ascertained.
2. Design and teach an introductory lesson on the skill to the subjects previously identified.
3. Design and teach two reinforcement lessons on the same skill to the same subjects.
4. Post-assess the subjects on the skill presented.

Participant's Instructions

1. Check with your instructor for any special directions.
2. Arrange five sessions, each at least two days apart, and a place to meet with (a) a student who will be your subject and (b) a classmate or other colleague who will be your observer.
3. Read the Participant's Checklist in this experience.
4. Give the Observer's Checklist in this experience to your observer. At each session have the observer complete the appropriate section.
5. Complete the five sessions.
6. After concluding the above steps, complete the Participant's Follow-Up.

Participant's Checklist

As you perform each task, record the date on the blank to the left of each number.

_____ 1. Turn to the Teacher's Checklist of Skills in this experience. Write in the names of the subjects that you will be pre-assessing in the space provided at the top of the page.
_____ 2. From the scope and sequence of skills in Chapter 10, select four skills on which you will pre-assess your subjects.
_____ 3. List the skill descriptors on the left side of the Teacher's Checklist of Skills.
_____ 4. On a separate sheet of paper, write a pre-assessment for each objective you have chosen. (For suggestions for writing pre-assessments, see Chapter 9, "Task 2: Pre- and Post-Assessing."

471

_____ 5. While you are administering the pre-assessment, ask your observer to complete the "Selection of Objectives and Use of Chart" and "Pre-Assessment Design" sections on the Observer's Checklist.

_____ 6. Administer the pre-assessment.

_____ 7. Using the symbols in the "Suggested Key" on the Teacher's Checklist of Skills or ones of your own design, record the results of your testing.

_____ 8. Did you find at least one skill on which one or more subjects have not achieved mastery? If not, repeat steps 3 through 7 until such a skill is found. If there was at least one skill on which one or more students did not perform on a satisfactory level, proceed to teach and post-assess that skill with those subjects.

Teaching and Post-Assessing a Skill

_____ 9. On a separate sheet, write a lesson plan for teaching the skill. It should include the objective, materials, a procedure that includes an initial teaching lesson and two reinforcement lessons, and a post-assessment. (For sample lesson plans, see Chapter 9.)

_____ 10. Teach the initial teaching lesson.

_____ 11. Teach the first reinforcement lesson.

_____ 12. Teach the second reinforcement lesson.

_____ 13. Administer the post-assessment.

_____ 14. Following the post-assessment, record the results on the Teacher's Checklist of Skills in this experience.

Participant's Follow-Up

1. Do you believe your pre-assessment was valid?

   (circle one)   yes   no   Why or why not?_____

   _____

2. Do you believe you taught your subjects a skill?

   (circle one)   yes   no   Why or why not?_____

   _____

3. Do you believe that subjects felt they had learned a skill?

   (circle one)   yes   no   Why or why not?_____

   _____

4. General comments:_____

   _____

   _____

Teacher's Checklist of Skills
for Experience 10

Subjects' Names

Descriptor

(e.g., Making Inferences)

Descriptor									

Suggested Key: Blank Space — Not Assessed

√ — Passed Pre-Assessment

◯ — Did Not Pass Pre-Assessment; Needs Instruction

◯√ — Did Not Pass Pre-Assessment; Has Received Instruction and Passed Post-Assessment

Observer's Checklist

This assessment was completed by: (circle one)

self   peer   cooperating teacher   course instructor   other_____

Selection of Objectives and Use of Chart

1. Did objectives selected appear appropriate to the content area?

    (circle one)   yes   no   Why or why not?_____

    _____

2. Are names and descriptors correctly recorded on chart?

    (circle one)   yes   no   If no, why not?_____

    _____

Pre-Assessment Design

3. Did each assessment question appear to assess the behavior described in the objective?

    (circle one)   yes   no   If no, why not?_____

    _____

4. Are there at least three questions for each objective or subobjective being assessed?

    (circle one)   yes   no

5. Did each test question appear to be on the correct level of difficulty? (i.e., Were selections on instructional level when instructional level was required?)

    (circle one)   yes   no   If no, why not?_____

    _____

6. General comments:_____

    _____

Lesson Plan Design

7. Did lesson plan include:

    a. an initial teaching lesson?   (circle one)   yes   no

    b. two reinforcement lessons?   (circle one)   yes   no

    c. a post-assessment?   (circle one)   yes   no

Initial Teaching Lesson

8. Did initial teaching lesson provide demonstration or explanation of the skill to be learned?

   (circle one)   yes   no

   If yes, how was it given? (teacher, audiotape, film, combination)

   _____

9. General comments:_____

   _____

First Reinforcement Lesson

10. Did the first reinforcement lesson provide practice and any necessary explanation regarding the skill to be learned?

    (circle one)   yes   no   Describe activity used._____

    _____

11. General comments:_____

    _____

Second Reinforcement Lesson

12. Did the second reinforcement lesson provide practice and any needed explanation regarding the skill to be learned?

    (circle one)   yes   no   Describe the activity used._____

    _____

13. General comments:_____

    _____

Post-Assessment

14. Did each test question appear to assess the behavior described in the objective?

    (circle one)   yes   no

    If no, why not?_____

    _____

15. Did each test question appear to be at the correct level of difficulty?

    (circle one)   yes   no   Explain._____

    _____

16. General comments:_____

_____

EXPERIENCE 11: CHAPTER 11

Prerequisite: Before performing this experience, the participant should have satisfactorily completed the objectives for Chapter 11.

Objectives: During this experience, the participant will do one or more of the following: (1) construct and utilize an instrument to diagnose the reading interests of adolescents and/or (2) utilize a checklist to help locate appropriate reading materials and/or (3) develop and use a game or activity designed to reinforce a reading skill within a content area.

Participant's Instructions

1. Check with your instructor for any special directions.
2. Arrange a time and place where you can work with (a) a student who will be your subject if you plan on completing Objectives 1 or 3 and (b) a classmate or other colleague who will be your observer.
3. If you plan on completing Objective 1, you may use the Reading Interest Inventory in Figure 11.1 or you may devise your own. If you plan on completing Objective 2, use the Checklist for Locating Reading Materials in Figure 11.3.
4. If you have planned on completing the first objective, give the Observer's Checklist—Form A in this experience to your observer. If you plan on completing the second objective, give the Observer's Checklist—Form B to your observer. If you plan on completing the third objective, give the Observer's Checklist—Form C to your observer.
5. Complete the experience you have prepared.
6. After you have concluded the above steps, complete the Participant's Follow-Up—Form A and/or the Participant's Follow-Up—Form B and/or the Participant's Follow-Up—Form C.

Participant's Follow-Up—Form A

After administering the Reading Interest Inventory found in Figure 11.1 or one you have constructed yourself, do the following:

1. State the name, age, grade, and content area for the student you worked with.

Name	Age	Grade	Content Area

2. From the results of your administration of the inventory, briefly describe the types of books you would suggest that the student read.

_____

_____

3. Give a specific example of a book that you feel the student might enjoy.

_____

Participant's Follow-Up — Form B

After using the Checklist for Locating Reading Material in Figure 11.2, do the following:

1. Briefly describe the name, publisher, purpose, and contents of at least one type of instructional material that you reviewed and that you feel would be particularly appropriate to the age, sex, and content area of the student with whom you are working.

    Name_____

    Publisher_____

    Purpose_____

    Brief summary of contents _____

    _____

    _____

    Age level intended_____

    Sex intended_____

    Content area intended_____

2. Briefly describe the name, publisher, purpose, and contents of at least one type of nontext material that you reviewed and that you feel would be particularly appropriate to the age, sex, and content area of the student with whom you are working.

    Name_____

    Publisher_____

    Purpose_____

    Brief summary of contents_____

    _____

    _____

Age level intended_____

Sex intended_____

Content area intended_____

Participant's Follow-Up — Form C

Do the following:

1. Briefly discuss the most effective aspect of your game or activity.

   _____

   _____

2. Briefly discuss the least effective aspect of your game or activity.

   _____

   _____

3. Briefly discuss how you might design a second game or activity to reinforce the same reading skill.

   _____

   _____

Observer's Checklist—Form A

This assessment was completed by: (circle one)

self   peer   cooperating teacher   course instructor   other_____

1. Was the interest inventory in a format that was easy to fill out?

    (circle one)   yes   no

    Briefly describe the format of the inventory. Give an example of an
    item, if you wish._____

    _____

2. For what age level was the inventory appropriate? (circle one or
    more)

    early adolescence—   middle adolescence—   late adolescence—
    age 11–14   age 15–16   age 17 through
                                                             adulthood

    Briefly explain your answer._____

    _____

3. Was the inventory appropriate to the age of the adolescent to whom
    the inventory was administered?

    (circle one)   yes   no

    Briefly explain your answer. _____

    _____

4. How did the adolescent react to the inventory?   (circle one)

    favorably   unfavorably   other_____

    Briefly explain your answer. _____

    _____

5. Did the content of the interest inventory reflect the following as-
    pects? (Put a check by those aspects that were included on the
    inventory.)

    _____ 1. mystery   6. family life

    _____ 2. supernatural   _____ 7. sex

    _____ 3. adventure   _____ 8. comedy

    _____ 4. violence   _____ 9. westerns

    _____ 5. romance   _____ 10. domestic animals

_____ 11. wild animals

_____ 12. sports

_____ 13. travel

_____ 14. social problems

_____ 15. philosophy

_____ 16. religion

_____ 17. biography and
autobiography

_____ 18. history

_____ 19. foreign countries

_____ 20. world affairs

_____ 21. local affairs

_____ 22. music

_____ 23. art

_____ 24. mathematics

_____ 25. applied science and
technology

_____ 26. physical science

_____ 27. biological science

_____ 28. vocations

_____ 29. avocations

_____ 30. adolescent life

_____ 31. personal problems

_____ 32. fairy tales and
mythology

Observer's Checklist — Form B

This assessment was completed by: (circle one)

self   peer   cooperating teacher   course instructor   other_____

1. Did the participant use the checklist in Figure 11.3 of the textbook to help identify appropriate instructional materials for a specific content area classroom?

   (circle one)   yes   no

   If no, briefly describe the checklist that was used by the participant.

   _____

   _____

2. Did you agree with the participant's categorization of instructional materials?

   (circle one)   yes   no

   Briefly explain why or why not._____

   _____

3. Did you agree with the participant's categorization of nontext materials?

   (circle one)   yes   no

   Briefly explain why or why not._____

   _____

Observer's Checklist—Form C

This assessment was completed by: (circle one)

self   peer   cooperating teacher   course instructor   other_____

1. Did the participant select a reading skill appropriate to the content area that he is teaching?

    (circle one)   yes   no   Tell why or why not and briefly identify

    the content area and the reading skill._____

    _____

2. Was the game or activity motivating, colorful, and durable?

    (circle one)   yes   no   Briefly describe why or why not._____

    _____

    _____

3. Did the student understand the directions for completing the game or activity?

    (circle one)   yes   no   Briefly discuss why or why not. _____

    _____

    _____

4. Did the student seem to enjoy the game or activity?

    (circle one)   yes   no   Briefly discuss the student's reaction.

    _____

    _____

5. Was the game or activity beneficial to the student in helping him learn or reinforce a needed reading skill?

    (circle one)   yes   no   Briefly discuss why or why not._____

    _____

    _____

EXPERIENCE 12: CHAPTER 12

Prerequisite: Before performing this experience, the participant should have satisfactorily completed the objectives for Chapter 12.

Objectives: During this experience, the participant will (1) design a reading lesson during which three different approaches to developmental reading are used with three different groups of students; e.g., one group by the textbook approach, one group by the individualized approach, and one group by the independent study approach and/or (2) design and teach a lesson based on an eclectic approach; e.g., the lessons for one group of students might include aspects of the language experience, the independent study, and the individualized approaches.

Participant's Instructions

1. Check with your instructor for any special directions.
2. Arrange a time and a place where you can work with (a) a student who will be your subject and (b) a classmate or other colleague who will be your observer.
3. Give the Observer's Checklist in this experience to your observer.
4. Complete the lesson you have prepared.
5. After you have finished all these steps, complete the Participant's Follow-Up.

Participant's Follow-Up

Answer the following questions:

1. Did your lesson that used a variety of strategies fit students' needs more closely than your regular technique did?

   (circle one)   yes   no   Why or why not?_____

   _____

   _____

   _____

2. Would you use a variety of strategies to teach reading in a middle, junior or senior high school classroom?

   Why or why not?_____

   _____

Observer's Checklist

This assessment was completed by: (circle one)

self   peer   cooperating teacher   course instructor   other_____

1. Participant designed a lesson that involved at least three different groups of students in different approaches to developmental reading?

   (circle one)   yes   no

2. Participant designed a lesson in which one group of students was exposed to more than one technique?

   (circle one)   yes   no

3. Which strategies were used? (Circle the appropriate strategies in the list below.)

   reading textbook approach

   language experience approach

   individualized approach

   independent study approach

   diagnostic-prescriptive technique

Appendixes

Teacher's Copy of the Informal Reading Inventory

Contents:

(1) Directions for administering and scoring the test.

(2) Selections to be used for oral and silent reading from each grade level—grades 1 through 12.

DIRECTIONS FOR ADMINISTERING

Before the informal reading inventory in Appendix A may be used with a student it needs some adaptation. To prepare the copy for student use, the teacher will need to tear out the passages along the perforated edges and then follow the procedure suggested below:

1. Make a photostatic copy in black, legible type (not purple spirit master because this affects readability) of the following twenty-four reading passages and twelve sets of questions.
2. Note the number on the upper, right-hand corner of each passage. The grade level is in code so that it can be identified by the classroom teacher but not by the student. For example, the codes for grade one are as follows: grade one oral reading selection = 312-1-159; grade one silent reading selection = 312-1-259. The fourth digit stands for the grade level of the passage and the fifth digit stands for whether the passage is to be read orally (1) or silently (2). Hence the fourth grade passages would be coded as follows: grade four oral = 312-4-159; grade four silent = 312-4-259.
   The teacher should black out this code on the front of each passage and write it on the back of each passage.
3. Cut the oral reading passage and the silent reading passage apart so that one sheet contains the passage for oral reading and the other contains the passage for silent reading and the accompanying questions. If the separated reading passages are smoothed out carefully and covered with clear plastic which has an adhesive backing, they will be more durable. If the teacher intends to use the same passages over and over again, such a protective covering would add to the length of time the passages would be useable.
4. As the student reads orally from the plastic covered copy, you should follow along on the original and note the oral errors that the student makes.
5. Note that the questions to the silent reading selection are on the back of the silent reading passage. Remind the students that after they have read the passage, they are to turn the passage over and answer the questions without looking back at the selection.

DIRECTIONS FOR SCORING

1. All the oral reading passages contain between one hundred and one hundred and sixteen words. Hence the number of errors that may be made in order that the passage be on the student's instructional level is five.
2. All the silent reading passages contain ten questions. Hence the maximum number of errors that may be made in order that the passage be on the student's instructional level is three.

496

The boy stood on the wall. He jumped down. He wore black shoes. The sand got on his shoes. It was very hot. The boy was back on the wall. The trees made him feel cool. He took off his shirt. He took off his pants. He had nothing on. He looked at the water.

He was twelve years old. His shoulders were wide. His mouth and eyes were gentle. He touched the tree and smiled. He stood on his head. He jumped down to the water again! The water felt good. He wanted to swim in the water.

———————————————— cut here ————————————————

The boy walked faster. He was late and had to hurry. The wind was blowing. It made his shirt touch his skin. His shirt felt very hard. The shirt scratched his skin. The edge of his shorts scratched his legs. They made his skin look pink. He felt dirty and did not like it. His hair had grown long and ugly. The sun was going down. He began to run.

The other boys were already at the beach. They were near the pool where they took their baths. They saw Mark coming. He had a frown on his face. They did not say anything to him.

1. What time of day was it?
2. Was Mark thinking of anything or just taking a walk?
3. Tell about his clothing.
4. Did the boy like the way he looked? Explain.
5. Why was Mark in a hurry?
6. What color were his legs? Why?
7. Tell about the weather.
8. Why did the other boys not say anything to him?
9. What time of day did Mark arrive at the beach?
10. Where on the beach were the other boys waiting?

He made his feet move until he was out on the neck of land. All around him there was only air. There was no place that he could hide but that did not really matter because he had to go on. He stopped on the skinny piece of land and looked down. It would take a long time, but someday the sea would cover this land. The castle would be under the sea. On one side was the lagoon. The lagoon had protected them from the Pacific. Mark could see the ocean as it rose and fell. It looked as if it were breathing.

———————————————— cut here ————————————————

Peter sighed because the rest of the boys could talk in the meeting just as if they were talking to one boy. They could say whatever they wanted to say. They were not afraid as he was. He stopped and looked back. There came Mark holding a spear. Peter slowed down until Mark was walking beside him. Mark looked down at him and smiled. That made Peter feel so good that he forgot to watch where he was going. He ran into a tree and got a cut on his head. Mark did not look at him, but Robert laughed. Mark sent Peter away and then started toward the castle again.

1. What could the other boys do that Peter could not do?
2. Why did Peter sigh?
3. Do you think Peter would be good as a teacher?
4. Was Peter walking ahead of or behind Mark?
5. Describe a spear.
6. Did Peter care what Mark thought about him? How do you know?
7. How did Peter feel before he hit the tree?
8. How do you think Peter felt after he hit the tree?
9. Who laughed when Peter hit the tree?
10. Where was Mark going?

He came at last to a sunny place. The vines did not have to go so far for light. They grew so thick that they had woven a great mat that hung at the side of an open space in the jungle. Here a patch of rock came close to the surface and would not allow more than little plants and ferns to grow. The whole space was surrounded with dark, sweet-smelling bushes. A great tree, which had fallen across one corner, leaned against the trees that still stood.

Peter paused. As he looked over his shoulder at Jeff he saw the beast behind the tree.

———————————————————— cut here ————————————————————

They set off along the beach walking in a line. Mark went first. He limped a little and carried his spear over his shoulder. Because it was so hot, he could only partly see things. His long hair and injuries even made it harder. The twins came behind him. They were worried now, but still full of energy. They said little and trailed the butts of their wooden spears. Brian had found that by looking down and shielding his eyes from the sun, he could see the trailing spears moving along the sand. So he walked between the twins and held the rock carefully between his two hands.

1. Where were the boys walking?
2. What were Mark and the twins carrying?
3. Why do you think Mark was limping?
4. What is the butt of a spear?
5. Why did Brian stand between the twins?
6. What kind of mood do you think the twins were in?
7. Who walked first in line?
8. Was it a sandy or rocky beach?
9. Why was it difficult for the boys to see where they were going?
10. What word or words can you think of to describe the way the twins walked?

Brian shouted at Mark and then jumped quickly into the sea. He was the best swimmer and liked the sea better than the others did. But he was angry at that moment and did not enjoy his swim very much. He was mad because one of the others ha   discussed the accident. He climbed out of the sea and threw his body on the beach. He stared at the distant shore for a long time before he finally noticed the sharks. He jumped up and shouted a warning to the others. In a few seconds most of the boys were swimming quickly for the beach.

———————————————————— cut here ————————————————————

The fat wolves enjoyed lying under the shadows of the trees. There was no wind and they had no idea anything was wrong. Mark had much practice at hiding in the shadows. He stole away and told his friends what to do. Soon they all began to inch forward. They sweated in the silence and the heat. Under the trees a tail wagged lazily. One wolf was a little apart from the others, lying there, apparently very content. She was black and gray and there was a row of baby wolves at her slender belly. Some were sleeping, some eating, and others were playing quietly with one another.

1. Where did the wolves like to lie?
2. Do you think something is going to happen to the wolves? What?
3. Why do you think one of the boys had "much practice at hiding in the shadows"?
4. Define the italicized word, "He *stole* away . . ."
5. Define the italicized word, "Soon they all began to *inch* forward."
6. What was the weather like?
7. Who was the leader of the group? How do you know this?
8. How did the wolves feel?
9. What color was the mother wolf?
10. Name two things that the baby wolves were doing.

While Mark was sitting, he was aware of the heat for the first time that day. He was very uncomfortable in his gray shirt. He sat and thought about washing his shirt. Sitting in what seemed an unusual heat even for this island, Mark planned how he could make himself better groomed. First he would like to have a pair of scissors to cut his hair. He flung his mass of filthy hair back and measured to half an inch where he would cut it. He passed his tongue over his teeth and decided that a toothbrush would come in handy too. He began to itch all over at the thought of the dirt.

———————————————— cut here ———————————————

312-5-259

Peter was not in the bathing pool as they had expected. When the other two had trotted down the beach to look back at the mountain, he had followed them for a few yards. Then he had stopped and had stood frowning down at a pile of sand on the beach. He turned around and walked into the forest as if he had something important to do. Peter was a small, skinny boy with a pointed chin and bright eyes. His course black hair was long and hid his low, broad forehead. He wore the remains of shorts and had no shoes. One foot was badly blistered.

1. What color was Peter's hair?
2. Why do you think Peter was frowning as he looked down at the pile of sand?
3. Where did the boys expect to find Peter?
4. Why do you think Peter wore no shoes?
5. At what did the boys look back?
6. What does the word *important* mean?
7. Define the italicized word, "He wore the *remains* of shorts . . . ."
8. Define the italicized word, "the other two had *trotted* down the beach . . . ."
9. What does the word *forehead* mean?
10. Why do you think Peter's foot was badly blistered?

Their bodies, from throat to ankle, were hidden by fur capes. The capes had a red mark on the left side and a snakeskin collar around the neck. The heat, the climb down, the search for food, and now this sweaty march along the hot beach had made them red in the face. The leader was dressed in the same way, but the mark on his cape was purple. When the boys were about ten yards from the platform, the leader shouted an order. The boys stopped, but they continued breathing heavily, sweating and swaying in the hot light. The stifling weather was too much for them.

———————————————————— cut here ————————————————————

Within the glittering haze of the beach something was stumbling around. Mark noticed it first and watched it until all the others looked in the direction of his gaze. Then the creature stepped into the clear sand. They saw that the animal was actually a party of boys marching in step in two straight lines and dressed in strange clothing. They carried knives and spoons in their hands and each boy wore a black woolen cap with a silver mark on it. Mark and his friends ran to the cabin to warn the others. The group huddled together to discuss what to do.

1. Who saw the "creature" first?
2. What did he see?
3. What was the "creature" wearing?
4. What were they carrying?
5. What color was the cap?
6. What material was the cap made of?
7. What was on the cap?
8. How many lines were the boys in?
9. Define the italicized word, "The groups *huddled* together . . . ."
10. What was Mark's feeling toward the "creature"?

The others were waiting for the signal and they came immediately. Some of the youngsters were aware that a canoe had floated down the river while the trap had been set. Any feelings of hope were quickly subdued because of Mark's anger. The other youngsters, including the toddlers, were impressed by the general air of seriousness. The meeting place filled quickly, and most of the hunters were on Mark's right, while the others were on the left, under the banana tree. Sidney came and stood outside the assembly. By this gesture, he showed that he wished to listen but would not speak. It was his way of expressing his disapproval for their carelessness.

———————————————— cut here ————————————————

When Mark awoke it was early morning. At first he was surprised to find himself sleeping with the bayonet, but then he remembered and jumped up and went to the edge of the beach with the cumbersome weapon clenched in his hand. The savage he had apprehended was still tied there. As Mark approached cautiously, the solitary savage did not turn his head to look, but kept staring straight ahead until Mark stood right in front of him. There was loathing in his eyes and a grimace on his face. He was an enormous man with bronze-colored skin. The lump was still on his forehead, and an old jagged scar ran across the top of his eyebrows and down one cheek.

1. What time of day did Mark wake up?
2. What was he sleeping with?
3. What had Mark remembered?
4. Where did Mark go as soon as he awoke?
5. Define the italicized word, "the *solitary* savage . . . ."
6. Define the italicized word, ". . . a *grimace* on his face."
7. Why do you think there was loathing in the savage's eyes?
8. Describe the way the savage looked.
9. Why do you think there was a lump on the savage's forehead?
10. Describe what sort of person you think Mark was.

About fourteen miles from the rapid stream they entered a part of the forest where the number of trees decreased. At first, they were cheered by the difference in terrain, because there was no undergrowth and the darkness of the forest was not so intense. In this spot there was a greenish glare around them and in some positions they could see quite a way into the forest. However, the light revealed only endless streams of green vegetation like the inside of a completely enclosed greenhouse. The sameness of all the trees gave them little hope of finding some landmark that they could use to find their way out.

———————————————— cut here ————————————————

312-8-259

With that thought agitating in his mind, his speed increased. He was alert all of a sudden to the sensation of urgency as well as to a little wind, produced by his speed, that breathed about his face. This wind crowded his gray shirt against his chest. His attention was aroused in this recent mood of comprehension—the folds of his clothes were stiff like cardboard and unbending, the frayed ends of his shorts were creating an uncomfortable pink area in the anterior of his thigh. With a convulsion of mind, Mark disentangled the dirt and decay. He comprehended how much he had lost.

1. What was Mark alert to? What sort of feeling?
2. What caused him to increase his speed?
3. Why do you think he felt uncomfortable?
4. What aroused his attention?
5. What was his recent mood? What word is used to describe it?
6. Why do you think the folds of his clothes were stiff?
7. Define the italicized word, ". . . *disentangled* the dirt and decay."
8. Define the italicized word, "with a *convulsion* of mind. . . ."
9. Why do you suppose the situation bothered him?
10. What words does the author use to convey Mark's feeling toward the situation?

Peter shifted direction away from the others and proceeded to where the just perceptible path led him into the eminent jungle. Towering trunks bore unexpectedly pale flowers all the way up to the dark canopy where the life force went on clamorously. The air was lured here and the creepers' ropes descended limply like the rigging of floundered ships. His feet left impressions on the damp, pliant soil, and the creepers shivered as he moved against their stretching lengths.

He came at last to where the sun had perceived an opening, its abundant rays warmed the creepers as they wove an intricate mat of weird green with their thrusting arms.

———————————————————— cut here ————————————————————

312-9-259

Mark's ordinary voice sounded whispery after the harsh note of the bugle as he laid it against his lips, breathing deeply and blowing once more. The note boomed again and then, at his firmer pressure, the note moved up an octave, becoming a strident blare, more penetrating than before. Sidney, with a pleased face and flashing smile was shouting something as the birds cried and small animals scattered. Mark's breath, failing with a rush of air, dropped the note an octave, making it rubbery. Mark's reddened face was dark with breathlessness as the bugle was silenced and became a gleaming tusk, leaving only echoes.

1. How did Mark's voice sound?
2. What made his voice change?
3. Do you think he felt tired? How do you know?
4. What was Sidney shouting?
5. Describe Sidney's appearance.
6. Describe Mark's appearance.
7. What was Mark doing?
8. What do you think his purpose for doing so was?
9. Define the italicized word, ". . . *strident* blare . . . ."
10. Define the italicized word, ". . . *making* it rubbery."

In vain they examined the bizarre cavern from both above and below. There simply was no passage by which they could exit, no sign of any other tunnel. Mark experienced a most excruciatingly painful flash of disappointment. He regained his composure enough to admit the negligible reality of possible escape. He stooped to his knees and looked above once more. The same barrier of granite was wedged in the opening. It was an obvious obstacle to their exit, and all previous attempts to disgorge it had failed. Peter used the lantern to examine all sides of the cavern in every direction, but to no avail. They both admitted that they had to relinquish all hopes of escaping.

———————————————— cut here ————————————————

312-10-259

He was perturbed at Brian's running around alone. On the following afternoon, he accompanied Brian when they went out to capture the wolves. Perhaps his presence gave the afternoon its peculiar quality of danger, which made it different from the other wolf hunts that summer. There were the same hunters, the same assortment of weapons, the same many-colored, many-keyed confusions, but there was an unpleasantness in the air, a pervading harshness that hadn't been there before. Perhaps the warning signs would have been noticed if the profusion of unusual events leading up to the hunt had not occurred. The first incident was the most bizarre of them all.

1. What was the main character perturbed about?
2. When did he go with Brian on the hunt?
3. What were they going to hunt?
4. What were the feelings of the main character about the day?
5. How many hunts had there been before this one?
6. What time of the year was it?
7. How many people went on the hunt?
8. Define the italicized word, ". . . a *pervading* harshness. . . ."
9. Define the italicized word, ". . . *profusion* of unusual events . . . ."
10. What do you think is going to happen?

Mark was the first to notice the surprising spectacle. The successive remains of what appeared to be generations and generations of men and animals
were compounded in one colossal, ancient cemetery. The great question that
presented itself to the boys was one which none of them actually wanted to
contemplate in terms of the totality of its implications. Had those once-
animated beings been buried underneath the earth because of some tremendous earthquake, after they had died a natural death? Or had they been
killed and then carried there by some demonical inhabitant of the island?
Who or what had placed this massive cemetery so far beneath the forest, and
so far beneath the entrance of the cavern?

———————————————— cut here ————————————————

The air was suffocating, while between flashing lightning the macabre
scene unrolled. The boys clamorously followed Scott and Eric, stumbling
through the viscid sand to the opening beyond the fire. Eric became the
enraged one, encouraging the others to draw back a bit, charging at Scott
who sidestepped; the excitement of the fight caused the group to make a
circle around the two who were quarreling; the emitted noises quickly lost
their first superficial excitement and became a titillating pulselike sound.
Under the lowering sky, Brian and Mark, like excited children on the outside
of the circle, began to feel an eagerness to become part of the foolish but
strangely intoxicating battle.

1. Describe the setting.
2. Define the italicized word, "the boys *clamorously* followed . . . ."
3. Define the italicized word, ". . . the *viscid* sand . . . ."
4. Give the names of the four boys in the passage.
5. Who would be the protagonist in the passage?
6. What was causing the "pulselike sound"?
7. Would the scene be the same without the "pulselike sound" and the "lowering sky"? Explain why or why not.
8. What was happening in the center of the circle?
9. Why do you think it was happening?
10. What were the feelings of the audience toward what was happening?

With deliberation, Mark parted the screen of grass and circumspectly looked out upon the few remaining yards of stony ground that preceded the area where the two sides of the island almost became indistinguishable. One expected to see a peak of headland but discovered instead a narrow projecting rock a few yards wide and possibly fifteen long that extended the island further into the sea, where it joined another of those pieces of pink squareness that underlay the structure of the island. This side of the castle, possibly a hundred feet high, was the pink bastion they had discovered from the mountain top.

———————————————————— cut here ————————————————————

Mark shuddered uncontrollably. The lagoon had protected them from the Pacific, and for some reason only Jeff had ventured completely down to the waters on the opposite side. Immediately, he was confronted with the landman's view of the swell, and it characteristically seemed like the breathing of some stupendous creature, as he solemnly watched the waters slowly sinking among the rocks, revealing pink tables of granite, unusual growths of coral, polyp, and weed. Down, down, down the waters continued, whispering like the wind among the heads of the forest, before it was sucked down on the four weedy sides of a large, flat, table rock.

1. What is the character's name in the passage?
2. What emotion does he feel at the beginning of the passage?
3. What words does the writer use to convey the character's emotion?
4. What body of water is mentioned near the beginning of the passage?
5. What sort of view of the swell did the character have?
6. To what does he compare the water?
7. What does the water appear to be doing?
8. As the water sinks into the rocks, what things are revealed underneath?
9. Define the italicized word, ". . . the *heads* of the forest . . . ."
10. What was the shape of the rock that was described near the end of the passage?

Concise Guide to Standardized Reading Tests

Concise Guide to Standardized Reading Tests

Test and Publisher	What it Measures (usually subtests)	Levels (grades)	Date of Publication or Latest Revision	Time (min.)	Brief Resume of Evaluation
SURVEY TESTS:					
Burnett Reading Series: Survey Test, Scholastic Testing Service	Vocabulary, comprehension, rate and accuracy	7–13	1967–70	50	Norms and validity data incomplete; problems concerning interpretation of some items; some cultural bias.
Cooperative English Tests: Reading Section, Educational Testing Service	Vocabulary, comprehension, speed of comprehension	9–14	1960	40	Perhaps not accurate for very high or low reading levels; normed mostly in Southern small town schools, but on the whole a satisfactory test.
Davis Reading Test: Psychological Corporation	Level and speed of comprehension	8–13	1961	40	Lacks vocabulary measure but well-constructed test.
Gates-MacGinitie Reading Tests: Surveys E & R, Teachers College Press, Columbia University	Speed and accuracy, vocabulary, comprehension	7–12	1970	46	Normative and reliability data inadequate; comprehension measures only use of context; but useful *Technical Supplement* and well-constructed test.
Metropolitan Achievement Tests: Reading, Advanced, Harcourt Brace Jovanovich	Vocabulary, comprehension	7–9	1970	46	Measures higher cognitive processes; one reading selection relevant to black culture; clear manual and well-constructed test.
Nelson-Denny Reading Test: Houghton Mifflin	Vocabulary, comprehension, rate	9–16	1960 (two new forms 1973)	40	Covers too great an age span: time restrictions create difficulty; literary emphasis; most suitable for college; insufficient reliability and validity data.
Nelson Reading Test: Houghton Mifflin	Vocabulary, comprehension,	3–9	1962	30	Covers wide range and takes little time; reliability and validity data insufficient; vocabulary dated.

522

Test	Areas Measured	Grades	Date	Time	Comments
Sequential Tests of Educational Progress: (STEP), Series II: Reading, Educational Testing Service	Comprehension	4–14	1969	45	Limited reliability and norming information; scanty manual; but appealing reading passages, pleasing format and high content validity.
Stanford Achievement Tests: Advanced Paragraph Meaning; High School Reading, Harcourt Brace Jovanovich	Comprehension	7–12	1965–66	40–45	Adequate norming and reliability data; excellent manual; high school test measures only literal and factual comprehension; very good series of reading tests.
Traxler High School Reading Test: Revised, Bobbs-Merrill	Comprehension, rate	9–12	1967	55	Measures lower level cognitive skills; paragraphs in social studies and science; inadequate norming and validity data; low reliabilities; possibility of answering questions without reading passages.
Traxler Silent Reading Test: Bobbs-Merrill	Rate, vocabulary, comprehension	7–10	1969	55	Useful test, but social class bias on some parts may reduce efficacy for lower-social-class students.
ANALYTICAL TESTS:					
California Achievement Tests: Reading California Test Bureau/McGraw-Hill	Vocabulary, study skills, comprehension in different types of materials	6–12	1970	50–75	Improved version for survey purposes; vocabulary words in context; content area passages; well standardized.
Comprehensive Tests of Basic Skills: Reading California Test Bureau/McGraw-Hill	Vocabulary, comprehension study skills	6–12	1968–69	60–65	Items classified in terms of intellectual process; minority groups represented in norms; variety of scoring reports; comprehensive manuals and well-constructed tests.

Reprinted with permission of the authors and the International Reading Association. From a "Concise Guide to Standardized Secondary and College Reading Tests," by Nancy A. Mavrogenes, Carol K. Winkley, Earl Hanson, and Richard T. Vacca, October 1974 *Journal of Reading*, pp. 12–22.

Concise Guide to Standardized Reading Tests (cont'd)

Test and Publisher	What it Measures (usually subtests)	Levels (grades)	Date of Publication or Latest Revision	Time (min.)	Brief Resume of Evaluation
Diagnostic Reading Tests: Committee on Diagnostic Reading Tests	Vocabulary, comprehension (silent and auditory), rate, word attack	7–13	1963	varies	Confusing manuals; technical information missing; but ambitious attempt.
Durrell Listening-Reading Series: Harcourt Brace Jovanovich	Vocabulary listening and reading, paragraph listening and reading	1–9	1969–70	140–195	Some questions raised as to design of test items and purpose of measuring degree of retardation, but compares very favorably with other tests of reading and listening abilities.
Dvorak–Van Wagenen Diagnostic Examination of Silent Reading Abilities: Van Wagenen Psycho-Educational Laboratories	Rate, perception of relations, vocabulary, information, details, central thought, inferences, interpretation, reading for ideas	4–16	1939–54	140–150	Useful for speed of comprehension and as a general measure of reading ability; diagnostic value limited by unreliability of differences among separate test scores.
Iowa Silent Reading Tests: Harcourt Brace Jovanovich	Vocabulary, comprehension, locating information, skimming and scanning, reading efficiency	6–12	1973	60	Carefully prepared and easy to use.
Monroe-Sherman Group Diagnostic Reading Aptitude and Achievement Tests: C. H. Nevins Printing Company	Comprehension; speed; word discrimination; arithmetic; spelling; visual, motor and auditory ability; vocabulary	3–9	1939	60–70	No data on reliability and no description of norming population.
Reading Test: McGraw-Hill Basic Skills System: McGraw-Hill	Rate, flexibility, retention, skimming and scanning, comprehension	11–14	1970	70	Lack of adequate norming samples, but high face validity and clear manual; promising test.
Silent Reading Diagnostic Tests: (Bond, Balow, Hoyt) Lyons & Carnahan	Words in isolation and in context, visual structural analysis, syllabication, word synthesis, beginning and ending sounds, vowel and consonant sounds	2–6	1970	90	Limited in value but provides some useful diagnostic information.

Test	Skills/Areas Measured	Grade Level	Date	Time (min.)	Strengths/Comments
SRA Achievement Series: (Multi-level Edition) Science Research Associates	Comprehension, vocabulary, work-study skills (references and charts)	1–9	1963	77	Strengths to recommend its use: ease of administration, clarity of format, over-lapping tests providing for large class-room range, and large standardization sample.
Stanford Diagnostic Reading Test Level II: Harcourt Brace Jovanovich	Comprehension (literal and inferential), vocabulary, syllabication, auditory skills, phonic analysis, rate	4.5–8.5	1966	90–110	Offers suggestions for grouping and remediation; carefully standardized and useful test.
DIAGNOSTIC TESTS:					
Botel Reading Inventory: Follett Educational Corp.	(Group test except for word recognition) Phonics, word opposites, reading and listening	1–12	1961–70	varies	Data lacking on norms, reliability and validity; but may be useful as informal test to determine instructional levels.
Classroom Reading Inventory: (Silvaroli) William C. Brown Book Co.	(Individual test except for spelling) Word recognition; independent, instructional and frustration reading levels; hearing capacity level	2–8	1965–69	varies	When judiciously used, a most valuable adjunct to a total reading program.
Durrell Analysis of Reading Difficulty: Harcourt Brace Jovanovich	Oral and silent reading; listening; word recognition and analysis; naming, identifying and matching letters; visual memory of words; sounds of words and letters; spelling; handwriting	1–6	1955	30–90	Complete analysis; clear directions; complete and useful check lists; most useful with less severe cases.
Gates-McKillop Reading Diagnostic Tests: Bureau of Publications, Columbia University	Oral reading test, word lists, phrase recognition, syllabication, letter names and sounds, visual and auditory blending, spelling (28 scores in all)	1–8	1962	30–60	Very inclusive; satisfactorily standardized; well-established test; but needs sophisticated judgment to use.

Concise Guide to Standardized Reading Tests (cont'd)

Test and Publisher	What it Measures (usually subtests)	Levels (grades)	Date of Publication or Latest Revision	Time (min.)	Brief Resume of Evaluation
Gilmore Oral Reading Test: Harcourt Brace Jovanovich	Accuracy, comprehension, rate of oral reading	1–8	1968	15–20	Among best standardized tests of accuracy in oral reading; usefulness of comprehension and rate scores is more questionable.
Gray Oral Reading Test: Bobbs-Merrill	Oral reading	1–16	1963	varies	Welcome addition to the limited number of reasonably satisfactory oral reading tests. Doesn't measure comprehension.
Standard Reading Inventory: (McCracken) Klamath Printing Co.	Recognition vocabulary, oral reading accuracy, oral and silent comprehension and speed, listening	1–7	1966	30–120	Not standardized, cumbersome manual and complex scoring; but reliability and validity data available and attractive materials.
Pupil Placement Tests: Houghton Mifflin	Word recognition, oral sight reading, timed silent reading, listening subtests. To determine independent, instructional, frustration and potential reading levels	1–19	1970	varies	
Reading Miscue Inventory: (Goodman & Burke) Macmillan	Psycholinguistically analyzes why miscues are made as reader extracts meaning; qualitative as well as quantitative analysis	All levels	1972	varies	
Roswell-Chall Diagnostic Reading Test of Word Analysis Skills: Essay Press	Consonant and vowel sounds and combinations, syllabication	2–6	1959	5–10	Quick but limited assessment.

Test	Areas Tested	Grade/Level	Date	Time	Comments
Spache Diagnostic Reading Scales: California Test Bureau/McGraw-Hill	Word recognition, oral and silent reading, phonics	1–8 (retarded readers, 9–12)	1963	20–30	Gives considerable information, but standardization leaves much to be desired.
Sucher-Alfred Reading Placement Inventory: Brigham Young, University Press	Word recognition and reading paragraphs, screening for placement	1–9	1971	20	
Wide Range Achievement Test: Guidance Testing Associates	Reading, spelling, arithmetic	1–12	1965	20–30	Overclaiming manual; perhaps useful for quick estimate of general level of ability (to determine appropriate level of a survey test).
SPECIAL TESTS:					
Adult Basic Reading Inventory: Scholastic Testing Services	(Group test) Sight words, sound and letter discrimination, word meaning (reading and listening), context reading	Functionally illiterate adolescents and adults	1966	60	Adult norms lacking; perhaps informal methods of diagnosis more useful for skilled reading specialists.
ANPA Foundation Newspaper Test: Cooperative Tests and Services	(Group test) Simulated newspapers to test newspaper reading ability	7–12	1969	40–50	Norms and reliability data based on pre-publication forms.
California Phonics Survey: California Test Bureau/McGraw-Hill	(Group test) Vowel and consonant confusions, reversals, configuration, endings, negatives-opposites-sight words, rigidity	7–16	1963	40–45	Useful to identify weaknesses in phoneme-grapheme understandings, but not reasons for misunderstandings.
Doren Diagnostic Reading Test of Word Recognition Skills: American Guidance Service	(Group test) Letter recognition, beginning and ending sounds, whole word recognition, words within words, speech consonants, blending, rhyming, vowels, sight words, discriminate guessing	1–9	1964	180	More valuable as individual rather than group test, but useful in the hands of a skilled teacher.

Concise Guide to Standardized Reading Tests (cont'd)

Test and Publisher	What it Measures (usually subtests)	Levels (grades)	Date of Publication or Latest Revision	Time (min.)	Brief Resume of Evaluation
Huelsman Word Discrimination Test: Miami University Alumni Association	(Group test) Use of length, external design and configuration in perceiving words. Can give approximate reading level	1–8	1958	15	No manual; no data on reliability.
Iowa Every-Pupil Tests of Basic Skills: Test B, Houghton Mifflin	(Group test) Map reading, use of references, use of index, use of dictionary, graphing	3–9	1947	55–90	Well-constructed test, using life-like samples.
Iowa Tests of Educational Development: Science Research Associates	(Group tests) Test 5: Ability to interpret reading materials in the social studies. Test 6: Ability to interpret reading materials in the natural sciences. Test 7: Ability to interpret reading materials in literature. Test 9: Use of sources of information	9–12	1942–61	70 70 60 35	Well-designed battery of widely used achievement tests with good norming and statistical information; however, length of time required to take the tests and the lack of uniqueness in these reading tests warrant close consideration.
McCullough Word-Analysis Tests: Personnel Press	(Group test) Initial blends and digraphs, phonetic discrimination, matching letters to vowel sounds, sounding whole words, interpreting phonetic symbols, syllables, root words	4–6	1962–63	70	Best single instrument for assessing mechanical aspects of word analysis. Can identify specific difficulties interfering with higher order cognitive processes.
Minnesota Speed of Reading Test for College Students: University of Minnesota Press	(Group test) Speed in reading History, Geography, Economics, Government, Psychology, Education, and Science	12–16	1936	6–15	Inadequate manual, but test has considerable merit.

Test	Description	Grade/Age	Year	Time (min.)	Comments
Purdue Reading Test for Industrial Supervisors: University Book Store, W. Lafayette, Indiana	(Group test) 14 reading passages from industrial material with 38 multiple-choice test items.	12+	1955	35	Well-constructed test, but a simple vocabulary test could do the same job.
RBH Scientific Reading Test: Richardson, Bellows, Henry & Co.	(Group test) Paragraphs from scientific disciplines with multiple-choice questions. For employees in technical companies	12+	1950–59	60–65	Needs more evidence of validity; unrealistic paragraph samples; poor typography and inadequate manual.
Reader Rater with Self-Scoring Profile: Better Reading Program	(Individual test) Speed; comprehension; reading habits; reading for details, inferences and main ideas; adjusting speed; summarizing, skimming, recall of information; speeded and unspeeded vocabulary	10–12	1965	60–120	No data on reliability; no norms.
Reader's Inventory: Educational Development Laboratories	(Group test) Reading interests, attitudes, habits, visual conditions, background, expectations in reading	9–16	1963	10–20	Useful for inexperienced teacher; manual gives interpretations of and suggestions for particular problems.
Reading Adequacy "READ" Test: Individual Placement Series Personnel Research Associates	(Group test) Reading rate, percent of comprehension, corrected reading rate. For adults in industry.	12+	1966	10–15	Yields quick estimate of reading speed, but needs more evidence on reliability and validity.
Reading Progress Scale: Revrac Publications	(Group test) Evaluates progress in reading: 4 paragraphs needing completion by choosing between pairs of test words	1–12	1971	15	Reliability and validity all right; test measures ability to decode, not necessarily understanding.
Reading Versatility Test: Educational Development Laboratories	(Group test) Rate, comprehension, skimming, scanning	5–16	1968	40–50	Poor test; dubious interpretations suggested.
Robinson-Hall Reading Tests: Ohio State University Press	(Group test) Reading ability for art, geology, history and fiction: Rate and comprehension measured	13–16	1949	15	Useful for obtaining in a reasonable length of time measures of differences in reading performance in different subjects.

Concise Guide to Standardized Reading Tests (cont'd)

Test and Publisher	What it Measures (usually subtests)	Levels (grades)	Date of Publication or Latest Revision	Time (min.)	Brief Resume of Evaluation
Survey of Study Habits and Attitudes: Psychological Corporation	(Group test) Efficiency, promptness, attitudes towards teachers, co-educational objectives	7–14	1967	20–25	Good teaching aid for teachers and counselors; useful to frank and motivated students.
Test on the Use of the Dictionary: Reading Laboratory and Clinic, University of Florida	(Group test) Pronunciation, meaning, spelling, derivation, usage	9–16	1963	30–40	No data on reliability; tentative norms.
Tests of General Educational Development: American Council of Education	(Group test) Test 2: Interpretation of reading materials in the natural sciences. Test 3: Interpretation of reading materials in the social studies. Test 4: Interpretation of literary materials. Used for candidates for high school equivalency certificates. *Special editions for the blind and partially sighted.*	9–16	1944–70	120	Superior tests, lacking some statistical data; itemized scores would appear desirable, but chief question is whether these tests contribute information not already obtainable from tests of intelligence and of general reading ability.
Tests of Reading: Inter-American Series Guidance Testing Associates	(Group tests in English and Spanish) Vocabulary, comprehension	7–13	1967	50	Could be useful in measuring vocabulary and comprehension of students entering U.S. schools from Spanish-speaking countries.
Watson-Glaser Critical Thinking Appraisal: Harcourt Brace Jovanovich	(Group test) Inference, recognition of assumptions, deductions, interpretation, evaluation of arguments	9–16+	1964	50–60	Useful instrument to understand and appraise critical thinking.
Wide Range Vocabulary Test: Psychological Corporation	(Group test) Reading vocabulary. Can give quick estimate of intelligence.	3–12+	1945	10	Norming and reliability information incomplete, but useful screening device.

Index